GATEWAY GESAMT-AUSGABE

Englisch für berufliche Schulen

von Hellmut Imsel,
Rosemary King, David Phillips,
Wolfgang Rosenkranz,
Graham Tucker und
Terence Wynne

unter Leitung und Mitwirkung
der Verlagsredaktion
Weiterbildung Fremdsprachen

Ernst Klett Verlag für Wissen und Bildung
Stuttgart · Dresden

GATEWAY Gesamtausgabe   Englisch für berufliche Schulen

von
Hellmut Imsel, Studiendirektor, Fachleiter am Seminar für Schulpädagogik (B), Stuttgart;
Rosemary King M.A., Fachlehrerin für Englisch an der Berufsbildenden Schule, Wesel;
David Phillips B.A., M.A., Lektor für Englisch an der Universität Hohenheim, Stuttgart-Hohenheim;
Wolfgang Rosenkranz, Diplom-Handelslehrer, Oberstudienrat an der Freiherr-vom-Stein-Schule, Bad Oeynhausen;
Graham Tucker B.A., Fachlehrer für Englisch an der Berufsbildenden Schule, Castrop-Rauxel;
Terence Wynne B.A., Lehrbeauftragter für Technisches Englisch an der Fachhochschule für Technik, Esslingen a.N.

an den Arbeiten nahmen ferner teil
Dr. Max Frank, Studiendirektor an der Technischen Oberschule, Stuttgart;
Shirley Lechler B.A., Lehrbeauftragte für Englisch an der Universität Stuttgart

unter Leitung und Mitwirkung
der Verlagsredaktion Weiterbildung Fremdsprachen;
Mitarbeit an diesem Werk:
Dr. Klaus Finger, Dr. Sabina Fleitmann, Karin Nowak.

Visuelle Gestaltung
Umschlag: Friedemann Bröckel, Stuttgart;
Illustrationen: Peter Schimmel, München;
Realien und technische Zeichnungen: Held und Rieger, Fellbach;
Bernd Salzer, Waiblingen.

Sprachcassetten

Zur Verbesserung der Aussprache und zur Schulung des Hörverständnisses empfiehlt es sich, die Begleitcassetten zu diesem Lehrwerk zu verwenden.

● *2 Compact-Cassetten* mit Lektionstexten und Hörverständnistexten. Beide Seiten besprochen, Klettnummer 80934.

Lieferung durch jede Buchhandlung oder, wo dies auf Schwierigkeiten stößt, zuzüglich Portokosten per Nachnahme vom Ernst Klett Verlag für Wissen und Bildung, Postfach 1170, 7054 Korb.

Symbole

	Einsatz der Cassette
	schriftliche Übung
♟♟	Partnerarbeit
♟♟♟	Gruppenarbeit
🎭	Rollenspiel

Gedruckt auf Papier, das aus chlorfrei gebleichtem Zellstoff hergestellt wurde.

1. Auflage   1   7   6   5   4 | 1996   95   94   93

Alle Drucke dieser Auflage können im Unterricht nebeneinander benutzt werden, sie sind untereinander unverändert.
Die letzte Zahl bezeichnet das Jahr dieses Druckes.
© Ernst Klett Verlag für Wissen und Bildung GmbH, Stuttgart 1990. Alle Rechte vorbehalten.
Druck: Partenaires Fabrication, Paris
Printed in France.
ISBN 3-12-809310-6 (kart.)
ISBN 3-12-809320-2 (geb.)

GATEWAY,

das neue Lehrwerk für den Englischunterricht an beruflichen Schulen, bereitet in 15 Units auf den mittleren Bildungsabschluß (Fachschulreife) vor. Es entspricht den Richtlinien der Lehrpläne für berufliche Schulen der verschiedenen Bundesländer.

Gateway Gesamtausgabe ist an der zweijährigen Berufsfachschule und an der Berufsaufbauschule einsetzbar.

Dem unterschiedlichen Kenntnisstand und den verschiedenen Voraussetzungen bei Schülerinnen und Schülern der angesprochenen Schultypen wurde durch eine flache Strukturprogression in den ersten fünf Units Rechnung getragen. Damit wird schwächeren Lernenden der Zugang zur englischen Sprache erleichtert.

Gateway Gesamtausgabe ist in fünfzehn Units gegliedert, nach jeweils fünf Units steht eine Revisionsunit, die relevanten Wortschatz und behandelte Grammatik der vorhergegangenen Units wiederholt.

Die erste Revisionsunit ermöglicht somit einen Quereinstieg, da der Lehrer gezielt lexikalische und strukturelle Unitinhalte überprüfen und vertiefen kann. Damit wird ein flexibler Einsatz bei heterogenen Lerngruppen möglich.

Die Units sind in Doppelseiten gegliedert. Nach einer Starterseite, die auf das Thema der Unit hinführt, wird der jeweilige strukturelle Schwerpunkt auf den ersten drei Seiten eingeführt (A-Block), weitere grammatische Erscheinungen sind in den folgenden Doppelseiten (B- und C-Block) dargestellt. Der Transferteil (T-Block) faßt Strukturen der Unit zusammen und wiederholt einen Großteil des Vokabulars. Eine Fun-Seite (F) im Anschluß an die Units 1–5 wiederholt Grundwortschatz und ergänzt den Unit-Wortschatz.

Das Lehrwerk setzt ca. 700 Wörter als Grundwortschatz voraus. Diese werden systematisch wiederholt und durch maßvolle lexikalische Neueinführungen auf einen Gesamtwortschatz von ca. 1900 Wörtern erweitert.

Fachwortschatz aus dem gewerblich-technischen, hauswirtschaftlich-sozialpädagogischen und kaufmännischen Bereich wird ab Unit 6 verstärkt vermittelt: berufsbezogene Spezialtexte dieser drei Bereiche (S 1, S 2 und S 3) bilden den Abschluß jedes Unittextteils.

Gateway bietet Themen aus britischen und U.S.-amerikanischen Gesellschaftsbereichen.

Als Orientierungshilfe ist die Grammatik unitbegleitend angelegt. Die Grammatikseite faßt die wichtigsten Grammatikregeln in leicht verständlichem Deutsch und englischen Beispielsätzen zusammen.

Die Übung aller vier Grundfertigkeiten ist sorgfältig geplant. Für die gezielte Schulung des Hörverständnisses stehen besondere, auf Cassette gesprochene HV-Texte zur Verfügung, die nur im Anhang abgedruckt sind. Die Schreibfertigkeit wird zusätzlich im Arbeitsbuch geübt.

Bei der Gestaltung des Übungsapparates wurde darauf geachtet, daß die Übungen über Imitation und Reproduktion bei wechselnden Sozialformen zur freien Textproduktion führen.

In der Konzeption von Gateway Gesamtausgabe ist eine intensive Prüfungsvorbereitung eingeplant. Mit zwei unterschiedlichen Workbook-Ausgaben im zweiten Teil ab Unit 11 (Workbook 2, A und Workbook 2, B) bereitet Gateway gezielt auf die jeweils unterschiedlichen Prüfungsanforderungen einzelner Bundesländer vor: Ausgabe A enthält neben unitbegleitenden Übungen insgesamt 12 Erweiterte Textaufgaben (ETAs); Ausgabe B neben unitbegleitenden Übungen vier ausgewählte ETAs und einen Sonderteil zu *Commercial Correspondence,* der in die grundlegenden Bereiche der englischen Handelskorrespondenz einführt.

Wir wünschen Ihnen viel Spaß und Erfolg bei der Arbeit mit diesem Lehrwerk.

Autoren und Redaktion

INHALT

	Themen/Situationen/Textsorten	grammatische Schwerpunkte	Seite
Unit 1	**Young people in Britain**		**Starter: 8**
A	Anmeldung am *Manchester College*; persönliche Daten, Herkunfts- und Ortsangaben; persönlicher Brief, privates Telefonat	personal pronouns; possessive determiners; Present Tense of *be* (statement, question, short answer)	9
B	*College students* im Gespräch; Verwandtschaftsbeziehungen; Freizeitangebote in Manchester	*have got* (statement, question, short answer); *there is .../there are ...* (statement, question, short answer)	12
C	Junge Leute im *Southampton Youth Hostel*; Nationalitätsangaben; Freizeitangebote in und um Southampton	personal pronouns (Subjektform); possessive determiners; plural of nouns (regular, irregular plurals); interrogative pronouns	14
T	Stadtrundfahrt in London: landeskundliche Informationen zum *United Kingdom*	Present Tense of *be*; *have got*; *there is .../there are ...*	16
F/G	Fun: *What have they got?*	Grammatikübersicht	18/19
Unit 2	**Jobs**		**Starter: 20**
A	Berufliche Bildung am *Manchester College*; Kursangebote; individuelle Stundenpläne; Uhrzeiten; *college students* im Gespräch	indefinite article *a/an*; Present Continuous – present meaning: (im Moment/zur Zeit) (statement, question, short answer)	21
B	Freizeitaktivitäten von *college students*; Verabredungen; *What's on in Manchester*	Present Continuous – future meaning; personal pronouns (Objektform)	24
C	Berufsorientierte Tätigkeiten am *Manchester College*; Fächerangebot und Schulordnung am College	modal auxiliaries *can/can't, must, needn't, mustn't*	26
T	Zeitungsannonce: *Youth Training Scheme* (staatl. Programm gegen Jugendarbeitslosigkeit in GB)	Present Continuous (present meaning – future meaning); modal auxiliaries	28
F/G	Fun: *Work it out!*	Grammatikübersicht	30/31
Unit 3	**Sports and all that**		**Starter: 32**
A	Interview mit einer Schwimmerin; Sportarten; Trainingsprogramme	Present Simple of main verbs mit *I, you, we, they* (statement, question, short answer)	33
B	Freizeit und Sport; Zirkeltraining	Present Simple of main verbs mit *he, she* (statement, question, short answers)	36
C	Die *Highland Games* in Schottland; Tips zum Fitbleiben; Verhaltensregeln im Schwimmbad	comparison of adjectives *(-er/-est)*; imperative	38
T	Zeitungsartikel: *American football* und *rugby* – zwei Sportler im Vergleich	Present Simple of main verbs; comparison of adjectives *(-er/-est)*	40
F/G	Fun: *Motor racing*	Grammatikübersicht	42/43

INHALT

	Themen/Situationen/Textsorten	grammatische Schwerpunkte	Seite
Unit 4	**Media**		**Starter: 44**
A	Konsumverhalten im Medienbereich – britische Statistik; *Radio Orwell* – Alltag im Funkhaus eines privaten Senders	Present Simple – Present Continuous kontrastiert	45
B	Britisches Fernsehen; Fernsehgewohnheiten; Fernsehwerbung; Fernsehkochkurs	comparison of adjectives *as ... as; more/most; less/least; better/best; worse/worst*; cardinal numbers; quantities; *how much ...?/how many ...?*	48
C	New York – Radiowerbung; Stadterkundung; Konzertprogramm der *Radio City Music Hall*	ordinal numbers; prepositions	50
T	Die Presse in GB; wie eine Zeitung entsteht; Zeitungsartikel mit Satzfehlern	Present Simple – Present Continuous kontrastiert; comparison of adjectives; numbers; *how much ...?/how many ...?*	52
F/G	Fun: *Have a look at this ...*	Grammatikübersicht	54/55
Unit 5	**Changes**		**Starter: 56**
A	Eine Kleinstadt im Wandel; zwei Generationen im Gespräch; persönlicher Brief; Leben in der Stadt und auf dem Land	Past Simple of *be* (statement, question, short answer); Past Simple of regular verbs (statement, question)	57
B	Gespräch über das *Torrey Canyon*-Unglück; Umweltbewußtsein und Umweltschutz	Past Simple of irregular verbs (statement, question, short answer)	60
C	Werbebroschüre der britischen Umweltschutzorganisation *Friends of the Earth*; Tips zum Umweltschutz; *Recycled Paper Products* – Katalog mit Bestellformular	Past Simple of regular/irregular verbs; modal auxiliaries *should/shouldn't*	62
T	Zeitungsartikel: *Greenpeace Action Against Air Pollution*; Schlagzeilen über Umweltprobleme	Past Simple of *be*; Past Simple of regular/irregular verbs	64
F/G	Fun: *What's wrong?*	Grammatikübersicht	66/67
Revision 1			**68–73**
Unit 6	**The British – a people of many nations**		**Starter: 74**
A	Indische Nachbarn in einer britischen Kleinstadt; Hausrenovierung; Zeitungsartikel: *Perfect Neighbours*	Present Perfect; Present Perfect mit Signalwörtern (statement, question)	75
B	Das *Citizens Advice Bureau (CAB)* hilft bei der Arbeitssuche	Present Perfect mit *since/for*	78
C	Kommunalwahlen: Rede eines *independent*	Present Perfect (short answer); *a/an, some, any*	80

three 3

INHALT

	Themen/Situationen/Textsorten	grammatische Schwerpunkte	Seite
T	Unterhauswahlen: Wahlkampf-Flugblätter von *Conservative*- und *Labour*-Kandidaten	Present Perfect	82
S 1	Gewerblich-technischer Fachtext: Werkzeuge		84
S 2	Hauswirtschaftlich-sozialpädagogischer Fachtext: Ausländische Restaurants in GB		85
S 3	Kaufmännischer Fachtext: Werbeanzeigen; Preis- und Zahlungsangaben		86
G		Grammatikübersicht	87

Unit 7 History – now and then   Starter: 88

A	Ein Amerikaner in London; Broschüre: *A Walk into the Past* – Britische Traditionen und Geschichte(n); persönlicher Brief	Present Perfect – Past Simple kontrastiert	89
B	Fernseh-Talkshow mit berühmten Gästen; Jane Fonda – Lebenslauf eines amerikanischen Filmstars	Present Perfect – Past Simple kontrastiert	92
C	Ein Besuch in Covent Garden; *It's party time…*	adjective – adverb; 's-genitive	94
T	Museumsbroschüre: Geschichte des Automobils	Present Perfect – Past Simple kontrastiert; adjective – adverb; *of*-construction	96
S 1	Gewerblich-technischer Fachtext: Autoinspektion		98
S 2	Hauswirtschaftlich-sozialpädagogischer Fachtext: Soziale Dienste in GB		99
S 3	Kaufmännischer Fachtext: Autovermietung		100
G		Grammatikübersicht	101

Unit 8 Services   Starter: 102

A	Ein junges Paar auf Wohnungssuche; die neuen Nachbarn und ihre Lebensumstände; persönlicher Brief	relative clauses *who/which* (als Subjekt)	103
B	Eine Hotelangestellte und ihre Arbeit; Werbebroschüre eines Hotels	relative clauses *who/which* (als Objekt); contact clauses; defining/non-defining relative clauses	106
C	Ein Busfahrer und seine Arbeit; ein Autounfall; Polizeibericht	-*ing*-Form (gerund); Past Continuous; possessive determiners – possessive pronouns	108
T	Broschüre zu britischen Notdiensten	relative clauses *who/which* (als Subjekt und Objekt), contact clauses; Past Continuous	110
S 1	Gewerblich-technischer Fachtext: Elektrizität		112
S 2	Hauswirtschaftlich-sozialpädagogischer Fachtext: Gesunde Ernährung		113
S 3	Kaufmännischer Fachtext: Privater Geldverkehr		114
G		Grammatikübersicht	115

INHALT

	Themen/Situationen/Textsorten	grammatische Schwerpunkte	Seite
Unit 9	**Man and technology**		**Starter: 116**
A	Umfrage in einer amerikanischen Zeitung: Zukunftsvisionen; Geburtstagswunsch – ein Computer	*will*-future (statement, question, short answer); *going to*-future (statement, question, short answer)	117
B	Handhabung eines Kassetterecorders; Erstellung eines Biorhythmus durch Computer; Freunde im Gespräch	conditional sentences mit *if* (I)	120
C	Amerikanisches Zeitungsinterview: Meinungen zu Mikrowellenherden; Mikrowelle in der Familie	*-ing*-Form (gerund); reflexive pronouns	122
T	Satellitengesteuerte Nachrichtenübermittlung; interkontinentales Telefongespräch	conditional sentences mit *if* (I); *will*-future; *going to*-future; *-ing*-Form (gerund)	124
S 1	Gewerblich-technischer Fachtext: *Computer aided design*		126
S 2	Hauswirtschaftlich-sozialpädagogischer Fachtext: Moderne Kücheneinrichtung		127
S 3	Kaufmännischer Fachtext: Moderne Bürokommunikation		128
G		Grammatikübersicht	129
Unit 10	**Trade and transport**		**Starter: 130**
A	Am britischen Zoll; Einfuhrbestimmungen; Geschäftsreise mit Notlandung	*have to/not have to; be allowed to/not be allowed to*	131
B	Transport einer Kakaoladung; Stadtsanierung im Londoner Hafengebiet	Past Perfect; *used to*	134
C	Perspektiven einer Londoner Import-Export-Firma; Geschäftsbrief	conditional sentences mit *if* (II); comparison of adverbs	136
T	Textilien-Produktion und Vermarktung; Bericht einer Boutique-Besitzerin	conditional sentences mit *if* (II); *used to;* comparison of adverbs; Past Perfect	138
S 1	Gewerblich-technischer Fachtext: Bauhandwerk		140
S 2	Hauswirtschaftlich-sozialpädagogischer Fachtext: Modedesign		141
S 3	Kaufmännischer Fachtext: Das britische Transportwesen		142
G		Grammatikübersicht	143
Revision 2			**144–149**
Unit 11	**The world of modern industry**		**Starter: 150**
A	Besichtigung einer Haushaltsgerätefabrik, Produktionsabläufe; Gespräch über Finanzierungsprobleme; Gerätebeschreibungen	Passive: Present Simple, mit modal auxiliaries	151
B	Bewerbung bei einer Haushaltsgerätefabrik; Firmenprospekt	Passive: Past Simple, mit *by*-agent	154

five 5

INHALT

	Themen/Situationen/Textsorten	grammatische Schwerpunkte	Seite
C	Rationalisierung in einer Schuhfabrik, Arbeitsplatzverlust; Argumente von Geschäftsleitung und Gewerkschaft	reported speech (I): Present Tense	156
T	Industrieansiedlung in der mittelenglischen Stadt Corby	Passive: Present Simple, Past Simple	158
S1	Gewerblich-technischer Fachtext: Industrieroboter, CAD/CAM		160
S2	Hauswirtschaftlich-sozialpädagogischer Fachtext: Computer-Einsatz im Supermarkt		161
S3	Kaufmännischer Fachtext: Wirtschaftsstatistik zu USA, Irland, BR Deutschland		162
G		Grammatikübersicht	163

Unit 12 Life and work in the United States   Starter: 164

	Themen/Situationen/Textsorten	grammatische Schwerpunkte	Seite
A	Besuchergruppe aus Irland im New York Irish Club; Eindrücke der Besucher in den USA; Club-Zeitung mit Programm	reported speech (II): Past Tense; reported question	165
B	Armut in den USA, soziales Netz; Soziale Einrichtungen	reported imperative	168
C	Erfolgsgeschichte zweier amerikanischer Eiskremproduzenten	relative clauses mit *who, which, whose* Present Perfect Continuous mit *since/for*	170
T	Ältere Arbeitnehmer in den USA; Broschüre des US-Gesundheitsministeriums; Gerichtsverhandlung	reported speech (II)	172
S1	Gewerblich-technischer Fachtext: Amerikanische Raumfahrt *(Kennedy Space Center)*		174
S2	Hauswirtschaftlich-sozialpädagogischer Fachtext: Probleme junger Schwarzer		175
S3	Kaufmännischer Fachtext: Bevölkerungsstatistik in den USA		176
G		Grammatikübersicht	177

Unit 13 Energy   Starter: 178

	Themen/Situationen/Textsorten	grammatische Schwerpunkte	Seite
A	Ölförderung in Alaska; Auswirkungen auf die Lebenswelt der Eskimos	Passive: Present Perfect, *will*-future	179
B	Gezeitenkraftwerke in Kanada	adverbial clauses	182
C	Energiesparmaßnahmen für Hausbesitzer und private Haushalte	phrasal verbs/prepositional verbs; irregular nouns	184
T	Nutzung verschiedener Energien in Neuseeland/USA/Australien	Passive: Present Perfect, *will*-future; adverbial clauses	186
S1	Gewerblich-technischer Fachtext: Alternative Energien		188
S2	Hauswirtschaftlich-sozialpädagogischer Fachtext: Energieverbrauch beim Menschen		189
S3	Kaufmännischer Fachtext: Bankkredite für Hausrenovierungen		190
G		Grammatikübersicht	191

	Themen/Situationen/Textsorten	grammatische Schwerpunkte	Seite
Unit 14	**The world of advertising**		**Starter: 192**
A	Einkaufsratgeber einer Verbraucherorganisation; Preisvergleiche; Abkürzungen	*to*-infinitive nach Verb + Objekt	193
B	Aufbau einer Werbeanzeige; Lexikonauszug	participle constructions (Partizip Präsens/Partizip Perfekt)	196
C	Kreditwerbung einer Bank	reported speech (III): Past Perfect	198
T	Ziele und Methoden von Werbung und Werbeagenturen; Radiowerbung	*to*-infinitive nach Verb + Objekt; participle constructions; reported speech (III)	200
S1	Gewerblich-technischer Fachtext: Müllverwertung und Recycling		202
S2	Hauswirtschaftlich-sozialpädagogischer Fachtext: Aufklärung über Salmonellen		203
S3	Kaufmännischer Fachtext: Jahresbilanz einer multinationalen Unternehmensgruppe		204
G		Grammatikübersicht	205
Unit 15	**English as an international language**		**Starter: 206**
A	Sprachschulen in GB; Schulprospekte	question tags	207
B	Eine deutsche Sprachschülerin bei einer westindischen Familie in GB; Gedicht von Linton Kwesi Johnson	conditional sentences (III)	210
C	Amerikanisches Englisch; persönlicher Brief; Zeitungsanzeigen	American and British English contrasted	212
T	Englisch als internationale Verkehrssprache; Englisch im Beruf	question tags; conditional sentences (III)	214
S1	Gewerblich-technischer Fachtext: Hoch- und Tiefbauingenieure		216
S2	Hauswirtschaftlich-sozialpädagogischer Fachtext: Entwicklungshilfe		217
S3	Kaufmännischer Fachtext: Fortbildung für Frauen in Wirtschaftsberufen		218
G		Grammatikübersicht	219
Revision 3			**220–225**
V	**Basic vocabulary** Grundwortschatz		226
	Contextual vocabulary Unitbegleitendes Wörterverzeichnis		234
	Alphabetical word list Alphabetisches Wortregister		269
✱	**Irregular verbs** Unregelmäßige Verben		280
	Listening comprehension texts Hörverständnistexte		282
	Cardinal and ordinal numbers Grund- und Ordnungszahlen		289
	Instructions for the exercises Arbeitsanweisungen		290
	Grammatical terms Grammatische Ausdrücke		292

UNIT 1

YOUNG PEOPLE IN BRITAIN

United Kingdom

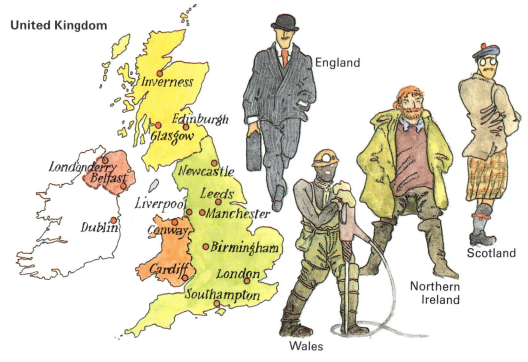

Where are they from?

Mary

She's from Glasgow. That's in Scotland.

Dave

He's from Conway. That's in …

Diana

She's from Manchester. That's …

Mark **Penny**

They're from Londonderry. That's …

Where are they from? How old are they?

Listen to the cassette.

Derek

Al **Jill**

Ann

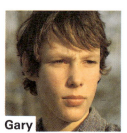

Gary

UNIT 1 A

1 A new student at Manchester College

Tom and his family are from Leeds. They live in Manchester now.
It is Tom's first day at college.

Tom: Good morning, my name's Baker.
Secretary: Oh yes, sit down, please.
Are you a new student here?
Tom: Yes, I am. It's my first day here at Manchester College.
Secretary: Well then – let's see. Can I have some information, please?
Tom: Of course.
Secretary: What's your first name?
Tom: Thomas.
Secretary: And how old are you?
Tom: I'm sixteen.
Secretary: What's your address?
Tom: 15 High Street.
Secretary: And your phone number?
Tom: 406 9971.
Secretary: Thank you, Thomas. That's all for now. Please go to ...

a What do you know about the new student?

▶ His name is ...
His first name is ...
His address is ...
His phone number is ...

b There is another new student at Manchester College.
What can you say about her?

▶ Her name is ...
Her first name ...
Her address ...
Her ...

REGISTRATION CARD

Baker, Thomas
Name, First Name

16
Age

15 High Street, Manchester
Address

406 9971
Telephone Number

REGISTRATION CA[RD]

Atkins, Susan
Name, First Name

17
Age

14 Chester Road, Stockport
Address

358 022
Telephone Number

c What about you?
Make a registration card. Then interview your partner and fill in the card.

▶ What's your name?   My name's ...
What's your first name?   My first name's ...
How old are you?   I'm ...
What's your address?   ...
What's your phone number? ...

d Now tell the class about your partner.

▶ His/her name's ...
...

nine 9

A UNIT 1

2 After some weeks Tom writes a letter to his old friend Chris.

> Dear Chris,
> How are things in Leeds? Manchester is such a big city and I'm not very happy. My new college is quite interesting. It's very large and the teachers are all right. My new friend Mark is here with me now. He's from Trinidad. We're in the same class at college.
> My parents aren't here at the moment. They are on holiday in France. But my sister's at home. She isn't at work today because she's ill. And you, Chris, how are you? Is work hard at the garage?
> Yours, Tom.

a Make sentences.

		in Manchester.
Tom		in Leeds.
His college		in France.
His teachers		on holiday.
His parents	is	at home.
His sister	are	at work.
Chris	isn't	from Trinidad.
Mark	aren't	interesting.
Tom and Mark		a small city.
Manchester		happy.
		very large.
		all right.
		ill.
		friends.

b Ask questions about Tom's letter. Give short answers.

▶ new college/interesting
Is the new college interesting?
Yes, it is.

▶ his parents/at home
Are his parents at home?
No, they aren't.

1 Chris/in Leeds
2 Tom's sister/at work
3 his teachers/all right
4 the college/large
5 Tom and Mark/on holiday
6 Manchester/a village
7 Tom's parents/in France
8 Mark/from Scotland

UNIT 1 A

3 Do you remember?
Answer the following questions. Use the correct prepositions.

▶ Where is Tom?
He's at college.

1 Where are Tom's parents?

2 Where is Mark from?

3 Where is Tom's sister?

4 Where is Chris?

5 Where are Tom and Mark?

6 Where is Tom from?

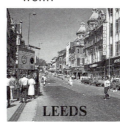

7 Where is Manchester?

4 On the phone

This is part of Tom's address book.

```
ADDRESSES
Chris Simpson
16 Wellington St
Leeds                488327
Harry Duncan
32 Bedford St
Leeds                413988
Rose Tucker
15 Queen Anne St
London             749 3478
```

```
ADDRESSES
Graham King
47 Mark Lane
Leeds                875531
Mark Bishop
34 Yarden St
Manchester        639 8431
Jeff Hartington
12 St Mary's gate
Manchester        799 6552
Mike Dale
55 Harrison St
London             439 4383
Alison Perkins
99 Peter St
Manchester        639 7864
Sally Roberts
53 Greengate
Manchester        624 7105
```

a Listen to the cassette and try to find out whose phone number it is.

b Tom rings his friend Chris in Leeds.

Chris: Leeds 488 327.
Tom: Hello, is that you, Chris? It's Tom here.
Chris: Hi, how are you, Tom?
Tom: Fine, thanks. And how are you, Chris?

Tom also rings his other friends. Play their roles.

B UNIT 1

1 Tom has got a new girlfriend, Alison. She is at college, too.
Here they are with some photos of his family. Listen to their conversation.

Tom: ... and this is my mother and father. My mother's from Leeds but my father's from Birmingham originally.
Alison: And who's this, Tom?
Tom: That's my cousin Derek. He's from Cardiff. He's got a job as a mechanic in Thornhill, a village nearby.
Alison: And who's this?
Tom: That's Jenny. Another cousin. She's from Newcastle.
Alison: How many brothers and sisters have you got, Tom?
Tom: Well, I've got a photo of them. This is my brother Brian. He's in London now, but he's out of work at the moment – and I've got a sister, Christine. She's here in Manchester, too. She's a nurse at the hospital here.

a Look at the dialogue again.
Ask and answer questions like this:

▶ cousin Derek
Where's his cousin Derek from?
He's from Cardiff.

Go on with:
father, mother, cousin Jenny.

b Now look at the dialogue again.
Ask and answer questions like this:

▶ a brother
Has Tom got a brother?
Yes, he's got a brother in London.

Go on with:
a sister, a cousin, a girlfriend.

c What about you?
Where's your mother/father/cousin ... from? Where are they now?

2 At the tourist information centre.
Tom asks his new friends about Manchester.

Tom: Manchester is a big city and I'm a little lost here at the moment.
Sally: Well, Tom – there are lots of things you can do in Manchester.
Jeff: Yes, we've got four cinemas in the city, for example.
Tom: Really? But how many are there near here?
Jeff: Well, there are two in Oxford Street and two in Deansgate.
Tom: Mmm ... and what about sports?
Jeff: There's a leisure centre in Moss Side with squash, table tennis, swimming-pools ...
Alison: Yes, and Manchester has got lots of good clubs and discos. Sandy's Club is a great place. They've got good music there. Look in the 'Manchester Evening News'. Have you got a copy?
Tom: No, I haven't.
Alison: Well, there are lists of clubs and discos in it.
Tom: But I'm really an ice-skating fan. Is there an ice-skating rink near here?
Sally: Yes, there's one in Devonshire Road. Have you got time this evening?
Tom: Sure, why?
Sally: Let's all go ice-skating, then.
Jeff: Great!
Tom: Yes, fantastic. What time ...?

UNIT 1 B

a Look at the text and the map in step **3**. Ask and answer questions like this:

▶ four cinemas
Have they got four cinemas?
Yes, they have.
▶ an ice-skating rink in Market Street
Have they got an ice-skating rink in Market Street?
No, they haven't.

1 many clubs and discos in Manchester
2 a leisure centre in Princess Street
3 good music at Sandy's Club
4 an ice-skating rink in Manchester
5 a leisure centre in Manchester
6 a squash centre in John Dalton Street

b Look at the text and the map again. Ask and answer questions like this:

▶ the leisure centre in Moss Side/ a swimming-pool
Has the leisure centre in Moss Side got a swimming-pool? – Yes, it has.
▶ Manchester/an ice-skating rink in Market Street
Has Manchester got an ice-skating rink in Market Street? – No, it hasn't.

1 Manchester/an evening newspaper
2 Manchester/six cinema centres
3 Manchester/a university
4 Tom/a copy of the 'Manchester Evening News'
5 Tom/time this evening
6 Sandy's Club/an ice-skating rink

3 The city – where to go, what to see

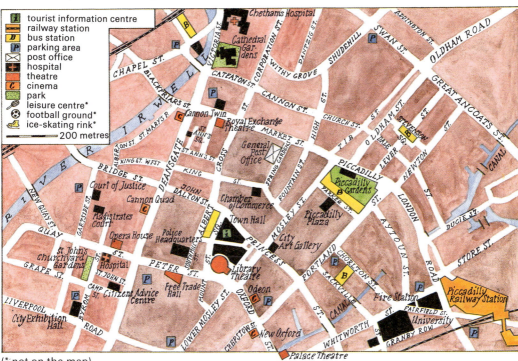

(* not on the map)

a Look at the map and the symbols. Ask and answer questions about central Manchester like this:

▶ Is there a cinema near the tourist information centre? – Yes, there is.
▶ Is there a railway station near the tourist information centre? – No, there isn't.
Go on: Is there ...?

b Now ask and answer questions like this:

▶ How many cinemas are there?
There are four cinemas.
▶ Where are they?
They are in Oxford Street and Deansgate.
Go on: How many ...? Where ...?

thirteen 13

UNIT 1

1 Travelling

In summer there are a lot of people in the British youth hostels.
It is dinner time at Southampton Youth Hostel.
Listen to the conversation ...

a True or false?

▶ Sabine's home is in Cologne.
That's true.
▶ Anna and Sven are from Norway.
That's false. They're from Sweden.

1 Anna's husband is Irish.
2 Jeanette and her boyfriend have got friends in Southampton.
3 Claude's English friends are in Italy now.
4 Claude's home is in France.
5 Marie and Mick are from Northern Ireland.
6 Marie and Mick have got three children.

b Who is it?
Listen to the cassette again.

▶ His wife is Irish.
Who is it?
It's Mick.

1 Their children are Swedish.
2 Their English friends are in America at the moment.
3 Her home is in Cork.
4 His girlfriend is German.
5 Her husband is Swedish, too.
6 She's from Cologne.
7 Their children are Patrick and Donna.

2 In the evening the guests help to lay the table in the dining-room.

Anna   Claude   Jörg   Jeanette

a Ask and answer questions like this:

▶ Who's got the knives?
Jeanette has.
Go on: Who ...?

b Ask and answer questions like this:

▶ What haven't they got yet?
They haven't got the apples yet.
Go on: What ...?

UNIT 1 c

3 The guests at Southampton Youth Hostel get some information about other youth hostels and the sights nearby.

SOUTHAMPTON YOUTH HOSTEL

461 Winchester Road · Southampton S01 7EH · Tel: 0703–769 607

WHERE TO GO AND WHAT TO SEE

Portsmouth Youth Hostel,
14 km, 🛏 58, closed on Sundays,
9 km to beach, ferry to Jersey
9 hours

Salisbury Youth Hostel,
28 km, 🛏 80, closed on Tuesdays,
cathedral (1258), famous for its
bell tower (130 metres high),
Stonehenge 17 km north

Whitwell Youth Hostel,
Isle of Wight, ferry 1 hour,
🛏 47, closed on Wednesdays,
3 km to beach

Winchester Youth Hostel,
13 km, 🛏 68, station 1 km,
closed on Thursdays and
Fridays

Winchester famous for its cathedral
(1079), Winchester College (1382),
28 km to beach

Windsor Youth Hostel,
90 km, 🛏 76, closed on
Saturdays

Windsor Castle (1078), Eton College
(1440)

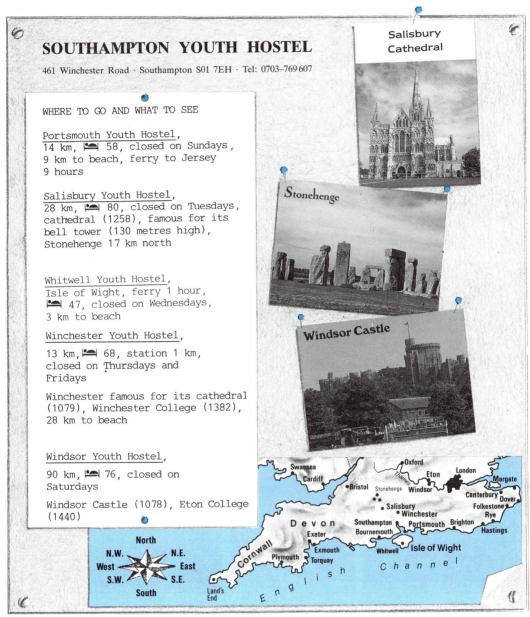

a Answer the following questions:

1. How many kilometres is it from Southampton to Portsmouth?
2. How old is Winchester Cathedral?
3. What is Salisbury Cathedral famous for?
4. When is Salisbury Youth Hostel closed?
5. Where is Stonehenge?
6. How many beds have they got at Portsmouth Youth Hostel?
7. When is Windsor Youth Hostel open?
8. What sights are there near Windsor Youth Hostel?

 b Ask your classmates more questions in the same way.

fifteen 15

UNIT 1

1 Bruce from Sydney, Australia, is with his English friend Cathy in London. It is his first visit to the British capital and they are on a sightseeing trip.

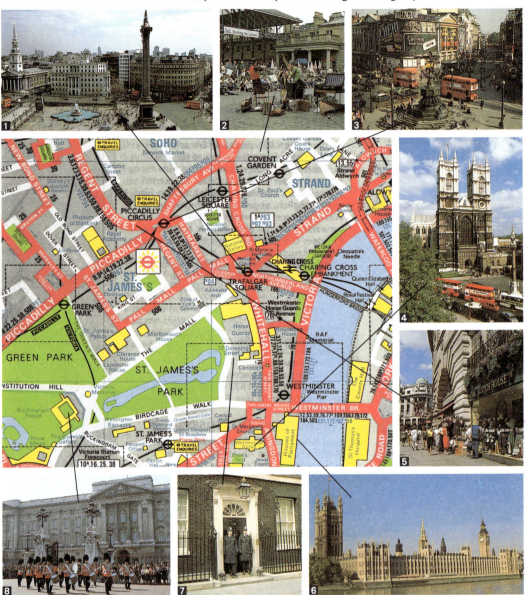

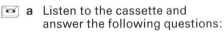 **a** Listen to the cassette and answer the following questions:

1. How many of the pictures are not part of their tour?
2. Which are they?
3. Which sights are part of their trip?
4. Put the sights in the order of the dialogue.

b Listen to the cassette again and answer the following questions:

1. What is Big Ben?
2. How old is Westminster Abbey?
3. Where is Nelson's Column?
4. How high is it?
5. What is Toni's Pizza Palace?
6. Where is a good place to go shopping?
7. How many rooms has Buckingham Palace got?
8. How old is it?

16 sixteen

UNIT 1 T

2 Here are Bruce's notes about the United Kingdom:

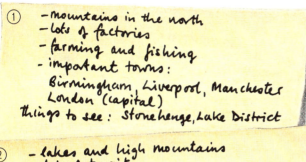

①
- mountains in the north
- lots of factories
- farming and fishing
- important towns:
  Birmingham, Liverpool, Manchester
  London (capital)
things to see: Stonehenge, Lake District

②
- lakes and high mountains
- lots of tourists
- fishing, oil
- famous for whisky and tweed
- important towns:
  Aberdeen, Glasgow,
  Edinburgh (capital)
things to see: Loch Ness (monster)
  Edinburgh Castle
  golf course in St Andrews

③
- lots of mountains
- sheep and cattle
- coal
- important towns:
  Swansea
  Cardiff (capital)
things to see: Devil's Bridge
  Conway Castle

④
- beautiful lakes
- farming and fishing
- important towns:
  Londonderry
  Belfast (capital)
things to see: Giant's Causeway
  old villages

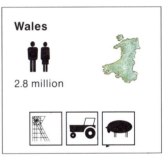

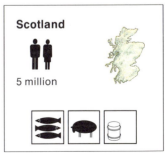

a Which country is which?

b Use Bruce's notes and talk about the different countries.
   You can use the expressions in the box.

| There's ... | There are ... |
| It has got ... | They've got ... |

c Ask and answer questions about the countries.
   Use the map on the inside cover of the book.

fishing   farming   wool

oil   mining   industry

seventeen 17

UNIT 1

1 What have they got?

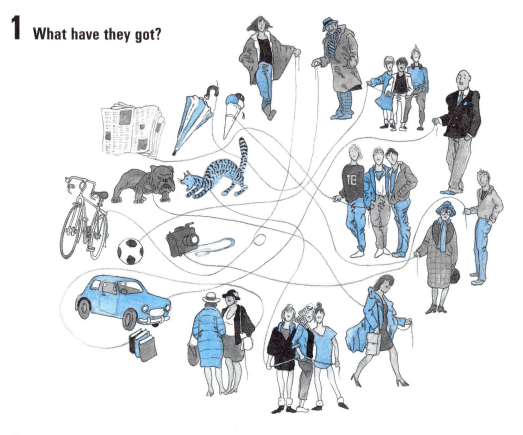

2 What can you see?

Find ten things.

UNIT 1 G

Personal pronouns

I	ich		we	wir
you	du, Sie		**you**	ihr, Sie
he	er		**they**	sie
she	sie			
it	es			

Possessive pronouns (determiners)

my	mein(e)		**our**	unser(e)
your	dein(e), Ihr(e)		**your**	euer(e), Ihr(e)
his	sein(e)		**their**	ihr(e)
her	ihr(e)			
its	sein(e)			

Present Tense of *be*

Statement

I	**am**			
You	**are**			
He / She / It	**is**	not	from Leeds.	
We / You / They	**are**			

Question

Am	I		
Are	you		
Is	he / she / it	late?	
Are	we / you / they		

Kurzformen werden meist im Gespräch oder z. B. in Briefen an Freunde gebraucht.

> How are you? – I**'m** fine.
> Mary**'s** from Liverpool. She**'s** a student.
> Tom **isn't** 18, he**'s** still 17.
> Where**'s** the car? – It**'s** in the garage.
> We**'re** late.

have got

Statement

I/you We/they	**have**	not	**got**	much time.
He She It	**has**			

Question

Have	I/you we/they	**got**	enough time?
Has	he she it		

I **haven't got** the tickets. – He**'s got** them.
Have you **got** the tickets? – Yes, I **have**.
Has Tom **got** the books? – No, he **hasn't**.

Beachte die Kurzformen!
In der Kurzantwort entfällt *got*; *have* wird nicht verkürzt.

The plural of nouns

Singular	Plural
cup	cup**s**
club	club**s**
glass	glass**es**
match	match**es**
city	cit**ies**
lady	lad**ies**

Pluralbildung:
– mit *-s*
– mit *-es* nach [s] und [ʃ]
– mit *-ies* bei Konsonanten + *y*

Singular	Plural
knife	kni**ves**
potato	potato**es**
child	child**ren**
man	m**e**n
woman	wom**e**n

Unregelmäßige Pluralbildung bei einigen Nomen!

UNIT 2

JOBS

What's their job?

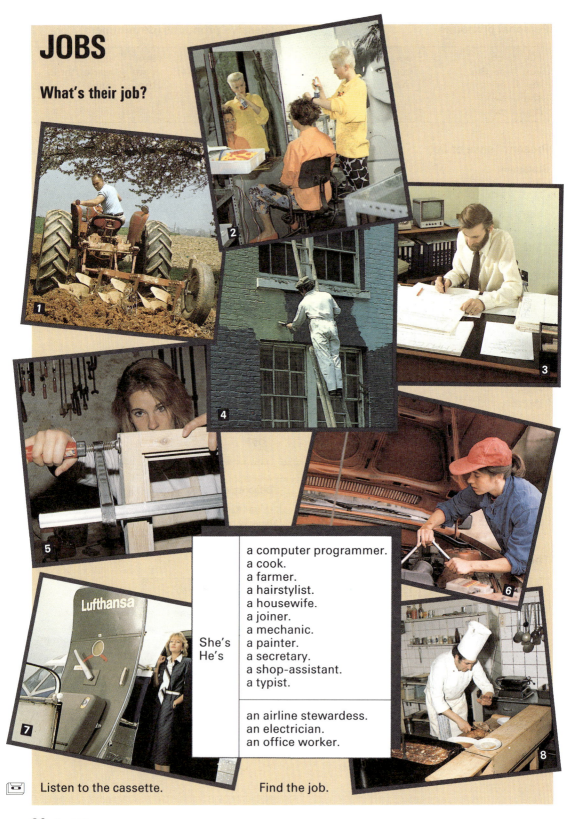

She's He's	a computer programmer. a cook. a farmer. a hairstylist. a housewife. a joiner. a mechanic. a painter. a secretary. a shop-assistant. a typist.
	an airline stewardess. an electrician. an office worker.

Listen to the cassette.   Find the job.

UNIT 2 A

1

Come to Manchester College

Learn to
repair electric cookers
type letters
program computers
make tools
plant vegetables
cook Italian meals
make a table
calculate prices
speak another language

Courses in
French
Metalwork
Business Studies
Home Economics
Woodwork

Courses in
Secretarial Studies
German
Electronics
Computer Studies
Farming

 Ask and answer questions like this:
▶ In which course can you learn to type letters?
In the Secretarial Studies course.
Go on: In which course ...?

2
John Kelly is now sixteen. His parents want him to go to Manchester College in September. At the moment he is going round the college to see what it is like there.

 a Look at the picture and make dialogues:

▶ John: What are you doing?
Carol: At the moment I'm calculating prices.
John: Oh, I see, so you're doing a course in Business Studies.

b Look at the picture. Ask and answer questions like this:

▶ What's Carol training to be?
She's training to be an office worker.
Go on: What's ...?

UNIT 2

3 Monday is always a busy day for Neil.

a Look at Neil's timetable and make sentences like this:

▶ In the morning he has Metalwork from quarter past nine to quarter to eleven. Then he has English from eleven o'clock to half past twelve.

Go on: In the afternoon he has Mathematics from ... to ...

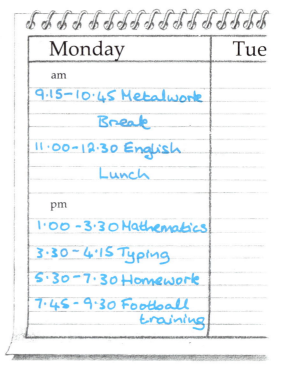

Monday
am
9.15–10.45 Metalwork
Break
11.00–12.30 English
Lunch
pm
1.00–3.30 Mathematics
3.30–4.15 Typing
5.30–7.30 Homework
7.45–9.30 Football training

Tue

b It's Monday. Let's look and see what Neil is doing at the moment:

 am — It's five past ten. He's doing a course in Metalwork.

 am — It's twenty-five to twelve. He's learning English.

 pm — It's five to one. He's having lunch.

 pm — It's ...   am

 am   pm   pm   pm

c What about you?
Talk about your timetable.

4 Jeff and Vera are in a coffee bar near the college.

Jeff: Coffee, Vera?
Vera: Yes, please.
Jeff: Wow, I'm really tired.
Vera: Why's that? Aren't you getting enough sleep?
Jeff: I'm doing this new computer course at the college.
Vera: Really? What's it like?
Jeff: It's not bad – we're learning how to program a computer.
Vera: Oh, that's great, Jeff.
Jeff: Yes, but it's hard work.
Vera: Look, there's Simon. Yoohoo, Simon!

UNIT 2 A

Simon: Hello, you two. Long time no see. How are things?
Vera: Not too bad, thanks. And how are you? Have you got a job?
Simon: Well, I'm not working at the moment, but I'm hoping to get a job as a painter next week. What about you, Vera? What are you doing these days?
Vera: Me? I'm working in a boutique. It's not a bad job but the money is terrible.
Simon: Well, it's better than nothing.
Jeff: Are you still going out with Sara?
Simon: Yes, I am. In fact, we're planning to go on holiday together.
Vera: What's she doing nowadays?
Simon: She's working as a joiner. Can you imagine that?
Jeff: Sure. Why not? She ...

a Can you find the questions? Answer them.

▶ – Sara – Is – working – a – as?

Is Sara working as a cook? – No, she isn't.

1 Jeff – – Is – as – working – an?
2 on – planning – holiday – Are – go – to – and – Sara – together – Simon?
3 computer – doing – Vera – Are – course – Jeff – a – and – together?
4 how – to – Is – 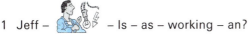 – program – Simon – learning – a?
5 a – in – Vera –  – working – Is?
6 Simon's – Is – girlfriend – Vera?
7 as – a – Simon – get – hoping – – Is – to – job – a?
8 Sara – Is – out – Simon – with – going?

b Listen to the cassette.
Make correct sentences.

▶ Sara/work/as a painter – as a joiner
Sara isn't working as a painter, she's working as a joiner.

1 Vera/work/in a bank – in a boutique
2 Simon/go out with/Vera – Sara
3 Jeff/learn/how to repair a TV – how to program a computer
4 Simon/hope/to get a job as a joiner – to get a job as a painter
5 Simon and Sara/plan/to take a computer course together – to go on holiday together

c Listen to the cassette and answer the following questions:

1 What are Vera and Jeff drinking?
2 What course is Jeff doing?
3 What is he learning in the course?
4 Is the course easy?
5 Has Simon got a job?
6 What is Simon hoping to get?
7 What is Vera doing these days?
8 Has Vera got a good job?
9 Is Vera's job well paid?
10 What is Sara working as?

twenty-three 23

B UNIT 2

1
Carol and Jeff are talking about their plans for next week.

Jeff's diary: Carol's diary:

Jeff's diary:
- Sun 15 pm 3.00 squash with Mark
- Mon 16 pm 7.15 coffee with Lynn
- Tues 17 am 10.30 computer course
- Wed 18 am 9.15 visit factory
- Thurs 19 pm 8.00 Mark's birthday party
- Fri 20 am 8.45 trainees from Germany
- Sat 21 pm 3.30 school concert

Carol's diary:
- Sun 15 pm 2.00 meet Susan at The Tea Rooms
- Mon 16 pm 5.00 tennis with Tom
- Tues 17 pm 7.30 german class
- Wed 18 am 9.15 shoe factory in Glendale
- Thurs 19
- Fri 20 am 8.45 meet trainees from Germany / birthday party at Mark's
- Sat 21 pm 8.30 disco ?? / 3.30 concert in school

a What is Jeff doing next week?

▶ On Sunday he's playing squash with Mark.
Go on: On Monday ...

b What about Carol?

c What are they doing together next week?

d Play the roles of Jeff and Carol.

▶ Carol: What are you doing on Sunday, Jeff?
Jeff: I'm playing squash with Mark.
Carol: When?
Jeff: At three o'clock.
Go on: What ...?

2
It is Wednesday. Carol is talking to Jeff on the phone.

Carol: Are you going to Mark's party tomorrow?
Jeff: Yes, I am. What time is the party exactly?
Carol: About eight. Listen, can you pick me up?
Jeff: Sorry, I'm meeting Sara and Neil at the station and taking them to Mark's.
Carol: What time are you meeting them?
Jeff: Quarter past seven.
Carol: Well, can't you pick me up on the way to the station?
Jeff: Errm ...
Carol: Come on, Jeff.
Jeff: All right. By the way, have you got a present for Mark?

Carol: Yes, I've got an LP for him – Rock 'n' Roll Man.
Jeff: Oh, no. I've got that record for him, too.
Carol: Well, you can change it tomorrow.
Jeff: No, you can. I haven't got the time.
Carol: OK. What time are you coming to pick us up then?
Jeff: Us?
Carol: Yes, Sally and me. I'm bringing Sally with me.
Jeff: Whew! You know Mark's not friends with her at the moment.
Carol: Yes, that's why I'm bringing her.
Jeff: You must be mad! OK, see you tomorrow at about seven.
Carol: See you.

a Look at the dialogue and answer the following questions:

1. Where are Sara and Neil going tomorrow?
2. Are they going by bus?
3. When is Jeff meeting Sara and Neil at the station?
4. Is Carol going to the party, too?
5. When is Jeff picking Sally and Carol up?
6. What has Carol got for Mark?
7. And what is Jeff giving Mark?
8. Who is changing the LP the next day?

b Neil and Carol are talking about their plans. Can you find the missing words?

Neil: What can I get you, Carol?
Carol: Can you get me a cup of tea, Neil? –
(Neil is back with a cup of tea and a cup of coffee.)
Neil: Here you are. Oh, what's that?
Carol: That's the new LP. I'm giving ① to Mark at his birthday party.
Neil: Sara and I are going, too. Jeff's picking ② up at 7.15.
Carol: Yes, I know. Jeff's taking you and us – Sally and ③, that is.
Neil: Mm, that's nice of ④. But another thing: what about the disco Friday night? Are you bringing the records?
Carol: Yes, I've got ⑤ here. Who's buying the drinks – you, Neil?
Neil: No, Tom's getting ⑥. Susan and I are looking after the food.
Carol: Susan? You're not going out with ⑦ again? You must be mad.
Neil: Oh, Susan's all right. Now what about Saturday's concert?
Carol: Are you taking ⑧ to the concert, too?
Neil: Of course, I am. But who are ⑨ taking, your brother?

3

CINEMA

- **New Oxford**
  Oxford St (234 8762)
  Ghandi
  2.05 pm, 5.05 pm, 8.05 pm
- **Cannon Quad**
  Deansgate (832 9215)
  1 **Roxanne**
  2.40 pm, 5.20 pm, 7 pm, 9.05 pm
  2 **Out of Africa** 8 pm
  Late Show Fri/Sat **The Rocky Horror Picture Show** 11.15 pm
  3 **Hanna and her Sisters**
  2.15 pm, 4.25 pm, 6.40 pm, 8.45 pm
  4 **The Color Purple**
  2.05 pm, 5.05 pm, 8.05 pm
- **Cannon Twin**
  Deansgate (832 5252)
- **Odeon Cinema Centre**
  Oxford St (236 8264)
  1 **Crocodile Dundee**
  1.45 pm, 3.55 pm, 6.05 pm, 8.25 pm
  2 **The Color of Money**
  1.50 pm, 4.05 pm, 6.20 pm, 8.40 pm
  3 **When the Wind Blows**
  1.55 pm, 4.45 pm, 7.45 pm

CONCERTS

- **Free Trade Hall**
  Peter St (248 6499)
  Queen in Concert 8 pm
- **Royal Northern College of Music** Oxford St
  **Liverpool Philharmonic Orchestra: Mozart –
  The Magic Flute** 7.30 pm
  Manchester Ticket Shop

THEATRE

- **Library Theatre**
  St Peter's Sq (236 7110)
  Hamlet 8 pm
- **Palace Theatre**
  Oxford St (236 9922)
  Double Double 7.30 pm
- **Royal Exchange Theatre**
  Royal Exchange (833 9833)
  Jesus Christ Superstar
  2.30 pm, 7.30 pm
- **Capital Theatre**
  School Lane, Didsbury (434 3331)
  Cinderella, 7.30 pm
- **Davenport Theatre**
  Buxton Road, Stockport (061-483 3801)
  Puss in Boots 7.30 pm
- **Tameside Theatre**

CLUBS/DISCOS

- **Fagin's**
  65 Oxford St (236 9971)
  Party Night with Dave Ward
- **Potters**
  300 Cheetham St (494 9234)
  The Gong Show
- **Jackie's**
  1–9 Albion St (236 1635)
  Dancing the Night Away

SPORTS

- **Football match**
  Manchester United vs Liverpool
  Old Trafford, Kick off 3 pm
- **Judo match**
  England vs Scotland
  Arcadia Leisure Centre, Hyde Road, 2.15 pm

a You are in Manchester for the weekend. Plan your programme for Sunday. Ask your partner what he/she is doing on Sunday.

▶ What are you doing on Sunday afternoon?
I'm going to the judo match.
Oh, I'm going there, too.
That's good. We can go together.

▶ What are you doing on Sunday night?
I'm going to Fagin's Disco.
Oh, I'm going to the cinema.
OK, see you on Monday then.

b Tell the class what you and your partner are doing on Sunday.

C UNIT 2

1

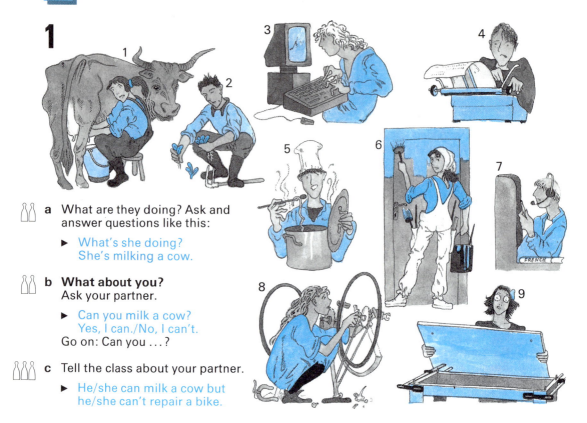

a What are they doing? Ask and answer questions like this:

▶ What's she doing?
   She's milking a cow.

b **What about you?**
   Ask your partner.

▶ Can you milk a cow?
   Yes, I can./No, I can't.
   Go on: Can you ...?

c Tell the class about your partner.

▶ He/she can milk a cow but he/she can't repair a bike.

2
Lynn is planning to do some work in her farming course.
But she has not got the right equipment for her job.

Look at the picture. Play the roles of Lynn and Mark.

▶ Lynn: Mark, I want to plant potatoes.
         Can you lend me a spade, please?
  Mark: Sorry, I haven't got one.
  Lynn: Mark, I want to cut flowers.
         Can you lend me a knife?
  Mark: Sure, here you are.

For other courses Lynn needs other equipment:
a brush, a cookbook, a pencil,
a pocket calculator, a pot, a screwdriver,
a spanner, a typewriter.
Go on.

26 twenty-six

UNIT 2 C

3 Sally has a problem. She must make her timetable for this term.

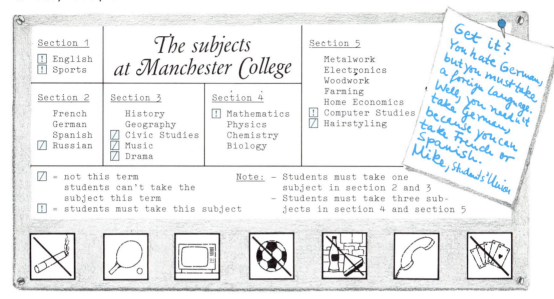

a Which subjects must Sally take?
Which subjects can't she take this term?
Sally is not good at the following subjects:
English, French, German, Mathematics,
Computer Studies, History, Geography
and Metalwork.

▶ She isn't good at Computer Studies
but she must take it.
She isn't good at History, she needn't
take it though.
Go on.

b **What about you?**
What can't/must/needn't you take at
your college?

c Look at the signs at Manchester College
and make sentences like this:

▶ You can photocopy.

▶ You mustn't drop litter.

Go on.

4 The principal of Manchester College is talking to the new students. Listen to the cassette.

a What is the principal talking about? Look at the bubbles.

b True or false?
Ann is one of the new students
at Manchester College.
Listen to the cassette again.

1 She mustn't smoke outside the college building.
2 She must clean the blackboard after class.
3 She can't have lunch at the college.
4 She must buy her lunch tickets on Fridays.
5 She mustn't eat or drink in the class.
6 She must wear overalls in the classrooms.
7 She can go to the study room in the free periods.
8 She needn't be in the classroom by nine o'clock.

c **What about you?** Talk about your college.
We mustn't/needn't/can/must ...

twenty-seven 27

UNIT 2

What is YTS?

The Youth Training Scheme (YTS) is a training course for 16- and 17-year-old school-leavers. They can learn a skill and earn money at the same time.

**WATCH OUT JAPAN
MICKEY HAWK IS COMING**

Our competitors in Japan and the rest of Europe are working hard. They are training their young people in a lot of skills and as a result they are taking trade away from us. But not much longer – young people in Britain are on their way.

Mickey Hawk is a typical British sixteen-year-old. He's leaving school in July, and in September he's starting a YTS course – with pay!

He needn't choose a skill at the beginning of the course – in the first weeks he can try different jobs. In this way he can find the right skill for him.

After two years he has a skill and he has a good chance to get a job.

At the moment over 100,000 firms in Britain are taking part in the YTS and they are looking for trainees like Mickey. The YTS is expensive but it is worth it. Because Mickey and about 360,000 British school-leavers are helping Britain to get trade back from our competitors abroad.

Watch out Japan, watch out Europe! Mickey Hawk is coming!

**TRAIN FOR A SKILL. THE NEW 2-YEAR-YTS.
NOW 16- AND 17-YEAR-OLD SCHOOL-LEAVERS CAN EARN WHILE THEY LEARN.**

a Here are six ideas taken from the text. Put them in the same order as in the text.

- A lot of young people in Britain are beginning to learn a skill. In this way they can help Britain to get trade back from countries in Europe and from Japan.
- Firms in Europe and in Japan are making a lot of money because they are training their young people.
- In two years Mickey's training course is over. His chances to get a job are not bad then.
- Many firms in Britain want to work with the YTS.
- Mickey is a typical British boy. He is starting the YTS this summer.
- Mickey can try different skills at first. Then after some weeks he must choose a skill.

UNIT 2 T

b Make sentences.

Britain's competitors in Europe and in Japan are working very hard	when	they are taking trade away from Britain.
Mickey needn't choose a skill at the beginning of the course	but	he can try different jobs first.
Mickey has a good chance to get a job	and so and so because	he has a skill in two years.
The training scheme is expensive		it is worth it.
British school leavers are taking part in the YTS		they are helping to get trade back from Britain's competitors.

c Which words in the text can replace the words in **bold type**?

1 **At present** firms are looking for trainees ...
2 You **get** money during the course ...
3 He is **finishing** school ...
4 Our competitors **abroad** ...
5 **Be careful**, Europe ...
6 He is **beginning** a course ...
7 Mickey Hawk is **on his way** ...
8 At the moment **more than** 100,000 firms ...

d Can you find the missing words?

Firms in Europe and Japan are ① hard.
These ② are training their young people in a lot of ③.
But now a lot of young ④ in Britain are on their way.
They are ⑤ YTS courses.
Two good points about this scheme are:
The trainees can learn a ⑥ and ⑦ money at the same time.
And after two years they have a ⑧ to ⑨ a job.
The YTS is ⑩, but it is worth it.
Many ⑪ in Britain are looking for ⑫ and the young people can help to get ⑬ back from Britain's ⑭.

e Answer the following questions in full sentences:

1 Who can take part in the YTS?
2 How many people are training with the YTS?
3 What is Mickey doing in July and what is he doing in September?
4 How can Mickey find the right skill?
5 What has Mickey got after two years?
6 Is the YTS cheap?
7 Why must Japan watch out?

twenty-nine 29

F UNIT 2

1 Work it out!

Sebastian Heldermann is principal of a commercial college in Munich.
He has a lot of problems. He must organize the timetable for class BS 1/3.

Class BS 1/3 must have the following lessons:

- 4 Mathematics,
- 2 Physics,
- 1 Chemistry,
- 2 Computer Studies,
- 4 English,
- 3 German,
- 2 Sports,
- 5 Economics,
- 1 History,
- 1 Politics.

They can take 2 lessons of Religious Instruction (RI) or 2 of Ethics,
but they must take place at the same time.
The students can also take 3 lessons of French, but needn't take them, though.

But look at this:

- There is no school on Saturdays.
- The class mustn't have afternoon school.
- The class mustn't have more than one lesson of the same subject a day.

Some teachers work at other schools, too:
- So the Maths teacher can't start before ten o'clock.
- The Physics teacher can only teach on Tuesdays and Thursdays.
- The Economics teacher must always finish before ten o'clock.
- The English teacher can't teach on Wednesdays.

 Can you help Sebastian Heldermann?

2 What are their jobs?

- JO RINE
  joiner
- NIC CHEAM
  mechanic

NAT RIECICLE

TRISHA SITLY

PAT RINE

RICK FEWROOFE

SISTAS PONSHAT

30 thirty

UNIT 2 G

Present Continuous

I	am	
He/she/it	is	working.
You/we/they	are	

hope	hop**ing**
sit	sit**ting**
plan	plan**ning**

Stummes -e entfällt.
Der letzte Buchstabe wird manchmal verdoppelt.

Jeff and Vera **are sitting** in a coffee bar.
Jeff **is learning** how to program a computer.
I**'m meeting** Carol tomorrow.

Das *Present Continuous* steht bei Handlungen:
– die im Moment des Sprechens stattfinden.
– die gegenwärtig stattfinden, nicht aber unbedingt im Augenblick.
– die in der Zukunft stattfinden (mit Zeitbestimmung).

Modal auxiliaries: *can, must, needn't, mustn't*

can/can't; must; needn't; mustn't + Infinitiv des Vollverbs

can	„können"	→ Fähigkeit
can …?	„können …?"	→ Bitte
can't/cannot	„nicht können"	→ keine Fähigkeit
must	„müssen"	→ Notwendigkeit
needn't/need not	„nicht müssen"	→ keine Notwendigkeit
mustn't/must not	„nicht dürfen"	→ Verbot

Eric **can** speak French.
Can you lend me your pencil?
Wayne **can't** speak French.
Every student **must** take maths.
We **needn't** take French.
Students **must not** eat in class.

The indefinite article *a/an*

It's **a** beautiful day.
It's **an** interesting course.

a + Konsonant
an + Vokal

He's **a** farmer.
She's **an** airline stewardess.

Vor Berufsbezeichnungen steht *a/an*

Personal pronouns

Subjektform		Objektform		
I	ich	me	mich	mir
you	du	you	dich	dir, euch, Ihnen
he	er	him	ihn	ihm
she	sie	her	sie	ihr
it	es	it	es	ihm
we	wir	us	uns	uns
you	ihr, Sie	you	euch, Sie	euch, Ihnen
they	sie	them	sie	Ihnen

I'm meeting Sara at the station.
She's playing tennis with Jeff tomorrow.
Can **they** beat Rose and Graham?

I'm meeting **her** at the station.
She's playing tennis with **him** tomorrow.
Can they beat **them**?

Die Subjektform des Personalpronomens steht:
– in Aussagesätzen vor dem Verb.
– in Fragesätzen nach dem ersten Hilfsverb.

Die Objektform des Personalpronomens steht:
– nach einer Präposition
– oder nach dem Verb.

UNIT 3

SPORTS AND ALL THAT

What's their sport?

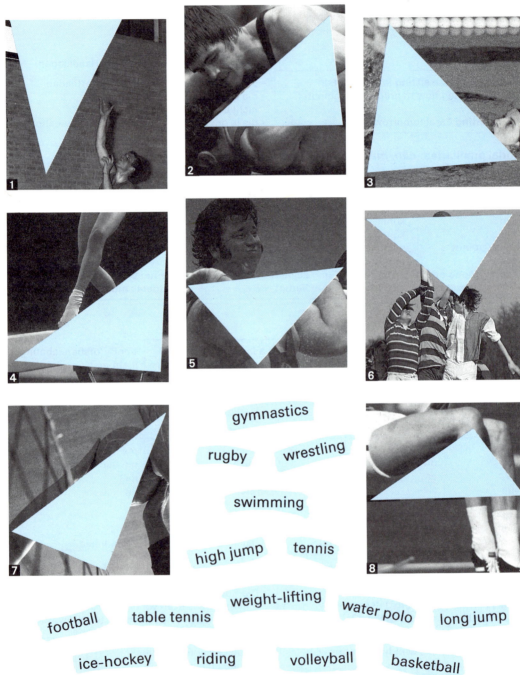

gymnastics

rugby   wrestling

swimming

high jump   tennis

weight-lifting

football   table tennis   water polo   long jump

ice-hockey   riding   volleyball   basketball

Listen to the cassette. Find their sport.

UNIT 3 A

1 A local hero

Interviewer: With us in the studio tonight we have Mary Read – the new women's 100 metres freestyle champion. Congratulations, Mary.
Mary Read: Thank you very much.
Interviewer: Mary's a local girl. Where are you from exactly, Mary?
Mary Read: I come from Clifton.
Interviewer: And do you train in Clifton?
Mary Read: No, I train at the leisure centre here in Bristol – they have a very good pool.
Interviewer: Do you train every day?
Mary Read: Well, normally I train five days a week.
Interviewer: Can you tell us something about your training programme?
Mary Read: Well, on Mondays I do fitness training and then I swim about 150 lengths of the pool. On Tuesdays I run 10 miles before school and in the afternoon I practise starts. Then on Wednesdays I just swim – long-distance or sprints. Thursdays I do weight-lifting – I don't like that very much. After training on Fridays we play a game - basketball or volleyball.
Interviewer: What about competitions?
Mary Read: We usually have competitions on Sundays.
Interviewer: You don't have much spare time. What about hobbies?
Mary Read: Well, I play tennis and I go riding. And I have to do my homework, too. But that's not a hobby.

Good evening ladies and gentlemen. Welcome to 'Sports at Home'...

Interviewer: OK Mary, thanks very much for this interview so far – we are now ...

a Which question goes with which answer?

1 Mary, where do you come from?
2 Do you train in Clifton?
3 Do you train every day?
4 How far do you swim on Mondays?
5 Do you have a hobby?
6 What do you do on Tuesday mornings?
7 What do you do on Wednesdays?
8 Do you like weight-lifting?
9 What games do you play on Fridays?
10 When do you have competitions?

No, I don't like it very much.
I swim about 150 lengths.
I come from Clifton.
I run about 10 miles before school.
No, I train in Bristol.

I just swim.
We play basketball or volleyball.
We usually have competitions on Sundays.
No, but I train five days a week.
I play tennis and I go riding.

A UNIT 3

b Which of these sports can you find in the interview with Mary Read?
Which are her hobbies?

c Make questions and write them in your exercise book.

What How often How far	do you	play on Fridays? practise on Tuesday afternoons? run on Tuesday mornings? swim on Mondays? train each week? practise on Wednesdays? have on Sundays? do in your spare time?

Use the questions in your exercise book and
play the roles of the interviewer and Mary Read.

▶ Interviewer: What do you practise on Wednesdays?
　Mary Read: On Wednesdays I just swim.
Go on.

d Mary Read is talking about her typical Mondays. Put the text into the right order and write it in your exercise book.

① I go to bed at nine o'clock.

② We finish morning school at half past twelve and then we have lunch in school. We have school every afternoon.

③ After school I go to the leisure centre for training.

④ I get up at quarter to eight and I go to school at half past eight.

⑤ I do my homework in the evening.

e What about you?
Contrast your typical Monday with Mary's.

▶ I don't get up at quarter to eight, I get up at ...
　We don't start school at nine o'clock, we start at ...
Go on.

UNIT 3 A

2 Mary's classmates Dennis and Jason are in Clifton swimming club, too. They have a different training programme.

Monday	Tuesday	Wednesday	Thursday	Friday	Saturday	Sunday
weight-lifting	football	starts	sprints	100 lengths	competitions	
200 lengths	fitness training	long-distance	basketball	basketball		

Ask and answer questions like this:
- What do they do on Fridays? – They swim 100 lengths.
- When do they have competitions? – They have competitions on Saturdays.

3 Put the sentences right.

- Ice-hockey players play with a round ball.
  Ice-hockey players don't play with a round ball, they play with a puck.

1. Rugby players play with a round ball.
2. Tennis players use sticks.
3. Soccer players play with an oval ball.
4. Windsurfers need snow.
5. Joggers wear skates.
6. Skiers need wind.
7. Hockey players use rackets.
8. Skaters wear running shoes.

4 What about you?

What sports do you do?
Ask and answer questions like this:

- Do you play football?
  Yes, I do.
- Do you go cycling?
  No, I don't.
  What sports do you do then?
  I do athletics.

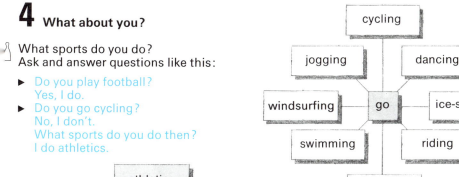

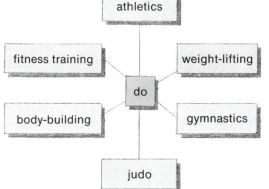

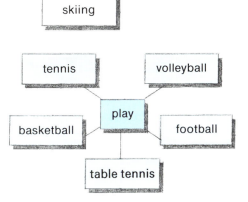

thirty-five 35

UNIT 3

1 How do they keep fit?
Which sentence goes with which picture?

This girl skates at the leisure centre once a week.
This boy goes jogging three times a week.
This man relaxes in front of the TV every weekend.
He plays tennis on Tuesdays and Thursdays.
He walks about ten miles every Sunday.
This woman dances at the local dancing club twice a week.
She does fitness training in the morning.
She swims ten lengths every other day.

2 Describe these two training programmes.

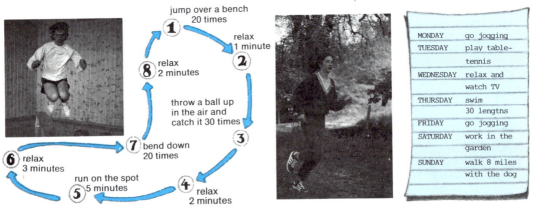

a What does the man do in his circuit programme?

▶ First he jumps over a bench 20 times, and then he ...
After that he ...
Go on.

b What does the woman do every week?

▶ She ... on Mondays, she ... on Tuesdays, ...
Go on.

UNIT 3 B

3

Beryl Thompson is slim because she watches her weight. Every day she eats fruit and vegetables. She only drinks fruit juices. She doesn't drink alcohol and she never eats chocolates. She tries to keep fit, so she does some kind of sport every day. She does fitness training every morning and she goes jogging once a week. Of course, she doesn't smoke. She works as a nurse and so she is always on the move. And don't forget: she carries all the shopping bags up to the third floor three times a week.

Wayne Smith is overweight because he eats spaghetti and cream-cakes nearly every day. He doesn't like fruit and he hates vegetables. He goes to the pub twice a week and watches TV every weekend. At work he sits at his desk all day. He doesn't do sports very often. He plays football with his friends from time to time. He knows he is not very fit but he still smokes a packet of cigarettes a day.

a True or false?

▶ Beryl doesn't smoke. – That's true.
▶ Wayne is slim. – That's false. He's overweight.

1 Beryl is overweight and doesn't watch her weight.
2 She eats a lot of apples, oranges, bananas, tomatoes and carrots.
3 She drinks a lot of wine.
4 She does fitness training every morning and goes jogging every weekend.
5 She never carries her shopping bags up to the third floor.
6 Wayne doesn't like vegetables.
7 He goes to the pub twice a week.
8 At his job he is always on the move.
9 He plays football from time to time.
10 He doesn't smoke.

b Put the sentences right.

▶ Beryl drinks alcohol every day.
  Beryl doesn't drink alcohol every day, she never drinks alcohol.

1 Wayne goes to the pub every night.
2 He plays football on Saturdays.
3 He watches TV on Wednesdays.
4 He eats spaghetti every Sunday.
5 Beryl goes jogging three times a week.
6 She does sports every other day.
7 She does fitness training every night.

c Ask and answer questions like this:

▶ Does Beryl work as a teacher? – No, she doesn't.
▶ Does Wayne sit at his desk all day? – Yes, he does.

Does	Beryl Wayne	go (to the) …? drink …? eat …? play …? smoke …? do …?

d Look at step **3b** again. Make questions with 'How often …?' and answer them.

▶ How often does Beryl drink beer? – She never drinks beer.
▶ How often does Wayne go to the pub? – He goes to the pub twice a week.
Go on.

thirty-seven 37

C UNIT 3

1 Come to the Highland Games

The Highland Games take place in many towns and villages in Scotland every year. There, local people take part in sports, dancing and piping competitions. Here is one of the events at the Highland Games.

Tossing the caber is a very old sport in Scotland.

The caber is very long – about 19 feet (6 metres). It weighs about 120 pounds (55 kilos).

The athlete has to throw the caber as far as he can. It must turn in a circle in the air before it hits the ground.

Answer the following questions.

1. Where do the Highland Games take place?
2. What can you see at the Games?
3. Who takes part in the Games?
4. How long is the caber?
5. How much does it weigh?
6. Look at the picture. What is the caber made of?

2 Here are three sportsmen from the Highland Games:

a Who says what? Which statement goes with which person?

	1	2	3
born:	27.04.1944	13.01.1906	01.11.1960
height:	1.65 metres	1.59 metres	1.93 metres
weight:	170 kilos	60 kilos	76 kilos

I'm Stanley MacLean. Some people say that I'm tall, but am I the tallest here?

I'm Jock Stewart. I know I'm fatter than most other sportsmen here, but I also think that I'm stronger.

Hallo! My name's Colin MacInnes. Do you think I'm too old for the Games?

b Ask and answer questions like this:

▶ How old/tall/heavy is Jock Stewart? – He's ...
▶ Who's the oldest/tallest/heaviest ...?
▶ How much does the youngest/shortest/lightest/thinnest ... weigh?

38 thirty-eight

UNIT 3 c

c Some of the following statements are wrong. Find them and correct them.

1. Stanley is taller than Jock.
2. Colin is older than Stanley.
3. Stanley is heavier than Colin.
4. Jock is younger than Stanley.
5. Colin is shorter than Jock.
6. Jock is thinner than Stanley.
7. Jock is older than Colin.

d What about you?
Ask and answer questions about your classmates.

3 Can you draw these people at the Highland Games?

Andy is the smallest and Rod is smaller than Ian.
Rod has got the shortest hair. Ian's hair is the longest.
He is also the tallest and has got the longest beard.
Rod's beard is shorter than Andy's.
Rod doesn't have a cap and Andy's cap is bigger than Ian's.
Andy is the fattest and Rod is thinner than Ian.
They are all wearing kilts.
Rod has got the longest and Ian has got the shortest kilt.
They all have jackets and scarves on.
Andy's scarf is the thinnest and the longest.
Rod's scarf is the shortest and the widest.
And all the shoes are the same.

Show your pictures to the class and explain them.

4 Tips on how to keep fit

- A good sportsman looks for an interesting sport.
- He doesn't try to do too much at once.
- He checks with his doctor before he starts.
- He doesn't start too fast.
- He always trains three or four times a week.
- He trains with other people – it's more fun.
- He doesn't eat too much – he never tries to train after a meal.
- He gets his pulse up to 130.
- He tries to get out into the fresh air.
- He never forgets to relax afterwards.

Look at this leaflet and give tips on how to keep fit.

▶ Look for an interesting sport.
▶ Don't try to do too much at once.
Go on.

5 At the swimming-pool. What do these signs tell you?

▶ Don't make a noise here.

 1   2   3   4

▶ Wear a bathing-cap.

 5   6   7   8

THE FORT AND THE FLEA

By David Moores

GEORGE ALLAN plays football – American football – for the Chicago Bears. American football is different from European football. In American football you can pick the ball up and run with it. And you can stop the other players with your hands.

American football is a hard game and American footballers wear helmets and padding.

The Fort

The Flea

GERRY WILLIAMS plays rugby football for Cardiff. Rugby is like American football in a way, but rugby players don't wear padding. The game is hard and rough but small players have a chance, too.

George Allan is one of the biggest players in American football – in more ways than one:

- he weighs 308 pounds (about 140 kilos) and he is one of the heaviest players in American football, although he is "only" 6ft. 3in. (about 1.90m).
- the Americans call him "The Fort" because he is so big and strong.
- at the age of 23, Allan is one of the biggest attractions in America.
- he earns a cool 2 million dollars a year and is one of the richest sportsmen in America.
- although he travels thousands of miles a year, he doesn't drive.
- he likes eggs and meat. His favourite food is hamburgers. He can eat up to 22 jumbo hamburgers in one meal.
- his greatest ambition? – To win the American championships.

Take 29-year-old Gerry Williams, for example:

- at 5ft. 2in. (about 1.57m) he's one of the smallest rugby players in Britain. Gerry weighs only 112 pounds (about 50 kilos), so he's one of the lightest as well.
- his nickname is "The Flea" because he's so quick and on the field he's all over the place.
- officially he doesn't earn any money because he's an amateur, but as everyone knows, amateurs can earn a lot of money, too.
- his hobby is motoring – he drives to all the matches.
- Gerry's favourite food is steak and spaghetti. He says that's all he needs to keep fit.
- his greatest ambition? – to play rugby until he's forty.

UNIT 3 T

a Here is some information about George Allan and Gerry Williams.

Name	George Allan	Gerry Williams
Sports	American football	rugby football
Country	America	Wales
Age		

Make a list like this in your exercise book. Find out about their age, weight, height, nicknames, food, earnings, hobbies, greatest ambitions.

b Compare the age, weight and height of George Allan and Gerry Williams.

▶ George is younger than Gerry.

c Can you find the missing words?

Allan is one of the ① attractions in America.
At 112 pounds Williams is ② than Allan.
At 23 Allan is ③ than Williams.
Williams is 5ft 2in – much ④ than Allan.
Allan's ⑤ ambition is to win the American championships.
At 308 pounds Allan is one of the ⑥ players in American football.
Williams weighs 112 pounds. He is one of the ⑦ rugby players.
Williams is 5ft 2in so he is one of the ⑧ players in Britain.

d Which words or phrases in the text can replace the words in **bold type**?

1 George Allan **makes** $2 million a year.
2 His favourite **meal** is hamburgers.
3 His greatest **wish** is to win the American championships.
4 George Allan is one of the biggest **stars** in American football.
5 On the field Gerry Williams is **everywhere**.
6 Gerry is very **fast**.
7 Gerry is one of the lightest players, **too**.
8 He **goes by car** to all the matches.

e You are a reporter for a local newspaper.
You want to write an article about George Allan.
Ask his manager about his weight, height, earnings, ambitions, hobbies and favourite food.
Play their roles.

▶ What's his weight?
How tall is he?
How much does he earn?
Go on.

Do the same for Gerry Williams.

f What about you?
Interview your partner. Put the information into a diagram.
Then introduce your partner to the class.

forty-one 41

F UNIT 3

Motor racing

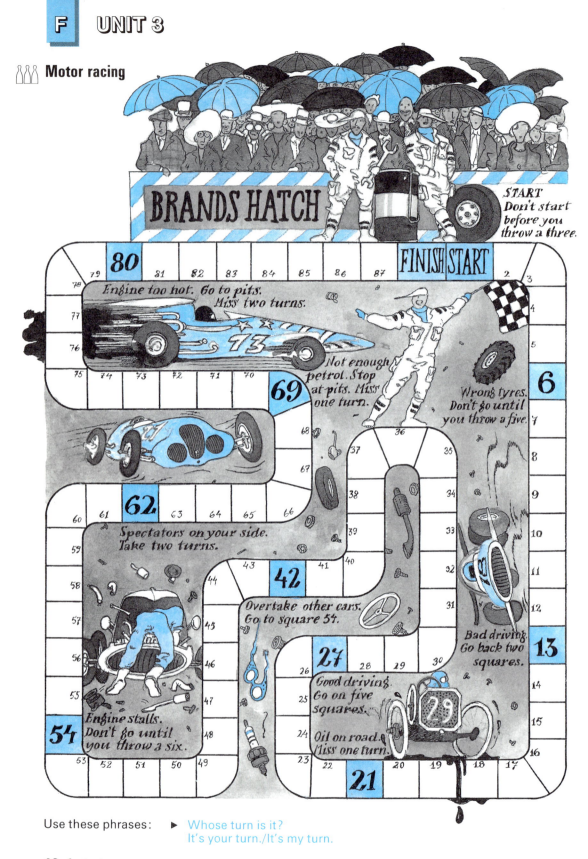

Use these phrases: ▶ Whose turn is it?
It's your turn./It's my turn.

UNIT 3 G

Present Simple of main verbs

Positive statement

I/you/we/they	**live**	in Chester.
He/she/it	**lives**	

Negative statement

I/you/we/they	**don't**	live	in Chester.
He/she/it	**doesn't**		

In der Schriftsprache findet man statt *don't/doesn't* auch *do not/does not*.

Positive question

Do	I/you/we/they	live	in Chester?
Does	he/she/it		

Negative question

Don't	I/you/we/they	live	in Chester?
Doesn't	he/she/it		

Short answer

Do you live in Chester?	Yes, I **do**.
Does she live in Leeds?	No, she **doesn't**.

Besonderheiten bei der *-s*-Endung

go, do	goes, does
watch, relax	watches, relaxes
carry, try	carries, tries
play	plays

go, do haben die Endung *-es*.
Nach den Lauten [ʃ], [s] steht *-es*.
y nach Konsonant wird zu *-ie*.
y nach Vokal bleibt erhalten.

| I **run** five miles every Sunday. |
| **Does** Mary always **train** in Bristol? |
| How often **do** you **train** each week? |
| What **does** the woman **do** every week? |
| She **doesn't smoke**. |

Das *Present Simple* steht:
– bei regelmäßigen Handlungen.
– bei wiederholten Handlungen.

– bei Gewohnheiten.

The imperative

| **Close** the door, please. |
| **Don't eat** too much. |

– Aufforderung = Infinitiv
– Verneinte Aufforderung = *don't* + Infinitiv

Comparison of adjectives

small	small**er**	small**est**
old	old**er**	old**est**
big	big**ger**	big**gest**
wide	wid**er**	wid**est**
heavy	heav**ier**	heav**iest**

Kurze Adjektive werden mit *-er/-est* gesteigert.

Der letzte Buchstabe wird manchmal verdoppelt.
Stummes *-e* entfällt.
-y wird zu *-ie*.

| The cat is **smaller than** the dog. |
| Her car is **faster than** my bike. |
| It's **the oldest** church in the country. |

smaller than = „kleiner als"

the oldest = „die älteste"

UNIT 4 A

1 Here is a print-out of questions and answers from a survey in Britain:

```
What's your favourite?              every day    now and then    never

Do you watch     television?           82 %         15 %          3 %
Do you watch     videos?               34 %         33 %         33 %
Do you listen to radio programmes?     54 %         39 %          7 %
Do you read      newspapers?           83 %         11 %          6 %
```

Look at the print-out and make sentences like this:

▶ The survey shows that 34% of the British watch videos **every day**.
▶ 39% of the British listen to the radio **now and then**.
▶ 6% of the British **never** read newspapers.
Go on.

2 The Wiggins family are a family with a lot of hobbies. Here they are:

a Ask and answer questions like this:

▶ Who reads comics? – Peter does.
▶ Who listens to pop music? – Linda does.
▶ Who watches westerns? – Mother does.

Go on with: videos, radio, books, television, thrillers, classical music, sports programmes, newspapers.

b What about you?
Ask about newspapers, television, radio and videos in your class.
Do a short survey and report about the results.

A UNIT 4

3 A radio day

All these people work for Radio Orwell in Ipswich.

Here is their typical Monday morning:

> disc jockey: play records
> cleaners: clean studios
> news editor: read telex reports
> technical engineers: service technical equipment
> editor of 'Teenage Magazine': watch music videos
> sports editor: write a report on the weekend football match
> secretaries: type answers to listeners' letters

Today there is a power cut. They can't do what they normally do. What are they doing?

Ask and answer questions like this:

▶ What does the disc jockey normally do on Monday mornings?
He normally plays records.

And what is he doing now?
He is smoking.

4

Joan is the 'Teenage Magazine' editor at Radio Orwell. Once a week she answers letters from listeners to the magazine. Here is her latest case:

```
Dear Joan,
We have two daughters. One of them is Louise. She is 19 and a super
girl. She has got a nice boyfriend and at the moment she is training to
be a shop-assistant. She never gives us any trouble. She is still living
at home and her boyfriend comes round regularly for a cup of tea with
us. But the problem is Tina. That's why we are writing to you today.
She is only 16 and is giving us a hard time right now. She is not
working at the moment and she is staying with some friends in a caravan.
She is now taking drugs, too. But she has her good points. For example,
she sometimes does unpaid work at the hospital. My husband and I talk
about her all the time and we write every week, but we are still waiting
for an answer. What can we do?
                                      Yours sincerely, Elizabeth
```

a Complete the sentences below and say whether it is Louise or Tina. Use the expressions from the box.

▶ **She** is not working …
Tina is not working at the moment.

sometimes	never
at the moment	right now
now	still	regularly

1 **She** is giving her parents a hard time …
2 … **she** is training to be a shop-assistant.
3 **Her** boyfriend comes round …
4 **She** is … taking drugs.
5 **She** … gives them any trouble.
6 … **she** is not working.
7 **She** is … living at home.
8 **She** is staying in a caravan …
9 **She** … does unpaid work.

46 forty-six

UNIT 4 A

b Talk about Louise, Tina and their parents.

Louise ... a nice boyfriend.
She never ... her parents any trouble.
She ... to be a shop-assistant at the moment.
She ... still ... at home.
Her boyfriend ... round regularly to have a cup of tea.

Tina ... a hard time.
She ... with friends in a caravan at the moment.
She ... now ... drugs.
Sometimes she ... unpaid work.

Their parents ...
Go on: They ...

c Can you translate Elizabeth's letter into German?

5 Making the news

Richard, Radio Orwell's news editor, likes to put some very personal stories in the news.
Listen to some parts of the news on Radio Orwell.

a Which picture goes with which story?

b Before he goes on the air, Richard makes notes. Can you take over Richard's role, use his notes and present this news again? Use the expressions in the box.

today	these days	this year
at the moment	just	now

Janet — play football with the boys — winner of the Football Lottery — train with the Chelsea team all this week — enjoy it

Deena — sheepdog — hate cats — run after them — look after 3 kittens — take over the role of a mother cat

Mr Scott — own village of Granraer — 21 empty houses — Scott — sell the village — offer it for £210,000

Firemen — risk their lives — work long hours — Billy Jenkins — do something for them — serve them free meals

Valentine's Day for Liz and Tom — work hard all year round — fly to Miami — Tom says — give each other the trip as a present

6

This is Paddy O'Brien's farm.

At the moment he is not at his farm,

he is on Majorca.

Richard wants to report on Paddy. Can you do his job again? Put a short story together.

Paddy O'Brien. — a farmer — get up early — milk the cows — feed the cows — clean the cowshed — take the milk to his customers — the winner of the Sun Travel Competition — enjoy a week's holiday on Majorca — lie in the sun — dream of a life without work

forty-seven 47

B UNIT 4

1 What sort of programme is it?

comedy religious programme quiz game film documentary sport educational programme show

▶ There's a film on Channel 4 at 8.15.
Go on: There's a ...

BBC 1
- 6.25 **News, Weather**
- 6.40 **Songs of Praise** From Coventry Cathedral
- 7.15 **Mastermind** This week's quiz game on the kings of England
- 8.00 **Wildlife on One**

BBC 2
- 6.30 **Money, Money, Money** An educational programme for all the family
- 7.15 **In the Kitchen** A cookery course, for men (and women)
- 7.40 **A Year with Fred** Series

LWT
- 6.00 **News**
- 6.40 **Places to Visit** Harry Poole looks at Brighton
- 7.15 **The Tina Turner Show**
- 8.30 **World in Action** The search for a cure for AIDS
- 9.00 **News**
- 9.30 **Relative Strangers**

C 4
- 6.15 **It's a Mad World** Have a good laugh with Benny Hill
- 6.45 **International Volleyball**
- 7.15 **The World at War:** August 1944 – March 1945
- 8.15 **The Swimmer** with Burt Lancaster (1968)

2 What the British think about TV:

m = viewers in millions   * = 'very poor'   **** = 'very good'

	how popular	entertaining	informative		how popular	entertaining	informative
sport	12 m	***	**	films	9 m	***	***
educational programmes	13 m	***	****	pop music	16 m	****	*
documentaries	7 m	**	****	religious programmes	6 m	*	**
shows	18 m	****	**	comedies	10 m	***	*
				plays	8 m	**	*

a Let's talk about the chart.

▶ Sport is more popular than documentaries.
▶ Sport is less entertaining than shows.
▶ Sport is as informative as shows.
Go on.

b Look at the chart again.

Which programmes are the most popular/entertaining/informative?
Which programmes are the least popular/entertaining/informative?

3 A time to advertise

The diagram shows you the viewing figures in Britain and the 'good' and 'bad' times to advertise.

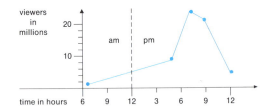

Mr Kelly from Kelly's Pies is phoning Mr Grace from MacLean's Advertising Agency to find out the best time to advertise his company's products.

Mr Grace: Well, 7.30 pm is the best time, and therefore it is also the most expensive time. It's still very good at 9 pm but cheaper.
Mr Kelly: Is it better to advertise in the morning than in the afternoon?
Mr Grace: No, you can't say that. 5 pm is bad but 9.30 in the morning is worse than 5 pm, but then again 6.30 am is the worst time of all. It's even worse than midnight.
Mr Kelly: Well, Mr Grace, what ...

UNIT 4 B

a Now answer the following questions:
1 Which is the worst time to advertise? Why?
2 Which is the best time to advertise?
3 Why does Mr Grace think it is better to advertise at 5 pm than at 9.30 am?
4 What is the problem about advertising at 7.30 pm?

b Work with your partner. Talk about the diagram. Use some of the following expressions and choose different times:

▶ What about 7 am? Is that a good time to advertise?
What do you think? Is ... all right?
Are ... and ... the same?
Can you compare ... and ...?
Well, what about ...?

c **What about you?**
Talk about the times to advertise on TV in your country.

4 Let's have a closer look at one of the programmes on TV.

Nora: More and more men are learning how to cook these days, and I think that's a very good thing, too. With us in the studio today is Jim Barnes. Hello, Jim.
Jim: Hello, Nora.
Nora: Jim, why are you learning to cook?
Jim: Well, now that my wife is working, I think it's only fair that we share the housework. And cookery is one of the nicest parts of it.
Nora: Well, today we're making Cornish Pasties. First of all the ingredients. You can write down the exact quantities at the end of the programme when we give you the recipe. Right Jim – what do we need for Cornish Pasties? ...

Now here is the recipe for 8 Cornish Pasties with the exact quantities.

For the pastry:
450 g flour
250 g margarine
15 ml water (6 spoons)

For the filling:
350 g cooked beef
8 potatoes
4 onions
salt and pepper
30 g butter
3 eggs

Ask and answer questions like this:

▶ How much flour do you need?
We need 450 grams of flour.
▶ How many eggs do you need?
We need 3 eggs.
Go on.

UNIT 4

1 New York – The Big Apple

Good afternoon, ladies and gentlemen. This is radio WNYK and my name is Tom Donovan...

 Listen to the following announcement.

a Which 4 stores are on the cassette?

1 Fred's Fun Store
2 Barron's Books
3 Macy's
4 Tracy's
5 The Black is Beautiful Salon
6 Frank's Fur Store
7 Parrot's Books
8 The Dog Beauty Salon

b Can you find the 4 stores on the map? Where are they?

 c Listen to the cassette again. Which is correct?

1 The radio station is in
New York State/San Francisco/
New York City.
2 The month is
November/December/October.
3 The time is
3.15 pm/2.15 pm/2.15 am.
4 The program is on
every day/once a month/once a week.
5 Macy's store is
on 69th Street/
on the corner of Broadway and 52nd Street/
on the corner of Broadway and 34th Street.
6 Macy's are selling
radios/TVs/fur coats.
7 Barron's Books is
on Second Avenue/
on Fifth Avenue/
on Third Avenue.
8 Barron's Books is giving away
a postcard/a map/a book.
9 Frank's Fur Store is
on East 32nd Street/
on West 23rd Street/
on South Street.
10 Frank's Fur Store is
opening/closing/
giving away fur coats.
11 The dog beauty treatment costs
less than $30/
more than $30/
exactly $30.

1 Guggenheim Museum	a–d:
2 Radio City Music Hall	4 stores
3 Rockefeller Center	
4 Times Square	
5 United Nations Building	
6 Madison Square Garden	
7 Empire State Building	
8 Washington Square	
9 Brooklyn Bridge	
10 World Trade Center	
11 Statue of Liberty	
12 New York City Museum	

UNIT 4 c

2 Famous places in New York

a Look at the map. Ask and answer questions like this:

> ▶ Can you tell me where the New York City Museum is?
> Yes, it's on Fifth Avenue between 103rd and 104th Street.

You can use the phrases in the box.

```
on ... in ...
on the corner of ... and ...
between ... and ...
near ...
```

1. the Empire State Building
2. the United Nations Building
3. Times Square
4. Madison Square Garden
5. the Rockefeller Center
6. Central Park
7. the Guggenheim Museum
8. the Radio City Music Hall

b You are standing in front of Macy's. Somebody asks you:

> ▶ Excuse me. Can you tell me the way to the Rockefeller Center?

Use your map and tell him/her the way:

> ▶ Go straight down 34th Street and turn left into Fifth Avenue. Go straight down Fifth Avenue. The Rockefeller Center is on your left.

Now people ask you the way to Madison Square Garden/the Empire State Building/Times Square. Find the positions and use your map to tell them the way. You can use the phrases in the box.

```
go straight down ...
turn left into ...
turn right into ...
... on your left/... on your right
```

c Now you are standing in front of the United Nations Building. People ask you the way to the World Trade Center/ the Guggenheim Museum/Central Park/the Radio City Music Hall. Can you help them?

3

Radio City Music Hall

Sixth Ave. at 50 St.   Tel: 246-4600

All concerts start at 8 p.m.
Summer break: July 29 – September 11

Program June 12 – July 27

Mon.	June 12	*David Bowie*
Wed.	June 14	*Eurythmics*
Sat.	June 17	*Prince*
Sat.	June 24	*Tina Turner*
Sat.	July 1	*Michael Jackson*
Fri.	July 7	*Queen*
Sun.	July 9	*Pet Shop Boys*
Sat.	July 15	*Depeche Mode*
Thu.	July 20	*Madonna*
Sat.	July 22	*George Michael*
Thu.	July 27	*Bruce Springsteen*

Ask and answer questions like this:

> ▶ When's Michael Jackson playing?
> On the 1st of July.

Go on.

UNIT 4

1 Newspapers

Everyone knows them – the newspapers. In Britain there are about 130 daily and Sunday papers. The most famous British newspaper is probably 'The Times'. The two most popular dailies are 'The Sun' and 'The Daily Mirror'. Over 20 million people read one of these newspapers every day. British newspapers are cheap – the 'Mirror' and the 'Sun' cost 18p and the 'Times' costs 32p.

Where do the newspapers get their news from? The large papers have reporters in many different parts of the world. They report on new events by telephone or telex. A lot of information comes from large news agencies such as UPI (United Press International) or dpa (Deutsche Presse-Agentur).

Let's take a look at the production of a large daily newspaper:

3.55 pm
The reporter is collecting information for a report.

5.57 pm
The report is coming in on the telex.

6.47 pm
An assistant editor is typing the article into the computer.

8.00 pm
The editors are choosing the articles for tomorrow's paper.

9.20 pm
The layout man is cutting texts and pictures to the right size.

10.02 pm
The page is finished. The proof-reader is looking for mistakes.

10.55 pm
The printer is operating the printing-press.

11.49 pm
The first edition is coming off the presses.

6.00 am
The van-driver is delivering the papers to the newspaper shop.

a What's going on here?

b What do these people do:

editors,
an assistant editor,
layout men/women,
reporters,
a proof-reader,
a printer,
van-drivers?

UNIT 4

c Look at the text and answer the following questions:

1. What is perhaps Britain's most famous newspaper?
2. Can you name two popular British newspapers?
3. Which newspaper is cheaper, the 'Mirror' or the 'Times'?
4. What is a daily?
5. What is a Sunday newspaper?
6. How many people read the two biggest popular dailies every day?
7. How many newspapers are there in Britain?
8. Where do newspapers get their news from?

d Which words in the text can replace the words in **bold type**?

1. The 'Times' is a **well-known** British newspaper.
2. The 'Daily Mirror' is a **well-liked** daily.
3. Newspapers get their **stories** from reporters and agencies all over the world.
4. **More than** 20 million people read the 'Sun' or the 'Mirror' every day.
5. British papers are **not expensive**.
6. Newspapers get **facts** from agencies.
7. A printer **works** the printing-press.
8. A van-driver **takes** the papers to the newspaper shops.

2 The proof-reader at the 'Rochdale Observer' is upset. He has got two articles full of mistakes. It is his job to put them right. Can you help him?

Isn't it a mad world?

Everyone wants to have this number

1 "Number-plates, these days, are pretty expensive," says Bernadette Sawyers, a loohcs teacher. "I spend much more money than before. I think that our
5 plate costs us nearly £200 a month. About £90 go to the ybabsitter. But like this, I can still work and earn a bit of money. We really love our little lingdar and he
10 gives us a lot of pleasure."

Don't they cost a lot?

B. Sawyers with her baby

1 Some people drive around in expensive cars. But the babies on them are even more evisnepxe than the cars. Why is that? The number-plate centre in
5 Swansea now has new rules. You can only take babies from other cars (not from motor-bikes or scooters) when they are still on the road. And there are no low numbers any more. So you
10 can't have a new **PIG 1**. You must buy it from another car-owner. And they pay up to £20,000 for a **JR 1** or a **2 BAD** or an **RR 1**.
"Isn't that enough?".

fifty-three 53

 **UNIT 4**

Have a look at this ...

When you describe a picture, you must say
 — where people and things are,
 — what the people are doing or wearing.

They can be ...

on the left-hand side in the foreground on the right-hand side

 Now look at the pictures. Then close your books and guess which picture one of the students in class is describing to you.

54 fifty-four

UNIT 4 G

Present Simple of main verbs

Positive question with *who*

| Who reads comics? |
| Who listens to pop music? |

Fragebildung ohne *do* bei Fragen nach dem Subjekt (*who* = „wer")

Present Continuous – Present Simple

Das *Present Continuous* wird verwendet für Handlungen, die im Augenblick oder gegenwärtig stattfinden. Deshalb mit den Signalwörtern:

| at the moment, now, today, just, these days |

Das *Present Simple* wird verwendet für Handlungen, die regelmäßig oder wiederholt stattfinden. Deshalb mit den Signalwörtern:

| always, never, normally, regularly, sometimes, every day/month/year, all the time, on ... |

| Janet's **working** in the garden today. |
| That's why we **are writing** to you now. |
| At the moment she **is training** to be a typist. |

| She always **works** in the garden on Saturdays. |
| She sometimes **writes** us a letter. |
| The players never **train** on Sundays. |

Comparison of adjectives

| popular | **more** popular | **most** popular |
| informative | **more** informative | **most** informative |

Längere Adjektive werden mit *more/most* gesteigert.

| Sport is **more popular than** plays. |
| Shows are **the most popular** programmes. |

more popular than = „beliebter als"
the most popular = „die beliebtesten"

| good | **better** | **best** |
| bad | **worse** | **worst** |

Einige Adjektive haben unregelmäßige Steigerungsformen.

| clear | **less** clear | **least** clear |
| popular | **less** popular | **least** popular |

Adjektive werden mit *less/least* vermindert.

| Mary's **less happy** about it **than** I am. |
| Documentaries are **the least popular** programmes on TV. |

less happy than = „weniger glücklich als"
the least popular = „die am wenigsten beliebten"

how much, how many

| How much sugar ...? | bei nichtzählbaren |
| How much water ...? | Begriffen |

| How many bottles ...? | bei zählbaren |
| How many eggs ...? | Begriffen im Plural |

Cardinal numbers, ordinal numbers

Grundzahlen		Ordnungszahlen					
one	seven	**first**	1st	seven**th**	7th	twenty-**first**	21st
two	eight	**second**	2nd	eigh**th**	8th	thirty-**second**	32nd
three	nine	**third**	3rd	nin**th**	9th	forty-**third**	43rd
four	ten	four**th**	4th	ten**th**	10th	fifty-four**th**	54th
five	eleven	fif**th**	5th	eleven**th**	11th	sixty-fif**th**	65th
six	twelve	six**th**	6th	twelf**th**	12th	seventy-six**th**	76th
...				...		...	

Die ersten drei Ordnungszahlen sind unregelmäßig.

Alle übrigen enden auf *-th*.

Beachte die besondere Schreibung von *fifth, eighth, ninth* und *twelfth*.

fifty-five 55

UNIT 5

CHANGES

Swanmouth today ...

... and 60 years ago

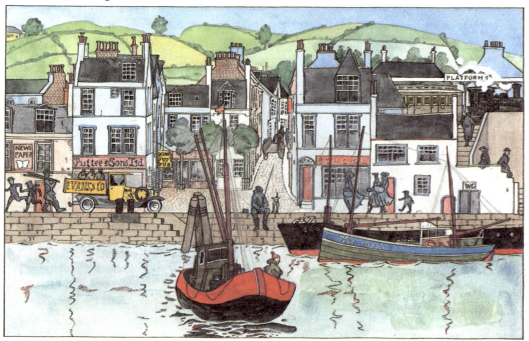

What can you see in the pictures? What is your town/village like?

UNIT 5 A

1 Jessica is spending her holidays with her grandfather in Swanmouth.
One evening she sees an old picture of Swanmouth and asks her grandfather about it.

Jessica: Grandad, what was it like when you were fourteen?
Grandfather: Well, our town was much smaller then. Everything was quieter here and there were only about 1,000 inhabitants.
Jessica: Were there any cars in the streets?
Grandfather: Hm, there were some old-fashioned cars but they were too expensive in those days. There were a lot of horses and carts. Today we have cars and lorries, of course.
Jessica: I see. – Do you think that people were happier when you were young?
Grandfather: Well, life was harder than it is now. For example, there was no central heating, no warm water, nothing like that at all, but we weren't unhappy. The streets were much safer and our town was more beautiful than it is now.
Jessica: But don't you think it's nicer today? There's a cinema and I can even go to the disco. – What were you interested in?
Grandfather: I was interested in hunting but there wasn't much time for that. You see, when I was your age, I was at work in the fields with my uncle George after school. He was a farmer.
Jessica: What about Grandma?
Grandfather: Oh, she was a wonderful wife. She was a good mother, too. She …

a Which question goes with which answer?

1 What were your hobbies?
2 No, but there were many horses and carts in the streets.
3 What was Grandmother like?
4 Life was harder, but I think we were just as happy as you are now.
5 Was it different here when you were young?
6 There was a lot of work so there was not much time for hobbies.
7 Were there many cars?
8 Oh, she was nice.
9 Were people happier 60 years ago?
10 Yes, it was quieter.

b Put the questions and answers in the order of the dialogue.

2 Look at the picture of Swanmouth 60 years ago.

a What was Swanmouth like?

▶ There was/were no …
▶ There were some …
▶ There was/were a lot of …

b Ask and answer questions like this:

▶ What was the river like?
   The river was clean.
▶ What were the streets like?
   The streets were safe.

Use words like these:

houses	trains	small	noisy
shops	cars	old	dirty
school	air	slow	beautiful
factory	clothes	clean	…

c Compare the two pictures.

fifty-seven 57

A UNIT 5

3 Jessica is still curious ...

Grandfather: ... you see, Jessica, I was born in 1920.
Jessica: Where were you born?
Grandfather: I was born in this house.
Jessica: What was your father's job?
Grandfather: He was a fisherman.
Jessica: How often was he out at sea?
Grandfather: He was out every day.
Jessica: What was his boat like?
Grandfather: It was just a small boat.
Jessica: What was your life like?
Grandfather: It was a lot of fun for us children.
Jessica: What were your hobbies?
Grandfather: My friends and I were good at hunting.
Jessica: How many children were there at your school?
Grandfather: There were about 70 pupils.
Jessica: What was your first job?
Grandfather: At first, I was a fisherman, too ...

a Take Jessica's role and ask questions.
Your partner should find the right answer.

▶ Where/you born?
Where were you born?
I was born in this house.
▶ What/your father's job?
What was your father's job?
He was a fisherman.

1 What/your first job?
2 What/your hobbies?
3 How many children/there at your school?
4 What/his boat like?
5 What/your life like?
6 How often/he out at sea?

b Listen to the cassette.
What else does Jessica's grandfather say?

4 Compare life today and sixty years ago.

There are many tall buildings **today**. Life is comfortable. The shops are big. In the shops there is a lot of fresh fruit from all over the world. There are not many children in the streets **nowadays**. There are many cars and they are very fast. **Today** it is easy to travel but it is noisy in the streets. The streets are dangerous **now**. There are not many trees. The air is dirty. Pollution is a big problem **today**.

Now say what life was like 60 years ago.

You can use the expressions in the box.

▶ There weren't many tall buildings **sixty years ago**. Life wasn't comfortable. The shops ...

| 60 years ago | then | in those days |

5 Play the roles of Jessica and her grandfather.

Ask and answer questions like this:

▶ life hard
Was life hard? – Yes, it was.
▶ parents rich
Were your parents rich? – No, they weren't.
▶ a cinema
Was there a cinema? – No, there wasn't.
▶ many horses
Were there many horses? – Yes, there were.

Go on with: town smaller,
everything quieter,
many big shops,
a school,
streets safer,
a hospital,
river dirty, many cars,
a supermarket,
Grandmother nice.

58 fifty-eight

UNIT 5 A

6 Back home in Midhurst, Jessica writes to her friend Jenny.

> and those two weeks with Grandad down in Swanmouth were really great. Oh yes, I wanted to tell you about our new neighbours, the Millers. They moved into the house next to us not long ago. When I was in the garden last week, I called to one of the children. Her name is Lucy and we talked for almost half an hour. Then she invited me in to meet the family. Well, it was quite a shock! When the Smiths lived there it was a normal house, but now it's full of bottles of funny-looking beans and things, and there's a windmill in the garden! The Millers are very nice though. And do you know where they lived before? They lived in London, but they hated the noise and the smell there. The air was too polluted and Lucy hated the dirty streets and the crowded buses when she travelled to school. So they decided to change their way of life and they moved to the country. They wanted to have lots of fresh air and only eat good wholefood. Above all, they wanted an alternative way of life. That's why they decided to have the windmill — it's to make electricity.
>
> Lucy's mother baked a cake for us while I was there, so I stayed for tea and we talked about London. She disliked London because their garden wasn't very big and so it wasn't possible to grow their own vegetables. Also there wasn't much time for the garden because she worked in an office and

a Look at Jessica's letter and say what the Millers hated about London.

▶ In London they hated the polluted air.
Go on.

Now say what they wanted to do in the country.

▶ In the country they wanted to have lots of fresh air.
Go on.

b Use the verbs in the box to complete the following text in the Past Simple Tense:

```
     want     stay
1 live    try    hurry
     look   2 watch
4 smoke    do    move
```

When the Millers were in London, they ① in a small house. They ② TV in the evenings. Mrs Miller only ③ her shopping in a supermarket. Mr Miller ④ twenty cigarettes a day. Mrs Miller ⑤ in the office for lunch. Mr Miller ⑥ to work in the mornings. Mrs Miller ⑦ to keep fit. They ⑧ a different way of life. They ⑨ at houses in the country. They ⑩ to Midhurst.

(handwritten answers: watched, wanted, lived, looked, smoked, hurried, did, moved)

c Can you answer the following questions?

1 When **did** the Millers **move** to Midhurst?
2 How **did** they **like** London?
3 Who **did** Jessica **talk** to in the garden?
4 Why **did** Mrs Miller **dislike** London?

Make more questions and answer them:

5 When/Jessica (talk) to Lucy?
6 Why/they (leave) London?
7 How/Lucy (travel) to school?
8 What/they (want) to do in the country?

fifty-nine 59

B UNIT 5

1 Last year the Browns from Southport spent their summer holiday at a bed and breakfast place in the seaside resort of Helston in Cornwall.

One evening they talked to Mrs Owen, the landlady. She told them about an oil tanker accident. It took place in 1967 and there was a lot of pollution because oil got onto the local beaches.

Mrs Owen: Well, it all started on a Monday. I can remember it so well because it was my birthday. We had a terrible storm the night before. I didn't want to go out but I had to do some shopping in the village. I met Mrs Gale on the way home and she told me the news. I can remember her voice still now...

"... an oil tanker, the Torrey Canyon, I think they said, sank last night near Shepherd's Rock. They sent an SOS signal from the tanker, and when the helicopters came, there was a lot of oil on the water. And you know, it's coming towards our beaches..."

That was true. Soon our beaches were full of oil. The government called in the army to clean up the beaches, but it was too late. Many sea-birds and fish died. Many tourists went home because they wanted nice clean beaches. You couldn't blame them, could you? Some other tourists wrote to me and said they didn't want to come to Helston that year. They planned their holiday somewhere else...

a What happened?
Complete the text.
Use the verbs in the box and put them into the Past Tense.

do	fly	meet	
get	send	have	be
tell	go	write	

Mrs Owen ① Mrs Gale on her way home.
Oil ② into the sea.
They ③ a terrible storm.
Tourists ④ to Mrs Owen.
Mrs Owen ⑤ some shopping.
The tanker ⑥ an SOS signal.
The beaches ⑦ polluted.
Tourists ⑧ home.
Mrs Gale ⑨ her the news.
Helicopters ⑩ to the tanker.

b Put the sentences above into the order of the text.

c Write down some questions about the oil tanker accident.

▶ Where did the accident take place?

where	Mrs Owen	take place
when	helicopters	say
what	the government	sink
why	tourists	go
who	Mrs Gale	meet
	accident	do
	the Torrey Canyon	send
		write to
		come
		stay

d Ask each other the questions and answer them.

UNIT 5 B

2 Not only big accidents cause pollution of the environment, tourists can do this, too. Helston put up signs last year to remind tourists to keep the village clean and tidy.

a Look at the picture.
  ▶ Some people didn't read the sign.
  ▶ Some people didn't take …
  Go on.

Please read this!
1. Take your litter home
2. Put your rubbish in the bins
3. Keep your dog under control
4. Park your car in the central car park
5. Leave the beach clean and tidy for other people

Helston Community Council

b The Smiths and the Bennetts went to Helston yesterday. Here is what they did:

The Smiths
- go to the beach / • have a swim
- spend a nice day on the beach
- have lunch on the beach
- meet their friends
- write postcards
- get home late

The Bennetts
- stay in town
- go to the tourist information centre
- visit a local museum
- have fish and chips
- do some shopping
- write some letters
- come back to their hotel late

Make sentences like this: ▶ The Smiths went to the beach.
The Bennetts didn't go to the beach, they stayed in town.
Go on.

3 Find out what your partner did or didn't do to keep the environment clean last week.

a Ask and answer questions.
  ▶ to college by bike last week?
  Did you come to college by bike last week?
  Yes, I did./No, I didn't.

Use the verbs in the box and give points for the answers.

| come | throw | take | drink |
| buy | put | speak | |

1 a plastic product last week? (Yes −1/No +2)
2 litter on the ground last week? (Yes −3/No +1)
3 your empty bottles to the bottle bank last week (Yes +2/No −2)
4 your old paper into a special container last week? (Yes +3/No −2)
5 out of a can last week? (Yes −1/No +1)
6 to your friends about the environment last week? (Yes +1/No −1)

b Now tell your partner his/her total points and what he/she must do.

+10 to +7	Our environment loves you. Keep up the good work.	−1 to −5	Our environment doesn't like you very much. Think more about what you do.
+6 to +3	Not bad. Our environment likes you, but you must try harder this week.	−6 to −10	You weren't very good last week. In fact, our environment doesn't like you at all. Read Unit 5 very carefully.
+2 to 0	You are not very active. Why not do something?		

sixty-one 61

UNIT 5

1 'Friends of the Earth' is a British environment group. It helps to protect the environment. The Millers work with their local group. Here is one of their information leaflets:

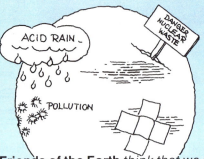

PROTECT THE EARTH

WORK WITH FoE

We at **Friends of the Earth** *think that we must protect the Earth because we want a healthy life.*

● Last year **Friends of the Earth** started 'Energy Action' groups. We helped to save more energy at home.

● We also protested about nuclear energy and fought for alternative forms of energy, for example wind energy.

● In May last year many **FoE** groups began a new project. We collected more waste paper than before and started bottle banks.

● We also protested about the use of dangerous chemicals on farms and at home.

● Last summer we started a project against pollution 'Stop Acid Rain'. It showed the dangers of cars and power stations to lakes, rivers and buildings.

● Last year the government wanted to make the M40 motorway longer. But in March **FoE** groups stopped these plans and so saved important woods in Oxfordshire.

● In the past, car firms showed pictures of fast and dangerous driving on TV. But after our protest last year this stopped.

a True or false?
1. After the FoE 'Energy Action' people used more energy at home.
2. Last year FoE fought for wind energy.
3. In September last year, FoE gave up their waste paper project.
4. The 'Stop Acid Rain' project was a danger to lakes, rivers and buildings.
5. Last year FoE were against the use of some chemicals.
6. In March last year, FoE protected the M40 motorway.
7. After the FoE protest, some car firms showed more pictures of fast and dangerous driving on TV than before.

b Last year FoE helped to protect the environment in a lot of ways. They were **for** some things and **against** others.

▶ They were **for** 'Energy Action' groups.
▶ They were **against** nuclear energy.
Go on.

c Look at the leaflet. How did FoE help to protect the environment?
Use the verbs in the box.

| protest | begin | fight | stop |

▶ They began 'Energy Action' groups.
Go on.

UNIT 5 C

2 Yesterday the Millers gave Jessica's parents, the Dixons, this leaflet from FoE. It says what people should or should not do at home to protect the environment.

Ten Things You Can Do to Protect the Environment

1. Take all your old bottles to the bottle bank.
2. Don't throw old batteries away.
3. Don't use too much water. Use rainwater for the garden.
4. Never throw old paper away.
5. Leave your car at home; ride your bike when possible.
6. Take your shopping bag with you when you go shopping. Don't accept plastic bags.
7. Buy recycled paper – writing paper, toilet rolls etc.
8. Talk about the environment to other people.
9. Never buy sprays.
10. Start a **Friends of the Earth** group at work, college or school.

Good luck!   For more details or help write to:
Friends of the Earth, 54–57 Allison Street, Birmingham 5.

a Later in the evening the Dixons talked about the leaflet.

▶ Mr Dixon: It says here we should take our old bottles to the bottle bank.
  Mrs Dixon: And it says here we shouldn't throw old batteries away.
Go on.

b Translate the leaflet into German.

3 The Dixons wrote to Friends of the Earth and FoE sent some more information and this price-list.

a The Dixons ordered 4 boxes of writing paper (white, A4) and 200 envelopes (white) and 1 large box of toilet rolls. Their daughter, Jessica, wanted 3 stickers (No 301, No 302, No 304). Copy the order form and write out their order.

b **What about you?**
Write down your own order.

UNIT 5

Greenpeace Action Against Air Pollution

By BERT HALLMOND

Yesterday morning a protest action by Yorkshire's Greenpeace Movement surprised managers and workers at the Ferrybridge Power Station, one of the biggest power stations in England.

It was early in the morning when 25 members of Yorkshire's Greenpeace Movement and friends from all over Europe started their protest action. They wanted to protest about the air pollution from the coal-fired power station. First some protesters stood in front of the main gate while others blocked the railway lines. All this just took ten minutes. Then two British demonstrators climbed up the tower of the power station and soon hung a banner from the tower to protest about acid rain. During this demonstration other protesters from Greenpeace gave leaflets to the workers. They explained the action, but some of the workers got angry: "Our jobs are in danger!" they shouted, "500 people work here, you shouldn't forget that!" "But we're not against people, we're fighting for more jobs in the field of alternative energy and for your health, too," answered one of the demonstrators. "Somebody should stop them", an old man shouted, "call the police!" This demonstration went on all day. Late in the afternoon, Alan Powell, the manager of the power station, spoke with the demonstrators and promised them a discussion on the problem soon. The demonstrators then left.

Greenpeace flag on Ferrybridge Power Station

a Answer the following questions in complete sentences:
  1 Where did the protest action take place?
  2 When did Greenpeace start the demonstration?
  3 How long did it take to block the railway lines?
  4 What did the demonstrators give to the workers?
  5 When did the protesters leave?
  6 Why did the workers protest?

b Complete the following sentences.

Some members of Greenpeace ① the railway lines.
They ② about air pollution.
The demonstrators ③ their protest action at 6.30 am.
Two people ④ up the tower.
Some workers ⑤ loud.
The manager ⑥ a discussion.
The protesters ⑦ leaflets to the workers.
They ⑧ a banner from the tower.
The demonstrators ⑨ the power station at 5.30 pm.

You can use the verbs in the box.

block		hang
	shout	
leave		start
	climb	
give		protest
	promise	

c Put the sentences above in the order of the text.

UNIT 5

d Make a summary of the text.
Use the following expressions in the given order:

1 in the morning
2 and
3 first
4 and then
5 soon
6 at the same time
7 but
8 when
9 after ten hours

e Which words in the text can replace the words in **bold type**?

1 The **demonstrators** were against air pollution.
2 The workers **began** to shout.
3 A member of Greenpeace **talked to** the workers.
4 Some workers did not like the **protest action**.
5 After ten hours they **went away**.
6 "When was the protest action?" she asked. "Yesterday", he **replied**.

f These were some newspaper headlines last year:

1 What happened?
2 How did these things damage the environment?
3 What do you think about protest actions against pollution?

You can use the phrases in the box.

In my opinion ...
I think .../I don't think ...
I agree with .../I don't agree with ...
I'm for .../I'm against ...
They should .../They shouldn't ...

What's wrong?

UNIT 5 G

Past Simple of main verbs

Das *Past Simple* wird verwendet für abgeschlossene Handlungen in der Vergangenheit, meistens mit Zeitangabe (zum Beispiel mit *last night, two weeks ago*).

Statement

I	**wanted** a new car.	Bei regelmäßigen Verben gilt für alle Personen:
You	**watched** TV last night.	Infinitiv + *-ed*
He/She/It	**moved** to London 2 years ago.	Stummes *-e* entfällt.
We/You/They	**tried** to get some exercise.	Konsonant + *y* wird zu *-ied*.
	stopped the car after 3 hours.	Konsonanten werden oft verdoppelt.

| They | **went** to Italy. | Unregelmäßige Verben bilden für das *Past Simple* |
| She | **wrote** a letter to Aunt Vera. | besondere Formen. |

| I | **didn't go** to the museum last night. | Verneinung für alle Personen: *didn't* + Infinitiv |
| They | **didn't stop** work in the morning. | (in der Schriftsprache *did not*) |

Question

Did		you	**watch** the TV show?	Fragebildung für alle Personen:
Did		the Thompsons	**move** to London?	*did* + Infinitiv
Where	**did**	he	**go** after the concert?	
What	**did**	the tourists	**write** to the landlady?	

| Who **watched** the TV show last night? | Aber: Kein *did* bei Fragen nach dem |
| Who **wrote** the letter to the landlady? | Subjekt (*who* = „wer") |

Past Simple of *be*

Statement

| I/he/she/it | **was** | not | in Exeter. |
| We/you/they | **were** | not | |

Question

| **Was** | I/he/she/it | in Birmingham? |
| **Were** | we/you/they | |

Frage und Verneinung werden nicht mit *did* umschrieben.
Kurzformen von *was/were* gibt es nicht.
Die Kurzformen von *was not/were not* sind *wasn't/weren't*.

Modal auxiliaries: *should/shouldn't*

You **should** take your glass to the bottle bank.	*should/shouldn't* werden gebraucht:
People **should** do more for the environment.	– um Ratschläge zu geben.
You **shouldn't** throw litter on the ground.	– um Vorschläge zu machen.
We **shouldn't** buy sprays.	– um Warnungen auszusprechen.

R REVISION 1

Unit 1

1 What are the possible answers?

1 Have you got a car?
2 Is there a theatre in Manchester?
3 Are you at Manchester College?
4 Is she from Glasgow?
5 Has he got a map?
6 Is the disco nice?
7 Are they from our college?
8 Have they got good music?
9 Are there museums in Manchester?
10 Has Manchester got an ice-skating rink?

Yes, it has.
No, they haven't.
Yes, there are.
Yes, they are.
No, I'm not.
Yes, it is.
No, I haven't.
Yes, she is.
Yes, there is.
No, he hasn't.

2 In the word list you can find the word 'glass' three times. What are the other words? How many can you find? Use 'there is, there are' in your answer.

Slsga, nichsawd, noops, patoto, salgs, nomaw, obx, otatop, krof, fnike, ihcld, chiwdans, sagsl, manow, leapp, ooaptt, dilch, xob, noitats, orenag, wichsand, efink, lichd, egnaro, latipsoh, nekif, etalp.

3 "My name's Mike. I'm at Manchester College and my sister's there, too. My hobby's football. I haven't got a car, but I've got a motorbike."

"My name's Rose. I'm from London. My parents have got a house there. We've got a dog. Our dog is very small, but my boyfriend is afraid of him."

Write about these people like this: ▶ His name is …

4 Find the missing words.

Dear Susan,
① am here in Bristol. Not alone, no. ② are three boys and a girl, Rose. ③ youth-hostel is in the centre of town. ④ is very modern and ⑤ have got nice rooms. ⑥ are big and clean. At the moment the others are in town. Rose is with ⑦ new boyfriend, Olaf. ⑧ is from Sweden. Graham and Mike are at a garage. ⑨ have got problems with ⑩ motor-bike. ⑪ have a problem, too. ⑫ are not here. Lots of love,
Tom

P.S. Tell ⑬ brother that ⑭ have still got ⑮ rucksack. ⑯ can have ⑰ back after the holidays.

5 Susan is new at Manchester College. Here is her conversation with Lynn. Rewrite it and put the verbs into the correct forms. Be careful with the word order.

Lynn: Are you new here?
Susan: Yes, I am.
Lynn: be/you/from/where?
Susan: I/from/be/Leeds.
and I/my parents/new/be/Manchester/in. you/have/a map/got/Manchester/of?
Lynn: No, why?
Susan: have/well,/I/two or three questions/got.
Lynn: Go on. be/here/I/from.
Susan: be/there/an ice-skating rink/Manchester/in?

Lynn: Yes. be/in Devonshire Road/it.
Susan: Good.
a music fan/be/my brother.
you/discos,/got/too/have?
Lynn: Lots.
and/have/got/nice music/they/there.
Oh, look. there/my bus/be.
Susan: Yes, but …
have/a telephone/you/got?
Lynn: Yes,/411 3862/be/my number./OK?
Susan: Good,/it/have/I/got. See you.
Lynn: See you.

Unit 2

REVISION 1

6 This is part of the programme at Bristol Youth Hostel:

Ask and answer questions like this:

▶ When's ...?
It's at ...
It's from ... to ...

THIS WEEK:
FRIDAY
8.15 - 9.15 BREAKFAST
12.30 - 1.15 LUNCH
5.45 - 6.45 TEA
10.15 BEDTIME
4.00 - 5.30 VIDEO: GOLDFINGER
A JAMES BOND CLASSIC
(RED ROOM)
7.15 - 10.00 TABLE TENNIS CUP!!!
(GAMES ROOM)
7.45 - 9.15 CONCERT:
TERRY AND HIS GUITAR
(MUSIC ROOM)

7 Fill in the missing modals.

can	can't
must	mustn't
	needn't

At Bristol Youth Hostel breakfast is from 8.15 to 9.15. So you ① have breakfast at 9.30. Bedtime is at 10.15. Everybody ② be in bed by then. There are 'No Smoking' signs in the building. So you ③ smoke in the youth hostel. There are no cleaners. The guests ④ clean their rooms. Sometimes in the evenings you ⑤ watch films, but you ⑥ do that, you ⑦ also listen to music or play games. There is a big cafeteria. You ⑧ eat and drink there. The meaning of the sign 'No bottles' on the bedroom door is clear. You ⑨ take drinks to your room.

8 Tom is a student. At the weekends he has got a job as a taxi driver.

Make dialogues:

▶ Passenger: Can you take **me** to the station, please?
Tom: Hello, Central 3414, I've got a passenger. I'm taking **him** to the station.

9 What are they doing?

10 You are standing in front of a phone box and you can hear parts of this conversation. Can you write down the possible questions?

– Hello Karen, this is Jerry speaking.
– ...?
– No, I'm not coming tonight, I'm coming tomorrow.
– ...?
– Yes, Jane's coming, too.
– ...?
– Oh no, we're not coming for lunch, we're coming later.
– ...?
– At 3.45.

– ...?
– Friday? – We're doing a sightseeing tour.
– ...?
– Bob? He's at college.
– ...?
– My parents are still living in London.
– ...?
– Our holidays this year? We're going to Spain.

R REVISION 1

Unit 3

11 Read what these people say.

Peter: I like disco music a lot. I go to Fagin's every night for an hour or so.

John: I hate Mondays. I always get up too late. I miss the bus every Monday morning.

Susan: I watch television every night. I really love it.

Ann: I go fishing sometimes. When I go, I always catch a big fish.

Mark: I hate French. I try hard. I always do my homework, but my grades* are still bad.

Alison: I help my grandfather with the shopping at the weekends. I always carry his bags for him.

Now write about them: ▶ Peter likes ...

* grades = Noten, Zensuren

12 Give short answers.

1 Does your mother cook every day?
2 Do you drive a car?
3 Do you like Maths?
4 Do your parents speak a foreign language?
5 Does your school sell food and drinks?
6 Do you speak Spanish?
7 Does your father smoke?
8 Do your teachers work hard?

13 What do these traffic signs mean? Give short negative or positive orders. Use the words in the box.

drive	overtake	
park	stop	turn

1 2 3

4 5 6 7 8

14 Something's wrong here. Put the sentences right.

▶ Computer programmers play with computers.

Computer programmers don't play with computers, they program computers.

1 A hairstylist pulls people's hair.
2 An airline stewardess shaves passengers.
3 Office workers plant vegetables in offices.
4 A painter builds a house.
5 Typists paint letters.
6 A cook serves the food.
7 A mechanic breaks cars.
8 Students forget to do their homework.

15 Compare the three pairs of sports shoes. You can use the words in the box.

high	flat	small
heavy	light	big

1 1250 g   2 480 g   3 380 g

16 Read this student's letter about his college. You can't read all the words. Ring him up and ask about them. For your questions use the words in the box.

what	where	why	what	where
how often		where	when	where

The German teacher is all right. He always wears ___. The physics teacher is very funny. He tells us a joke every ___. And our maths teacher! She tries to park her car in the ___ in the mornings. I don't like the food in the cafeteria because it's ___. My friend Tom always leaves his tools on his ___. Sometimes we even find them in the ___. I really like the ___ in the workshop. They are so practical. Lunch breaks are great. We have them at ___. Then we always go down to the ___. Well, I hope you can read everything.

Unit 4

REVISION 1

17 Arsenal is a famous football team from London. These are the dates of their matches in December and January.

Make sentences.

```
Away matches:        Home matches:
Dec 21  Everton      Dec 23  Chelsea
Dec 26  Chelsea      Dec 31  Leeds United
Jan  2  Manchester United   Jan  5  Liverpool
Jan 12  Watford      Jan 15  Wimbledon
```

▶ They have an away match on ... against ...

18 People want to sell their cars. Compare the cars. Use the words in the box.

```
expensive      noisy
    bad in winter
modern         elegant
  good on fast roads
  dangerous on snow
```

Jaguar XJ, elegant, £25,000, 1987, blue, 32,000 miles, top speed 145 mph, Tel 687 531

Austin Mini, 1957, 347,000 miles, defective heating, £1,500, **Tel 69 342**

Landrover Jeep, Turbo Diesel, 12,000 miles, 1985, good on snow and ice, £21,000, Tel 69 745

19 Say what these people do in their jobs and what they are doing at the moment.

1    2    3    4    5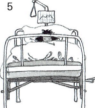

Tom is a taxi driver.   Joan is a cook.   Ian is an electrician.   John is a teacher.   Mary is an editor.

20 Lynn Nink is a nurse. Her husband George is a lorry driver. Look at this chart about their working lives.

Ask and answer questions with 'how much' and 'how many'. Use the verbs in the box.

```
work    have got    do    earn    be
```

	Lynn	George
working days a week	4	5
free days a week	3	2
hours a day	8	7
overtime a month	6 hrs	2 hrs
money a week (in £)	150	250
breaks a day	2	1
nurses in the hospital	58	–
drivers in the firm	–	12

21 Look at the text below. Rewrite it with the correct forms of the verbs and adjectives.

Daley Thompson is a very good British athlete. We even think that he is the (good) British athlete of all times. Winner of two Olympic Gold Medals in the decathlon*! But how does he live? First of all he (train) a lot. He (not drink), and he (not smoke). He (not be) on a diet, but he (watch) his food. He (go) to bed early and (get up) early. He knows that he (be) a professional and he (do) everything to show he (be) the (good) in the world.
Usually he (live) in Britain. But at the moment he (train) in California. For him, it is (good) to train there than in Britain, because the weather in Britain is (bad) than in that part of America.
What do people think about him? David Phelps, a sports fan from Bournemouth, says: "I think, he is a charming young man. Whenever he (open) his mouth, he (say) something funny. He is (funny) than most other sportsmen. His competitions are (interesting) to watch than other competitions, because he (do) a lot of different sports. I don't know how to say it – but he also looks much (elegant) than most other sportsmen! Next week he (run) here in Bournemouth."

* decathlon = Zehnkampf

seventy-one 71

REVISION 1

Unit 5

22 On Radio Orwell, Tony Simpson has a show from 8 till 9 and Sue Baker and Tina Brown have a show from 10 till 11 o'clock.
Some things went wrong in their programmes last Monday morning. (A ✓ means that they did and a !!! means that they did not do what they wanted to do.) Make sentences. Say what they did or did not do in their programmes.

```
Tony - 'Meet your neighbours'

play top ten ✓
speak to principal of Ipswich College
    about school meals !!!
report about Mr Black's front garden ✓
give weather report ✓
try a new game with listeners ✓
phone British Rail about new fast trains to London !!!
stop music at 8.30 to give travel news ✓
```

```
Sue & Tina - 'Home cooking'

introduce Mrs Fields (new cook at Intercontinental) ✓
ring a supermarket about meat prices !!!
explain the best way to cook fish ✓
correct mistakes in Friday's recipe ✓
help listeners to choose the right wine !!!
list the cheapest fruit of the week ✓
```

23 Where was it?
Look at the picture for ten seconds. Then close your books and say where the things were.

24 Read this report about a road accident in Birmingham...

The accident was in Drake Street.
Two lorries damaged a car.
People called the fire-brigade at 7.45 am.
The fire-brigade came because of the fire.
They fought the fire for 30 minutes.
They put sand on the road because of the petrol.
The police interviewed the drivers.

Now ask questions about the accident yesterday. Be careful with the word order.

1 Where/the accident/be?
2 How many lorries/there in the accident/be?
3 damage/What/they?
4 When/call/the fire-brigade/they?
5 Why/come/the fire-brigade?
6 they/get/When/fire under control?
7 sand on the road/put/they/Why?
8 do/What/the police?

25 John Newman is a famous film star. This is what he says about his normal working day:

"I get up at 7.30. Then I have my breakfast. After that I go to the film studio. I stand in front of the camera for two hours and then I go for lunch. I eat in the cafeteria and speak with other actors about new roles. In the afternoon I fight against sleep. How? I drink two good cups of coffee at around two o'clock. Then, I meet a reporter from a newspaper or magazine. We have a bit of a laugh and then I go back to work again. Around five o'clock I take my coat and go home. In the evening, I sit down and write to my fans and read a newspaper. When I go to bed I think 'What a hard day again!'"
What did John do yesterday? Write about it.

26 Bruce wants to lose weight. Say what he should or should not do/eat/drink.

REVISION 1

Units 1–5

27 You know six ways of forming the plural in English:

-s	o → oes	y → ies	irregular	f → ves	-es

1. Put the plural forms of these words into the six different groups:
   pot**a**to, **c**ar, b**o**x, **l**orry, m**a**n, tom**a**to, stati**o**n, church,
   c**i**ty, **l**ife, **ch**ild, **r**ecord, addr**e**ss, **f**actory, fish**e**rman, b**i**ke,
   glass, **f**erry, **s**helf, **d**ay, ste**w**ardess, poli**c**ewoman, **c**lass

2. Use the letters in **bold type** to make a word from each group.

3. Make a sentence with the six words about Radio Orwell.

28 Compare.

▶ elephant – big – mouse
An elephant is bigger than a mouse.

1. Rolls Royce – expensive – Mini Cooper
2. motor bike – heavy – bike
3. pizza – good – hamburger
4. wood – beautiful – beach
5. television – interesting – radio
6. Italy – hot in summer – Britain

29 From the Book of World Records: What are they famous for?

Use the words in the box:

| high | intelligent | fast |
| | pretty | elegant |

1. Marylin Mach (IQ 230)
2. Ben Johnson (9.84 seconds for 100 m)
3. Ulm Cathedral (161.60 m)
4. Miss United Kingdom
5. Princess Di

30 Three members of the Greenpeace group in Colchester say why they became members. Fill in the correct form of the verbs in the boxes.

"My name ① John. When I ② a child I ③ in the forest near our house. Years later I ④ out that they ⑤ to build a motorway through it. That ⑥ the moment when I …"

| be | want | be |
| play | be | find |

"I ⑦ Judy. At the moment I (not + ⑧) so I have a bit of time for other people. Yesterday, for the first time, I ⑨ out with the group. We ⑩ the beaches. It is shocking to see what people ⑪ there at weekends."

| be | leave | go |
| clean up | | work |

"Ten years ago I ⑫ a tanker accident on television. The tanker ⑬ and the oil ⑭ the beaches. And lots of birds ⑮, too. What ⑯ people for the environment in those days?"

| do | see | die |
| sink | | pollute |

31 Pollution problems

Complete these sentences and use the words in the box.

its	there	his	it's
where	their	he's
	it's	were

– Old factories are a big problem. The smoke from ① chimneys is very dirty so ② is always some dirt in the air.
– I think we should use recycled paper. ③ not cheaper but ④ better for the environment. We use it in our college although we don't like ⑤ colour.
– ⑥ are all our information leaflets about the bottle banks? They ⑦ still here yesterday.
– We shouldn't shout at the director of the power plant. It's not ⑧ plant, ⑨ not the owner.

32 Do you think the following statement sounds right?

"I think we needn't look after our environment. We can't think about it all the time. When we have an empty bottle, we must throw it away, because we can't always find a bottle bank. In winter we must turn our heating up to 26 degrees. We can't live without a red-hot room. We needn't discuss our environment. In fact, we shouldn't talk about it all the time, because nature can fight pollution without our help."

What did the speaker really want to say?

seventy-three 73

UNIT 6

The British – a people of many nations

Spot the Brits

Five of the following are British.
Can you find them?

1. Rajib Singh
   26 Smithfield Terrace,
   Manchester
   born: 23.08.1965/Calcutta
   father: British passport
   mother: British

2. Brendan McDowell
   22 Clive Street,
   Liverpool
   born: 16.03.1967/Dublin
   father: Irish
   mother: Irish

3. Kathleen Harris
   5 Blackwell Road,
   Earls Court, London
   born: 27.02.1965/Sydney
   father: Australian
   mother: Polish

4. Abram Sahir
   12 Medway Avenue,
   Bristol
   born: 13.08.1969/Bristol
   father: Pakistani
   mother: Pakistani

5. Mi Chang
   27 Bedford Close,
   Southampton,
   born: 24.10.1971/Peking
   father: Chinese
   mother: Chinese

6. Daniel David
   308 High Street,
   Colchester
   born: 24.07.1972/Cape Town
   father: South African
   mother: British

7. Doreen Czembella
   45 Stockport Road,
   Nottingham
   born: 03.07.1975/Nottingham
   father: British
   mother: British

8. Barry Smith
   23 Newbury Road,
   Aldershot
   born: 27.07.1976/Winchester
   father: British
   mother: British

UNIT 6 A

1 Neighbours

It is a beautiful day in the small town of Southport. Mrs Joan Lewis is working in the garden. Ron Hart, a neighbour from the next street, passes by.

Mr Hart: Hello Joan, I hear that some Indians have moved in next door to you.
Mrs Lewis: Yes, that's right – the Vaziranis – very nice people.
Mr Hart: Really? Come on, Joan. You know what these foreigners are like – they're lazy, they're dirty ...
Mrs Lewis: Wait a minute, Ron. Do you remember the Walkers? They had the house before – they really let the house go to the dogs. And just look at it now – the Vaziranis have done so much work on it – they've even renovated part of the house. You can't call that dirty and lazy.
Mr Hart: Yes, I've noticed that they've painted the windows. But what else have they done to the house?
Mrs Lewis: Well, come round the corner and see.
(They go round to the back of the house.)
Mrs Lewis: You remember those broken windows – well, they've fixed them. And Mrs Vazirani has made new curtains. They look lovely, don't they?
Mr Hart: Yes, well, perhaps you think so.
Mrs Lewis: They've mended that hole in the back door, too. And Mr Vazirani has even painted the dustbin to make it look nice. I think they've done a great job.
Mr Hart: Have you met your new neighbours then?
Mrs Lewis: Well, I've talked to Mrs Vazirani a few times but I haven't had the chance to speak to her husband. But Tom has met him. Look, there he is now. Yoohoo, Mr Vazirani ...

a Put the sentences right.

▶ An Indian family have moved into Joan's house.

They haven't moved into Joan's house, they've moved in next door.

1 The Vaziranis have renovated the whole house.
2 The Vaziranis have painted the roof.
3 The Vaziranis have broken the windows.
4 Mrs Vazirani has bought new curtains.
5 Mr Vazirani has made a hole in the door.
6 Mr Vazirani has bought a dustbin.
7 Joan Lewis has talked to Mr Vazirani a few times.
8 The Vaziranis have done a terrible job on the house.

b Let's have a look at what the Vaziranis have done inside the house.

▶ Mr V./paint/all the doors/in ...
Mr Vazirani has painted all the doors in the house.

1 They/paint/windows/in ...
2 They/paper/walls/in ...
3 Mr V./mend/pipes/in ...
4 Mr V./put in/new lights/in ...
5 Mrs V./wash/ceiling/in ...
6 Mr V./repair/bath/in ...
7 They/paint/ceiling/in ...
8 They/buy/new chairs/for ...
9 Mrs V./make/new curtains/ for ...
10 They/renovate/...

seventy-five 75

UNIT 6

c What have the Vaziranis done to their house?

▶ They've fixed the broken windows.
Go on.

They ...

1 They ...

2 Mrs V. ...

3 They ...

4 Mr V. ...

5 They ...

2 Meet Umesh Vazirani

Mr Vazirani: Good afternoon. Mrs Lewis, I believe.
Mrs Lewis: That's right, Mr Vazirani. This is Ron Hart. Ron lives in the next street.
Mr Vazirani: How do you do.
Mr Hart: How do you do.
Mrs Lewis: Mr Vazirani, I think you've done a great job on the house.
Mr Vazirani: Thank you very much, Mrs Lewis, but we certainly haven't finished yet.
Mrs Lewis: But you've already done more in five weeks than the Walkers in five years. The house has never looked better.
Mr Vazirani: Well, yes, I have a lot of spare time, you see, because I'm unemployed at the moment.
Mrs Lewis: I'm sorry to hear that. Have you tried the Job Centre yet? They can help sometimes.
Mr Vazirani: Yes, I've just come back from there. They say it's very difficult to find jobs at the moment.
Mr Hart: That's true, three factories have closed down in Southport this year, you know.
Mr Vazirani: Yes, it's very unfortunate. I've applied for at least twenty jobs but I've had no luck so far.
Mrs Lewis: Oh dear, I'm sorry to hear that, I hope you find something soon.
Mr Vazirani: Yes, I hope so, too. We've already spent all our savings on the house. – Well, Mrs Lewis, Mr Hart, goodbye for now.
Mrs Lewis: Goodbye.
Mr Hart: Goodbye.

a Complete the following sentences.
You can use the expressions in the box.

never	already
yet	so far	just
just	already
already	this year

Mr Vazirani has not found a job ①.
He has ② come back from the Job Centre.
The Vaziranis have ③ done more in five weeks than the Walkers in five years.
The house has ④ looked better.
Mr Vazirani has ⑤ applied for at least twenty jobs.
He has had no luck ⑥.
The Vaziranis have ⑦ spent all their savings on the house.
They have ⑧ moved to Southport.
Three factories have closed down in Southport ⑨.

UNIT 6 A

b The Vaziranis must do a lot of things. They have made lists and have already done some of the things, but they have not done everything yet.

This is Mr Vazirani's list.

fix broken windows ✓
repair roof
mend hole in back door ✓
paint dustbin ✓
paint pipes in kitchen
repair bath
talk to bank manager

This is Mrs Vazirani's list.

make curtains for bedrooms ✓
buy new cups and saucers
make new table-cloth
wash ceiling in kitchen ✓
paint windows in living-room ✓
paper walls in dining-room
paint kitchen

Ask and answer questions like this:

▶ Has Mr Vazirani fixed the broken windows yet?
Yes, he's already fixed them.
Go on.

▶ Has Mrs Vazirani bought new cups and saucers yet?
No, she hasn't bought them yet.
Go on.

3 Tom Crosby from the 'Southport News' has written an article about the Vaziranis. Can you complete it? You can use the verbs in the box.

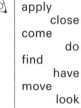

apply	
	close
come	
	do
find	
	have
move	
	look
renovate	
	spend
try	

Perfect Neighbours

A new family ① to Southport. Mr and Mrs Umesh Vazirani and their two children ② here from Manchester. Mrs Joan Lewis, the Vazirani's next door neighbour, says:

"The Vaziranis are perfect neighbours. They are always very friendly and they ③ the house – inside and out. The house ④+never better. They ⑤ a marvellous job. The only problem is – Mr Vazirani is unemployed. He ⑥+not a job yet. He ⑦ the Job Centre but they couldn't help him. He ⑧ for over 20 jobs but he ⑨ no luck so far. And time is running out. They ⑩+already all their savings on the house…"

Everybody would agree that the Vaziranis are a good example to us all. Perhaps somebody can help them. The job situation is difficult – three factories ⑪ down this year – but perhaps someone can do something for Joan Lewis's perfect neighbours.

4 Your youth club is in a bad state. You and your friends want to do some repairs. Someone has made a list of the repairs and the costs of the materials:

Repairs	Costs in £
repair roof	345.00
mend pipes	150.00
paint 12 windows	5.00 per window
paint 5 doors	15.00 per door
make new curtains for 4 rooms	28.50 per room
paint dustbin	4.00
fix 3 broken windows	23.00 per window
paper walls in 3 rooms	56.00 per room
repair toilet	88.00
put in 6 lights	5.00 per light

You have £780. You cannot repair everything with the money and therefore you and your friends must decide what to repair. Try and use as much of the budget as you can. When you have finished, tell the class what you have repaired and how much you have spent.

B UNIT 6

1 The Citizens Advice Bureau (CAB) has over 900 offices throughout Great Britain. Every year its advisers help thousands of people with problems, and the advice is free.

Mr Welch is one of the advisers at the Southport office. He has worked there for nearly ten years and has dealt with immigrant problems for the last two years.

Mr Vazirani: Good morning, my name's Umesh Vazirani.
Mr Welch: Good morning, Mr Vazirani. Take a seat, please. – Now, what can I do for you?
Mr Vazirani: Well, I've just moved into Crescent Avenue. We live in the house next to Mr and Mrs Lewis. They're very nice neighbours and they've helped us a lot since our arrival.
Mr Welch: How long have you and your family lived in Britain?
Mr Vazirani: We've lived in Britain since 1983, but many of our relatives and friends have lived here in Southport for more than ten years.
Mr Welch: So you know quite a lot of people here, then. But what's your problem, Mr Vazirani?
Mr Vazirani: Well, I'm looking for a job. I've written about twenty letters since March and I've had about ten interviews, but I never get the job. I think it's because I'm not white.
Mr Welch: I know it's difficult sometimes to find the right employment, and there are quite a number of unemployed immigrants here in Southport, but maybe we can help you. Now, let me see …

Answer the following questions:

1 What do the advisers at the Citizens Advice Bureau do?
2 How much does the information at the CAB cost?
3 How many letters has Mr Vazirani written to find a job?
4 How long have Mr Vazirani's relatives lived in Southport?
5 What is Mr Welch's job at the CAB?
6 Mr Vazirani hasn't found a job yet. What reason does he give?
7 How many Citizens Advice Bureaus are there in Great Britain?
8 How many years has Mr Welch worked for the CAB?
9 How many interviews has Mr Vazirani had?

2 The neighbours and their jobs

Ask and answer questions like this:

▶ How long has Mr Lewis worked at the factory?

   He's worked at the factory since 1972.

▶ How long has Mrs Billard worked at the Town Hall?

   She's worked there for two years.

Mr Lewis  1972

1 The Browns  1985

2 Miss Brian  8 months

3 Mr Hart  1987

Mrs Billard  2 years

4 Mr Jenkins 1979

5 Mrs Smith  5 years

6 Mr Cook  6 months

UNIT 6 B

3 All these people live in Crescent Avenue:

a Make sentences like this:

▶ The Browns have lived there since 1968.
  Mr Jenkins has lived ...

b Ask and answer questions like this:

▶ How long have the Browns lived in Crescent Avenue?
  They've lived there for ... years.

4 Ask and answer questions like this:

▶ How long have you had that car, Mr Lewis?
  Oh, I've had it since 1988.

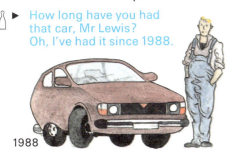

1988

6 months   1988

1987

9 months

10 years

1938

5 What haven't they done for ages?
Look at the cartoons. What can you say about them?

▶ The man hasn't shaved for six days.

6 days

① 2 weeks

② 6 months

③ Christmas

④ a long time

⑤ weeks

⑥ Easter

⑦ last year

seventy-nine 79

UNIT 6

1 Allan Blackhead is standing as an independent in the local elections of his home town Southport.

Here are parts of his speech at his election meeting in front of the Town Hall.

... Have you had a good look round our town? Have you really had a look at it? Well, I have and do you know what I've seen? I've seen some rich people in Jaguars and Rolls-Royces, but I haven't seen any jobs for our 3,000 unemployed. – You can still find work in some of the factories near London, but that doesn't help any of us here in Southport. The town has built a modern congress centre. Has it built a modern hospital, too? No, of course it hasn't. – There are some plans for new hotels, but there aren't any plans for new houses for the old people. – The council haven't provided any new playgrounds for our children since 1968. – Oh yes, the council are good to us, they've built some new tennis courts in the best part of town. – And the council have bought some expensive furniture for their offices. But, have they bought any sports equipment for our youth centre, though? – We really need some new nursery schools, we don't need any wider roads for the people in big cars. You can help me to change all this ...

a Listen to the cassette again. Which is correct?

1. Allan thinks it is better to spend some money on a new congress centre/new hotels/houses for old people/big cars/a hospital in Southport.
2. Allan thinks that the town of Southport should provide new tennis courts/more jobs for the unemployed/better roads/more money for the sports teachers at the youth centre.
3. Allan thinks it is better to build houses for the unemployed/a swimming-pool/a hospital/some playgrounds/some nursery schools.

b Listen to the cassette again. Allan contrasts some things in his speech. Match them.

▶  He contrasts ... with ...

UNIT 6 C

c Ask and answer questions like this:

▶ Have they built/provided/bought any ...?
Yes, they have./No, they haven't.
▶ Is there any ...?
Yes, there is./No, there isn't.
▶ Are there any ...?
Yes, there are./No, there aren't.

d Make sentences.

▶ They have built/provided/bought some ...
They haven't built/provided/bought any ...
There is/are some ...
There isn't/aren't any ...

2 Talk about Allan and the town of Southport.

▶ He has seen some rich people in Jaguars and Rolls-Royces, but he hasn't seen any jobs for the 3,000 unemployed.
Go on.

| he
the council
they | provide
build
buy
see | a
some
any | new playgrounds
rich people in Jaguars and Rolls-Royces
sports equipment for the youth centre
work in their own town
tennis courts
plans for new houses for old people
modern hospital
expensive furniture
jobs for the 3,000 unemployed
plans for new hotels
congress centre |

3 Allan is not very happy about the situation in his town. What about your town? Do a survey.

a Ask your partner about his/her town or village.

Give points* as shown in this example:

▶ Have they built any new houses?
No, they haven't built any. (0 points)
Yes, they have built one. (1 point)
Yes, they have built some. (2 points)
Yes, they have built a lot. (3 points)

* for a village multiply by 3
for a small town multiply by 2

Now go through 1 to 8 and do the same:

1 build houses for old people
2 buy computers for their schools
3 build swimming-pools
4 have sports competitions
5 provide bottle banks
6 renovate old buildings
7 build new playgrounds
8 repair roads

b Report your results.

UNIT 6

1 Normally the British people elect their Members of Parliament (MPs) every four or five years. The MPs decide on political problems.

The two biggest parties are the Conservatives and the Labour Party. In the 1987 elections in Britain, Clive Clements tried to win votes for the Conservatives in Bedford.

Clive Clements

YOUR CONSERVATIVE CANDIDATE FOR BEDFORD

I believe that the Conservatives have shown that they can run the country.

We all know that unemployment is far too high. But it is going down. This year the number of unemployed people has gone down by 50,000 and since March 1983 the number of jobs has gone up by over one million.

We need the police. Let us not forget that. Within the last 8 years we have spent 50% more on the police and the number of police has increased by 15,000. So when we say that we want to reduce crime we mean it.

Our students are our future. Thousands of young people want to get a job after school. We are giving them the money to get good skill training. The money for the Youth Training Schemes (YTS) has increased by 78%. The chances of getting a good education and training have become much better and the number of young people without a skill has decreased.

We must accept people from Asia or Africa. But we must also be fair to our own people. We are trying to slow down immigration. The result: it has decreased by 35%.

Old people need our help. After 40 years of work they should have enough money to buy food and clothes. They should also live in nice houses. Under the Conservative Government the pensions have gone up 4½ times faster than under the last Labour Government.

Vote Conservative!
Yours sincerely,

a Which headings from the leaflet go with which paragraph?

- Pensions
- Unemployment
- Immigration
- Education and Youth Training
- Law and Order

b Complete what Clive Clements says:

the money for the YTS ①
the number of jobs ②
the chances of getting a good education and training ③
the number of unemployed people ④
the number of police ⑤
the pensions ⑥
the number of immigrants ⑦
the number of young people without a skill ⑧

UNIT 6 T

2 Can you find the nouns for the words in **bold type**?

In July 1987 there were about 3 million **unemployed** people in Britain. ① was very high then.

At present a lot of young people want to **study** at colleges and universities. But these cannot accept all the ②.

The British normally **elect** their Members of Parliament every four or five years. The ③ always takes place on a Thursday.

A German car in Britain is a **foreign** car. As a German you are a ④ there, too.

A lot of Asians and Africans have come to Britain. They have **immigrated** because they hope for a better future. ⑤ has become a big problem for the British.

The Conservatives and the Labour Party **decide** how to solve political problems in Great Britain. They, not the Queen, make the important ⑥.

In Britain it is sometimes **difficult** for a coloured person to get a job. But this ⑦ also exists in Germany.

3 In the same elections, David Newman tried to win votes for the Labour Party. He said in his leaflet:

LABOUR

FIVE REASONS WHY THE CONSERVATIVES MUST GO:

1. Unemployment figures have gone up from two million to three million in the past eight years. The unemployment of young people has gone up by 50%.

2. Pensions in Britain have come down to the second lowest in Europe.

3. The pay for teachers is terrible. Thousands of teachers have left schools and colleges because of low pay. Today there are more students, but the number of teachers is smaller.

4. The crime rate has increased by 20% under the Conservative Government.

5. Our present government has turned away tens of thousands of people from Africa and Asia. They wanted to be with their families in Britain.

VOTE LABOUR!

David Newman

a You have found the headings for Clive Clements' leaflet. Which of them go with David Newman's points in his leaflet?

▶ The heading 'Unemployment' goes with point ...
Go on.

b Compare what they say about the different subjects.

▶ They don't agree on unemployment: Clive Clements says that ... but David Newman says that ...
Go on.

UNIT 6

DIY means 'do it yourself' ...

The magazine 'The Homeowner' recommends that every homeowner should have a basic tool-kit and some machines so that he can do repairs. Here are some of them:

an angle-grinder

a jigsaw

a screwdriver

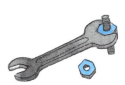
a spanner

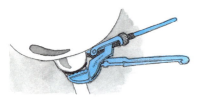
a pipe wrench

a power drill

a test lamp

a hammer

jump leads

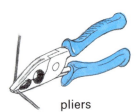
pliers

Copy the crossword puzzle frame into your exercise book.

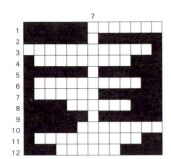

Now do the crossword puzzle:

1. It fits on nuts. You can turn them with it.
3. It is a very practical machine. When you put a special disc on, you can cut metal or stone with it.
4. Your car does not want to start? Put them on the battery of your car and on the battery of another car.
6. Use it when you want to drill a hole.
7. Knock a nail into a wall with it.
8. You can bend a piece of wire with them.
10. You can use it to check an electric wire.
11. You can make it bigger and smaller. Then you can tighten and loosen all sizes of pipes.
12. You can cut wood with it.

Now complete line 7 from top to bottom. These tools can help you to tighten and loosen screws.

84 eighty-four

UNIT 6 S2

Foreign Food

For over forty years, the British have been able to enjoy their food in thousands of foreign restaurants. Since the end of the British Empire, millions of people from all over the world have come to live in Britain, especially from places like India, Pakistan, the West Indies and Hongkong. Many of them have opened restaurants and foreign food has become more and more popular amongst the British.

Here are four London restaurants:

Do you know the correct answer?

1. Can you say which is an Indian and which is a Chinese restaurant?
2. It is 4 pm and you are hungry. Which of the restaurants can you go to?
3. You are getting married and you want to invite 60 guests for a meal. Which of the restaurants caters for large groups?
4. It is Sunday lunchtime and you are very hungry. You have £6 in your pocket. Which restaurant is the best for you?
5. You want an Indian meal to eat at home. At which restaurant can you get a meal to take home?
6. It is Saturday and you have no cash. But you have 'plastic money' – a credit card. Where can you go for a meal?
7. All the restaurants are 'fully licensed'. That means one can get certain kinds of drinks. What kind?

eighty-five 85

UNIT 6

Consumer problems

a At which shops can you buy the above products? Look at the advertisements again.

b Which expressions in the advertisements have the same meaning? Find them.

1 what you have to pay for a product
2 part of the payment; you have to make it for several months
3 letting someone take goods now but pay after half a year
4 time when a shop sells things at lower prices than normal
5 money in coins or banknotes
6 part of total payment at the time when you buy a product
7 what you can take off the full price
8 an offer at lower prices for only a few days

c Which of the above products are they talking about?

1 – You see, I need it at home and for my shop as well.
   – Well, I think this machine is ideal for private and business letters.
2 – Is it my size?
   – We offer trousers in all sizes and colours.
3 – Where can I turn it on?
   – When you want to watch a programme, you just press this button.
4 – Is it really so good?
   – It gets your shirts as white as snow.
5 – I'm a beginner. Do you think it's the right one for me?
   – It's an all-round model for every player.
6 – I want to move to a new flat and I must do most of the jobs myself.
   – No problem. Our new product can do the most difficult jobs.

d Now try and make an advertisement of your own. You want to sell: a washing powder, a video recorder, a typewriter, T-shirts.

UNIT 6 G

Present Perfect

Statement

I/you/we/they	**have**	not	**gone** ...
He/she/it	**has**		

Question

Have	I/you/we/they	**asked** ...?
Has	he/she/it	

have + 3. Form *(past participle)*

They **have repaired** the roof.
She **has** already **painted** the windows.
Has he **fixed** the windows yet?
We **have lived** in London since 1983.

Das *Present Perfect* steht:

– bei Handlungen in der Vergangenheit ohne Zeitangaben
– bei Handlungen in der Vergangenheit mit den Signalwörtern *already, just, never, so far, this week/month/year, yet*
– bei nicht abgeschlossenen Handlungen und Zuständen mit *since, for, how long*

since + Zeitpunkt

for + Zeitraum

| We have lived in London **since 1983**. |
| Wir wohnen seit 1983 in London. |

| We have lived in London **for six years**. |
| Wir wohnen seit sechs Jahren in London. |

Beachte den abweichenden Gebrauch des Präsens im Deutschen!

a/an, some, any

They have got **a** car. They haven't got **a** car.	*a/an* + zählbare Begriffe im Singular
They have written **some** letters. They haven't written **any** letters.	*some/any* + zählbare Begriffe im Plural
They have given us **some** information. They haven't given us **any** information.	*some/any* + nichtzählbare Begriffe

Bejahte Aussage → some

Verneinte Aussage → any

Frage → any

| They have given us **some** information. | They haven't given us **any** information. | Have they given us **any** information? |

UNIT 7

HISTORY – NOW AND THEN

Who or what can you see in the pictures?
Where can you see these people or things?
What can you say about them?

88 eighty-eight

UNIT 7 A

1 In the pub

Alan and Sally have invited their American friend Greg for a drink in an English pub. Greg has just arrived in London from the States.

Alan: All the best.
Sally: Cheers.
Greg: Cheers. – I've been here in London since Tuesday and this is the first time I've been to an English pub. It's quite different to our bars. What about these strange opening hours here?
Sally: Oh, that law has changed. Up until August 1988, pubs closed from 3.00 to 6.00 in the afternoon. But now they can open all day from 11.00 am to 11.00 pm.
Greg: Oh, that's good. But, you know, I still think you British are very traditional. When I think of Britain, I think of tea, driving on the left, school uniforms and that sort of thing. I've just read a book on British history and ...
Sally: Have you been to the tourist information centre at Victoria Station?
Greg: No, I haven't. Should I?
Sally: Well, they have a lot of interesting leaflets and books about old British traditions there.
Greg: That sounds a good idea. I mean, I've already been to British Rail for more travel information, but I ...

a True or false?
1 Greg is from Canada.
2 Alan and Sally are in a restaurant with Greg.
3 This is Greg's first visit to an English pub.
4 English pubs aren't open all day.
5 The tourist information centre offers many interesting things.
6 Greg is interested in British traditions.

b Make sentences like this:

▶ Greg – to Britain
Greg has never been to Britain before.

Use the words in the box.

| already | not ... yet | never ... before |
| just | since | for ... years | now | just |

1 Greg – from America
2 Greg – an English pub
3 He – in London
4 English pubs – open all day
5 Greg – a book about Britain
6 He – to the tourist information centre
7 Greg – to British Rail

c What about you?
Ask and answer questions like this:

▶ visit Britain
Have you ever visited Britain?
Yes, I have./No, I haven't.

1 drink tea with milk
2 listen to an English record
3 read a British/an American newspaper
4 listen to British/American radio
5 buy British clothes
6 speak to an Englishman/American
7 see a British/an American car
8 hear anything about the Highland Games
9 watch British or American TV

d Report your answers to the class:

▶ Susanne has visited Britain./Susanne hasn't visited Britain yet.

A UNIT 7

2 Greg got this information leaflet about Britain's history and traditions from the tourist information centre.

A Walk into the Past

Bread Street is the name of a street in the City of London. But how did it get its name? The answer is easy. In the past all the bakers lived there. All the shoemakers lived in Shoe Lane and the butchers in Meat Road and so on ...

Street names can tell you a lot about local history. Other things in the street can tell you a lot about the past, too.

Hundreds of years ago almost every shop had a sign with a picture outside. Pictures were necessary because most people could not read. Now only pubs still have signs. A pub's sign often shows how old the pub is. Some are very old and have, for example, a picture of St George and a dragon on their sign.

St George lived a long time ago and he is famous because people say he killed a dragon.

In Britain, tea was a drink only for rich people in the seventeenth century. Later, tea shops like this brought the price of a cup of tea down and everyone started to drink it.

How many people know how a 'Bobby' got his name? In the nineteenth century Robert Peel started the police in London. So people called the first policemen 'Peelers'. Later the name changed to 'Bobby' – the short form of Robert.

And why do the British drive on the left? Well, some people say it is because in the past horse riders often had to fight on the road. They rode on the left side of the road because most of them carried their swords in their right hands.

a Look at the text. Each expression in the left box goes with another expression in the right box. Make pairs.

| cup   St George   Peel   baker   shop |
| right hand   Meat Road   horses |

| Bread Street   butcher   dragon |
| policeman   sword   sign   tea   traffic |

b True or false?
1 A long time ago the bakers of London lived in Meat Road.
2 In the past shops had signs with pictures outside because people liked pictures.
3 It is often easy to find out how old a pub is.
4 When tea first came to Britain, everyone started to drink it.
5 People called the first policemen 'Bobbies'.
6 People rode their horses on the left side of the road in the past.

c Look at the following descriptions and find out what they are:

1 Bakers lived there.
2 In the past it hung outside a shop.
3 St George killed it.

Now describe these in the same way. The rest of the class must find out what it is.

4 Meat Road
5 St George
6 policeman
7 tea
8 sword
9 Robert Peel

UNIT 7 A

3 A week later, Alan and Sally met Greg again.

a Alan: Well Greg, have you enjoyed your first week in London?
Greg: Yes, it's been great. I've seen some interesting things and learnt something about British traditions.
▶ Sally: Have you been to Piccadilly Circus yet?
Greg: Yes, I have.
Sally: When did you go there?
Greg: I went there last Monday.

Look at the dialogue and play the roles of Sally and Greg.

1 Buckingham Palace – two days ago
2 Big Ben – last Wednesday
3 Harrods – the day before yesterday
4 Hyde Park – three days ago
5 The Tower – Friday morning
6 City of London – last Tuesday
7 Westminster Abbey – Thursday afternoon
8 London Transport Museum – yesterday

b Sally asks what else Greg has done.

▶ Sally: Have you taken the boat to Greenwich yet?
Greg: Yes, I have. I took it last Friday.

Play their roles in the same way.
You can use the verbs in the box.

see	visit	eat	take
try	be	drink	visit

1 Houses of Parliament – five days ago
2 Madame Tussaud's – on Tuesday
3 a cup of English tea – yesterday afternoon
4 the British Museum – at the beginning of the week
5 to the flea market in Portobello Road – last Saturday
6 a traditional English breakfast – yesterday morning
7 the boat to Hampton Court – three days ago
8 fish and chips – on Tuesday lunchtime

c What about you?
Ask and answer questions like this:

▶ eat a hamburger
Have you eaten a hamburger this week?
Yes I have./No, I haven't.
When did you …?

1 go for a walk
2 make a cup of tea
3 take photos
4 watch TV
5 read a newspaper
6 buy a magazine
7 meet your friends

4 After two weeks in Britain, Greg wrote a letter home to America.

Can you complete it?

You can use the verbs in the box. Put them into Past Simple or Present Perfect.

go	meet	learn
	see	
be		have
	start	
be		go
	give	
take		learn

Dear Ken,
I am enjoying my stay in London very much. I (1 + already) a lot of interesting things. Last Wednesday I (2) my friends Alan and Sally. They (3) me to a nice pub in the evening. On Thursday I (4) to the tourist information centre. They (5) me an interesting leaflet. As you know, I (6 + never) to Britain before. But I (7 + already) a lot about its history and traditions. I (8) to a tea shop with my friend Janice last week. We (9) a real English tea with sandwiches and cakes. But I (10 + not) how to make a good cup yet. The weather (11 + not) very good yesterday, but now it's much better. Oh yes, and by the way, I (12 + just) to understand their funny English accent. Best wishes, Greg

B UNIT 7

1 The Jerry Hogan Show is a popular talk show on television. Jerry Hogan, the programme's interviewer, is talking about the guests for next week's show.

Jerry Hogan: One of our guests next Tuesday is Bob Geldof, the famous Irish rock singer and charity promoter. Up till now he's had many different jobs. In the sixties he worked as a lorry-driver, an English teacher and a journalist.
In the seventies he became a pop star and had his own group. They made many hit records together.
Well, and from 1984 to 1986 he organized a lot of charity programmes. I'm sure you remember Band Aid, Live Aid or Sport Aid. In this way he helped to collect over £100 million for people in the Third World. In 1986 the Queen made him Sir Bob Geldof. He hasn't been on TV for a couple of years and we're glad to have him on our show.

Our next guest then is Clare Francis, the famous English sailor and writer. As we all know, she sailed across the Atlantic on her own in 1973 and became the first woman sailor to do this. Before Clare took up sailing, she went to university and in the seventies she spent all her time sailing, but in 1982 she decided to give it up. Since then she's talked about sailing on radio and TV and she had her last TV show a week ago. She has also written two books about her main occupation. Clare has just moved to London and we are very happy that she can come on the show …

a Who could this be? Give reasons.

▶ This person is a pop star. It's Bob Geldof, because Jerry Hogan tells us that he is a rock singer.

1 This person has had a lot of different jobs.
2 This person spent a lot of time at sea in the seventies.
3 This person lives in London.
4 This person got a title in 1986.
5 This person hasn't appeared on TV for quite a while.
6 This person writes about the sea.
7 This person is from Ireland.

b Another guest on the next talk show is Neil Armstrong, the famous American astronaut.
Can you complete Jerry Hogan's introduction?

Neil Armstrong ① born in 1930 in Ohio, USA. In the early fifties he ② to the University of California. Later he ③ a test pilot and then an astronaut for NASA. In July 1969 he ④ to the moon in Apollo XI. From 1971 to 1979 Neil Armstrong ⑤ as a professor of engineering at Cincinnati University. Since 1982 he ⑥ the chairman of an international company and he ⑦ very hard in this job for many years. He (8 + just) in London on business.

You can use the verbs in the box.

teach	be	go	fly	work
	become	be	arrive	

92 ninety-two

UNIT 7 B

c Ask and answer questions like this:

▶ Bob Geldof/When/work/as an English teacher?
When did Bob Geldof work as an English teacher?

1 a pop star/become/Bob Geldof/When?
2 organize/What/from 1984 to 1986/he?
3 When/as a lorry driver/work/he?
4 make/What/he/in the seventies?
5 since last year/appear/he/on TV/ How often?

▶ Where/just move/Clare Francis/to?
Where has Clare Francis just moved to?

6 Clare Francis/When/on her own/ the Atlantic/sail?
7 What/become/she/in 1973?
8 she/before/go/a sailor/Where/she/become?
9 How/already write/many books/she?
10 just/move/she/to London?

2 Russel Parker, a journalist, is talking to Jerry Hogan about his career as a TV interviewer. Complete the dialogue and use the expressions in the box.

Russell: I've ① seen a video of your last show with Jack S. Low, the racing driver.
Jerry: Oh, have you? I have ② had a chance to see it ②.
Russell: By the way, ③ did you ask Jack to come on your show?
Jerry: I asked him about 3 weeks ④.
Russell: That was good work. I've tried ⑤ months to get an interview with him. – ⑥ have you worked on TV, Jerry?
Jerry: ⑦ about 10 years. In fact, I've been with the BBC ⑧ 1980. You get a lot of experience over the years.
Russell: That's true. ⑨ did you do your first talk show?
Jerry: That was ⑩.
Russell: Tell me, what was the best programme you have ⑪ done?
Jerry: I think that was ⑫ with Jack.

not ... yet	
for	since
how long	
when	ever
last week	
in 1985	
when	ago
just	for

3 Jane Fonda, the American film star, is another candidate for Jerry Hogan's show. Here is part of her biography:

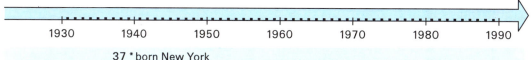

```
1930    1940    1950    1960    1970    1980    1990
        37 * born New York
        38 _____ 47 live California
              47 _____ 54 live Greenwich
        42 _____ 54 go school
                    55 __ 59 college
                        60 * be at Broadway theatre
                        make films 61 _____
                                69 * win Oscar
                                    73 * get married
                                do TV fitness programmes 85 ____
                    interested in politics 60 _____
                                    70 * protest against Vietnam war
                                protest against atomic bombs 80 __
                        live in Los Angeles 60 _____
```

a Introduce Jane Fonda. Use the information above.

▶ Jane Fonda was born in 1937. She ...

b Now you think of a famous person. Write down some information about his or her life and play the role of this person. The rest of the class must guess who you are.

c What about you?
Do your own biography in the same way. Write about date of birth, birthplace, schools, college, interests, where you live, English, hobbies, ...

UNIT 7

1 Greg has met an English girl, Anna. She has invited him to a party. Right now, they are in Covent Garden, looking for some old-fashioned clothes for the party.

Anna: That's the Central Market Hall over there. I think they've renovated it beautifully.
Greg: Yes, they've done it very well. But tell me: Why is it called Covent *Garden?*
Anna: Well, a long time ago this area was all fields. Monks lived here and they grew fruit and vegetables. After that Henry VIII ...
Greg: Ah, now he was the one with all the wives, wasn't he?
Anna: That's right. Anyway, he threw the monks out. Then people from the country simply began to sell fruit and vegetables here. This market grew very fast and until 1974 it was the centre for London's fruit and vegetable trade. So you see, in a way it has always been a garden.
Greg: And it still has a market feeling now. I like that. You can easily see why it's become so popular. There are street entertainers, too, and small shops and stalls where you can buy all sorts of things. You can buy old furniture and old books and ...
Anna: ... and clothes! Come on, it's time to go shopping.

a Look at the pictures. What was Covent Garden like in the past – and today?

b Put the following sentences into the same order as in the text:
1 Later on Henry VIII threw the monks out.
2 Many years ago Covent Garden was all fields.
3 In fact, it has been a shopping centre since then.
4 Between Henry VIII's time and 1974, Covent Garden was an important fruit and vegetable market.
5 In those days monks grew fruit and vegetables in these fields.
6 After 1974 Covent Garden was no longer a fruit and vegetable market.

c Look at the text and complete the following sentences:
1 They have renovated the Central Market Hall ...
2 Greg thinks they've done the job very ...
3 People from the country ... started to sell fruit and vegetables in Covent Garden.
4 Covent Garden market grew very ...
5 Greg says you can ... understand why Covent Garden has become so popular.

UNIT 7 c

2 Greg is at Anna's party now. It's a special party because everyone must wear old-fashioned clothes.

Mike   Sally   Mary   Jane   Paul   Sam   John   Carol   Pete   Dave

a Greg and Anna are talking about some of Anna's friends:

▶ Jane/beautiful/dancer
  Jane's a beautiful dancer.
  Yes, she dances beautifully.

Go on with:
1 Paul/terrible/dancer
2 John/noisy/guitar-player
3 Sally/quiet/talker
4 Sam/wonderful/cook
5 Mike/heavy/smoker
6 Pete/bad/guitar-player
7 Mary/fast/talker
8 Carol/good/dancer

b Now you talk about the following people:

▶ John makes a lot of noise when he plays the guitar.
  He's a noisy guitar-player.

You can use the words in the box.

| good | noisy | bad |
| heavy | wonderful | quiet |

1 Alan smokes forty cigarettes a day.
2 Janet never plays a wrong note on the piano.
3 You can't hear Dave when he speaks.
4 You must put your fingers in your ears when Tom sings.
5 When Elaine cooks, the food is always very tasty.
6 When Sam dances, he steps on people's toes.

c Now talk about how the same people do things.

▶ John makes a lot of noise when he plays the guitar.
  He plays the guitar noisily.

Go on.

d After the party Greg helps Anna to clean up the room. They find all kinds of things. Look at the picture above and talk about the following things:

▶ Whose is it?
  It's Paul's hat.

▶ Whose are they?
  They're Dave's gloves.

e Now make sentences like this:

▶ the Browns/key
  It's the Browns' key.
▶ the children/toys
  They're the children's toys.

1 our neighbours/plates
2 my sister/pen
3 the students/dictionary
4 the Scotsmen/bagpipes
5 my parents/tickets
6 my brother/cassette

ninety-five 95

UNIT 7

1 A visit to a motor museum

Have a look at this leaflet and find out some interesting facts of the history of the world's most popular vehicle: the car.

CARS

Cars have played an important part in our lives for many years. But hundreds of years ago there were no cars, so people travelled by stage coach. Of course the horses could only go at about 15 km per hour.

The first coach without horses had a steam-engine. The steam coaches needed a lot of water, so these vehicles could only travel a short distance. Then they had to stop for water.

In 1885 Carl Benz invented the first car with a petrol-engine. It had only three wheels and it was very slow. It could not even go up hills. Some years later Gottlieb Daimler built the first car with four wheels. It was much safer than the Benz car. At that time cars were usually open and had no heating, so they were not very comfortable.

The first cars were of course very expensive and only few people could buy them. But then in America Ford began to build the famous 'Model T' cars in 1913. That was the start of mass production and since then lots of people have been able to buy cars.

The Volkswagen 'Beetle' has been one of the most popular cars. You can still see it in the streets although production stopped a few years ago. Modern compact cars consume much less petrol than cars did 100 years ago. They are less expensive and so many people can buy them. As a result the millions of cars on our roads today have become a big problem.

a Look at the pictures and name the vehicles.

b Make sentences.

The first steam coach	built a much safer car.
The first petrol cars	needed a lot of water.
Mr Daimler	have become very important.
Few people	have produced millions of cars.
The steam-engine	produced the 'Model T'.
The 'Beetle'	went very slowly.
Mr Ford	worked badly.
The car firms	could buy the first cars.
Cars	was one of the most popular cars for a long time.

UNIT 7

c Answer the following questions in complete sentences:

1. How did people travel two hundred years ago?
2. How fast could they travel then?
3. What was one of the problems of the steam coaches?
4. When did Carl Benz invent the motor car?
5. Why was Gottlieb Daimler's car safer than the Benz car?
6. Why was it not very comfortable to travel at that time?
7. What are the good points of the modern compact car?
8. Why have cars become a big problem these days?

d Write the correct sentences into your exercise book and fill in the missing words.

1. by 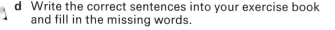 – Two hundred – people travelled – years ago.
2. 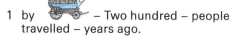 – They needed – to pull it.
3. but it was – About 200 years ago – the 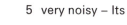 engine – too heavy for cars – James Watt invented.
4. the 19th century – the first motor car – Then at the end of – Carl Benz built – – It had three.
5. very noisy – Its – was.
6. a lot of – It consumed – 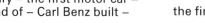.
7. not strong enough – because it was – go up – It could not.
8. was very high – people could buy them – the first 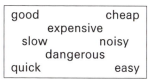 – so only very rich – The  of.

e Adjective or adverb?

Use the correct form of the words in the box and put it in the right place:

good	cheap
expensive	
slow	noisy
dangerous	
quick	easy

The first steam-engines did not work very ①.
It was not ② to travel long distances.
The cars could only go ③ so there were not many accidents.
The engines were very ④ so people found it difficult to talk to each other.
As cars were very ⑤, only rich people could buy them.
Car production changed ⑥.
Soon car firms could sell their cars much more ⑦ than at the end of the 19th century.
As there are so many cars today, driving has become more ⑧ than years ago.

2 Look at this card and complete the text below.

BRANDS HATCH RACES

Grand Prix races at Brands Hatch since 1964. Grand Prix races many years earlier. Top speed today of 250 mph. About 1900 top speed 70 mph. First races – few cars. Since then much faster cars. Racing very popular now.

You can use the verbs in the box.

start	become	take place
be	build	reach	be

1. Since 1964 …
2. Of course, Grand Prix racing …
3. In the first races …
4. At the beginning of the 20th century, …
5. Since then engineers …
6. In the last few years some racing cars …
7. Car racing …

ninety-seven 97

S1 UNIT 7

At the garage

Look at the picture and name the parts of the car. You can use the expressions in the box.

| bonnet | wheel | headlights | tyre | mirror | boot |
| windscreen-wiper | | exhaust | bumper | number-plate | |

Every 7,500 miles cars come into the workshop for a service. Here is part of a service check for a Jaguar XJS. The owner has just brought his car to the garage for a service.

JAGUAR Daimler

JAGUAR SERVICE LIST	1,500 km / 1,000 miles	12,000 km / 7,500 miles	24,000 km / 15,000 miles	
1 Check tyres (pressure and tread)	✓	✓	✓	
2 Check lights	✓			
3 Remove wheels (front and rear)			✓	
4 Balance wheels (front)			✓	
5 Change oil	✓	✓	✓	
6 Check windscreen wipers		✓	✓	
7 Fill up battery				
8 Check mirrors	✓			
9 Check exhaust		✓	✓	
10 Clean car (bonnet, boot)	✓	✓	✓	
11				

a Later the owner of the Jaguar asks the mechanic about the service:

▶ Owner: Have you checked the tyres?
Mechanic: Yes, we've just checked them.
Owner: And have you checked the lights?
Mechanic: No, not this time. We checked them at 1,000 miles.

Play the roles of the owner and the mechanic. Use the check list above.

b Look at the bubbles. What's wrong? What could it be?

① IT DOESN'T OPEN. I CAN'T GET THE SPARE WHEEL OUT.
② THE CAR DOESN'T START VERY WELL.
③ IT'S FLAT.
④ THEY ARE TOO HIGH.
⑤ THEY AREN'T BALANCED.
⑥ THEY DON'T WORK WHEN I NEED THEM – WHEN IT RAINS.

c Can you remember?
Draw a car and name as many parts as you can. Do not look at this page.

UNIT 7 S2

The district nurse is on her way

A home help at work

Nowadays, thanks to motor transport, many old or sick people can have a more independent life than they could in the past.
The social services and voluntary organizations use cars and vans to visit and help old people in their own homes.

Meals on wheels: the Women's Royal Voluntary Service

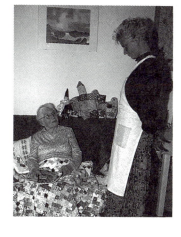

For five years Mrs Sanderson has lived alone. She is 85 years old and now she cannot do much for herself. But there's a voluntary Meals on Wheels organization in her town, so she always gets at least one hot meal every day. Mrs Sanderson also has Charlotte, a home help. She comes in and does her housework once a week. Charlotte can also do Mrs Sanderson's shopping in her car.

It is Tuesday morning, Mrs Sanderson and Charlotte are talking about the work.

Mrs Sanderson: Have you done the shopping?
Charlotte: Yes, I've just done it.
Mrs Sanderson: And have you hoovered the carpet?
Charlotte: Yes, I hoovered it two hours ago.
Mrs Sanderson: And have you cleaned the bath?
Charlotte: No, I haven't done that yet.

Now play the roles of Mrs Sanderson and Charlotte as in the dialogue above.

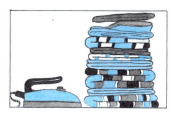

1 do the ironing
   yes/just

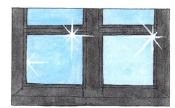

2 clean the windows
   yes/two weeks ago

3 polish the furniture
   yes/last week

4 tidy up the bathroom
   no/not yet

5 wash the kitchen floor
   yes/half an hour ago

6 do the washing up
   yes/just

ninety-nine 99

UNIT 7

Renting a car

Fred Sinclair has just arrived at Heathrow Airport and has gone to the Strawberry Fields Car Rental desk to rent a car for his trip to Edinburgh:

Clerk: **Good afternoon, sir.** Can I help you?
Fred: **Good afternoon,** I'd like to rent a car **for a week.**
Clerk: What kind of car would you like to rent?
Fred: Have you got a **Mitsubishi Colt**?
Clerk: No, I'm sorry we've already hired all the **Colts** out. But we can offer you a **Fiat Uno**.
Fred: How much does it cost **for a week**?
Clerk: **£110.**
Fred: Well, by the way, can I pay **by American Express card**?
Clerk: Of course you can, **sir**.

Some other customers want to rent cars at Strawberry Fields Car Rental.

Rita Jones wants a Metro for two weeks. She arrives in the morning and wants to go to Bristol. She has got a cheque book.

Joe Hill from New York wants to rent a Vauxhall Cavalier for a weekend. He arrives on a Friday evening and would like to pay cash. He wants to make a trip to Leeds.

Strawberry Fields Rent-A-Car

Group 1
Mitsubishi Colt
Fiat Uno

Daily £20
Weekend £35
Weekly £110

Group 2
Honda Civic
Metro Automatic

Daily £25
Weekend £45
Weekly £130

Group 3
Ford Sierra
Vauxhall Cavalier

Daily £30
Weekend £55
Weekly £160

Group 4
Ford Granada
Rover 3500

Daily £40
Weekend £75
Weekly £220

Includes: full insurance, VAT at 15%, 100 miles free (at weekends: 200 miles free).

Hirer pays for petrol and 10p per mile (if more than 100 miles).

Tom Tanner arrives at Heathrow Airport on Monday afternoon and wants to rent a Ford Granada for two days. He has got a Diner's Club card and wants to travel to Glasgow.

 a Now you and your partner are Rita Jones/Joe Hill/Tom Tanner and the clerk. Read the dialogue above again and replace the words in **bold type**.

 b What do the four customers have to pay? Look at the mileage chart and make out a bill for each of them.

The bill should include
– price per day/weekend/week
– price for extra miles
– final amount.

c **What about you?**
You want to rent a car at Heathrow Airport and you want to visit other towns in Great Britain.

Play the roles of the clerk and the customer with your partner.

Do not look at the text.

How much is your bill?

Mileages

	Aberdeen	Birmingham	Bristol	Cardiff	Edinburgh	Glasgow	Leeds	Liverpool	Manchester	Portsmouth	Salisbury	Southampton	LONDON
Birmingham	420												
Bristol	493	81											
Cardiff	491	103	45										
Edinburgh	125	292	373	385									
Glasgow	145	292	273	385	44								
Leeds	327	113	194	220	202	215							
Liverpool	341	93	161	169	216	216	75						
Manchester	340	80	161	172	215	215	40	35					
Portsmouth	560	141	97	142	435	433	244	234	221				
Salisbury	514	111	52	93	397	395	215	195	190	40			
Southampton	547	128	76	121	421	420	232	211	208	18	22		
LONDON	503	105	115	167	378	397	189	202	185	70	84	77	

UNIT 7 G

Past Simple – Present Perfect

Das *Past Simple* steht:

- bei Handlungen in der Vergangenheit mit genauer Zeitangabe (z.B. *in August 1961, two weeks ago, last Friday*).
- bei Fragen nach einem genauen Zeitpunkt in der Vergangenheit (z.B. mit *when ...?*).

Das *Present Perfect* steht:

- bei Handlungen in der Vergangenheit ohne Angabe des Zeitpunkts.
- bei Handlungen in der Vergangenheit mit den Signalwörtern *just, never, already, ever, so far, not yet, today, this week/month/year*.
- bei noch andauernden Handlungen mit *since, for, how long*.

Susan **left** school in 1979.
When **did** he **live** here?
He **lived** here three years ago.

Tom **has repaired** his house.
He **has** just **put** in new doors.
He **has lived** here for three years now.

Adjective – Adverb

Adjektiv	Adverb
bad	bad**ly**
easy	eas**ily**
terrible	terri**bly**
good	well
fast	fast
hard	hard

Das Adverb wird gebildet aus:

Adjektiv + *-ly*
-y wird zu *-ily*
-le wird zu *-ly*

Einige Adverbien bilden abweichende Formen.

Adjective

He is a **bad piano player**.
John, **be careful**, please.

Adverb

He **plays** the piano **badly**.
Read this **carefully**, please.

- Das Adjektiv bezieht sich auf das Nomen.
- Das Adjektiv steht nach Formen von *be*.

- Das Adverb bezieht sich auf das Verb.

's-genitive – of-construction

's-genitive bei Personen

Mrs Miller**'s** hat the girl**'s** bike	Im Singular: Nomen + *'s*
the Millers**'** house the girls**'** bikes	Im Plural: Nomen + *'*
the men**'s** club the children**'s** problems	Ausnahme: *men's/women's/children's*

of-construction bei Sachen

the price **of** the book the girl **of** his dreams	Im Singular und Plural: *of*

one hundred and one 101

UNIT 8

SERVICES

Can we help you?

Which picture goes with which advertisement?

ASHGROVE HOTEL
FULLY LICENSED
FAMILY RUN HOTEL
* SINGLE ROOMS WITH SHOWERS
* ALL OTHER ROOMS WITH FULL FACILITIES
* FUNCTION ROOM AVAILABLE FOR WEDDING RECEPTIONS AND CONFERENCES
* LARGE CAR PARK * MEMBER OF CROESO
CARDIFF 488144
193 NEWPORT ROAD, CARDIFF

SAMARITANS
24 hr emergency service for the suicidal and despairing.
75 Cowbridge Rd East, Cardiff, CF1 9AF.
☎ Cardiff 44022. /3/4.

BREWERS MOTOR SERVICES COACH HIRE
19–53 SEATER LUXURY COACHES
PRIVATE HIRE TOURS & EXCURSIONS
NATIONAL & INTERNATIONAL
MAESTEG 734204 & 734077
Caerau Garages, Caerau, Maesteg, Mid Glam

METRO CABS CARDIFF
24 HOUR TAXI SERVICE
CARDIFF 464646

Kemps
Chartered Surveyors   Estate Agents
154 Holton Road
Barry (0446) 721111

PADFIELD'S
ESTABLISHED 60 YEARS
EVERYTHING FOR THE DIY MAN OR BUILDER
• BUILDING & DECORATING MATERIALS
• PLUMBING MATERIALS
• TIMBER • HAND TOOLS
• PRICE COMPETITIVE
• FREE EXPERTISE AND ADVICE
MON–FRI: 8–5 (LUNCH 1–2)
SATURDAY 8–12 NOON
• TOOLS, TIMBER
• PAINT, WALLPAPER
• TILES, CERAMICS
• HOMEBREW, TEXTILES
• PLUMBING, GREENHOUSES
CARDIFF 563393
VICTORIA PARK CARDIFF

BROOKLYN MOTORS
24 HOUR RECOVERY SERVICE
(CARS & LIGHT COMMERCIALS)
MOT's — 7 DAY SERVICE WHILE-U-WAIT
* ACCIDENT DAMAGE REPAIRS
* MECHANICAL
* SERVICING
* BODYWORK — PANEL BEATING
* RESPRAYS * FREE ESTIMATES
NEWPORT (GWENT) 852345
NEWPORT (GWENT) 276650 (AFTER HOURS)
29A PANT ROAD, NEWPORT

HOSPITALS
BUPA Hospital Croescadarn Rd Pentwyn--Cardiff 735515
Barry Community Hospital Windham St-----Barry 733372
Caerphilly District Miners Hospital
  St Martins Rd--------------------Caerphilly 887811
Cardiff Royal Infirmary Newport Rd-----Cardiff 492233
Cefn Mably Hospital St Mellons---------Cardiff 777241
Children's Ear Nose & Throat Hospital
  Cowbridge Rd West-------------------Cardiff 561371
Dewi Sant Hospital Rhiwfelin Annexe--Llantrisant 224209
  Albert Rd---------------------------Pontypridd 404121

You are in one of these situations. Who do you ring?

1 You are helping to organize a class trip for 25 people.
2 The last bus has already left, but you must get home tonight.
3 You are in the middle of painting the living-room in your flat, but you haven't bought enough paint. You need some more of the same colour – quickly!
4 It is late at night, your car has broken down and you haven't got any tools.
5 You are looking for a flat.
6 Your boyfriend/girlfriend has finished with you. You feel very alone and you have no one to talk to.
7 Your grandmother is coming to visit, but there is no extra bed for her in your house.
8 You are baby-sitting one evening. Suddenly the baby goes red in the face. He has swallowed a 5p piece.

UNIT 8 A

1 Andy, a bus driver, and Carol, a receptionist, are looking for a flat. So yesterday they went to an estate agent's. The agent gave them information about several flats. They went to look at them in the afternoon and talked to the people who wanted to let the flats.

a Describe the flats in complete sentences.

Nice flat, 2 bedrooms, kitch. + bath, balcony, centr. heat., near shops, £40 per w.

Modern flat, 3 bedrs, k. + b., op. fireplace, tel., near football ground, £75 p.w.

Quiet flat, 1 bedr., 1 liv.rm., mod. kitch., WC, near bus stop, only £55 p.w.

Lge flat, nice k. + b., tel., c.h., near city centre, £175 p.m.

b In the evening Andy and Carol talked about the flats:

Andy: The **first** flat was **nice**, wasn't it?
Carol: Yes, and it even had a **balcony**.
Andy: Oh yes, I remember. You mean the one which was near the **shops**.
Carol: The rent was **£40** per **week**.
Andy: Do you remember the **landlord**?
Carol: Wasn't **he** the one who was wearing those **old jeans**?

What did they say about the other flats? Replace the words in **bold type** and read the parts of Andy and Carol.

c Now play their roles.

2 The couple talked about the advantages and disadvantages of the different flats.

Carol's ideal flat:

- should have central heating
- shouldn't be too far from the city centre
- should have a bathroom
- shouldn't be too near a football ground

Andy's ideal flat:

- shouldn't be too small
- should have a telephone
- shouldn't be too expensive

a What did Andy and Carol say? Make sentences like these:

▶ Carol: I'd like a flat which has got ...
Andy: I don't want a flat which is ...

b Which flat did they choose? Can you say why?

one hundred and three **103**

A UNIT 8

3 At the end of that month, Andy and Carol moved into their new flat. Have a look at the rest of the people who live in their house.

Ask and answer questions like this:

▶ Where does Mr Jones live?
He lives on the first floor.
How do you know?
He's the man who smokes a lot.

104 one hundred and four

UNIT 8 A

4 The next evening Carol wrote a letter to her grandmother in Cardiff and told her about the new flat.

Complete the text with 'who' or 'which'.

> is the latest news about Andy and me!
> We've made it at last! We've found the flat ① is ideal for us. Most of the furniture is in the flat, but you know there are so many things ② are necessary. It's difficult for people ③ haven't saved much, but I still think that we can buy the things ④ are most important.
> There's a cooker in the flat, but I also want a fridge and – if possible – a washing-machine.
> Yesterday we met some of the people ⑤ live in the house. The man ⑥ lives downstairs has offered us a second-hand fridge for only £30. Andy has just gone to the do-it-yourself shop ⑦ is round the corner. He wants to buy some cheap wallpaper.
> You must come and see us soon.
> Love, Carol

5 People and things in the house where Andy and Carol live:

1

2

3

4

5

6

7

8

a What can you see in the pictures?

b Describe the people or things in the pictures. You can use the verbs in the box.

| wash | record | serve | wake up |
| take up | drive | control | work |

A	...	is a	woman person machine thing	who ... which ...
	...	are	people	

one hundred and five 105

B UNIT 8

1 Carol is the daytime receptionist at the Lawrence Hotel in Exeter. Sometimes guests have complaints. What are they saying?

put in my room | repair for me | serve me | send up to my room | leave in my room | wash for me

▶ The television which you put in my room is broken.

2 It is the 23rd of June.

Here is what some guests at the Lawrence Hotel are doing:

Mr Donovan | Mr Allan | Mr Thompson | Ms Johnson | Mr Kelly | Ms Stewart

 The next day Rose, Carol's colleague, asks her about the guests.
Use the phrases below and play the roles of Rose and Carol.

Mr Atkins

▶ take to the airport
Rose: What about Mr Atkins?
Carol: He's the gentleman we took to the airport.

1 promise to meet at the station
2 speak to on the phone
3 lock in his room
4 put in room 248
5 try to wake up
6 tell to see the manager

3 Carol's daily routine is different ...

a What is she doing at the moment?

b Make sentences with 'who' or 'which'.

▶ In the first picture I can see some guests, who Carol is greeting at the reception.

UNIT 8 B

4 Here is part of a brochure about the Lawrence Hotel which Carol sends to the British Tourist Authority in London every year.

Exeter is an interesting city in the south west of England with 2,000 years of history. You can visit old city walls which the Romans put up. The famous cathedral, which the Normans built in 1112, is also worth a visit. Moreover, Exeter is an ideal centre for tourists who want to visit the south west of England.
When you come to Exeter you stay at the attractive Lawrence Hotel, which you can find in the centre of the city. It is one of the best hotels in town – modern rooms, an excellent restaurant and friendly service. Our hotel staff, who we train personally, are here to make your stay most enjoyable. For more information just contact Mr Parkin. He is our hotel manager, who you can talk to anytime.

Make sentences with either 'who' or 'which':

You can read a brochure about Exeter There are old city walls You can visit a beautiful cathedral, The Lawrence Hotel is an attractive hotel, Stay in the Lawrence Hotel, The Lawrence Hotel has an excellent staff, Mr Parkin is the hotel manager,	who which	the hotel trains. is one of the best in town. Carol sends to the British Tourist Authority. the Romans put up. you can contact. you can find in the city centre. the Normans built.

5 If you prefer camping to hotels, you can also spend your holidays in caravan parks, which you can find near the coast.

a What does this place offer?

1 neci wlkas

2 lelvoy bahec

3 frlydine plopee

b What does this caravan park offer?

1 feer smigiwnm ploo

2 dogo fastf

3 lephluf gamrane

c Ask and answer questions like this:

▶ What is it?
  It's/They're …

1 The tourists can enjoy them.
2 The guests can talk to him anytime.
3 The caravan park trains them especially for you.
4 The children love it.
5 It is close to the harbour.
6 You see them in town.

d Make sentences with 'who' or 'which'.

▶ The town offers nice walks, which the tourists can enjoy.
Go on.

UNIT 8

1 Andy is a bus driver in Exeter. The bus he drives is not one of those typical red double deckers. In Exeter, as in many British cities, they have now introduced a mini bus service.
These buses are much smaller but there are a lot of them. So it is a better service for the passengers. Andy talks about a typical day:
"This new mini bus service has made my job very busy, you know. Now I have to take the fares *and* drive the bus. That's the thing I don't like about the job. But then again, I enjoy driving and meeting different people. Sometimes in the summer, when there are a lot of foreign visitors here in Exeter, I wish I could speak a foreign language. You see, I like talking to all kinds of people.
I don't enjoy driving on Saturdays. Sometimes, when I see those football hooligans, I get a little worried. Last Saturday, for example, some of them got on my bus and didn't want to pay. But I've got my two-way radio in the bus and the police soon arrived.

The friendliest people seem to be the old age pensioners. I suppose they've got more time.
The old double decker buses always stopped at the normal bus stops. Now in the mini bus I have to stop when someone wants to get on or off. Just like a taxi. It means I have to be more careful, but I suppose it's better for the passengers. All in all I preferred driving the double deckers but those days are gone."

a What do you call the people in these pictures? Find out from the text.

b Answer the following questions:
1 What kind of bus does Andy drive?
2 Why have they introduced this service in Exeter?
3 Andy wishes he could speak another language. Why?
4 What happened one Saturday?
5 Why did Andy prefer driving the old double deckers?

c Make a list of the things Andy likes/doesn't like.
▸ Andy likes driving the double decker bus.
Andy doesn't like ...ing ...

d Now translate into German what Andy says about his job.

2 Last week Andy was driving his mini bus down Cowick Street when a small child ran out in front of his bus. Andy was able to brake in time, but the little boy fell down and hurt his leg. Of course Andy had to call the emergency services. Later the police interviewed the witnesses.

UNIT 8 C

a Play the roles of the police officer and the other people.
Look at the pictures on page 108.

▶ Officer: What were you doing when the accident happened?
Lady: I was walking down Cowick Street.

b Later the police officer made his accident report:

> At 9.30 am on the 24th November Mr Andrew Phillips of 13 Paris Street, Exeter, was driving his minibus, reg. C673 AFJ, down Cowick Street when a little boy, Tony Short of 21 Ferndale Road, Exeter, ran out in front of the bus. The boy fell down and hurt his leg. Witnesses told me that Mr Phillips was driving at about 25 mph. I talked to Mr and Mrs James Perkins

Can you continue the report?

1 At that time Mr and Mrs Perkins/sit/in/café/when they/see/accident.
2 Then I spoke to Mr Barnes. He/talk to his friend/when/boy/run out.
3 I also interviewed Mr and Mrs Bennett. When/accident/happen/they/wait/at the bus stop.
4 After that I spoke to Miss Jones. She/go into the shop/when she/see/accident.
5 Finally I interviewed Mr McLean. When/accident/happen/he/walk down/Cowick Street, too.

3 Have a look at this. Make sentences from these pictures.

▶ type/ring
The girls were typing when the fire bell rang.

1 make/cut
2 wash up/break
3 hang up/hit
4 carry/fall down

4 The vehicle you can see in the picture is a coach. The people here are collecting their luggage. John Law is confused.

Look at the picture and play the roles of John and Anne Law.

▶ my case – Kate's/hers
John: Hey, is that my case?
Anne: No, it's Kate's. The label says it's hers.

1 Mary's surfboard – the Shaws'/theirs
2 David's racket – Steve's/his
3 Kate's umbrella – mine
4 Steve's case – ours
5 the Shaws' bag – yours

UNIT 8

1 Emergency Services

Richard, Andy's colleague, works for the St John's Ambulance Service in his free time. This is an organization which trains young people to help in emergencies. While he was doing his training, he got this information leaflet.

Dialling the Emergency Services

In an emergency you may need the police, the fire-brigade, or an ambulance. To get one of these services, in Britain you dial '999'. There are, of course, more services which help in other emergencies: mountain rescue, air-sea rescue, lifeboat and coastguard.

But for all these services the number you want is '999'. Then just tell the operator the service you need.

That's easy to remember, isn't it? But in an emergency?

This is what you do!

1. In an emergency keep calm.
2. Lift the telephone handset and dial '999'. The call is free.
3. When the British Telecom operator answers, listen carefully to what he/she asks. Tell the operator the emergency service you want.
4. The operator then wants to know the number of the telephone you are using. Give it clearly and correctly.
5. Then the operator connects you to the emergency service you want. Tell the person who answers what the trouble is, where it is and where you are phoning from.
6. When you finish the call, remember to replace the handset.
7. Never make a false call. It is against the law and risks the lives of people who really need help.

1. What number do you dial in an emergency?
2. Do you need to pay for the call?
3. Something is wrong in this sentence, put it right: "Never make a afels lacl."
4. The emergency services include the following: fire-brigade, mountain rescue, ambulance service, lifeboat and coastguard, air-sea rescue and what other service?
5. What information must you give the British Telecom operator?
6. When the emergency service answers, what information do they need?
7. Find the missing words:
"When you make an emergency call, you must keep ①, speak ②, and then at the end of the call ③ the handset".

a Test yourself.
Look at the questions above, which were on the back of the leaflet.

UNIT 8 T

b Look at the picture and join these sentences with 'who' or 'which'.

▶ The man is an air-sea rescue man.
  He is pulling up the man.
  The man who is pulling up the
  man is an air-sea rescue man.

▶ The boots are made of rubber.
  The firemen are wearing them.
  The boots which the firemen are wearing
  are made of rubber.

1 The man is a policeman. He is standing by the sign.
2 The vehicle is a fire-engine. It has a ladder.
3 The man is afraid. The air-sea rescue men are pulling him up.
4 The men are firemen. They are wearing white trousers.
5 The woman is hurt. The ambulancemen are carrying her.
6 The helmets are made of plastic. The firemen are wearing them.
7 The woman is a doctor. She is wearing a white coat.
8 The sign is a police sign. It tells you to drive slowly.

2 Strange events ...
Listen to the cassette.

Answer the following questions about their experiences:

1 Do you think they dialled '999'? Why/Why not?
2 Which service did they ask for?
3 Retell the stories, say what happened.

one hundred and eleven **111**

UNIT 8

1 Electricity in the home

When we press a switch to turn on a light, we do not think of all the cables which bring the electricity from the power station to our homes. We get electricity through a main cable. This cable can be underground or, in country districts, it can hang above ground on pylons. The cable goes to a meter in the building. A meter measures the electricity we use in the building. Near the meter we can find a master switch where we can cut off the electricity. There are also fuse boxes near the master switch. Fuses break the circuit when there is a fault. The wires take the electricity to each of the switches in the building (lights etc.). All these wires, fuses and switches are part of the wiring circuit.

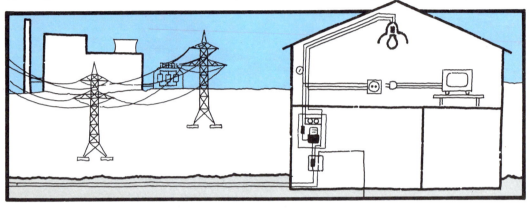

a What can you see in the picture? Explain how electricity gets to the lights in your home.

b What function do they have?

1 cable 3 fuses 5 wires
2 master switch 4 switch 6 meter

2

We measure the voltage in volts (V). In Great Britain this is usually 240 volts. The voltage sometimes falls in winter when a lot of houses are using electricity at the same time. When this happens, the TV picture shrinks or lights flicker.

We measure the energy an appliance uses in watts (W). The more watts you use the higher your electricity bill will be. Some appliances use little but others use a lot (see table in step 3). We measure the current which flows through the circuit in amps (A).

Remember this from your physics class?

$$\frac{\text{watts}}{\text{volts}} = \text{amps}$$

What is it?

1 We measure it in amps.
2 This tells you how much electricity you have used.
3 Some appliances, like a refrigerator, use very little of it.
4 When it falls, some appliances do not work properly.

3

Your electricity bill tells you the price for one unit. A unit is the electricity which a 1,000 watt appliance uses in one hour.

appliance	watts	time for one unit
light bulb	100	10 hours
oven	4,000	–?–
refrigerator	–?–	10 hours
TV (b/w)	150	approx. 7 hours
TV (colour)	350	approx. –?–
washing machine	–?–	20 minutes

a Look at the table. Can you find the missing figures?

b All the appliances on the left are on at the same time. What fuse do you need?

UNIT 8 S2

Food for thought

Joy Davies works in the kitchen of a large London hotel. She looks after everything there. She checks the food, they must have enough and it must be fresh. She plans the meals and sees that everything is ready on time.

Here is what she says about her job:

"Nowadays people are much more interested in what they eat. So they know more about food and what is good for them. When they eat in a hotel or restaurant, they expect to have a good, well-prepared and well-balanced meal. I have to make sure that they are happy with what they get. So I plan every meal carefully. We must have a balance of five things in our food, proteins, carbohydrates, fats, minerals and vitamins. Animal products and vegetables are a good source of proteins for example. Cereals and sugar supply us with carbohydrates, and dairy products are a good source of fats. Most foods contain vitamins and minerals, but good sources are fruit, vegetables and animal liver.

I keep this list of foods in our kitchen. It helps me when I'm planning the meals."

peas

pork

onions

liver

lentils

lamb

nuts

beef

rice

noodles

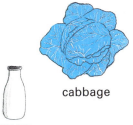
cabbage

cream

sausages

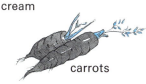
carrots

lettuce

PROTEIN	CARBOHYDRATES	FATS	VITAMINS AND MINERALS
eggs	bread	butter	apples
fish	potatoes	cheese	beans
meat	sugar	ice-cream	tomatoes

a What about you?
Can you do part of Joy's job? Copy the list into your exercise books. Look at the food Joy has bought this week and add it to your list.

b Use your list to plan balanced meals for three days.

one hundred and thirteen 113

UNIT 8

Bank Services

WHY IS GIROBANK BETTER? BECAUSE WE MADE IT FOR YOU!

When we opened Girobank – the newest British Bank on the High Street – we said, "Let's make this a bank which is really easy to use." So first we put Girobank in around 20,000 local post offices. They are open long hours and Saturday mornings.

OUR SERVICES:

1. With our current account you get a cheque-book and can draw up to £50 at two post offices of your choice every other business day.
2. With a cheque card in addition, you can get up to £50 cash at any of the 20,000 post offices every business day, and you can buy goods and services almost anywhere by cheque up to £50 a time.
3. And with a LINK card you can draw up to £100 a day from any Girobank LINK cash machine day and night.
4. A credit card can give you buying power when you haven't got enough cash. You can even enjoy a month's credit completely free. You can use VISA throughout the UK and 160 other countries – in about 4 million shops, restaurants, garages and other places worldwide. It is one of the most popular credit cards.

a Look at the text. Where would you use these things?

| At a | post office
restaurant
cash machine
shop and a post office | I'd use
take | a VISA card.
a cheque book.
a cheque card.
a LINK card. |

b Answer the following questions:
1. Why is it easy for people to find Girobank in every town or even in villages?
2. On which day of the week is there no service at Girobank?
3. How much money can you draw from your account if you have a cheque book?
4. What do you need to get cash on a Sunday?
5. How much cash can you get on a Sunday?
6. How can you pay for a pair of shoes which cost £30?
7. How can you pay a bill of £200 at a travel agency?

c What do you think?
1. What are the advantages and disadvantages of cash and of 'plastic money' like cheque card, LINK card, credit card?
2. Why should people who work have accounts?

d What about you?
Have you got a current account or savings account?
What for?

Relative clauses – relative pronouns

Relativsätze werden verwendet, um eine Person oder Sache näher zu beschreiben. Sie werden mit einem Relativpronomen eingeleitet.

Das Relativpronomen als Subjekt des Relativsatzes

The man **who** works in the hotel is very nice.	– bei Personen *who*
The girls **who** serve in the restaurant are very friendly.	
This is the road **which** leads to the castle .	– bei Sachen *which*
The rooms **which** have a private bath are more expensive.	

Das Relativpronomen als Objekt des Relativsatzes

This is the **guest who** we forgot to wake up .	– bei Personen *who*
The **car which** I rented was very good.	– bei Sachen *which*
This is the guest we forgot to wake up .	Ist das Relativpronomen Objekt eines notwendigen Relativsatzes, so kann man es weglassen.
The car I rented was very good.	

Possessive determiners – possessive pronouns

possessive determiners stehen vor einem Nomen. *possessive pronouns* stehen allein.

possessive determiners		
This is	my your his/her/its	book.
These are	our your their	cases.

possessive pronouns	
It is	mine. yours. his/hers/(its).
They are	ours. yours. theirs.

– Is this your **case**, Anne?
– Yes, I think it's **mine**.
I've found my **case**. Have you found **yours**?

Mit einem *possessive pronoun* kann man die Wiederholung eines vorausgegangenen Nomens vermeiden.

-ing-Form (gerund)

learn	learn**ing**	Infinitiv + *-ing*
drive	driv**ing**	Stummes *-e* entfällt.
get	ge**tting**	Manchmal wird der letzte Buchstabe verdoppelt.
lie	**ly**ing	*-ie* wird zu *-y*.

I like **driving**.
Do you enjoy **learning** English?

Nach den Verben *enjoy, like, love, prefer* steht die *-ing*-Form. Sie hat den Charakter eines Nomens.

Past Continuous

| I/he/she/it | **was** | watching TV. |
| We/you/they | **were** | |

was ⟩ + *-ing*-Form des Vollverbs
were ⟩

I **was watching** TV last night.
We **were having** breakfast early in the morning.
– Did you go to the match on Saturday?
– No, I **was working** in the garden all weekend.

I **was watching** TV when the phone rang.
We **were having** breakfast when the post arrived.

Das *Past Continuous* steht:

– bei abgeschlossenen Handlungen in der Vergangenheit; der Verlauf, das Andauern der Handlung wird betont.

– bei einer Handlung, die schon im Gang war, als eine andere einsetzte.

UNIT 9

MAN AND TECHNOLOGY

Describe the four cartoons.

Which cartoon do you think is the funniest?
Which cartoon do you think is the most critical?

Which picture goes with which?

 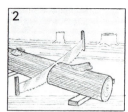 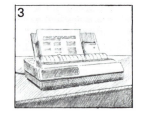 

 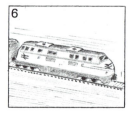 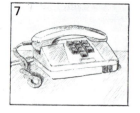 

What kind of noises do you hear?
Listen to the cassette. What can you say about the differences?

UNIT 9 A

1 In 1970 the 'Seattle News', a newspaper in Seattle, Washington, asked its readers to make predictions about the future. Here are some of the results:

1. Cars will use water instead of gas.
2. Robots will do people's jobs.
3. People will live in space.
4. There will be a lot of unemployment.
5. Cars won't need as much gas as today.
6. There won't be any more illnesses.
7. Airliners will fly faster than sound.
8. There won't be any more pollution.
9. Nobody will use cash any more – people will use credit cards.
10. People won't eat animals any more.
11. Trees will die because of acid rain.
12. Every home will have a computer.

a Here are headlines from the newspaper report about the predictions.
Can you match the predictions with the headlines?

Transport   Food   Employment

Space travel   Environment

Computers   Money   Medicine

b Which of the predictions have already come true? Which haven't come true? Which do you think will come true? Which do you think won't come true?

c Look at the things below. Ask and answer questions about their future.

▶ Will people still make war in the future?
Yes, they will./ No, they won't.

2 Chuck, a boy from Seattle, sees this ad in the local newspaper:

ALBATROSS PC 20
You could win this fantastic computer

Specifications:
CPU: 68000
Memory: 512 K Byte
Hard disk: 20 M Byte
Disk drive: 5 ¼"
Printer: 120 cps NLQ
Price: only $ 550

What this computer will do for you:

The Albatross PC 20 will
- organise your pocket money.
- help you learn your vocabulary.
- teach you math.
- check your spelling.
- play chess with you.
- draw for you.

And remember:
Program it yourself and it will do anything you want it to.

1. Floppy disk 2. Printer   3. Monitor
4. Mouse   5. Screen   6. Cursor
7. Keyboard   8. On/Off switch 9. Disk drive

All you have to do:
Match the letters with the numbers.
Write the answers on a postcard.
Take it to your local dealer and ask him about the fantastic

Albatross PC 20

UNIT 9

a Look at the ad on page 117 again and answer the following questions:

1. How do you turn the computer on?
2. Where do you put the floppy disk?
3. What can you see on the screen?
4. What can you move with the mouse?
5. What do you do with the keyboard?
6. What can you do with a printer?
7. What is the difference between a monitor and a television?

b These people have decided to buy the Albatross.
Will the computer help them? Look at the ad to find the answers.

Cathy   Jill and Graham   Doreen   Dennis   Gladys and Linda   Clive

Now make 5 short dialogues like this:

▶ Clive wants to buy the Albatross.
Really, why's that?
He wants to write English texts correctly.
How will the Albatross help him then?
It will check his spelling.

3 Breakfast talk in a Seattle suburb ...

Mabel: George.
George: Mmmm.
Mabel: George, what are we going to get Chuck for his birthday?
George: I'm not going to get him anything! He's got enough already.
Mabel: Aw, come on, George. You know you don't mean that.
George: Well, what does he want?
Mabel: He said something about a computer.
George: A computer – that's much too expensive.
Mabel: He's saved quite a bit. I think he has saved about $400 already.
George: But what's he going to do with a computer – play all day?
Mabel: He says he's going to learn how to program it.
George: Well, that sounds reasonable. What kind does he want?
Mabel: I don't know and there are so many of them.
George: Well, perhaps the best thing is to give him some money towards it, and he can buy the thing himself ...

UNIT 9 A

a Answer the following questions:
1. Who do you think Mabel and George are?
2. Whose birthday is it?
3. Why does George say: 'I'm not going to get him anything'?
4. What does Chuck want?
5. What do Mabel and George think about Chuck's idea?
6. How much has Chuck saved?

b You can see the problem from different sides. Listen to the cassette.
1. Who do you think Carrie is?
2. When is Chuck's birthday?
3. What can Chuck have for his birthday and what are the alternatives?
4. Why can't he have a party and a big present?
5. What are Mabel and George going to give Chuck for his birthday?

4 Right or wrong? Follow the flow chart.

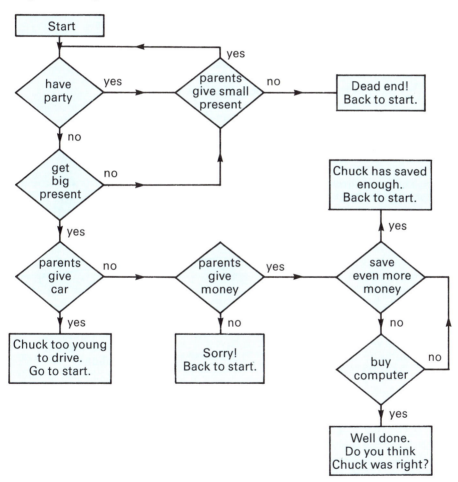

a Make statements like this:
- Chuck's going to have a party.
  Yes, that's right./No, that's wrong.
- His parents are going to give him a small present.
  Yes, .../No, ...

b Ask and answer questions like this:
- Is he going to have a party?
  Yes, he is./No, he isn't.
- Are they going to give him a small present?
  Yes, .../No, ...

one hundred and nineteen 119

B UNIT 9

1 The world of multi media

a Talk about the people, the animals and the media equipment.

▶ If ○ (bite) the cable, * (get) an electric shock.

If the dog bites the cable, it will get an electric shock.

If ① (put) the earphones on, * (hear) music.
If ② (drop) the box, * (damage) the video recorder.
If ③ (buy) the video camera this week, * (be) cheaper.
If ④ (fall off) the shelf, * (hit) the dog.
If ⑤ (break) the LP, the salesman (shout).
If ⑥ (see) the bird on the screen, ...

b Ask and answer questions like this:

▶ What will happen if the dog bites the cable?
It will get an electric shock.
Go on.

2
Carrie Dixon and her girlfriend want to make a recording for Chuck's birthday. They want to speak some sentences on the cassette. But just look at their new digital cassette recorder.

a Match the statements with what you can see in the picture. What's wrong?

The recorder won't work The cassette deck won't close The cassette won't turn The recorder won't be ready for recording	because	they haven't put in the cassette the right way. they haven't connected the microphone. they haven't closed the deck. they haven't plugged it in.

Why won't it work?

Carrie hasn't released the PAUSE key She hasn't pressed down the PLAY key She hasn't turned up the VOLUME level She hasn't pressed the RECORD key	and so	their voices on the cassette won't be loud enough. it won't record. the PLAY key won't work. the cassette won't work.

b Now say what won't happen if ...

▶ The PLAY key won't work if Carrie doesn't release the PAUSE key.
▶ The recorder won't be ready for recording if they don't connect the microphone.
Go on.

UNIT 9 B

3 Computer rhythms

This is a print-out of a biorhythm chart. It belongs to Carrie and a computer has worked it out for her. It can show her good and her bad days of a coming month. That means it shows when she'll be fit or weak – her physical highs and lows and when she'll feel happy or sad – her emotional highs and lows. It tells us whether her mind will work well or badly. This is the mental curve in the chart.

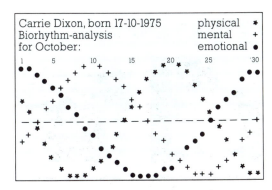

Carrie and Chuck are talking about the practical side of Chuck's computer. Listen to the cassette.

Carrie: Chuck, you're doing a computer course, aren't you?
Chuck: Yeah, why?
Carrie: Well, I wonder, you know, whether you could work out my biorhythm.
Chuck: Your what?
Carrie: My b-i-o-rh-y-thm.
Chuck: Oh, I've heard about that. What do you want it for, though?
Carrie: Well, you see, I've got a lot on next month and I don't know how to pick the right days.
Chuck: OK, I'll do it. But it'll take me a week and I need your birthday.
Carrie: The 17th of the 10th, you stupid ...

a Answer the following questions:
1 How can Chuck help Carrie?
2 Why does Carrie want to know about her biorhythm?
3 Chuck is going to work out Carrie's biorhythm. How long will it take?
4 What does Chuck need to work out Carrie's biorhythm?
5 What does he use to work out her biorhythm?

b Can you answer these questions, too? Listen to the cassette again.
1 According to Chuck, what will happen if Carrie goes climbing on the 10th?
2 When is her physical high?
3 Do you think Chuck and Carrie are very serious about biorhythms?

c Play computer for Carrie. Use her list of plans. Decide first whether the things which she wants to do are mainly physical, mental or emotional. Then look at the lines in the chart and say what will happen if she does the things in her list.

- go to a dinner-dance with Paul (Oct. 8 or 21)
- go to a party with Tom (6 or 19)
- start driving lessons (12 or 28)
- take a test in French (14 or 29)
- go for a day's climbing (10 or 20)
- take part in a 10-mile fun-run (8 or 22)
- help Dad plant new rose bushes (19 or 30)
- take part in a chess competition (2 or 23)

4

You can see these signs every day. What kind of advice or warning can you give to somebody who has not seen these signs yet?

▶ If you drop ..., ...

1

2

3

4

5

6

7

C UNIT 9

1 An interviewer from the 'Seattle News' is asking people in the street what they think about microwave ovens.

A: Brenda
B: Colin
C: Mr Duncan
D: Mr King
E: Mr and Mrs Paul Smith
F: Mrs Bishop

EXCUSE ME, I'M DOING A SURVEY FOR THE 'SEATTLE NEWS' ON MICROWAVE OVENS. DO YOU HAVE ONE AT HOME?

① NO, I THINK THEY'RE FAR TOO DANGEROUS. I WORK IN A RESTAURANT AND WE'VE GOT FOUR OR FIVE BUT I HATE USING THEM. THEY'RE CERTAINLY BAD FOR YOUR HEALTH.

② YOU MUST BE JOKING. I'M NEARLY 80, DEAR, AND MUCH TOO AFRAID OF TRYING NEW THINGS LIKE THAT.

④ WELL, I ENJOY EATING WHAT PAUL COOKS. HE TRIES ALL KINDS OF NEW RECIPES NOW THAT HE'S GOT HIS MICROWAVE.

⑤ WELL, AS YOU CAN SEE I LIKE EATING VERY MUCH BUT I THINK IT'S ALL TOO NEW — MAYBE WE'LL BUY ONE IN A COUPLE OF YEARS' TIME.

③ NO, WE DON'T. BUT MY MOTHER'S TIRED OF KEEPING THE DINNER HOT FOR ME UNTIL I COME HOME FROM SCHOOL SO PERHAPS WE'LL GET ONE.

⑥ A MICROWAVE OVEN — ME? NO, AND I'M NOT INTERESTED IN BUYING ONE EITHER. FOOD'S NOT IMPORTANT — IT'S ONLY MUSIC THAT COUNTS.

⑦ YES, WE'VE GOT ONE I DISLIKE WASTING ENERGY....

... AND USING A MICROWAVE OVEN IS A GOOD STEP IN THE RIGHT DIRECTION.

a Look at the photos and write down who says what.

b What do you know about each of the people?

c What do the people say they like or dislike?

Mr King	dislikes	buying a microwave.
Paul Smith	hates	trying new things.
Brenda's mother	likes	keeping the dinner hot.
Karen Smith	enjoys	using a microwave.
Colin	is tired of	wasting energy.
Mrs Bishop	is afraid of	eating very much.
Mr Duncan	is not interested in	eating what Paul cooks.

UNIT 9 c

2 Likes and dislikes

love
like
not mind
dislike
hate

a What do they like or dislike?

buy — make → (clothes)

▶ He hates buying clothes.
  She doesn't mind making clothes.

1 cook — cook
2 eat — eat
3 read — read
4 bake — eat
5 eat — cook

b What about you? Now talk about what you like or dislike.

3
The 'Seattle News' has completed the survey on microwave ovens. Here are some statements other people made:

Replace the parts in **bold type** and use the verbs in the box.

| dislike | interested in |
| enjoy | tired of | prefer |

1 **I think it's great fun to cook** a large dinner every Sunday.
2 **I think it's a waste of time to try** and keep the food hot.
3 **It's not much fun for me to cook** for my family because they all come home at different times.
4 **I'd buy** a microwave but my wife/husband doesn't agree.
5 **We think it's better to eat** fresh vegetables. They're better for our health.

4
Complete the text. Use the words in the box.

yourself	ourselves
myself	himself	herself
yourselves	themselves

Lucy: You needn't prepare the dinner for me, Mom. I can do it ① when I come home from school.
Nora: Now that we've got a microwave cooker, we can easily look after ②.
Mom: Well, I'm not so sure — Danny's only six. He certainly can't cook a meal ③.
Nora: No, of course not, but Mom, you must stop doing everything ④ and let us do more.
Mom: That's easily said, Nora. But look at the Bugattis. They thought they could do everything ⑤ when their mother went to hospital.
Nora: Yes, I know, but they haven't got a microwave and Mrs Bugatti did everything ⑥, too.
Mom: All right! But do you all really think you can look after ⑦ just because we've got a microwave?
Lucy: Of course, that's the only reason we bought the microwave six months ago, remember?

UNIT 9

Satellite communication

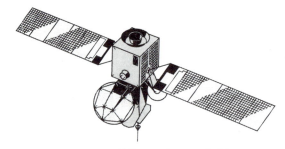

This is the place where we all live – the earth. Have you seen the picture before? Do you know who took it? –

No, it wasn't an astronaut. A satellite took it. One of the many in space which move round the earth. These satellites help us in many ways. For example, they help to predict the weather, they show us where to find fresh water or even oil. And we can use the pictures to make very exact maps. But satellites do not only take pictures. Today we can communicate by satellite from one side of the world to the other. We can transmit telephone conversations, television pictures, drawings and diagrams and lots more.

In 1962 engineers sent TELSTAR – the first communication satellite – into space. A satellite is like a large mirror in the sky. If you transmit a signal to it from the aerial of one earth station, it will reflect the signal back to a different earth station. Some satellites carry more than 20,000 telephone calls and up to four TV programmes at one time. With the help of new technologies, engineers will be able to increase the number of calls to more than 100,000 in the near future.

Solar cells cover most of the satellite. When the sun's light hits them, they start producing the energy the satellite needs. If a satellite goes off course, engineers will use the satellite's small motors to bring it back on course. If they do not succeed, they will lose the satellite forever.

a Can you answer the following questions?

1 There is a picture of the earth at the top of the page. Who took this picture?
2 What can we transmit with the help of a satellite?
3 What was the name of the first communication satellite?
4 In what way is a satellite like a mirror?
5 What will be different about the satellites of the future?
6 Explain the importance of solar cells for the satellite.
7 How can engineers bring a satellite back on course?
8 If you are planning to go on a bicycle tour tomorrow, what information from the satellite will help you?

b The opposites of these words are in the text. Can you find them?

1 after
2 lose
3 wrong
4 last
5 same
6 less
7 decrease
8 past
9 stop
10 large

c Put in the correct prepositions.

Today we can communicate ① satellite ② one side of the world ③ the other. If you transmit signals ④ the satellite from one earth station, it will reflect them back ⑤ another. These satellites are ⑥ space and move ⑦ the earth very quickly. They get the energy they need ⑧ solar cells. If a satellite goes ⑨ course, its small motors will bring it back ⑩ the right place.

124 one hundred and twenty-four

d Find the mistakes and correct them.

"You see, a satellite is like a flying saucer. It takes video tapes, which it transmits to special earth stations. The satellite shows us where to find exact maps. It is also very good at making drawings and telephone conversations. Solar energy covers most of the satellite. This energy is very important for the engineers if the satellite goes off course. The small motors produce all the energy the satellite needs to transmit pictures. Future satellites will never transmit more than 100,000 telephone calls and 2 radio programmes at the same time."

e Chuck is talking to his aunt in Britain on the telephone.
You can hear him but not his aunt. Try to complete their conversation.

Aunt Mary: Chester 535128.
Chuck: Hello, Aunt Mary, this is Chuck.
Aunt Mary: ...
Chuck: I'm fine, thanks. And how are you?
Aunt Mary: ...
Chuck: A cold? Oh, I'm sorry to hear that. Listen, Aunt Mary – about your visit next month. Pa wants to know what date you're going to arrive so we can pick you up at the airport.
Aunt Mary: ...
Chuck: Right. And what time will the plane arrive here in Seattle?
Aunt Mary: ...
Chuck: OK. Got it.
Aunt Mary: ...
Chuck: Aw, school's all right, I guess. But we'll be on vacation when you come. Before I forget – do you like sun-bathing and swimming? Mom says, if you do, we'll go to the coast for a few days.
Aunt Mary: ...
Chuck: That's good. What else do you like doing?
Aunt Mary: ...
Chuck: OK. Mom's going to make a program for your visit.
By the way, thanks very much for the money for my birthday.
Aunt Mary: ...
Chuck: I'm going to put it together with the money from my parents and my savings, and I'm going to buy a computer.
Aunt Mary: ...
Chuck: I'm going to learn how to program it. OK, see you soon. Bye!
Aunt Mary: ...

f Imagine you are going to make a call to an aunt in America. Look at the pictures and say what will happen after you have dialled her number.

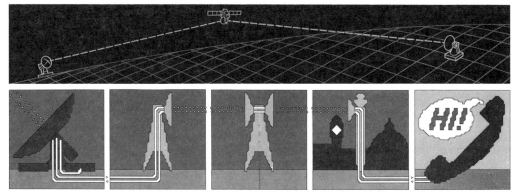

g Translate the text about satellite communication into German.

UNIT 9

Computers work it out ...

CAD stands for **c**omputer **a**ided **d**esign. It means that draftsmen do not only work at their drawing-boards with pen and pencil, but they can use a computer, which is faster and more exact. So it is quite simple to change the shape and size of an object with the help of a computer. Let's have a look at some two-dimensional drawings first. As you can see in the figures 1, 2 and 3, you have a circle with an area of 25 square centimetres (cm^2) first. If the draftsman selects the right commands, it will only take a few seconds to enlarge or to reduce the circle area or to change the circular shape into square or rectangular shapes.

Industrial designers, however, need a lot of three-dimensional drawings. To design the new brake shoe (fig. 4), the draftsman first draws the brake shoe in two dimensions. Then, different colours will create a three-dimensional effect and give the brake shoe depth. If the drawing is wrong, the draftsman will not lose much time. He can change it quickly into the shape he wants. He need not draw the whole brake shoe again. He must only change one or two parts in his drawing, and the computer screen will show him the new three-dimensional drawing.

a Can you answer these questions?

1. Which shapes are the objects in figures 1, 2 and 3?
2. Replace the words in **bold type** with expressions from the text: If the draftsman chooses the right commands, he can **make** the circle area **smaller**, he can **make** it **bigger** or he can **make** the shapes **different**.
3. In how many dimensions does an industrial designer start to draw when he wants to get a three-dimensional drawing?
4. What creates the three-dimensional effect of a drawing on the computer screen?

b What about the following objects?
Are they two-dimensional or are they three-dimensional?
An egg, a square, a ball, a rectangle, a circle, a box, a case.

c Give the measurements of this object in full sentences.

▶ Its height is .../
It's ... high.
Go on.

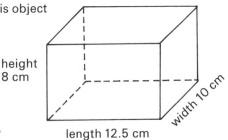

height 8 cm
length 12.5 cm
width 10 cm

How much water will it hold?

d Draw an object of any size. It should have straight sides.
Put down its height, width and length.
Now ask for the measurements of your partner's drawing and draw it according to his/her answers.
Compare your drawings: What height/width/length is it?

UNIT 9 S2

A kitchen for you!

Appliance	Function
microwave oven	keep food fresh
dishwasher	clean air and remove kitchen smells
fridge-freezer	heat up food in seconds
fan cooker with ceramic hob	store food and utensils
cooker hood	wash your clothes
washing-machine	wash dishes and cutlery automatically
sink and draining-board unit	cook food and boil water
cupboards	provide work area for cleaning pots, pans and other utensils

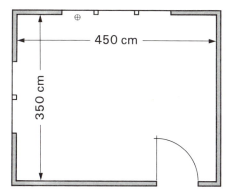

1 stool
2 chair
3 table
4 sink and draining-board unit
5 sink
6 fan cooker with ceramic hob
7 fan cooker with cooker hood
8 dishwasher
9 fridge
10 fridge-freezer
11 freezer
12 washing-machine
13 bottom cupboards
14 top and bottom cupboards

a Match the appliances with the correct pictures and functions.

b Imagine you and a partner are going to move into a new flat. Copy the kitchen and use the appliances to design your own supermodern kitchen.

c Discuss your ideal kitchen with the rest of the class. Whose kitchen is best?

one hundred and twenty-seven 127

UNIT 9

The office in the year 2000

Nearly all offices in the year 2000 will use modern technology. The office staff ...

... will send copies of letters and other documents overseas in seconds by TELEFAX.

Employees will use video systems and will see and talk to people in different parts of the world.

People will use the TELETEX to send letters, memos, plans and pictures to one or a number of 'receiver mail boxes' at the same time.

The company will need very little space to store large amounts of information.

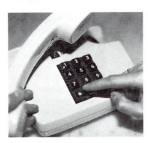

The staff will use
- short code dialling which keeps long phone numbers in a memory:
  * 1 = 001 212 – 936 4215 (WIPS Corp – a New York number)
  * 2 = 051 789 6789 (K-Tools Ltd – a Liverpool number)
- a 'ring-when-free'-system: if the person you want to speak to is already talking, you put the receiver down. As soon as the other person puts his receiver down, your phone will ring. When you pick up the receiver, the other telephone will ring.

What about you?

Imagine you work in an office like this and find the following notes on your desk:

1 Send a plan of JR 21 machine to our partner in Boston by 8.30 am.
2 Send memo to all our UK factories.
3 Organize a round-table discussion with our suppliers from overseas.
4 Get addresses of all customers in Switzerland.
5 Phone back to K-Tools Ltd in Liverpool.

What are you going to do? What equipment are you going to use?

will-Future

I/you	will	
He/she/it	'll	+ Infinitiv
We/you/they	will not / won't	

Der Zukunftsaspekt wird häufig durch Signalwörter wie *in (the) future, in 1998, next week, tomorrow* verdeutlicht.

Every home **will have** a computer.
There **won't be** any more pollution in 1998.
I'**ll help** you with the washing-up.

– Have you written the letter?
– No, not yet. I'**ll do** it tomorrow.

Das *will*-Future steht zum Ausdruck der Zukunft bei Vorhersagen oder Versprechen.

going to-Future

I	am/'m	
He/she/it	is/'s	going to + Infinitiv
You/we/they	are/'re	

They'**re going to give** him some money.
Chuck **isn't going to have** a party.

Das *going to*-Future steht zum Ausdruck der Zukunft bei persönlichen Absichten und Vorhaben.

Conditional sentences (I)

if-Sätze drücken Bedingungen aus.

if-Teil	Hauptsatz
If he **goes** to bed late,	he **will be** tired tomorrow.
If he **doesn't go** to bed late,	he **won't be** tired tomorrow.
Present Simple	*will*-Future

Für den Sprecher ist das Gesagte erfüllbar.
Er betont, daß er keinen Zweifel daran hat.

Hauptsatz	*if*-Teil
Carrie **will have** a good time	if she **goes** skiing next week.
Carrie **won't have** a good time	if she **doesn't go** skiing next week.
will-Future	Present Simple

Der *if*-Teil kann auch am Satzende stehen.
Er wird dann nicht durch Komma abgetrennt.

-ing-Form (gerund)

Ebenso wie nach *enjoy, like, love, prefer* steht die *-ing*-Form nach folgenden Verben:

Verb	+	*-ing*-Form
hate **dislike** **(not) mind**		*-ing*-Form

Verb	+	Präposition	+	*-ing*-Form
be afraid **be interested** **be tired**		of in of		*-ing*-Form

Reflexive pronouns

Singular	Plural
myself	**ourselves**
yourself	**yourselves**
himself	**themselves**
herself	
itself	

Lucy is old enough.
She can look after **herself**.

The children are old enough. They can prepare the dinner **themselves**.

Das Reflexivpronomen ist:
– eine notwendige Ergänzung. Ohne *herself* wäre der Satz unverständlich.
– eine nicht notwendige Ergänzung. *themselves* dient zur Verstärkung.

UNIT 10

TRADE AND TRANSPORT

Where do we get the goods from?
How do we transport them?

UNIT 10 A

1 Anna Simpson is an American who lives in London. She has just arrived by ship at London's passenger docks. She has been on a tour of Europe with a group of Americans, and now she is waiting with other passengers to go through customs.

Lady: Excuse me, do we have to go through the red or the green channel?
Anna: It depends – you don't have to go through the red channel if you have nothing to declare.
Lady: Well, I've bought some perfume. How much are we allowed to have duty-free?
Anna: I think you're allowed to have 50 grams of duty-free perfume.
Young man: But I don't think you can take in all those cigarettes duty-free. How many have you got?
Lady: 400 – they're my favourite sort.
Young man: Yes, but you aren't allowed to take in more than 200 duty-free cigarettes.
Lady: Oh dear! I hope he doesn't notice.
Customs Officer: I'm sorry, madam, but you've got too many cigarettes. You needn't pay duty if you have 200 or less, but 400! Now, I'll just have a look in your shopping basket. Good heavens, madam, is that a dog? I'm sorry, but regulations are very strict about animals. You mustn't try to smuggle a dog in with you. Please go to the desk over there!
Next please! I'm afraid I must ask you to open your case, too, madam.
Anna: Here you are, sir. I haven't got anything to declare. I only bought a few presents on the boat.
Customs officer: I see, and how much are they worth?
Anna: Let me think ... about £50.
Customs officer: Well, I'm sorry, madam, but the limit is £28. I'm afraid you must pay the duty!

a Several more passengers have problems at the customs. Complete the statements of the customs officers and the passengers.

Use the modals in the box.

mustn't	
must	can
	needn't

– Well, I'm sorry but you ① try to smuggle goods into the country.
– That's all right, madam, if your presents are only worth £20, you ② declare them.
– That's fine, sir. You ③ close your case again now.
– I'm not sure, but I think you ④ go through the red channel if you have something to declare.
– No, sir. You ⑤ declare less than 200 cigarettes.
– Sorry, sir, if you want to keep all those cigarettes, you ⑥ pay the duty.
– No, I'm sorry. You ⑦ bring in any animals at all.
– Excuse me, but I don't think you ⑧ take in more than 200 duty-free cigarettes.

A UNIT 10

b

DUTY- AND TAX-FREE ALLOWANCES

	duty-free		duty-free
Alcoholic Drinks		**Tobacco Goods**	
over 38% proof (whisky, gin etc)	1 litre	Cigarettes	200
or		Cigars	50
not over 38% proof	2 litres	Tobacco	250g
plus table wine	2 litres	**Other Goods**	£28
Perfume	50g	**Not allowed** animals; plants; gold coins; explosives	

Use the information above and talk about the duty-free allowances like this:

▶ You are allowed to bring in 250 grams of tobacco.
You aren't allowed to bring in more than 250 grams of tobacco.
You have to declare over 50 grams of perfume.
You don't have to declare under 50 grams of perfume.

c Go through the text in step **1a** again. Use '(not) have to/(not) be allowed to' this time.

2 Back home, Anna meets her friend Liz Tucker. Liz works for KTR Impex, a large import-export firm in London.

Liz: ...Well, did you enjoy your holiday?
Anna: It was terrific! By the way, I've brought you a little present.
Liz: Oh, thank you! But you didn't have to get me anything!... Oh, it's lovely!
Anna: I had a lot of trouble at the customs with the things I bought. I had far too much and I wasn't allowed to bring everything in duty-free. Luckily, I didn't have to pay in cash though.
Liz: I had the same problem once. I was only allowed to bring in about £28 worth of duty-free goods, I think.
Anna: That's right. It's the same now. But some people weren't even allowed to keep their things. One man had a cactus with him and a woman even had a dog. Of course they weren't allowed to take them through. The lady had to pay a lot for all the cigarettes she had, too. Imagine, she ...

True or false?
Correct the statements if they are false and then put them in the order of the text.

1 The man with the cactus was allowed to bring it into the country.
2 The lady with the dog had to leave her dog at the customs.
3 Anna didn't have to pay duty on her presents.
4 Liz wasn't allowed to bring in over £28 worth of duty-free goods.
5 Anna had to pay the duty in cash.
6 All the passengers who arrived with Anna were allowed to bring their goods into the country without paying duty.

UNIT 10 A

3 Anna and Liz start talking about travel. Liz tells Anna about a flight back to London after a business trip to Lagos.

Use the expressions in the box and make a sentence for each part of the journey.

| be allowed to | have to |
| not be allowed to | not have to |

▶ check in at 1.00 am
  We had to check in at Lagos at 1.00 am.

▶ take all our luggage into the plane
  We weren't allowed to take all our luggage into the plane.

15 walk miles to the bus
14 unpack our cases at the customs luckily
13 wait hours for our luggage

12 wear seat-belts
11 use the washroom
10 leave our seats

9 get into a different plane at 12.30 pm
8 leave the airport
7 get out of the plane

6 stay in our seats
5 wear seat-belts
4 smoke

3 read the emergency instructions
2 take the airport bus to the plane
1 buy duty-free goods

one hundred and thirty-three 133

B UNIT 10

transport: the carrying of goods from one place to another.
cargo: the goods which ships, planes or other vehicles carry.
dock workers: they load or unload the cargo from the ships at a port.
warehouse: a building in which companies can store their goods before they deliver them to their customers.

a What can you see in the picture?

b A cargo of cocoa from Nigeria arrived at the port of London last month. Mr Smith, the import manager of Kencocoa, wrote this report.

Say what happened:

▶ 2 April/workers/load/cocoa onto lorries

On 2nd April workers loaded the cocoa onto the lorries.

Go on.

April
3 lorries/take/cocoa/to port of Lagos in Nigeria
4 dock workers/load/cocoa onto/MS Seaworthy
6 ship/leave/port of Lagos
11 ship/arrive/at/port of London
12 dock workers/unload/cargo
12 cargo/go/through/customs
12 dock workers/take/goods to/warehouse
14 company/sell/cocoa to their customers
16 workers/load/cocoa onto lorries
17 lorries/deliver cocoa to/shops

c Now make sentences like this:

▶ After workers had loaded the cocoa onto the lorries, the lorries took the cocoa to the port of Lagos.
After the dock workers had loaded ...

2

Nowadays most of the goods which arrive at the ports come in large containers. The container system has several advantages:
It is faster, safer and cheaper than the transport system in the old days.

a Changes at the port of London:

	then	now	
Type of packing:	crates	containers	(companies/pack goods)
Time in port:	for 14 days	for 36 hours	(ships/stay in port)
No. of dock workers:	28,000	2,500	(dock workers/work)
No. of docks:	5	1	(London/have)
Loading/unloading:	4,000 tonnes a week	4,000 tonnes a day	(dock workers/load)
Amount of container goods per year:	2 million tonnes	5 million tonnes	(container goods/pass through the port of London)
Imports/exports:	from/to Commonwealth countries	from/to EC countries	(Britain/import-export)

Make sentences like this: ▶ Years ago companies used to pack goods in crates, but nowadays they pack them in containers.

UNIT 10 B

1 What can you see in the picture?
2 Now make sentences with 'used to'.
3 Describe a modern port.

3 The changing face of London's docklands

In 1968 there used to be 28,000 dock workers at the port of London. With the introduction of container ships most of them lost their jobs. Now there are only 2,500 dock workers. By 1983 most of the 20 square miles of docklands had turned into a slum area. Then in 1983 the London Docklands Development Corporation (LDDC) decided to invest a lot of money in the area. From 1983 to 1988 they built or modernized 12,000 flats. A typical example is Oliver's Wharf. It used to be a tea warehouse and is now a modernized block of flats. However, the rent in this area is very high (£50 per month per square metre), and

a lot of the people who used to live and work here have left. Since 1983 over 300 firms have moved to this area. Most of them are so-called 'hi tech' companies.
The LDDC also cleared a lot of the older houses to build the new London City Airport for small jets.

a Answer the following questions:
1 Why did many dock workers lose their jobs?
2 What happened to the docklands between 1968 and 1983?
3 When did the LDDC start to invest its money in the docklands?
4 What is Oliver's Wharf?
5 What was Oliver's Wharf at first?
6 Why did the LDDC decide to clear a lot of the older buildings?

b What do you think?
1 What kind of people live in Oliver's Wharf now?
2 What has happened to most of the dock workers?
3 Why did they need a new airport?

c Make five sentences from each box.
Match a sentence in the left box with a sentence in the right box.

Start your sentences like this: ▶ After the LDDC had decided to invest money in the docklands, the docklands became ...

1 LDDC/decide/invest money/docklands	the docklands/become/attractive place to live again
2 companies/introduce/container ships	a lot of the dock workers/lose jobs
3 many companies/leave docklands	the area/turn into/slum area
4 they/modernize/flats and warehouses	many dock workers/move away
5 they/knock down/older houses	they/build/a new airport

C UNIT 10

1 KTR Impex Ltd is an import-export company in London.

a At a meeting the managing director of KTR Impex spoke to the heads of the departments about his plans for the future:

We're not making enough profit. What can we do? – Just think of our cotton sales.
▶ We would make more profit if we imported cotton from China.
We would make more profit if ...

And he has got some more ideas. Go on in the same way:

1 use private transport
2 invest money in a new warehouse
3 sell Irish beef
4 buy shoes in Spain
5 install American video typewriters
6 buy Italian fruit
7 import Californian wine

b The heads of the departments had something to say as well. So the head of the General Administration started like this:

▶ We would save more energy if we installed a modern heating system. We would save more money if we ...
Go on.

You can use these verbs:

import	install
buy	sell
order	invest in

General Administration:

we	save	more money more time	video typewriters personal computers
	offer	more products better service	a bigger warehouse new lorries

Non-Food Department:

we	have	lower prices better designs	shoes from Spain shoes from Italy
	get	lower prices better service	cotton in China cotton in Sri Lanka

Food Department:

transport quality	become	cheaper better	Irish beef beef from Argentina
products transport	be	here early in the year faster	Italian fruit French fruit

UNIT 10 C

c What about you?
What would you do if you were the managing director of KTR Impex? Use the same verbs as in step 1b.

▶ chairs/Italy/£48 – chairs/Austria/£45
If I was the managing director, I wouldn't buy chairs in Italy, I'd buy them in Austria.
Go on.

Goods to be compared*	country of origin	price per unit (£)	country of origin	price per unit (£)
fish	Norway	1.50	Portugal	1.80
tea	China	0.90	India	0.85
jackets	Taiwan	15.00	South Korea	17.00
wine	France	2.00	Italy	1.50
shelves	GDR	35.00	Sweden	49.00
computers	South Korea	350.00	Japan	410.00

*The quality of the goods is the same.

2 Mr Morris, the head of the KTR Non-Food Department, dictated his secretary a letter to World Export Services in Hong Kong, who had delivered goods to KTR Impex.

KTR IMPEX LTD
21 Downstream,
London E2, England
Telephone: (01)312394
Telex: 82436

World Export Services Ltd (WES)
5 - 7 Yee Wo Road,
Central, Hong Kong

24th August 1989

Dear Mr Kimyang,

Delivery of toy engines

We have now received your delivery of 10th August, but we must say that we had expected it three weeks earlier.

Please try harder to deliver on time in future. I am certain we would sell your products more easily if we got them more quickly.

23 of the boxes were damaged, so please pack them more carefully next time. We would also be grateful if you transported the goods more cheaply

We hope that you will cooperate better in future.

Yours sincerely,

D. H. Morris (Non-Food Dep.)

---

a Make sentences like this:

▶ WES/pack/the engines (carefully)/they/not/be damaged
If World Export Services packed the engines more carefully, they would not be damaged.

1 they/send/the goods (quickly)/KTR/get/them/on time
2 they/deliver/the goods (cheaply)/KTR/sell/them/at a lower price
3 KTR/get/the products (early)/Mr Morris/be/happy
4 WES/try (hard)/cooperation/be/better
5 the workers/at WES/work (well)/their customers/be grateful

b After Mr Kimyang had received the letter he talked to some of the staff members at World Export Services:

▶ You don't work hard enough. Our customers are angry.
If you worked harder, our customers wouldn't be angry.

1 You don't write carefully enough. You make too many mistakes.
2 We don't send the goods fast enough. They arrive late.
3 You don't transport the products cheaply enough. They are too expensive.

UNIT 10

1 From the cotton fields to the boutiques

Almost 50% of the world's cotton comes from China and the Soviet Union.
In the old days people used to pick cotton by hand and they had to work very hard. Today modern machines pick the cotton far more quickly and of course more cheaply than people can.

Other machines press the cotton into big bales. Lorries or trains transport the bales either to the nearest port for Great Britain or to a company in South East Asia. Today many Asian countries produce a lot of clothes for the European market because they can work more cheaply than British companies do. If British companies made normal clothing, they would lose a lot of money. That is why they mainly make very exclusive clothing these days.

When the bales of cotton arrive at the factory, modern machines clean and spin the raw cotton, sometimes together with acrylic. Then the companies weave the cotton into cloth. After that machines cut out the pieces for a T-shirt or a jacket, and very often other machines sew them together. Today most of the production is automatic.
In the past hundreds of workers used to do the work, but now there are machines which do the job faster and sometimes even better. Of course, there are still some workers in the factories, mostly women, who earn very little money.

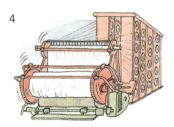

When the clothes leave the factory, import and export agencies try to find customers all over the world. They transport most of the clothes to their customers by plane. When the goods arrive at the airports, workers load them onto lorries. Then the clothes go to warehouses or directly to department stores or boutiques.

a Put the pictures in the order of the text:

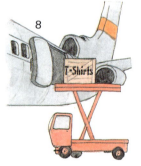  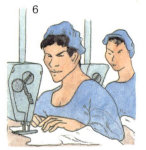 

b Describe the production and transport of a jacket with the help of the pictures.

c Answer the following questions:

1. Why are there not so many workers in the cotton fields these days?
2. What can modern machines do in the production of clothes today?
3. Why do British textile factories mainly produce expensive clothes?
4. Why have many factory workers lost their jobs?
5. What would happen if the import and export agencies sent the goods by ship?
6. What would it be like if production was not automatic?

UNIT 10 T

2 Linda Williams has got some boutiques in London. She has sold clothes to young people for a couple of years now. She tells us about how it all started ...

a Listen to the cassette. In which of these shops did Linda work?

What did she sell there?
When did she start there?

b Listen to the cassette again. Which is the correct answer?

1. Linda left Liverpool because
   she did not like it/
   she was unemployed/
   her parents moved to Birmingham.
2. Linda got the money for her own boutique from
   an old friend/her parents/her bank.
3. Linda sells jeans because
   she gets cheap jeans from Asia/
   she always wears jeans/
   the bank manager told her so.
4. Linda has got
   three boutiques/a shoe shop/
   four boutiques.

c Complete the following sentences:

1. Linda moved to Birmingham after ...
2. She did not find a job in Liverpool because ...
3. She prefers ...
4. Linda opened a boutique after ...
5. Linda had to work hard ...
6. If she had no business connections with India, ...

3 What articles can you find in the shop window of Linda's boutique? Name them.

4 What about you?

What would you do if
– your parents bought you a boutique?
– you worked in an import and export agency?
– you were unemployed?
– the bank lent you £1,000,000 at 2% interest?

one hundred and thirty-nine 139

S1 UNIT 10

Trades

a Look at these different types of houses:

detached

semi-detached

terraced

block of flats

What type of house is it?

It is one of a row of houses.
It stands alone.
It is a large building with several apartments.
It is joined to another house on one side.

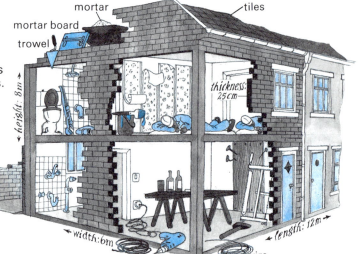

b Look at this picture:
1 What kind of house is this going to be? Give reasons.
2 Where do you think the living-room, kitchen, toilet, bedrooms and garage are going to be?

c On a building site you can find different kinds of workers:

There are
– electricians
– carpenters
– bricklayers
– plumbers
– roofers
– painters and decorators

They
– build the walls
– put in the pipes
– install the wiring
– make the wooden parts of the building
– paint and paper the walls
– put the tiles on the top of the building

1 Who does what?
2 Which materials do they use?
3 Which tools do they use?

d Look at the picture in step **b** again.
1 What have they finished?
2 What do they still have to do?

Fashion

1 Who designed this dress?

Most people in Britain could tell you at once: It's a Laura Ashley.
The dress is typical of her style. A style which has become very successful. A pretty, flowery, cotton material, with long sleeves, a tight waist and a full skirt.
Laura Ashley and her husband started their business in 1953 with only £10. The first dresses only cost £6 and they soon became so popular that the Ashleys started to export them to France, Holland, the US and Australia. Laura Ashley got some of her ideas for the design of her first dresses from the beautiful Welsh countryside where she and her husband had their first factory. Soon you could see this 'country-look' in High Streets all over Britain. Later the look became so popular that the Ashleys started making and selling materials for interior furnishing and decoration. Today there are more than 450 Laura Ashley shops all over the world.

a Look at the picture and say what is typical of a Laura Ashley dress.

b Now answer the following questions:
1 How much money did the Ashleys have to start their business with?
2 Why did the Ashleys start to export their dresses to other countries?
3 Where did they have their first factory?
4 The Ashleys do not only produce clothes. What else do they sell?
5 How many Laura Ashley shops are there in the world today?

2 Have a look at this picture.

A fashion student designed this dress last year. It is quite a different style to Laura Ashley's dresses. It is short and loose-fitting. It is made of metallic thread and has got short sleeves. Underneath it the model is wearing a cotton blouse and shorts.

a Describe the differences between a Laura Ashley model and this dress. Which one do you like better? Why?

b **What about you?**
Now you are a fashion designer. Draw a dress in a style which you like, and label its features.

UNIT 10

Transport in Britain

Britain has always been a trading nation, but in the 20th century international trade and with it international transport have increased more than ever before.

Britain became a member of the European Community (EC) in 1973. Since then British companies have found many new markets in Western Europe.

Britain has a good network of railway lines and motorways. In many cases the companies use their own lorries for a door-to-door service. Of course, if you have to transport hundreds of tonnes from London to Aberdeen, it is more economical to use trains or sometimes even ships.

As Britain depends on the import and export of oil, machinery, electronic products, food etc, her ports are still important these days. Britain is an island and so ships and ferries play a part in the transport of people and goods. British companies also use lorries and trains for fast connections between the United Kingdom and the Continent. As many companies use containers today, they can even deliver their goods more quickly and cheaply than they used to.

Of course, transport by plane is even faster, and although air freight is more expensive than shipment by sea, it has become more and more popular in international trade, because – time is money.

a Can you do these tasks?
1 Find all the means of transport mentioned in the text.
2 List them under the headings land, water, air.
3 What other means of transport can you put into the lists?
4 Name some member countries of the European Community.

b What about you? How would you transport computers from London to Aberdeen/Paris/Hong Kong?

UNIT 10 G

have to, be allowed to

Die Hilfsverben *must, needn't, can, mustn't* haben nur eine Form. Ihre Ersatzformen können in allen Zeitformen, zum Beispiel *Past Simple, will-Future, Present Perfect,* gebildet werden.

must	„müssen"	→ **have to**	We **have to** declare these goods.
needn't	„nicht brauchen"	→ **not have to**	I **didn't have to** pay duty.
can	„können, dürfen"	→ **be allowed to**	You **are allowed to** bring in 200 cigarettes.
mustn't	„nicht dürfen"	→ **be not allowed to**	She **wasn't allowed to** keep her dog.

Past Perfect

| I / You / He/she/it / We / You / They | **had + 3. Form** (past participle) | After MS Seaworthy **had arrived** at the port of London, the dock workers unloaded the cargo. | Das *Past Perfect* steht bei einem Geschehen, das schon vor einem bestimmten Zeitpunkt in der Vergangenheit abgeschlossen war. |

used to

| **used to** + Infinitiv | Companies **used to** deliver their goods in crates. | *used to* wird verwendet, um in der Vergangenheit gültige Gewohnheiten auszudrücken. |

Conditional sentences (II)

if-Sätze drücken Bedingungen aus.

if-Teil	Hauptsatz	
If we **used** personal computers,	we **would save** money.	Für den Sprecher ist das Gesagte erfüllbar. Er betont, daß er es für denkbar oder möglich hält.
If we **bought** beef from Argentina,	transport **would become** cheaper.	
Past Simple	**would** + Infinitiv	
– What **would** you **do** if you **were** the managing director of KTR Impex? – If I **was** the managing director, I **would buy** chairs in Austria.		Für den Sprecher ist das Gesagte nicht erfüllbar. Er betont, daß es sich um rein theoretische Überlegungen handelt.

Comparison of adverbs

hard	hard**er**	hard**est**	Kurze Adverbien werden mit *-er/-est* gesteigert.
fast	fast**er**	fast**est**	
early	earl**ier**	earl**iest**	*-y* wird zu *-i*.
cheaply	**more** cheaply	**most** cheaply	Längere Adverbien werden mit *more/most* gesteigert.
easily	**more** easily	**most** easily	
carefully	**more** carefully	**most** carefully	
well	better	best	Einige Adverbien haben besondere Steigerungsformen.
badly	worse	worst	

REVISION 2

Unit 6

33 Describe what has happened in and around Swanmouth in the last twenty years.

Use the verbs in the box and put them into the Present Perfect.

go up	be	build
become	look for
come	leave	sell

Pollution ① a big problem. The number of accidents ② to 250 per year. They ③ a modern hospital. The car companies ④ many cars. There ⑤ a lot of demonstrations against the pollution from the power plant. Many people from Asia ⑥ to Swanmouth. Many young people ⑦ the town and ⑧ work in bigger cities.

34 Sam has moved to London. His old friend Mark has written him a letter. Use the words in the box.

| already | just | this year |
| yet | never | so far |

I've ① received your letter and I'm happy to see that you've ② found some new friends in London. Hey, have you heard about the big tanker accident near our coast? Oil has polluted our beaches. They have closed three beaches ③. I have ④ seen so many dead sea-birds! Of course a lot of tourists have stayed away ⑤. I haven't planned my holidays ⑥. What about you?
Yours, Mark

35 Make questions and answers. Use 'how long', 'since' and 'for'.

1 Mary/live/in Edinburgh? – six years
2 Tom/work/for the newspaper? – five months
3 Susan/have/a cottage in Granrear? – 1988
4 the tourists/be/there? – two weeks
5 they/not be/to the beach? – Monday
6 Mary/not eat/fish and chips? – Christmas
7 Dave/have/a computer? – his birthday
8 Peter/collect/stamps? – many years

36 Have a look at this picture and describe it. Use the expressions in the box.

| a | some | any | a lot of |

Are there ① cars in the picture? Yes, there are ② cars, but there aren't ③ motor-bikes. ④ people are waiting for the bus. On the left you can see ⑤ children who are looking at ⑥ shop window. Why aren't there ⑦ bicycles in the street? Because ⑧ thief has stolen them.

37 Make questions and find the right answers.

1 Susan ever (be) to Glasgow?
2 you (hear) about the accident yet?
3 How long the Browns (live) there?
4 you (read) any books about pollution?
5 the boys (collect) old bottles?
6 How long Mr Davis (work) for the tourist information centre?
7 Why the tourists (stay away) this year?
8 you (enjoy) your holidays so far?

Yes, I (read) some interesting books.
Yes, they (collect) old paper as well.
No, she only (be) to a town nearby.
Because the beaches (be polluted) his year.
Yes, I just (hear) it on the radio.
No, I (not enjoy) them very much.
They (live) there/3 years.
He (work) there/1981.

REVISION 2

Unit 7

38 Describe Umesh Vazirani's life.

Umesh Vazirani was born in Calcutta in 1948. His parents (move) to England when he was four. He (start) school at the age of five. Umesh (take) three O-levels in 1963. He (do) a lot of different things since then. From 1966 to 1971 he (be) a painter and a taxi driver. And he (work) in a restaurant up till last year. He (get married) 12 years ago. Last summer his family (move) into an old house in Southport. They (already repair) a lot of things there. They (not renovate) the second floor yet. But they (do) a good job up to now.

39 Adjective or adverb?

When Umesh Vazirani and his family moved in, the house was in a (bad) state. Now you can see that they have renovated it (careful). They have painted the walls (beautiful). They have bought (nice) curtains and the front garden is also (beautiful) now. They have really done everything (good) and have finished their work (quick). Last week they had a (wonderful) party with all their friends and neighbours. They spent a (nice) time together and sang and danced (happy).

40 Is it the lady's …?

student / lady / lorry-driver / children / tourists / American footballers

▶ Whose hat is it? It's …

41 A letter to Marie

When we landed here in Sydney yesterday afternoon, I was very happy to see my old friend Charly again. He drove us to his house where his wife served us with wonderful Australian food and wine. She's a good cook! You know, I can't believe that our plane left Heathrow only 2 weeks ago! First we flew to Tokyo, then to Hongkong and to Djakarta. In Djakarta I took a taxi to go on a sightseeing tour but I didn't enjoy the trip very much. The car was at least 30 years old and the driver drove much too fast. On Saturday I want to fly to New Zealand. But first I'd like to see as much as possible of Australia because it's my first stay here, you know. Australia is great! See you next week. Yours, Ann

Make questions and answer them in complete sentences. Ask

1 if Ann has ever been to Australia before.
2 when Ann arrived in Sydney.
3 who she met at the airport.
4 where she is staying.
5 how Charly's wife cooks.
6 how long she has been on holidays so far.
7 which cities she has already seen.
8 which country she has not visited yet.
9 how she got to the sights in Djakarta.
10 what the trip in Djakarta was like.

REVISION 2

Unit 8

42 Join these sentences with 'who' or 'which':

1. Piccadilly Circus is in the centre of London.
2. Bob Geldof is a pop star.
3. James Watt came from Scotland.
4. Covent Garden still has that market feeling.
5. Neil Armstrong was the first man on the moon.
6. Shops had signs with pictures.
7. Gottlieb Daimler built the first car with four wheels.

They showed people what they could buy there.
He helped to collect a lot of money for people in the Third World.
He is now chairman of an international company.
It was the centre of London's fruit and vegetable trade.
It was much safer than other cars.
It is a popular meeting place for tourists.
He invented the steam engine.

▶ Greg comes from America. He is interested in history.
Greg, who is interested in history, comes from America.

43 Define the words on the left. Use 'who' or 'which' or leave them out when possible.

▶ A ... is someone/something who/which ...

1. A receptionist
2. A central heating
3. A bus driver
4. Hotel brochures
5. A bill
6. Policemen
7. An operator

He takes the fares.
You get it when you leave the hotel.
You call them after an accident.
She looks after the guests.
You turn it on when it is cold.
You can phone this person in an emergency.
We can read them when we want to find out more about hotels.

44 What were they doing when it happened?

1. he/wait at bus stop/friend come in car
2. he/have bath/phone ring
3. she/sit in disco/boy ask to dance
4. they/write test/bell ring

5

6

7

8

45 After midnight.
What were they doing when Tom's parents came home?

Carol   Mike   Brian   Joan   John   Tom

46 Look at the picture in step **45**.
Say what the people like/don't like/prefer doing.

1. Carol and Mike
2. Brian
3. Joan (prefer) classical music
4. John
5. Tom

Unit 9

REVISION 2 R

47 What will happen in the future? Make sentences.
Start with 'people', 'robots', or 'computers'.
Use the phrases in the box.

1 This firm is introducing robots into its factory.
2 Engineers are developing a new 'video-phone'.
3 I have a computer. I want to write English correctly.
4 More and more satellites are going into orbit.
5 Britain and France are building the 'Chunnel' (Channel tunnel).

> help to check spelling
> watch more foreign TV programmes
> do the work
> see each other on the phone
> travel by train directly from Paris to London

▶ Credit cards are becoming very popular. – pay by credit card
People will pay by credit card.

48 What are these people – or you – going to do first?

1 John has just bought a new computer.
buy some interesting programs/
read the instructions/
look for another computer
2 Carol and Andy have just moved into a new flat.
buy some new furniture/
go out for a meal/
unpack their things
3 They have just done an English test.
have a rest/
look up the words they did not know/
prepare for the next test
4 You have planned a class trip. The teacher is ill. – …?
5 You and your friends have just played football. You are very dirty. – …?
6 It's your birthday. – …?

49 Tom is doing a survey about leisure.
Answer the questions.
Use the words in the box.

> enjoy   hate   dislike   prefer
> be tired of   be interested in

1 What are your interests? – I …
2 What else do you like doing in your free time? – I …
3 What do you enjoy doing most? – I …
4 What don't you like doing? – I …
5 What do you dislike doing most? – I …
6 Do you mind answering all these questions? – Yes, I do. Actually, I …
7 OK then. What do you really love about school? – Oh, I love …

50 Andy writes this letter to Ron. Put the sentences right.

> you for your nice letter. Why don't you come over next weekend? If you (catch) the 10 o'clock train, Jane and I (meet) you at the station. If the train (arrive) late, I (not be) there because I have to go to the dentist's. But my sister (wait) at the station if the train (not be) on time. – If you (like), we (go) for a ride in the country. I (show) you the lake where we can go swimming if it (not rain). By the way, have you seen the new program on bio-rhythms? If I (have) enough money, I think I (buy) it. It's really

51 Here is part of Ron's answering letter. Put in the reflexive pronouns.

> a party. We enjoyed ① very much. The food was very good. John and his girlfriend Sally prepared the cold buffet ②. Unfortunately, Sally cut ③ while she was making the sandwiches. Later, John had an accident, too. He fell off a chair while he was putting up the loudspeakers. Luckily, he didn't hurt ④ very much. But all in all it was great and I enjoyed ⑤ a lot… Now you know everything about the last few weeks. So when we meet, you must tell me everything about ⑥. OK?
> Bye, Ron
> P.S. Is 10 o'clock at the station still alright? Get ⑦ organized, you two!

REVISION 2

Unit 10

52 Brenda's parents have bought a microwave oven. Brenda is allowed to use it sometimes. This is what her mother said to her yesterday before she went out.

1. You needn't cook the dinner, I've already done that.
2. You must heat it up in the microwave.
3. You can use the special new microwave plates.
4. You mustn't use the old plastic dishes.
5. You must shut the oven door carefully.
6. You needn't stay in the kitchen all the time.

Make sentences: ▶ You must take the food out after two minutes.
Yesterday, Brenda had to take the food out after two minutes.

53 Carrie and her friend have made a recording for Chuck, but something went wrong. Make sentences and put the verbs into the correct form.

1. After they (press) the RECORD switch, they (not release) the PAUSE key.
2. After they (start) talking, they (press down) the PAUSE key.
3. After they (put) the cassette in, they (unplug) the cassette deck.
4. After they (start) recording, they (unplug) the microphone.
5. After they (plug) the cassette deck in, they (not press down) the ON/OFF switch.
6. After they (put in) the cassette, they (not turn up) the volume.

 54 Nowadays we have technical devices to do all sorts of jobs for us. In the past people used to do things differently. Look at the pictures and make sentences to compare the past and the present.

▶ In the past we used to travel by stage coach, now we travel by car.

1 cook/
   food/
   large stove

4 draw/
   things
   by hand

2 write/
   letters
   by hand

5 buy/
   tickets/
   ticket office

3 wash/
   clothes
   by hand

6 dial/
   telephone
   numbers

 55 Sometimes people have problems with their technical devices. Here are parts of some letters to the magazine 'Crazy Repairs':

1. I find that the computer doesn't always store the information.
2. When I take the food out of the microwave, it is often still cold in the middle.
3. We set the video, but it doesn't always record at the right time.
4. I have stored my friend's phone number, but I always get the Seattle Dog's Home when I ring it.
5. My word processor doesn't know how to spell.
6. Our dishwasher doesn't clean the dishes well.
7. My new CD player always plays the disks backwards.

Here is some of the advice the magazine gave:

take it to a TV repair man
try a new disk
leave it in 20 minutes longer
check your friend's number
put in more baking powder
stand on your head
buy it a dictionary

Make sentences: ▶ If you took it to a TV repair man, it would record at the right time.

REVISION 2

Units 6–10

56 A hotel manager is worried. Business is bad. He wants to buy a computer.

He knows:
1 We run the hotel badly in a number of ways. – run well
2 We get our brochures out too late. – get out early
3 Some of our staff don't work hard enough. – work hard
4 We sometimes take too long to reply to letters. – reply quickly
5 We sometimes make mistakes with our bookings. – do the bookings* carefully

Use the comparative form of the adverbs and make sentences like this:

▶ If we had a computer, we ...

* bookings = Buchungen

57 Mr Vazirani has written a letter to his parents in India.
Put the verbs into the correct form.

> Well, we (move) into our new house here in Southport some months ago and we are very happy here. Since then we (do) a lot of work on it and now it looks very nice. Only two days after we (move) in, I (meet) Mrs Lewis, our next-door neighbour. Well, I (talk) to her in the garden one day last week, when she suddenly (have) an idea. She told me to go to the Citizens Advice Bureau to look for a job. So I (not waste) any time and the next day I (make) an appointment. This man there knows a lot about the problems we Indians have because he (work) in the office for nearly ten years now. Well, after I (see) him, I (feel) much better. He

58 What is it? Can you remember who these persons or what these things are?
Make definitions using 'who' or 'which':

neighbour, Rolls-Royce, nursery school, Member of Parliament, pension, Henry VIII, steam coach, estate agent's, ticket, football hooligan, foreign language.

59 Adjective or adverb?

In an emergency it is (important) to do the (right) thing and to keep very (calm). Of course, it is (good) if you aren't afraid of helping someone yourself. But you must do it (good). If someone is (bad) hurt, it is better to call the emergency services as (quick) as possible. The number you want is **999**, that is (easy) to remember, isn't it? The call is (free), so you needn't be afraid of not having enough money. When you talk to the operator, make sure you give your phone number (clear). And remember:
Do not get excited, speak (slow).

60 Jeff is from Texas and he is on holiday in Britain. He planned to stay for four weeks, but there is so much to see, he has decided to stay longer. He calls his parents. Here is what he says. Put the verbs into the correct form.

– Hi Mom, this is Jeff.
– Yeah, I'm fine. Listen, I don't think I'll be home next week after all. No really, there's so much to see that I'll have to stay on longer if I (want) to see everything. If my money lasts long enough, I (not return) until next month.
– No, you needn't send any yet. If I need some, I (write) to you.
– No, I'm sure I'll be alright, yes really. If I wasn't sure, I (not say) so.
– Why? Well, there's so much to see. So far I've only seen London. I want to go up to Scotland. If I had enough money, I (fly) – it's much quicker. But I'm going to take the train – that's a lot cheaper.
– No, I haven't booked a hotel yet. If the weather's good, I (camp), if not, I (find) a hotel when I get there. I've arranged to meet Sam there and we are going to travel through the Highlands together.
– Now, come on Mom, don't be silly. If he (not be) a responsible sort of guy, I wouldn't go with him.
– Yes sure, I know, but if I (come) home now, I would miss so much here.
– Yes, I'll ring again soon. Bye!

UNIT 11

THE WORLD OF MODERN INDUSTRY

What products can you see in the pictures?
What can you say about the production?
Where would you prefer to work?

UNIT 11 A

1 At the factory

Some weeks ago Mr Harris, an economics teacher at Manchester College, arranged a visit to Ronsons Ltd. Yesterday he went there with his class. Ronsons produce a wide range of fridges and other household equipment. When the students arrived, the manager welcomed them and started to show them round the factory.

Here is what he said:

... Here we are in the stores. This is where the steel for the casing and all the other parts come in. First everything is checked and then stored here until it is needed. Then the steel sheets are transported to the shop-floor where the metal casing is produced. As the material is very heavy, we use fork-lift trucks for this ...

... This is the shop-floor. First the casing parts are pressed here and then they are taken to the production line. There we put them together. Of course, nowadays we don't need so many people on the shop-floor as in the past because machines can produce a lot of things faster and more cheaply than people can.
Well, the casing is sprayed and afterwards the paint is dried in a special oven. This only takes a few minutes. Over there the motor is put in the casing ...

... Finally we check all the fridges – as you can see here – and then they are packed in boxes and taken to the warehouse. We sell our fridges to many dealers in Great Britain. Maybe you've got one of our fridges at home. However, we export more than 30 per cent of our products to other European countries and even to Australia ...

a Put the pictures in the order of the text.

b Make sentences like this:

> ▶ paint/dry
> The paint is dried.
> ▶ casing parts/take/to the production line
> The casing parts are taken to the production line.

1 motor/put/in the casing
2 fridges/pack
3 fridges/take/to the warehouse

A UNIT 11

c Make sentences as in **b**. You can use the verbs in the box.

1 fork-lift trucks
2 casing parts
3 all the fridges
4 a lot of fridges
5 about 30 per cent of the fridges

> check   put together   use in the factory   export   sell in Britain

d Look at the following pictures and make sentences as in **b** and **c**.

1 check

2 store

3 press

4 spray

5 pack

2 Can you remember how a fridge is produced?

a Look at **1b–d** again and describe the whole production of a fridge. Use the words in the box.

> first, then, afterwards, after that, and then, finally, later

b Ask and answer questions about the text in **1**.

▶ Where/casing parts/put together?
Where are the casing parts put together?
They're put together on the production line.

1 How/paint/dry?
2 Where/fridges/store?
3 Why/fork-lift trucks/use?
4 Where/casing/produce?
5 Where/fridges/sell?

c Put the following sentences right:

▶ The fridges are exported to the North Pole.
The fridges are not exported to the North Pole, they're exported to European countries and to Australia.

1 The fridges are packed in toilet paper.
2 Fork-lift trucks are used to transport the breakfast.
3 The fridges are produced at a leisure centre.
4 The casing is put in the motor.
5 The fridges are stored on the production line.
6 The paint is dried with a hair-drier.
7 The casing is made of wood.

UNIT 11 A

3 After their visit to the shop-floor, the students went to the manager's office where they talked about the money that Ronsons Ltd earned.

Manager: We had some problems last year, but this year we're doing well. Of course, not all our income can be seen as our company's profit. Don't forget, wages have to be paid and some money has to be invested in new machines. And last but not least, taxes have to be paid.

a You know that taxes are used for many different purposes. Today you have to decide what to do with the taxes.

Look at the list on the right. Write down four things which are very important to you and have to be done first. Then write down four more things from the list which can also be done with the rest of the money if we spend less money on other things.

- build hospitals
  Hospitals have to be built.
- employ more nurses
  If we spend less money on other things, more nurses can be employed.

```
provide old people's homes
stop pollution
build new roads
find jobs for school-leavers
develop alternative forms of energy
build more youth clubs
buy more toys for kindergartens
organize pop concerts
increase pensions
provide better sports facilities
```

b Now report to the class.   **c** Say what else should be done with the money.

4 What is it?

a Describe the things in the box on the right. Ask the class what it is.

- It's a device which is used for washing clothes. What is it?
- It's a product which is made of paper. What is it?

```
            fork-lift truck
     taxi                drier
   photo-copier        typewriter
     bottle       pan        chair
       telephone      magazine
```

vehicle	transporting		goods	people
device	making copying	drying writing	clothes documents	calls letters
product	metal glass	wood paper		

b Now describe one of the following things and ask your partner what it is: hair-drier, dishwasher, oven, warehouse, production line.

UNIT 11

1 Mary Stewart, one of the students from Manchester College, applied for a job as a machine operator at Ronsons Ltd. She was invited for a test and a job interview with the personnel manager.

a In the evening she told her boyfriend about it:

First I was given a registration card.

give

Then we were all taken to the training centre.

take to

1 give a test in

2 send to

3 ask about

4 give

5 show

6 give a test in

7 call in

8 offer

b Mary was also tested in General Knowledge. This is part of the test. Can you find the right answers in the box?

1 When was America discovered?
2 When were the first steam-engines built?
3 When was George Bush elected President of the US?
4 When was the telephone invented?
5 When was Michael Jackson born?
6 When were the first books printed?

1988	1958
19th century	
18th century	
1492	1452

UNIT 11 B

2 At her interview Mary Stewart was given an information leaflet about the company. Here is a page which describes the new offices.

Welcome to Ronsons Ltd

Ronsons Ltd has some of the most modern offices in the country. Several years ago we recognized the importance of electronic communication for the future. In May 1984, plans for new offices were suggested by a group of our top managers. Modern offices were designed by the best architects. In November 1986, the new buildings were opened by Princess Margaret.

People liked the new buildings very much. Modern work areas replaced our old offices, and word processors and computers were introduced to replace the old office equipment. They greatly reduced the time it takes to do routine office jobs. A telefax system was also installed. This brought our communications system up to date.

The workers' relaxation areas were not forgotten, either. The old restroom was completely redecorated by one of the best local firms and the canteen was also improved. At the same time a new, wholefood menu was introduced by our new cook. The only thing which was not replaced was our tea-lady. She still supplies our workers with a "real" cup of tea in their breaks.

Our special thanks go to these firms:

Olaf of Sweden – office furniture
File-It – office equipment
Pineapple Electronics – computers
Quick Communications Ltd – telefax system
Westminster Carpets – carpets
Soft Interiors – curtains
Greenfingers Ltd – plants and flowers
Safe House Ltd – safety equipment

a Look at the text and make pairs.

1. modern offices
2. old restroom
3. new, wholefood menu
4. new buildings
5. plans for new offices

Princess Margaret
our new cook
best architects
a group of top managers
one of the best local firms

b Now make complete sentences from your pairs.
Use the verbs in the box.

| suggest | redecorate |
| introduce | open |

▶ design
Modern offices were designed by the best architects.

c Look at the list of firms in the text which helped with the work.

Ask and answer questions like this:
▶ Who supplied the office furniture?
The office furniture was supplied by Olaf of Sweden.

d True or false? If the sentence is false, put it right.

▶ The best architects suggested plans for new offices.
Plans for new offices were suggested by the managers.

1. The offices at Ronsons Ltd are really up-to-date now.
2. Princess Margaret designed the modern offices.
3. The best architects opened the new buidings.
4. The tea-lady introduced a new, wholefood menu.
5. People really liked the new buildings.
6. Word processors and computers reduced the time it takes to do routine office jobs.
7. The old office equipment brought the communications system up to date.

UNIT 11

1 Family Footwear Ltd is a shoe company in the Midlands. 400 machine operators are employed in their Birmingham factory. The **company** is **facing financial difficulties** so the **management** have made plans to reduce the **number of staff** and to **introduce** more **automation** in the factory. This means that many of the **employees** will **become redundant**. The union, which supports them, is against these plans.

a Replace the words in **bold type**.
Use the following words:

1 workers
2 managers
3 lose their jobs
4 bring in
5 firm
6 losing money
7 robots
8 work-force

b Here are some of the comments you can hear at the factory. Report what the managers and the union leaders say.

▶ "In the next few years we are going to introduce robots in our factory."
The managers say that in the next few years they are going to introduce robots in their factory.
Go on.

Managers:
1 "Automation has become necessary – we're losing too much money."
2 "We need fewer machine operators and more robots."
3 "We lost too much trade last year."
4 "We've tried to find jobs in our Northampton factory for some of the younger workers."

Union leaders:
1 "We want to save all the jobs – we are against automation."
2 "We're going to fight against the management's plans."
3 "We support all the workers here – both young and old."
4 "The firm made a big profit last year."

c Here are some more comments from managers and union leaders.
Find out who says what. Then report what they say. Use the words in brackets.

1 "We don't like doing it, but we have to make some of the staff redundant." (say)
2 "We don't need robots. We want jobs for our members." (are of the opinion)
3 "The young workers should have a right to finish their training." (think)
4 "Not all of the workers will become redundant." (believe)
5 "A lot of our members are too old to find new jobs." (think)
6 "We are losing markets to our competitors." (say)

2 Here are some of the reactions of the workers to the management's plans.

a Report what these people say.

▶ David says/thinks/is of the opinion (that) ...

David: We'll all lose our jobs soon.
Julie: We should support the union.
Robert: The union can't help me.
Patrick: I've worked here all my life. I'm too old to find another job.
Sally: They won't let me finish my training.
John: The management is right. I'm against the strike.
Mary: We should fight for better working conditions.
Fiona: My husband works here, too. We don't know what we're going to do.
Ben: I've talked to the shop-steward. He represents us in discussions with the management.
Carol: We mustn't give up. I'm going to support my union.

UNIT 11 C

b Now listen to the cassette. These people are all facing financial difficulties.
Say what their problems are.

Linda

Linda says (that) she has bought some new furniture for her flat. She says (that) she will have to sell it if she loses her job.

Bill

Liz   Phil

Brenda

Jack   Jill

3 The staff at the factory have a lot of questions about the automation plans. The shop-steward, David Mills, goes to the manager and discusses their problems.

a Here are some of the workers' questions. Report what David asks the manager.

▶ Are we all going to lose our jobs?
The workers want to know if/whether they are all going to lose their jobs.
▶ Does automation mean any new jobs?
The workers want to know if/whether automation means any new jobs.
Go on.

1 Does the management have any other plans for the future?
2 Is the company prepared to invest money in new jobs?
3 Can all the young workers finish their training?
4 Will the older workers get their full pensions?
5 Will some of us get jobs at the Northampton factory?
6 Does the company still make a profit?
7 Do the managers agree with any of our ideas?
8 Have the managers worked out any alternative plans?

b David Mills has collected some more questions from the workers.
He writes the following letter to the manager:

```
Dear Mr Boot,

It seems that there are still a number of other points
which we should discuss. Would it be possible to
arrange another meeting?
Some of the questions the workers have asked are:

1. Why is the firm introducing robots?
2. How many of us will become redundant?
3. Where can we get new jobs?
4. How much money is the company losing?
5. Why do the managers earn so much?
6. What do you think about exporting to China?
7. What does the management think about our ideas
   for new products?
8. When exactly was it decided to introduce robots?

Could we meet this Wednesday?
Thanking you, I remain
                              David Mills
                              Shop-steward
```

When they meet, David asks the manager like this:

▶ The workers want to know why the firm is introducing robots.
Go on.

UNIT 11

1 During the seventies the crisis in the steel industry in Britain meant that a number of steelworks were closed and many jobs were lost. One of the towns which was hit by this crisis was Corby in Northamptonshire. So Corby had to plan a new future. Here is part of a publicity leaflet which was produced to interest new business and industry in Corby.

CORBY WORKS

"When we first heard of Corby, we had to look for it on the map," says Gary Freetone, Manager of Freetone Music Ltd. "But now – well, who hasn't heard of Corby? Corby is an ideal spot for a new business as it is in the centre of the country, not too far from London and near important motorways." Freetone Music Ltd is the name of one of the many firms which have recently moved to Corby.

"When the steelworks closed in 1979, it seemed to be a catastrophe," says Joe Bloggs of the Industrial Development Office. "After the steelworks was built in the 1930s, Corby needed the steel to live. When 6,500 jobs were lost in the steel industry between 1979 and 1981, it was hard to see how the town could continue."

But the people of Corby did not simply sit around and wait for help. They helped themselves. Work on new projects was begun almost immediately. They wanted to increase the small number of non-steel companies in the area.

"New factories were built very quickly," says Mr James of the Planning Office, "and new jobs and new industry soon began to arrive. Four industrial estates were developed around the town and some 250 new projects were started by companies which moved to Corby. Now a large number of different products, from computers to cosmetics, from plastic bottles to potato crisps are produced there. I wonder how many other towns have had the same success?"

Not long ago, the town's most difficult scheme was completed. The steelworks itself was pulled down and a big shopping and leisure centre was developed. For industry and local people, it's good to know that Corby still works!

a Make one sentence for each picture. Use the information from the text.

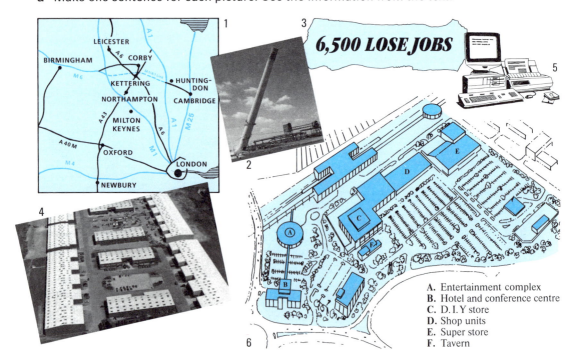

A. Entertainment complex
B. Hotel and conference centre
C. D.I.Y store
D. Shop units
E. Super store
F. Tavern

UNIT 11 T

b Make correct sentences to show what is done/was done at Corby.

1. the steelworks/build
2. steel/produce
3. 6,500 jobs/lose
4. the steelworks/close down
5. work on new projects/begin
6. new factories/build
7. many different goods/produce
8. the steelworks/pull down

Use the words in the box.

> not long ago
> between 1979 and 1981
> there now
> very quickly
> between 1930 and 1979
> in the 1930s
> in 1979
> almost immediately

c Now answer these questions:

1. Why did some people in Corby lose their jobs in the seventies?
2. What did the people of Corby do to plan a new future?
3. Why is Corby a good place to start a new firm?
4. Which new projects replaced which old industry in Corby?
5. What was the town's most difficult scheme?

d Can you find the opposites of these words in the text?

1. open
2. decrease
3. slowly
4. win
5. large

e Can you find the words which have the same meaning as these words?

1. in the middle of
2. difficult
3. at once
4. large
5. a short time ago
6. go on

f Find the corresponding verbs and nouns.

1. development
2. completion
3. building
4. (to) help
5. (to) produce
6. (to) succeed

g Define the following words:

1. steelworks
2. leisure centre
3. industrial estate

2

These young people all found jobs in four of the firms which moved to Corby. You can see pictures of them and the firms below.

a Listen to the cassette. Where does each person work?

Jimmy   Jane   Nancy   Eric

b Listen to the cassette again and answer the following questions:

1. Where do the four people come from?
2. What do they say about their parents?
3. Do they like Corby? Why?/Why not?
4. What do they like about their jobs?
5. What do they dislike about their jobs?

UNIT 11

Robots

1 Most industries nowadays use robots in their manufacturing processes. Many of these robots in factories only have simple mechanical arms with a tool at the end. They are programmed by computers to do the work on the production line. They cut, weld, install, lift, pack and do jobs which are necessary to make all sorts of products from cars to biscuits.

There are other robots which are more flexible. They are equipped with audio, visual and touch sensors so they can do more complex things. They can be programmed to move around the factory and do other complicated jobs.

Answer the following questions:

1. What can you see in the pictures?
2. What is a simple robot?

2 The more modern systems even connect computer aided design (CAD) with computer aided manufacture (CAM). This means that a computer is used to get the best design for a product. This information is then fed into a program which gives instructions to the computer-controlled machines and robots. They then make and store the finished product.

Here is an example of how a washing-machine is designed, produced and stored. The whole system is monitored by computers, which also respond to feedback.

cut steel sheets
design washing-machine
take products to warehouse
feed design into program
store washing-machines
put in motor

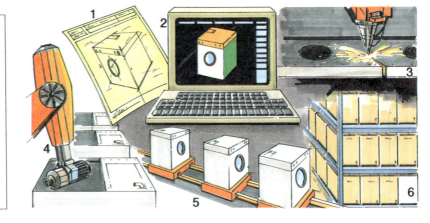

 a Describe the pictures. What is happening there? Use the words in the box.

b "Computers respond to feedback." What does that mean?

UNIT 11   S2

Computer shopping

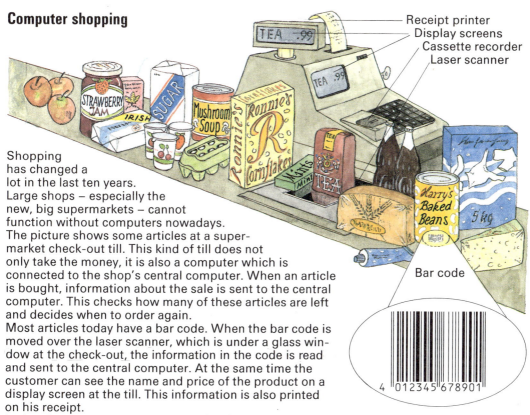

Shopping has changed a lot in the last ten years. Large shops – especially the new, big supermarkets – cannot function without computers nowadays. The picture shows some articles at a supermarket check-out till. This kind of till does not only take the money, it is also a computer which is connected to the shop's central computer. When an article is bought, information about the sale is sent to the central computer. This checks how many of these articles are left and decides when to order again.
Most articles today have a bar code. When the bar code is moved over the laser scanner, which is under a glass window at the check-out, the information in the code is read and sent to the central computer. At the same time the customer can see the name and price of the product on a display screen at the till. This information is also printed on his receipt.
In the picture you can see an example of a bar code. The bar code is on a tin of Harry's baked beans. With the help of the code the central computer can tell: 1. that it is a Harry's product, 2. that it is baked beans and 3. the size of the tin. The price is not included as this can change. Information about the prices of goods is stored in the check-out till's memory.

a Answer the following questions:
  1 How has shopping changed recently?
  2 What do modern supermarket check-out tills do?
  3 What does the laser scanner at the check-out do?
  4 Which two things show the customer the name and price of the product he has bought?
  5 What information cannot be found in the bar code?

b Fill in the missing words. You can find them in the text.

The ① has black and white stripes like a zebra.
The laser scanner is ② the glass window at the till.
The assistant puts your money in the ③.
You buy beans in a ④.
The picture shows an ⑤ of a bar code.
The laser scanner ⑥ the information on the bar code.

c The first letter of each of the missing words in **b** will give you the name of an article which is shown in the picture. What is it?

d True or false? Here are some statements about the article in **c**.
  1 It is made from milk.   4 You eat it with cornflakes.
  2 It is pink in colour.   5 If you leave it in the sun, it melts.
  3 You put it on bread.   6 Some people say it is bad for your health.

e Now make similar sentences about another article which you can see in the picture.

UNIT 11

The Economy

1

1987	US	Ireland	West Germany
Population in millions	250	3.5	61

Goods and services
   produced in billion $
   per head in $
	4,440
	18,050
		29
		8,280
			1,120
			18,360

Inflation in % Unemployed in %	+ 1.9 8	+ 3.2 19	+ 0.2 8
People employed in agriculture in % Land used for agriculture in %	3 46	17 84	5 49

Production of
   cars in 1,000
   steel in million tons
	7,080
	80
		0
		0
			4,000
			36

Cars per 1,000 inhabitants Doctors per 1,000 inhabitants	500 2.5	200 1.3	440 2.5

True or false?

1. In the US there are six times as many inhabitants as in West Germany.
2. The production of goods and services per head is nearly the same in the US and in West Germany.
3. West Germany has the highest inflation rate.
4. In Ireland more than 50 per cent of the land is used in agriculture.
5. There is no steel produced in Ireland.
6. In the US more cars are produced per head than in West Germany.

2 The Irish economy

Ireland is a small country with a small population. It belongs to the EC. Its inflation rate is almost twice as high as that in the United States and unemployment is a big problem. Ireland is an agricultural country. Every sixth job can be found in agriculture. There is no production of cars or steel. The standard of living is rather low. Compared with the United States, less than one third of goods and services are produced per head. Only every fifth Irishman has got a car and there is only about one doctor for 1,000 inhabitants. Because of the economic situation many people have left Ireland.

a Compare the text with the table in **1**.
   Which are the exact figures for the statements in the text?

▶ small population
   Ireland has got
   3.5 million inhabitants.

b Now write a similar report about the US economy.

UNIT 11 G

The passive: Present Simple

Das Passiv wird hauptsächlich in der Schriftsprache und bei offiziellen Gesprächsanlässen gebraucht, vor allem wenn der Träger einer Handlung nicht bekannt oder dem Sprecher nicht wichtig ist.

Statement

> The steel **is checked** in the stores.
> The steel sheets **are transported** to the shop-floor.
> The paint **is not dried** with a hair-drier.
> The fridges **are not exported** to Alaska.

Das Passiv wird gebildet aus: *Present Tense*-Form von *be* + Partizip Perfekt (3. Form).

Question

> **Is** the steel **checked** in the warehouse?
> **Are** the fridges **exported** to Alaska?
> How **is** the paint **dried**?
> Where **are** the fridges **stored**?

In der Frage gilt die Reihenfolge: *Present Tense*-Form von *be* – Subjekt – Partizip Perfekt (3. Form).

The passive: with modal auxiliaries

> Pollution **can be stopped**.
> More hospitals **should be built**.

Nach modalen Hilfsverben steht der Infinitiv von *be* + Partizip Perfekt (3. Form).

The passive: Past Simple

> I **was taken** to the training centre.
> When **was** America **discovered**?

Das Passiv wird gebildet aus: *Past Simple*-Form von *be* + Partizip Perfekt (3. Form).

The passive: with *by*-agent

> In 1987 a new, wholefood menu **was introduced by our new cook**.
> In 1986 the new buildings **were opened by Princess Margaret**.

Der Träger einer Handlung wird mit der Präposition *by* eingeführt.

Reported speech (I) – Einleitendes Verb im Present Tense

Steht das einleitende Verb (z. B. *say, think/ask, want to know*) im *Present Tense,* bleibt die Zeitform des Verbs in der indirekten Rede erhalten.

	Statement	Reported statement	
Patrick:	I **have worked** for Ronsons all **my** life.	Patrick **says** that **he has worked** for Ronsons all **his** life.	*I* wird zu *he/she.* *my* wird zu *his/her.*
Mary:	**I am** against the strike.	Mary **says** (that) **she is** against the strike.	*that* wird häufig weggelassen.
Workers:	**We will lose** our jobs.	The workers **think** that **they will lose their** jobs.	*we* wird zu *they.* *our* wird zu *their.*

	Question	Reported question	
Workers:	**Is** the company **going to give** us new jobs?	The workers **want to know if** the company **is going to give** them new jobs.	Indirekte Entscheidungsfragen werden mit *if* oder *whether* eingeleitet.
Managers:	**Does** the union really **plan** a strike?	The managers **want to know whether** the union really **plans** a strike.	Die Umschreibung mit *do/does* wird in der indirekten Frage durch die Aussageform des Verbs ersetzt.
Workers:	**Why do** the managers **earn** so much?	The workers **want to know why** the managers **earn** so much.	Indirekte *wh*-Fragen werden mit demselben Fragewort eingeleitet.

UNIT 12

Life and work in the United States

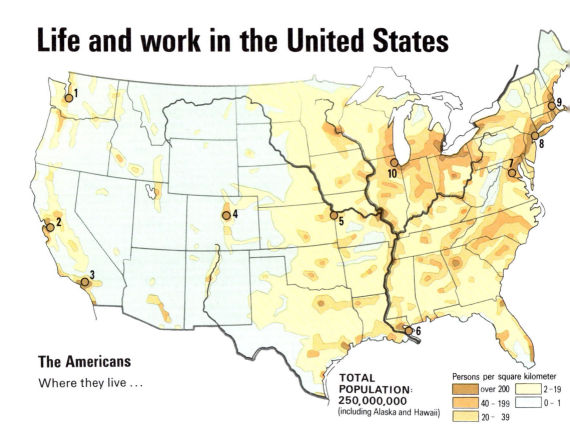

The Americans
Where they live ...

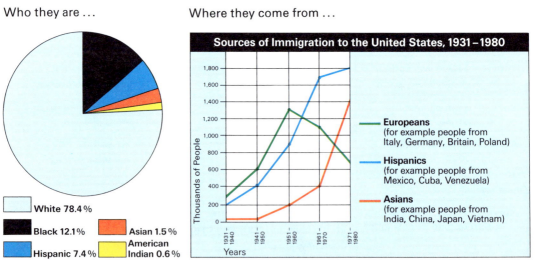

Who they are ...

Where they come from ...

Look at the map and the graphs. Answer the following questions:
1. What is the total population of the US?
2. Name five big cities and a few states. Say where they are.
3. Where do a lot of people/only few people live?
4. What is the smallest/the second largest population group in the US?
5. Where did most of the people who live in the US come from?

UNIT 12 A

1 A group of young people from Cork, Ireland, are on a tour of the United States. At the moment they are in New York at the Irish Club (NYIC). John J. Johnson, the director of the Club, has invited the group to report on their impressions of America.

Here are some of their comments:

Director: ... our Irish friends will now tell us about their impressions of America ... Yes, Carole ...
Carole: Hmm ... in my opinion there are too many murders and robberies in American cities. I'm not surprised, really. Anybody can walk in a shop and can buy a gun. Some people have five guns ...
Director: Yes, that's a big problem. Perhaps that will change in the future. People are protesting against the free sale of guns – that's why we have a strong anti-gun movement in the States. Yes, Judy?
Judy: I like America and I love the Americans. People are so friendly and helpful. I'll never forget their kindness. And the people in the US don't only talk about helping others. I know a lot of Americans who do voluntary work. That's what I call charity.
Director: Well, it's nice to hear something positive. What's your impression, Steve?
Steve: Outside the big cities, land is fantastically cheap here in the US. That's great. Nearly everybody can afford to buy their own home.
Director: They can if they have enough money. Nearly 10 million Americans are out of work. A lot of them don't get any money. All over this town, you can see hungry people who are searching through the garbage cans outside restaurants.
Sometimes there is not enough social security. Most workers don't get more than two weeks paid vacation and some don't have health insurance. Yes, Heather?
Heather: ... but America has a lot of good things, too. The Americans often think up good things such as windsurfing and jogging, pizza and T-shirts ... No, it's true. And I think the speed-limit on the motorways is a good thing. It's certainly helping to protect the environment ...

a Which speakers make positive statements and which make negative statements about America?

b Here are some other statements by the speakers. Who do you think said what?

1 Sports are very interesting for me.
2 The crime rate is much too high.
3 The friendliness of the Americans is fantastic.
4 It is a good thing to own a house.
5 Some employees in America have a bad time.
6 The unemployment rate is very worrying.
7 Americans believe more in action than in words.
8 Driving more slowly is good for the world around us.

2 A week later there was a report about the visit in the NYIC newsletter.

NEW YORK IRISH CLUB NEWSLETTER NO. 4

GROUP FROM IRELAND AT CLUB

Last Wednesday a party of young people from Cork, Ireland, visited our Club. John J. Johnson, the NYIC director, welcomed the party and asked the guests to talk about their impressions of America.

The first speaker, Carole King, said that in her opinion there were too many murders and robberies in American cities. She added that she was not surprised – anybody could walk into a store and could buy a gun. She said that some people had 5 guns. The director agreed with her. Perhaps, he said, that would change in the future because they had

A UNIT 12

a Who said it?
Look at the comments in **1** again and complete the sentences on the right.

▶ I love the Americans.   ① said that she loved the Americans.
   Judy said that she loved the Americans.

What they said:

What the newsletter reported:

There are too many crimes.	② said that she liked America.
I'm not surprised.	③ said that that would change in the future.
Some people have five guns.	④ added that the people in the US didn't only
That will change in the future.	talk about helping others.
I like America.	⑤ added that she wasn't surprised.
The people in the US don't only	⑥ said some people had five guns.
talk about helping others.	⑦ said there were too many crimes.

b Look at **1b** again and ▶ One of the people said (that) …
report what the people said.   Another said (that) …

3

Welcome to the Irish Club!

Dear Friends,

we hope you had a pleasant Christmas holiday and wish you all the best for the New Year.
Here are some statistics for this year. We now have over 17,000 members at the Club. With the new building we have a total floor space of about 8,000 square feet. For the summer we are planning to build two new tennis courts. These are, of course, very expensive. We will get money from the city of New York but we also need your help. Please give as much as you can.
This year we will offer new courses in Aerobics and Computer Studies.

Looking forward to seeing you at the Club soon,
sincerely,

M. O'Donnell   *John J. Johnson*

Marie O'Donnell   **John J. Johnson**
President   Director

P.S.
Don't forget the St. Patrick's Day Parade on 17 March!

Fees

Youth (under 18 yrs) – $130
Adult (18–59 yrs) – $300
Senior (60 yrs and older) – $120

How to get to the Club

BY BUS
Bus stops outside the Club building:
Lines 6, 12 & 14
BY CAR
Follow the signs from the city center.
Limited parking available in the car park next to the Club building (fee: $1.20/hr).

Where to find what at the Club

Pre-School programs 3
Language Classes 3
Seniors 4
Irish film series 5
Health & fitness 5
Squash & tennis 6
Dancing classes 6
Swimming-pool 7
Trips for adults 7
Trips for kids 7
Camp holidays (ages 8–17) 8

UNIT 12 A

During their visit to the NYIC, the young people from Cork talked to John J. Johnson a second time. Here are some of the questions which they asked him:

Steve: How much is the membership fee for children?
Who is the President of the Club?
What are you planning for the summer?
Judy: How can people get to the Club?
Where can people park at the Club?
Carole: What new courses will you offer this year?
Where will you get the money for the tennis courts from?
Heather: How many members does the Club have?
How much do adult members pay?
How many bus lines stop in front of the Club?
How much does the car park cost?

a Look at the NYIC leaflet. Can you find John's answers?

b Now report the various people's questions.

▶ Steve: How much is the membership fee for children?
Steve asked how much the membership fee for children was.
Go on.

c Here are some more questions which the group from Cork asked. Look at the NYIC leaflet again. Can you find John's answers?

Judy: Are there trips for grown-ups?
Are there holidays for kids?
Heather: Can small children be members of the Club?
Can members play squash at the Club?
Can you learn to dance at the Club?
Carole: Do you show films?
Does a bus stop in front of the Club?
Does the Club have courses for very young children?

d Now report the questions from **c**.

▶ Judy: Is there a swimming-pool at the Center?
Judy asked whether there was a swimming-pool at the Center.
▶ Carole: Do you offer language classes?
Carole wanted to know if they offered language classes.
Go on.

UNIT 12

1 Poverty in the US

	Who are the poor?
Total work-force in the US: 120,000,000 **Unemployed:** About one out of every 12 Americans **Poor:** About one out of every 9 Americans **Poverty level:** A family of four who has an income of less than $8,400 a year	1 out of every 11 Whites 1 out of every 3 Blacks 1 out of every 5 Hispanics 1 out of every 7 people, 65 or older

Look at the figures above and answer the following questions:

1. How is the poverty level in the US defined? How much would that be in your money?
2. In which group do we find the most poor people?
3. How many people are unemployed?

2 Social security in the US

Unemployment benefits are only given for up to a year. Pensions depend on how much money people paid into a pension scheme while they were still working. People who cannot work – handicapped people or mothers who have to look after their children – can get welfare benefits, mostly in the form of food stamps.

Meet some people from Cleveland, Ohio.

Jaime Gonzales, 46 years old

Chuck Brown, 22 years old

Mickey Gladowski, 47 years old

Brenda and Randolph Forster, both 67 years old

a Look at the photos and listen to the cassette. Who is the first/second/third/fourth speaker?

b Look at the figures in **1** again. Which speaker belongs to which group of poor people?

c Listen to the cassette again and put the following sentences right:
1. Chuck cannot get into the labour market because he has got the wrong skill.
2. Brenda and Randolph have not got a retirement pension.
3. People who did not pay into a pension scheme only get a low pension.
4. Mickey has never worked and so he has never had any unemployment benefits.
5. Jaime has had an American passport for three years.
6. Jaime depends on food stamps.

d Listen to the cassette again and report what the speakers say about unemployment benefits and pensions.

▶ Chuck says (that) he can't get into the labour market.
▶ Brenda says (that) their retirement pension is very low.

UNIT 12 B

3 In Cleveland, Ohio, the Food Forum is trying to help those who find it very hard to buy themselves one warm meal a day. Bob Rogers, a social worker, is giving instructions to new helpers.

... we don't have much time now so I'll have to be brief. Joe, go down the line and sell the tickets. It's just one dollar. Don't let the dog in, though. Florence, collect the tickets and hand out the soup. Give everybody one ladleful. Err, just a second. I think we'll ... err ... Yeah. Don't take those bowls there, take the paper cups. What next? Yeah, I'll take the big plates and put the hamburgers into this big section here. Then I'll pass the plates to you, Gretchen. Put a big spoonful of French fries in the section next to the hamburgers and then a small spoonful of peas in the little section. Err ... that's it, I guess ... err ... no, it isn't. Mike ... the gravy. Be careful with that. Don't pour it all over. Just pour it on the hamburgers. And as a general rule to all of you: Be nice to everybody, don't shout. Give everybody a friendly smile, but don't smile all the time. OK. Let's start then ...

a Listen to the cassette and look at the photos of the helpers. Number them in the order in which Bob mentions them.

Gretchen   Joe   Mike   Florence

b Report what Bob told his helpers to do.

▶ Joe, open the door.
   He told him to open the door.
▶ To all of you. Don't serve anybody without a ticket.
   He told them not to serve anybody without a ticket.
   Go on.

c The first day was difficult for the new helpers. They tried to help each other, though. Take over their roles and report to Bob Rogers.

▶ Gretchen to Mike:
   Please be careful with the gravy.
   Mike:
   Gretchen asked me to be careful with the gravy.
▶ Mike and Joe to Gretchen and Florence:
   Please help us clean the dishes.
   Gretchen and Florence:
   Mike and Joe asked us to help them clean the dishes.

Florence to Joe:	Please give me more time to collect the tickets. Help me with the soup for a while, please.
Mike to Gretchen:	Don't put the French fries in the little section on the plate. Please pass that plate to me.
Florence and Gretchen to Mike and Joe:	Give us some time to breathe, please. Don't eat all the French fries yourselves. Come over and have a cigarette with us.

UNIT 12

1 The Ice-Cream Kings

Bennett Cohen and Jerry Greenfield, whose HOMEMADE INC. sold more than $40 million of ice-cream last year, can be looked upon as an example of those who have 'made it'. The two friends from Long Island, both now 37, are – almost to their own surprise – really successful.

Their success story started less than 10 years ago. Ben, whose college career ended after two semesters, had worked as a cleaner, a taxi-driver and a baker's assistant before he decided to take a one-day course in ice-cream making. And he has been making ice-cream ever since. Jerry, who had wanted to get into medical school but had never made it, first worked as a technician. Then, he decided to try his luck with ice-cream, too.

But what is the secret of their success? "We make an excellent product," says Ben, "and are full of bright ideas. The latest is the 'Mother's Day promotion' – any mother gets a free ice-cream and an expectant mother gets two. Or in winter our POPDUZ, which stands for Penny Off Per Degree Under Zero!"

In addition, Ben and Jerry look at business in a completely new way. As Jerry explains, "We believe that a successful business must support the community".

It was because of this that they started a foundation three years ago. The Ben and Jerry

Foundation, whose income is 7.5% of the company's earnings, gives a lot of money every year to community groups and social organizations throughout the North-east. As Ben says, "Our aim is to help people".

Could this be the secret of Ben and Jerry's success?

a True or false?

1 Homemade Inc have sold more than 40 million dollars of ice-cream for the last five years.
2 Ben went to college for two semesters to learn how to make ice-cream.
3 Jerry, who is from Long Island, is three years older than Ben.
4 Ben wanted to go to college to train to be a doctor.
5 On Mother's Day, all women get a free ice-cream at one of the Homemade Inc shops.
6 One of Ben and Jerry's ideas is to sell ice-cream more cheaply when it is cold outside.
7 Jerry thinks that the community must support a successful business.
8 The Ben and Jerry Foundation helps communities in the Northeast.

b Join these sentences with 'who' or 'which'.

▶ Ben and Jerry's company has become very successful. They started it in the late seventies.
Ben and Jerry's company, which they started in the late seventies, has become very successful.

▶ Ben started selling ice-cream from an old van. He did not expect to become a millionaire.
Ben, who did not expect to become a millionaire, started selling ice-cream from an old van.

1 The company sells ice-cream in 35 states. It employs more than 200 people.
2 Ben and Jerry have never finished college. They are both 37 years old.
3 Jerry worked for many years as a technician. He wanted to be a doctor.
4 The Ben and Jerry Foundation gives a lot of support to the community. Ben and Jerry started it in 1986.
5 Ben and Jerry sell more than 40 million dollars of ice-cream. They now have more than 60 shops.
6 One of their ideas is called 'Mother's Day promotion'. It is very popular with families.

UNIT 12 c

c Join these sentences with 'whose'.

▶ Ben worked as a cleaner. His career at college ended after two semesters.
Ben, whose career at college ended after two semesters, worked as a cleaner.

1. Ben and Jerry are very popular. Their ideas about business are different from most other people's.
2. These young businessmen now own 63 shops. Their first shop opened in Burlington, Vermont, seven years ago.
3. The Ben and Jerry Foundation got over $560,000 last year. Its income is 7.5% of Homemade Inc's earnings.
4. The foundation gives a lot of money to community groups every year. Its aim is to help people.
5. Ben and Jerry receive hundreds of letters of thanks every week. Their story has become famous throughout America.
6. Jerry worked as a technician. His dream was to become a doctor.

d Complete this newspaper article. Use 'who', 'whose' or 'which'.

STRAW SUPPORTS FIGHT AGAINST ILLITERACY By Caren Kavon

The unemployment rate for June, ① is now as low as it was in May 1974, shows that 12% of the unemployed are white teenagers. However, 28.4% are black teenagers.

The Manager of the Labor Department, Sam Straw, ② gave a press conference in Vermont yesterday, said, "Many of the young people without jobs cannot read or write. Thousands of jobs, ③ of course we offer to both Blacks and Whites, are for people with a skill. But a large number of unemployed people, ④ families are very poor, just do not have a skill. Thousands of students, ⑤ need our help, try to find work during the holidays. A few companies, ⑥ names you will find on the list below, are willing to give jobs to black students. One company, HOMEMADE INC., ⑦ is well-known in Vermont, has given jobs to over 100 black unemployed in the last five years".

2 How long?

Join these sentences with 'since' and 'for'.
Use the Present Perfect Continuous.

▶ Ben and Jerry: We make ice-cream. We started in 1979.
Ben and Jerry have been making ice-cream since 1979.

▶ Colin White: I sell newspapers and cigarettes. I opened my business 10 years ago.
Colin White has been selling newspapers and cigarettes for 10 years.

Greg and Tom: We make ladders. We started in 1976.
John Davies: I manufacture toothbrushes. I started my business in 1962.
Greg Brown: I sell foreign cars. I opened my first showroom 12 years ago.
Carol and Joan: We produce computer software. We started back in 1983.
Henry Moore: I now make films. I began 6 months ago.
The Bellugis: We build houses and factories all over the US. Our grandfather built the first factory about 90 years ago.

UNIT 12

1 If a person over 55 loses his or her job, it is very often impossible for them to get another one. And some people over 65 want to go on working because they do not have enough money. Other over-65s have enough money but want to go on working because they enjoy it. However, a lot of companies think it is not good to employ older people. They say that they are not a charity but a firm whose aim it is to increase productivity. That is why the US Department of Health and Human Services published this leaflet. It presented four myths about older workers and showed how older workers could make a positive contribution to a firm. They defined 'older workers' as persons 55 years or older whose health enabled them to work.

U.S. DEPARTMENT OF HEALTH AND HUMAN SERVICES
Office of Human Development Services
Administration on Aging

hds
human development services

OLDER WORKERS: MYTHS AND REALITY

Myth No. 1: Older workers are less productive.

Statistics show that productivity does not decrease with a worker's age. Older employees work as well as younger employees in most jobs.

Myth No. 2: Older workers are ill more often.

Data show that workers age 55 and over are not sick more often or longer than other age groups of workers.

Myth No. 3: Older workers have a high rate of accidents at work.

The opposite is true. Data show that older workers have only 9.7% of all accidents although they make up 13.6% of the work-force.

Myth No. 4: Older people have enough retirement income.

For many people this statement is simply not true. Although the income of older persons has been improving in the last three years, one out of seven older persons still lives in poverty.

Think it over – give older people a chance.

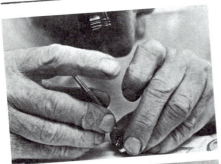

a Can you find the corresponding nouns in the text and the leaflet?

1 real
2 produce
3 retire
4 poor
5 employ
6 work

b Can you find the opposites of the following words in the text and the leaflet?

1 healthy
2 get worse
3 low
4 go up
5 negative
6 wrong

c Define the words on the left. Make sentences.

A myth		a fact or the truth about something.
Reality		numbers which represent facts.
Retirement income	is	an organization which helps poor people.
A work-force	are	a story which is not based on facts.
A charity		the money older people get as a pension.
Statistics		all the people who work in a factory.

d Answer the following questions:
1 Why do some people over the age of 65 want to go on working?
2 Why did the US Department of Health and Human Services publish the leaflet?
3 How did they define 'older workers'?
4 Do all old people in the US get enough retirement income?

e An American friend of yours has the following opinions about older workers:

1 They're too slow.
2 They have a lot of money.
3 They cause a lot of accidents.
4 They're always ill.

Tell him/her what the leaflet said.
Start your answers like this:

▶ I'm not so sure. Somebody gave me a leaflet last week and there it said ...

2 The right to work

This is the story of a 66-year-old office worker from Los Angeles. When he reached the age of 65, everybody thought he would retire. But Harry didn't want to retire – he wanted to go on working. His firm said he should retire to make way for younger workers. When Harry still refused, they simply fired him. Harry did not agree and so he took them to court.

In the court case you can hear the office worker, his ex-employer and the judge speaking.

 a Listen to the cassette. Who is Mr Smith and who is Mr Hall?

 b Listen to the cassette again. Who used these arguments?

1 I want to keep my job.
2 After a lifetime of work people deserve a rest.
3 This is a very difficult case to decide.
4 Top managers carry on working long after 65.
5 Don't forget young people who're looking for a job.
6 Everyone in this country has a right to work.
7 There just won't be enough jobs free if everybody works until they're 70.

c Now report what Mr Smith, Mr Hall and the judge said in **b**.

d How would you decide the case? Say why.

UNIT 12

Kennedy Space Center

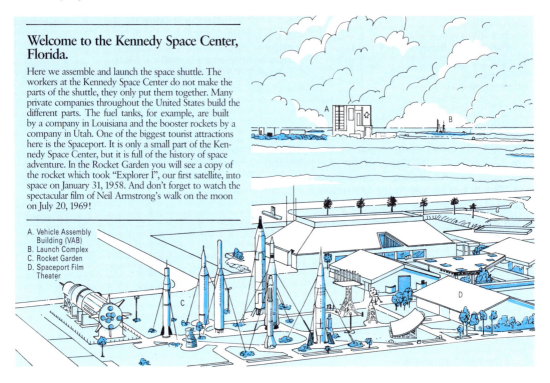

Welcome to the Kennedy Space Center, Florida.

Here we assemble and launch the space shuttle. The workers at the Kennedy Space Center do not make the parts of the shuttle, they only put them together. Many private companies throughout the United States build the different parts. The fuel tanks, for example, are built by a company in Louisiana and the booster rockets by a company in Utah. One of the biggest tourist attractions here is the Spaceport. It is only a small part of the Kennedy Space Center, but it is full of the history of space adventure. In the Rocket Garden you will see a copy of the rocket which took "Explorer I", our first satellite, into space on January 31, 1958. And don't forget to watch the spectacular film of Neil Armstrong's walk on the moon on July 20, 1969!

A. Vehicle Assembly Building (VAB)
B. Launch Complex
C. Rocket Garden
D. Spaceport Film Theater

a Look at the picture above and answer the following questions:

1. Where exactly at the Space Center is the space shuttle put together?
2. Where is the shuttle launched?
3. What is the Rocket Garden?
4. What film is shown at the Spaceport? Where?

b Which description goes with which picture? One description is left. Which one?

flight deck   space shuttle at liftoff   special heat tiles   Rocket Garden

1. It has one external tank and two solid rocket boosters and weighs nearly 2,000,000 kilograms at liftoff and has a maximum crew of 7.
2. This is part of the space shuttle's crew compartment. Two astronauts, the pilot and the commander, sit in front at the flight controls.
3. This is part of the Spaceport. Authentic rockets from different periods of America's space program can be studied here.
4. The various parts of the shuttle are tested and put together here. The shuttle is 37 metres long and 17 metres high. Its wings can be 24 metres across.
5. These are small, about 20 cm x 20 cm, but very important. They can become red-hot on the one side, but the other side stays cool. They are put on the nose and the wings to give the space shuttle a heat shield against temperatures of up to 1,650 degrees Celsius.

UNIT 12 S2

Working for a better future

1 The 'Save the Children' campaign was started in 1988 to draw special attention to the problems of young Americans. The basic problem is poverty – people have little or no money. This and a general lack of motivation can lead to difficulties at school and often result in illiteracy – the fact that a lot of young people are very bad at reading and writing. And people who do not have these skills are faced by the next problem – unemployment. Unemployed youths who hang about the streets with no money and no prospects are then confronted by the biggest problem of all – drugs.

Let us take a look at a model school in a Black community in Austin, Texas, that is fighting these problems.

At Alice Owens Kindergarten and Elementary School, teachers and children work against the myth that low income, inner-city Black youth cannot learn.

By "normal standards" the children at Owens would not have the chance to reach the top. Owens' pupils are 98% Black and many are from poor, single-parent homes. However, Owens' pupils are above average in mathematics and reading tests.

Kindergarten teacher Ms Tina Adams explains why the school is so successful. Last year, for example, Ms Adams introduced a reading and writing competition for the 295 children. Every pupil who takes part gets a prize.

Owens also invites volunteers – successful local Black people – to come and read fairy tales for an hour or two each week. These volunteers also act as a role-model for the children.

Another part of the plan is the sports program – children can learn different sports in free after-school courses. "If we can get the kids off the streets and into the sports clubs, the danger they will start taking drugs is lower", says Ms Adams.

Answer the following questions:

1. When was the 'Save the Children' campaign started? Why?
2. Where is Alice Owens School?
3. What are Alice Owens children better at than most young Americans?
4. What reasons does the teacher give for the school's success?
5. What happens very often to poor young Blacks in big cities?

2 The story of seventeen-year-old Bernard M. Ballman

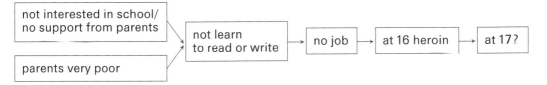

a Retell the story of Bernard M. Ballman.
What do you think happened to him at the age of 17?

b Each of the six parts in the flow chart has the same meaning as one of the words in the box. Can you find them?

| unemployment | no prospects | poverty |
| lack of motivation | drugs | illiteracy |

c For which of Bernard's problems has Wheatley found a solution?
What solutions would you suggest? Discuss.

UNIT 12

Past and future development of the American population

1 In 1950 the total American population was about 155 million. By 1990 it had risen to around 250 million. It will increase to 305 million by 2030 and to 310 million by 2050. The number of people aged 65 and older went up from 14 million in 1950 to 40 million in 1990. Their number will go up even more, namely to 74 million by 2030 and to 83 million by 2050. The development of the number of people younger than 65 looks a bit different, though. It went up by nearly 70 million between 1950 and 1990, namely from 141 million to 209 million. From then on the increase will slow down. For the year 2030 we predict 231 million. After that their number will decrease. It will fall to 227 million by 2050.

A chart or a bar graph can give you the same information much more quickly. A line graph can be a better solution if you want to show the ups and downs of the population development.

a Complete the missing figures in the chart with the help of the text above.

Year	Total population	Age 65 and older	Younger than 65
1950	155	14	141
1990	250	②	209
2030	①	74	231
2050	310	83	③

(in Millions)

b Compare the two graphs. What do the three lines in the line graph stand for?

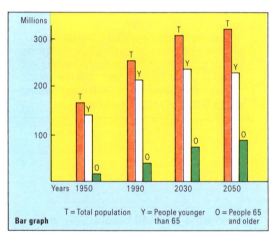

T = Total population Y = People younger than 65 O = People 65 and older
Bar graph

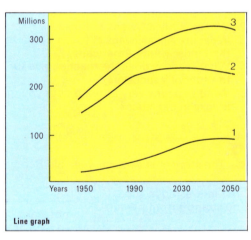

Line graph

2 Development of the work-force in the US (1952–1982)

a Talk about the chart in full sentences.

b Show the development of the work-force in a bar graph and in a line graph.

Year	Total	Blue Collar	White Collar	Service	Farm
1952	60	25	22	6	7
1982	110	34	59	14	3

(in Millions)

UNIT 12 G

Reported speech (II) – Einleitendes Verb im Past Tense

Steht das einleitende Verb (z. B. *say, think/ask, want to know*) im *Past Tense*, erfolgt beim Verb in der indirekten Rede eine Rückverschiebung zur *Past Tense*-Form.

Statement	Reported statement	
Harry: I **am** not surprised.	Harry **said** that he **was** not surprised.	*Present Tense*-Formen werden zu *Past Tense*-Formen.
John: People **are protesting** against guns.	John **said** that people **were protesting** against guns.	
Judy: The Americans **don't** only **think** about helping others.	Judy **said** the Americans **didn't** only **think** about helping others.	*that* wird häufig weggelassen.
John: Things **will** change.	John **said** things **would** change.	*will* wird zu *would*.
Carole: Anybody **can** buy a gun.	She **said** anybody **could** buy a gun.	*can* wird zu *could*.

Question	Reported question	
Judy: **Is** there a swimming-pool?	Judy **asked if** there **was** a swimming-pool.	Indirekte Entscheidungsfragen werden mit *if* oder *whether* eingeleitet.
Carole: **Do** you **show** films?	Carole **asked whether** they **showed** films.	Die Umschreibung mit *do/does* wird in der indirekten Frage durch die *Past Tense*-Form des Verbs ersetzt.
Heather: **What does** NYIC **stand** for?	Heather **asked what** NYIC **stood** for.	

Imperative	Reported imperative	
Bob: Joe, **open** the door.	Bob **told** him **to open** the door.	Indirekte Aufforderung: *(to) tell* + Person + Infinitiv mit *to/not to*
Bob: **Don't take** the bowls, Florence.	Bob **told** her **not to take** the bowls.	
Bob: **Come** again, please.	Bob **asked** us **to come** again.	Indirekte Bitte: *(to) ask* + Person + Infinitiv mit *to/not to*
Mike: **Don't look** so serious, please.	Mike **asked** me **not to look** so serious.	

Relative clauses – relative pronouns

Ben, **whose first shop was opened in 1986**, now owns over 60 shops.	*whose* bezieht sich auf Personen oder Sachen.
The company, **whose aim is to help the poor**, sells more than $40 million of ice-cream.	*whose* = „dessen, deren"

Present Perfect Continuous

I **have been making** films **for two years**. She **has been selling** cars **since 1988**. How long **have** they **been building** houses?	Das *Present Perfect Continuous* wird mit *for/since/how long* verwendet, um eine Handlung zu beschreiben, die in der Vergangenheit begonnen hat und in der Gegenwart immer noch andauert.

UNIT 13

ENERGY

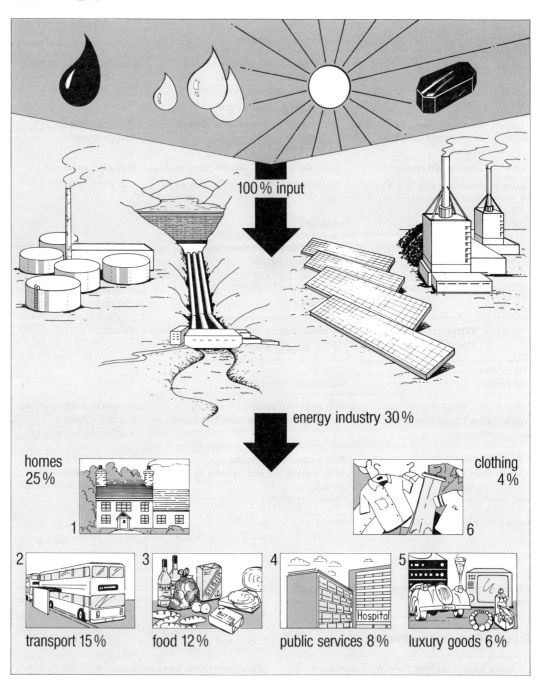

What sources of energy can you find above?

30% of all energy produced from these sources is used simply for the production of the energy itself. What is the other 70% used for?

How is energy used? Look at pictures 1–6 and talk about production, heating, lighting etc.

UNIT 13 A

1 Oil in Alaska

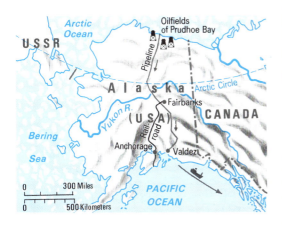

In 1867 Alaska was sold to the United States by Russia for 7.2 million dollars. Because of the cold climate Alaska remained a relatively unproductive area for over 100 years with a total population of 60,000 in 1900.
The people there lived mainly from fishing, lumbering and mining. Now over 540,000 people live in Alaska.

Since the discovery of oil in 1968, Alaska's economy has been transformed.
The oil reserves there are not only the largest in the US but also about a quarter of all the oil reserves in the US.
Oil companies started to invest a lot of money, and between 1974 and 1977 the Trans-Alaska Pipeline was built. Since then oil has been transported from the oilfields in the North (Prudhoe Bay) to the port of Valdez in the South. Technologically this pipeline project has been compared with the first moon landing. Since the start of oil production, 200,000 newcomers have been attracted to Alaska. Most of them are men who have come from other parts of America. They have been attracted by the high wages which the oil companies offer in Alaska. Nearly all the newcomers live and work in either Anchorage or Fairbanks.

Prudhoe Bay

Port of Valdez

a True or false?

1 They discovered oil in Alaska in 1968.
2 The pipeline runs from Valdez in the North to Prudhoe Bay in the South.
3 The oil reserves in Alaska are the biggest in the United States.
4 People compare the pipeline project with a famous space project.
5 200,000 newcomers have moved to Anchorage.
6 Most of the newcomers work in the fishing industry.

b Make sentences.

▶ economic face of Alaska – transform
The economic face of Alaska has been transformed.

1 a lot of money – invest
2 oil – find in the North
3 a long pipeline – build
4 new jobs – create
5 a lot of people – attract to Alaska
6 oil – transport to Valdez in the South
7 a railway – build between Anchorage and Fairbanks
8 most of the newcomers – offer jobs by the oil companies

one hundred and seventy-nine **179**

A UNIT 13

2 Workers in Alaska

Fairbanks is America's most northern city, only 100 miles from the Arctic Circle. It is a place of extremes. It is the land of the midnight sun and of long dark winters. The temperatures can be extreme, too (−55°C to +50°C). Working in these conditions is difficult and often dangerous. That is why the oilmen earn good pay.

Neil Scot, an oilman in Alaska, is writing a letter home.

> Fairbanks
> January 23
>
> Dear Marge,
>   Just a few lines to let you know I'm OK. The weather has been terrible for the last few weeks. It's −30°F today. But I'm lucky, I'm only on stand-by today. The rest of the crew have been called out on an emergency. There's a leak in the pipeline north of here. They haven't repaired all the damage yet. And do you remember Gary? Well, he had a bad accident this morning. He took off his gloves while he was working outside and burnt his hands on a piece of ice-cold metal. They've taken him to the hospital in Anchorage by helicopter. I hope he'll get better soon.
>   By the way, there have been some changes here: They've built a new leisure center in Fairbanks. The oil company has also modernized our accommodation here a bit. They've made our bedrooms bigger and they've also renovated the rest rooms

a Answer these questions. Make active sentences.

1 Why has Neil not been called out?
2 Why has the rest of the crew been called out?
3 Has the damage been repaired?
4 Why has Gary been taken to hospital?

b Answer these questions. Make passive sentences.

1 Where have they taken Gary?
2 What have they built in Fairbanks?
3 What have they made bigger?
4 What have they also renovated?

c Now listen to what two other oilmen, Mike Rollerson and Ron Meyer, say about their jobs. Answer the following questions:

1 What is Mike's job?
2 Where does he work?
3 How long has the pipeline been monitored from Valdez?
4 How much does he earn?
5 What doesn't he like in Alaska?
6 What is Ron's job?
7 How long has he been employed in Alaska?
8 How many times has he been called out recently?
9 How much does he earn?
10 What is one of the dangers of working in Alaska?

UNIT 13 A

3 Oil and the Eskimos

Since the beginning of the oil boom in Alaska, the life of the Eskimos there has changed greatly.
This is what an Alaskan Eskimo says about their situation:
We used to be a proud nation. Before the oil companies came, our main activities were hunting and fishing. In this area we lived in wooden huts. Only Eskimos in the North lived in igloos. Our traditional clothing was furs, parkas and anoraks which we made ourselves. We ate food which we hunted or fished for ourselves. We were completely self-sufficient.
Now everything's changing. A lot of our men have stopped hunting and fishing and have moved to the cities because they want to work for the oil companies. But I'm not so sure that we'll be given jobs by the oil companies. They usually prefer to employ oilmen from other parts of the States. In my opinion, we'll become outsiders in our own

country, just like the Indians all over America. Many Eskimos don't agree with me but I'm sure that our culture will soon be destroyed completely. If this development goes on, more and more foreign things will be introduced into our lives. More and more apartment houses will be built. Our clothes will be imported from abroad. Soon hamburgers and other types of fast food will be sold here. More and more bars will be opened in the towns, so alcohol will become a big problem. Even our native language won't be spoken in the future. We'll soon feel like strangers in our own country.

a Look at the text and answer these questions with the help of the words in the box.

1 What was Eskimo life like in the past?
2 What will it be like in the future?

kind of work		homes
clothes	food	language

b What predictions can be made about Eskimo life in the near future? Make sentences like this. You can use the verbs in the box.

▶ their culture – destroy
   Their culture will be destroyed.

1 apartment houses
2 traditional food
3 foreign-made clothes
4 bars
5 more alcohol
6 their language
7 new jobs in the oilfields

open	sell	build
wear	not eat	
offer	not speak	

c The oil companies look at this problem in a different way. They believe that this development will bring a lot of advantages to Alaska. What promises do the oil companies make there? Make sentences like this. You can use the expressions in the box.

▶ build – better houses
   We will help to build better houses.

1 improve   5 raise
2 attract   6 make
3 install   7 increase
4 provide

more TV stations   living conditions
   the standard of living
leisure time   more telephones
   more doctors to Alaska
   life in Alaska much easier

d Now look at c again and make passive sentences.   ▶ Better houses will be built.

UNIT 13

1 CANADIAN TV NEWS

Channel 2

9.30 Using the Tide

Second part in our series on alternative energy in Canada. This week the program is presented by David Jones and looks at a tidal energy project in the Bay of Fundy. In projects like these, turbines in the dam can turn one way as the tide comes in and the other way as it goes out in order to generate as much electricity as possible from the tide. 'Annapolis Royal', one small test project, is already functioning and there are plans to build a much larger dam across the bay near Truro. This dam would be eight kilometers long. With its 100 turbines it will cost between 22 and 25 billion dollars to build.

Answer the following questions:

1. What part of a coastline is a good place to start a large tidal energy project?
2. What will be built across the Bay of Fundy near Truro in order to help produce electricity?
3. What comes in and goes out and can be used to help to produce electricity?
4. What must be built into a dam in order to generate electricity?

2

Here is part of an interview. David Jones is talking to various people about the tidal energy project in the Bay of Fundy.

D. Jones: Welcome to tonight's program on alternative energy. With us in the studio we have Jane Grey, Energy Minister, Dan James, Mayor of Truro, and John Smith, a local resident. Now, I'd like each of you to give your opinions on the Truro project. Minister, can we begin with you? Why tidal energy in the Bay of Fundy?

J. Grey: When we look for alternative sources of energy, it's important for each country to make the best use of the resources it has. Here in the Bay of Fundy we're lucky because it's one of only about fifty sites in the world where tidal energy can be produced. You see, there has to be a tidal range of at least 5 meters in order to produce tidal energy. Parts of the Bay of Fundy have a range of up to 17 meters so that we should make the most of our special position. Solar energy, on the other hand, is not such a good idea here because there simply isn't enough sun.

D. Jones: Mr Smith, I believe you think that there may be some disadvantages to the project.

J. Smith: Yes ... Although I'm very happy that the government is now looking at alternative sources of energy, I'm worried about the effects the

UNIT 13 B

D. Jones: project will have on the wildlife in the bay. Large areas of land will be permanently flooded so that for example a lot of birds will lose their feeding grounds.

D. Jones: You are a local resident, too, Mr James. Do you share Mr Smith's worries?

D. James: No, not completely. I'm sure the project can only improve life in the area although as a bird lover I understand his point of view. You see, a dam like this takes a long time to build and employs a lot of people so that the job situation will certainly improve. All in all, if I didn't think there were more positive than negative sides to this project, I certainly wouldn't support it.

a Look at the text. Whose opinions are these?

1 We must protect the wildlife in the bay.
2 Tidal energy is a better idea for this part of Canada than solar energy.
3 The project will bring more work to the area.
4 We should build the dam here because the bay is an ideal place for it.
5 There are more advantages than disadvantages to the project.

b Make correct sentences.

1 Building a dam creates a lot of work		there will be less unemployment in the area.
2 Solar energy is not the best form of alternative energy for this area		this part of Canada doesn't have enough sun.
3 The difference between high and low tide has to be at least 5 metres	because although in order to so that	generate electricity.
4 Large areas of land will be flooded		birds won't find enough food.
5 Most people support the project		some of the wildlife will suffer.
6 Tidal energy is a good source of energy for this area		there is a big tidal range.

c Here are five people who live in the area where the dam will be built. They are talking about the project.
Make sentences as in **b**. Use 'because', 'although', 'so that' or 'in order to'.

1 create new jobs – have less unemployment — Mrs Smith, new supermarket manageress
2 more people come – house prices rise — Mr Owen, homeowner
3 fishing industry earn less – catch fewer fish — Mr Black, fisherman
4 dam look ugly – tourists come — Ms Brown, hotel-owner
5 build new houses – give workers new homes — Mr Thumb, builder

UNIT 13

1 Save your energy. Fill in the coupon.

The way you heat your home can be a massive waste of energy ... and money. But it needn't be. We've got the solution. Your Energy Council will look at your house and heating system and talk about ways you can save energy. Together we'll find out how much you can save. And the advice is free.
When we call on you, we'll look at your home first and check your roof, windows and walls. Your chimneys and outside doors will also be checked for drafts. You can ask us about ways you can improve the insulation of your house at low costs.
Old heating systems use up a lot of energy. We can explain to you how little it costs to put in a new central heating system. And it pays for itself within a short time!

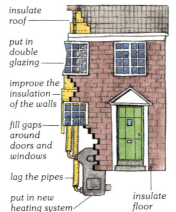

insulate roof
put in double glazing
improve the insulation of the walls
fill gaps around doors and windows
lag the pipes
put in new heating system
insulate floor

If you're looking for a solution to your energy problems, this is your first step:
– dial 100
– ask for Freefone Energy Council
– talk to one of our "energy doctors" or
– send in the coupon for more information.

My home and I would like to save energy. We are mainly heated by: ☐ electricity ☐ oil ☐ gas ☐ coal
Name: _____
Address: _____
_____

---

a What promises does the Energy Council make in the advertisement?

▶ They will look at your house. Go on.

b Mrs Storm meets Mrs Owen on her way to the market place. Complete the dialogue and use the correct forms of the verbs in the box.

ask about	ask for	call on
find out	look at	look for	pay for
put in	talk about	talk to

Mrs Storm: Hello, Dolly. Sorry I didn't call you yesterday, but the man from the Energy Council ① us and he stayed with us for more than two hours.
Mrs Owen: Oh really? He did a good job then.
Mrs Storm: Well, first he ② the house, you know, questions like how old it was, and such things. And then he ③ the house and heating very carefully.
Mrs Owen: So he ④ gaps around the doors and windows?
Mrs Storm: Yeah, and he also wanted to ⑤ if the insulation of the roof and walls was thick enough.
Mrs Owen: And did you ⑥ some advice?
Mrs Storm: Of course, I did. And I must say he had some good ideas. He ⑦ how we can save money. If we ⑧ a central heating system, it will ⑨ itself in a few years. I think it's worthwhile. Why don't you ⑩ him, too?

 c Look at the picture of the house in the leaflet. Some things have to be done at Mrs Storm's house in order to save energy. Find solutions to the following problems:

1. There is no snow on the roof, but there is snow on the neighbour's house.
2. The curtains move, even when the windows are closed.
3. The family always have cold feet.
4. Mrs Storm's gas bill is very high.
5. The hot water cools down very quickly.

UNIT 13 C

2 The news about energy is "Save It". Here is some information from the Department of Energy. It is about how to save energy in the house.

Fuel is expensive, don't waste it!

A lot of electricity is used when you use the air conditioning. Our advice is – draw your curtains and pull the blinds down, do without it if you can.

Cooking in a microwave saves a lot of energy. Use it whenever you can.

Think before you use it! People often use gadgets which aren't really necessary. Sometimes it's more fun to do the job by hand.

Wait until there are enough clothes to fill your washing-machine before you use it. It saves energy, even though it may mean your favourite jeans are out of action for a bit longer!

Perhaps you've forgotten, but your hair also dries naturally. Energy is saved when you do without a hair-drier, and it's better for your hair, too.

Energy sense is common sense.

a Make complete sentences.

Jeans Information Advice The news Hair	is are	helpful information. information about things which happened recently. what grows on your head. trousers made of blue material. facts about something.

b Complete the following sentences with the correct form of the verbs in the box:

| mean | cost | be | save | waste |

The news about energy ① we must learn how to save it.
Electricity ② money.
People ③ energy when they use unnecessary gadgets.
Energy sense ④ using the microwave instead of the oven.
Washing a lot of clothes together ⑤ energy.

c Look at the text again. Find the missing nouns and put the verbs into the correct form.

The ① from the Department of Energy (be) about how to save energy.
When your ② (be) wet, don't use a hair-drier.
When there (not be) enough ③ to fill your washing-machine, don't use it.
Microwaves save your time. That (be) good ④!
Our ⑤ (mean) your electricity bills will be lower.

d Now translate the information leaflet.

UNIT 13

1 Energy – chances and risks

"Do not walk in the dark without a light," says a warning sign near Rotorua. Walking there can be dangerous because there are geysers, hot springs and even volcanoes all over the place. "The heat is right below our feet," says Ken Wilton, who lives in Auckland in the middle of the North Island. "This is an area of geothermal energy, that means that we can use both hot water and steam from the earth."

For many years now hot steam from the earth has been used to produce electricity. There is also enough warm water so that houses can be heated. "Our aim is to use nature's power for man, but not to harm our environment," says Ken.

Los Angeles Today: How do you think we can stop pollution, Mr. Johnson?
Johnson: We must develop cleaner forms of energy. Although alternative technologies will become more important, I still believe that the answer to most of our problems will be nuclear energy.

Los Angeles Today: But don't you think there are too many risks?

Johnson: Of course, some big problems haven't been solved yet. There is still the risk of an accident, and we don't know where to put our nuclear waste at the moment. But I'm certain that some day these problems will be solved and nuclear energy will be made absolutely safe.

"Our energy of the future will be solar energy," Mike Douglas from Sydney explained to me when I visited him 'down under'.

"We've introduced two ways of using the sun's energy: A lot of families already heat their water with the help of solar collectors. We're also planning some new projects near the west coast where sunlight will be converted into electricity by solar cells. Of course, solar energy systems can be used efficiently here because we've got a lot of sunshine."

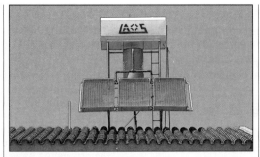

UNIT 13 T

a Which of the following sources of energy are mentioned in the texts?

> wind energy   coal   solar energy   water power
> geothermal energy   oil   nuclear energy   gas

b In which countries can you find these sources of energy according to the texts?

> Scotland   United States
> New Zealand   Austria
> Australia   Canada

c Answer the following questions:
1. What does the countryside look like near Rotorua?
2. How can the hot water from the earth be used?
3. According to Mr Johnson, what are the solutions to today's energy problems?
4. What two big problems are caused by the use of nuclear energy today?
5. What do you need if you want to convert sunlight into electricity?
6. Why will solar energy be used more in Australia than in Northern Europe?
7. What sources of energy can be called alternative?
8. Which alternative sources of energy would you use in Denmark, which in Brazil? Why?

d Can you find the words in the texts which have the same meaning?
1. the world around us
2. difficulties
3. sure
4. region
5. with good results
6. turn into

e Find the opposites of these words in the texts.
1. safe
2. cold
3. above
4. few
5. dirty
6. small

f Complete these sentences. Use 'because', 'although', 'so that', 'in order to'.
1. Solar energy can be used in Australia ...
2. Most people pollute the air ...
3. Alternative technologies will be developed ...
4. In many countries they have installed solar energy systems ...
5. Many politicians say that nuclear energy is safe ...
6. It may be dangerous to walk in the dark in Rotorua ...
7. In New Zealand a lot of hot water comes from the earth ...
8. They have started to use the sun's energy very late in Australia ...

2 Listen to the cassette and answer the following questions for each of the three interviews.
1. What kind of energy is the person talking about?
2. What is the person's job?
3. Where does the person live?
4. What problem is mentioned?

3 Describe a source of energy in about five sentences. Do not mention its name. The rest of your class have to find out what you are talking about.
Say something about:
air/climate/environment/countryside/risks/pollution/energy/reserves/waste/costs.
You can use the words in the boxes.

> clean/dirty
> safe/dangerous
> limited/unlimited
> important
> cheap/expensive
> high/low

> pollute
> cause
> damage
> develop
> lead to
> use

UNIT 13

Energy problems – any alternatives?

Imagine you own a farm and you are worried about your fuel costs. Your farm uses 20,000 litres of light heating oil and 50,000 kW-hr electricity per year. You want to install a new system.
Here are five alternatives:

1. **a solar energy system**
   - produce hot water
   - no sunshine – no energy!
   - save 3,000 litres of light heating oil
   - investment costs: about £20,000

2. **a windmill**
   - produce electricity
   - no wind – no energy!
   - save 30,000 kW-hr
   - investment costs: about £45,000

3. **a bio-mass system**
   - produce gas from dung
   - only large systems available
   - save 10,000 litres of light heating oil/ 10,000 kW-hr
   - investment costs: about £33,000

4. **a heat exchanger system**
   - cool cowsheds and heat water
   - difficult to install
   - save 5,000 litres of light heating oil/ 10,000 kW-hr
   - investment costs: about £48,000

5. **a solid fuel system**
   - use your own resources of wood, straw etc.
   - own resources used up soon
   - save 10,000 litres of light heating oil
   - investment costs: about £14,000

a Describe the alternatives.

b Talk about the advantages and disadvantages of each system.

c What do you think is best for your farm? You can choose one system or a combination.

The body's energy givers

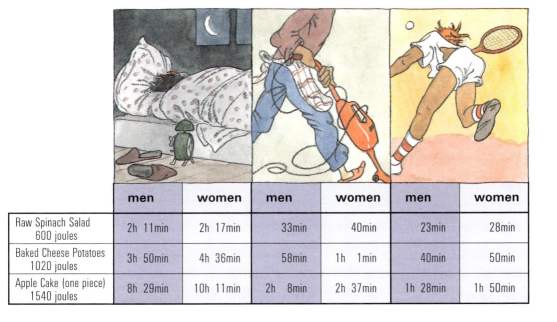

	men	women	men	women	men	women
Raw Spinach Salad 600 joules	2h 11min	2h 17min	33min	40min	23min	28min
Baked Cheese Potatoes 1020 joules	3h 50min	4h 36min	58min	1h 1min	40min	50min
Apple Cake (one piece) 1540 joules	8h 29min	10h 11min	2h 8min	2h 37min	1h 28min	1h 50min

Your body needs energy in order for you to live. Even if you are not doing anything, you need a certain amount of energy just to keep your heart and other organs working. As soon as you start to do something, you need more energy. You get your energy, of course, from the food you eat. The amount of energy it gives you is measured in joules. All food gives you energy, but some types of food give you more than others.

The chart above gives you examples of some types of food and the amount of energy they provide you with. It also shows how long it takes to use up this energy. The reason why people become too fat is that the food they eat contains more joules than their body can use. This extra food is turned into fat. Experts have worked out that the average woman has an energy output of 9,240 joules per day, and the average man an output of 12,600 joules per day. Even 420 joules a day more than you need can add about 5kg a year to your weight. If you want to be healthy, it is important not to be too fat. But, of course, it is not good to be too thin either. You need some body fat as a reserve of energy.

a Look at the chart. How long does it take to use up the energy in

1 raw spinach salad for a man who is doing the housework?
2 a piece of apple cake for a woman who is sleeping?
3 baked cheese potatoes for a woman who is playing tennis?

b Now ask and answer similar questions.

c Can you find the solution?

1 You eat it and it gives you energy.
2 The unit which measures energy in food.
3 It pumps the blood around your body.
4 It gives you a reserve of energy.
5 The number of joules the average woman needs every day.
6 What happens to a person who eats 420 joules too many a day for a year?
7 Why does everybody need some body fat?

S3 UNIT 13

THE ROSE CANADIAN BANK

HOME IMPROVEMENT LOANS:
Simple to arrange · Planned repayments
Free life insurance

YOU WANT TO RENOVATE YOUR HOME?
This leaflet explains in simple terms what you need to know.

JUST DECIDE HOW MUCH
We can lend you up to $15,000 straight away – or even more if we can have some security. Repayments can be made over periods from 2 to 25 years.

PROTECTING YOUR REPAYMENTS
When you take out a RCB loan, you can also be insured against sickness, accident or unemployment.

FREE LIFE INSURANCE
You will automatically be protected with free life insurance. This means that if you die, your family will not have to make any more payments.

HOW DO YOU GET A LOAN?
After reading this leaflet have a word with your local RCB branch manager or agent. You then fill in a form, pay a fee and you will soon be offered a loan.

NEW! OUR "SAVE ENERGY PROGRAM"
Now we can offer you a special "Save Energy Program" at very low interest rates. If you want to put in a new heating system or wish to insulate your home, please contact us. In most cases we can help you.

Mr Woodstock, a customer, is talking to a clerk at the Rose Canadian Bank.

Clerk: Good morning, sir. Can I help you?
Customer: Yes, I've read your leaflet about improvement loans. I'm especially interested in your "Save Energy Program" because we're planning to put in a new central heating system.
Clerk: Well, our new program could be suitable for you. At the moment, we can offer you loans at 8% interest for up to 10 years.
Customer: That sounds good.
Clerk: And we can lend you up to $15,000 as a personal loan or even more if your house can be the bank's security.
Customer: Well, I've saved about $10,000 and I'd like to borrow the same amount.
Clerk: No problem. You just have to fill in this personal loan application form, and I think we can give you the money in a few days.

a Answer the following questions in complete sentences:
   1 What do most people need who want to renovate their house or want to buy a new car?
   2 Why is a life insurance good for the bank and for the customer?
   3 How much money can Mr Woodstock get as a personal loan?
   4 How much money does he want to borrow?
   5 In what way can Mr Woodstock's house be a security for the bank?
   6 What does the customer have to pay on top of the repayment of the loan?

b Find the corresponding nouns for the following verbs from the text:
   1 pay
   2 insure
   3 manage
   4 live
   5 lend
   6 program
   7 improve
   8 employ

c You want to insulate the roof of your house. It will cost $8,000. You have saved $4,000. The interest rate at your bank is 7,5% for up to 8 years. Play the roles of the bank clerk and the customer.

d You want to put in new double glazing. What do you have to do? Put the following steps into the right order and make complete sentences.

   ▶ look/advertisements
   First I look for advertisements for double glazing.

   1 fill in/application form
   2 decide/suitable windows
   3 contact/bank
   4 go/different firms
   5 have to repay/loan
   6 compare/prices
   7 get/loan
   8 buy/new windows

UNIT 13 G

The passive: Present Perfect

> A lot of money **has been invested**.
> Where **have** the oil reserves **been found**?

Das *Present Perfect* Passiv wird gebildet aus:
have/has been + Partizip Perfekt

The passive: *will*-Future

> New jobs **will be created**.
> Our culture **won't be destroyed**.

Das *Future* Passiv wird gebildet aus:
will be + Partizip Perfekt

Adverbial clauses

Einfache Sätze können mit Konjunktionen wie *because, so that, although, in order to* zu komplexen Sätzen verbunden werden. Diese Konjunktionen leiten adverbiale Nebensätze ein.

Nebensätze mit *because* drücken einen Grund aus:

> Tidal energy is a good idea in this area **because** **it has a big tidal range**.

Nebensätze mit *so that* drücken ein Ergebnis aus:

> The project employs a lot of people **so that** **the job situation will improve**.

Nebensätze mit *although* drücken eine Einschränkung aus:

> Some people will profit from the dam **although** **the wildlife will suffer**.

Nebensätze mit *in order to* drücken einen Zweck/eine Absicht aus:

> They want to build a big dam **in order to** **generate electricity**.

Phrasal verbs – prepositional verbs

> We want to **put in** a new central heating system.
> Energy experts will **find out** how much you can save.
>
> **Talk to** our energy experts if you **are looking for** a good solution.

Viele Verben können durch das Anfügen von z.B. *after, for, in, on, out, to* ergänzt werden und damit eine veränderte Bedeutung erhalten.

Irregular nouns

Nomen nur mit Pluralform

> – Where **are** my **jeans,** Dad?
> – Your **clothes are** in the bedroom.

Bei diesen Nomen steht auch die Verbform im Plural. Dazu gehören insbesondere Paarwörter, z.B. *trousers, jeans, glasses, scissors*.

> The **news is** good.
> **Physics is** difficult.

Bei diesen Nomen steht die Verbform im Singular.

Nomen nur mit Singularform

> Let me give you some **advice**.
> Your **hair** is too long.
> Have you received any new **information**?

Manche Nomen haben keine Pluralform. Dazu gehören *advice, hair, information, progress*.

UNIT 14

THE WORLD OF ADVERTISING

Here comes Mr Icicle

The WINNEX Solid Gold Quartz – it even ticks like watches used to do.

Describe the different methods of advertising you can see in the pictures.
Which methods appeal to the eyes, which to the ears?
Which other methods of advertising can you think of?

UNIT 14 A

1 If you shop carefully, you can buy more for your money. This brochure from a consumer organization shows you some of the ways to become a careful shopper.

TIPS AND TRAPS OF SHOPPING

1. Are you an impulsive shopper? Do you go into a shop and buy things suddenly without thinking about the price? Can the attractive shape or bright colour of a product persuade you to by it? Be careful! Make a shopping list and only buy those things which are on your list. In addition, we advise you not to do your shopping on an empty stomach.

2. A discount is a price reduction. Discount stores buy large quantities of products at one time. This enables them to sell many of the items a lot cheaper. Some of these items are not of top quality. So remember, some shopkeepers want you to believe that all of their products are of good quality. Don't forget to check them carefully.

3. A bargain can be a quality item which is sold at a lower price than normal. But be careful! Remember, bargains are there to attract you, and the shopkeeper expects you to buy other articles at their regular price.

4. The prices of summer clothes are reduced near the end of July or August, and those of the winter collection in January. Sales can help you to save a lot of money. Ask the shop-assistant to show you the original price tag because often low quality items are produced especially for the sales.

5. Check the unit price of foods and other items. The unit price is the cost of 1 kilo of an item. So, if 300g of cheese cost £1.20, then the unit price is £4.00. Many shops expect you to work out the unit price yourself. Remember, products in large-size containers do not always cost less per unit than products in smaller ones.

6. WHICH is a monthly consumer magazine. Its staff test products like washing-machines in laboratories and report on their quality and safety. So, before you buy a product, try to get as much information as possible. Be careful, too. The same product is sometimes sold under different names at different prices.

a Which heading goes with which paragraph? Give reasons.

LOOK IN DISCOUNT STORES, TOO

HIGH QUALITY NEED NOT ALWAYS BE EXPENSIVE

WORK OUT THE UNIT PRICE

GET INFORMATION BEFORE YOU BUY

DON'T JUST BUY BECAUSE IT LOOKS GOOD

BUY AT THE SALES

A UNIT 14

b True or false?

1. Not all products which are cheap are of low quality.
2. Only buy things you have written on your list.
3. All products which are sold at sales are of good quality.
4. Take the time to calculate the unit price.
5. Low quality products which are sold cheaply are bargains.
6. Shops must show the unit price of each article on their shelves.
7. Consumer organizations want you to compare prices.
8. Products in large containers are usually more expensive.

c What does the text say about influences on customers? Make sentences.

Consumer organizations and magazines Advertisers and shopkeepers The colours of articles	help advise expect persuade	customers shoppers consumers	to work out the unit price. to buy at sales. to compare products. to check the price tag. to buy more than they really need. to buy without thinking. to believe that everything is good quality. to get a lot of information.

d Complete the following sentences.
You can use the expressions in the box.

Consumer organizations ① the best product for their money.
A shopkeeper ② things because they think they are cheap.
In some countries the government ③ the unit price.
Buying in large quantities ④ items more cheaply.
Clever advertisements ⑤ about the price of a product.
Consumer Advice Councils ⑥ carefully and save money.
Shopping without care ⑦ more money than they have got.
Careful shopping ⑧ money for something you have always wanted.

> wants customers to buy
> expects shop owners
>   to show
> causes people to spend
> persuade people not
>   to think
> enables discount stores
>   to sell
> advise people to shop
> help people to find
> helps you to save

2 Write complete sentences.

▶ Fred: This container looks bigger and cheaper than that one.
June: Look at the unit price, Fred. (tell)
June told him to look at the unit price.

1. June: My washing-machine has broken. I need a new one.
   Fred: Try BROWN'S. They've got a special offer. (advise)
2. Fred: I'm going to town this afternoon. Can I get you anything?
   June: Bring some of that French cheese, please. (ask)
3. June: I put this new cream on my face and it's gone all red.
   Fred: You should see a doctor, June. (advise)
4. Fred: Look, this suit has got a small hole in the trousers.
   June: You'd better not buy it. (warn)
5. June: I need a microwave, Fred.
   Fred: I'd go to DAVE'S. They've got good quality at reasonable prices. (persuade)
6. Fred: I'll go shopping before dinner.
   June: No, Fred. It's better for you to do the shopping in the morning after a good breakfast. (want)
7. June: I'm going to the sales tomorrow.
   Fred: Yes, I'm sure you'll get some good bargains. (expect)
8. Fred: Oh, look! JOHN'S have got 50% off electrical goods.
   June: Be careful, Fred. Look for quality. (warn)

UNIT 14 A

3 Careful shoppers

a Which goes with which?

p	This is the smallest unit of British money.	minimum
min	This is the smallest possible number.	per person
v	This is one way of measuring electricity.	volt
pp	This is the price which each guest has to pay.	postage and packing
VAT	This is a tax you have to pay on everything you buy.	pence
d.b.b.	The price is for a room, breakfast and an evening meal.	including
p&p	This is the cost of sending it to you.	Value Added Tax
incl	There are no additional costs.	dinner, bed and breakfast

b What is your advice?
You can use the information from the advertisements.

Your girlfriend Your boyfriend Your parents	wants to want to	buy an alarm clock. buy some washing-powder and yoghurt. go on holiday to Bournemouth. buy some chicken pies and potatoes.

Start your sentences like this: I'd advise/expect/tell ...
Give reasons.

UNIT 14

1 An ad and how it works

THIS WATCH DOESN'T DO MUCH – IT JUST TELLS THE TIME BUT IT DOES THAT SUPERBLY

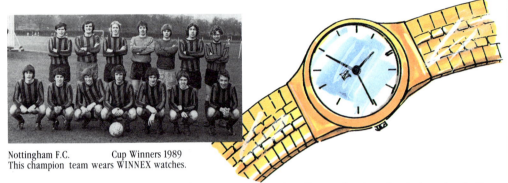

Nottingham F.C.   Cup Winners 1989
This champion team wears WINNEX watches.

Do you like watches squeaking and bleeping at you? Do you like a watch flashing at you and speaking to you? You don't? That's what we thought. That's why we designed the Solid Gold Quartz.

It only tells you the time, but it does that better than any other watch in the world. A superb product designed and manufactured by the best British craftsmen. Especially for you.

WINNEX *every one a winner*

a Answer the following questions:
1 What is the watch in the advertisement made of?
2 Where is it made?
3 What can the watch do?
4 What can't the watch do?
5 Why is the football team in the picture?
6 Do you think the watch in the ad is a good watch?
7 What do you think of watches which squeak or bleep?

b Here are some extracts from a dictionary of advertising:

body copy:	a longer text giving more details about the product Function: to inform the reader
headline:	a short text containing the basic message of the ad Function: to persuade the reader to read the body copy
logo:	the symbol or the brand name of a product Function: to help the reader to recognize the product quickly and easily
slogan:	a short and catchy phrase Function: to help the reader to remember the product
visual:	an illustration showing the product and/or people who use the product Function: to persuade people to look at the ad

Look at the Winnex advertisement and say what the body copy, the headline, the logo, the slogan and the visual are.

196 one hundred and ninety-six

UNIT 14 B

2 Form relative clauses.

▶ The body copy is a text giving information.
 The body copy is a text which gives information.

1. Headlines are short texts containing the main idea of an ad.
2. The logo is an element helping the reader to recognize the product.
3. The visual is an illustration showing the product and/or people who use the product.
4. Do you like a watch squeaking at you?
5. Some people like a watch flashing at them.
6. I do not like a watch bleeping at me every few minutes.

3 Replace the relative clauses.

▶ An illustration which gives the reader detailed information is often better than a long text.
 An illustration giving the reader detailed information is often better than a long text.

1. An advertisement which shows Princess Di in the bath has been banned.
2. The film star who appears in this commercial is very popular.
3. A woman who lives in Chester has won the first prize in the Albatross Computer competition.
4. People who work in advertising agencies must be very flexible.
5. A letter which contains all the necessary product information will be sent to all our customers.
6. Customers who ask for more detailed information can get a special leaflet.

4 Here are some tips for advertising. Make sentences.

▶ a symbol/use/as a trade mark/easy to remember
 A symbol which is used as a trade mark should be easy to remember.
 A symbol used as a trade mark should be easy to remember.

1. a slogan/invent/for a product/short and catchy
2. a logo/choose/for a product/clear and simple
3. commercials/show/on television/funny
4. product information/give/to the consumer/correct
5. advertisements/publish/in newspapers/controlled by the government
6. a headline/print/in an ad/not too long

5 Here is an advertisement from an English paper.
It has been shortened to save space.

Can you give the full version?

Jeeps made in Japan cheaper than last year.

Dyson's is one of the biggest companies selling Harakiri jeeps in Liverpool. And as everybody knows, jeeps manufactured in Japan are comfortable and reliable. And what's more – the jeeps sold at Dyson's are actually cheaper than last year! Anybody wanting more information should **call us on 313 778**.

C UNIT 14

1 This is a newspaper advertisement by MINI BANK offering loans to young people. It tries to persuade you to become one of the bank's customers.

Do you need £ 2,000?

We like young people to grow bigger, not smaller.

MINI BANK
The bank for the little people

a Match the young man's answers with the questions in the advertisement.

1. No, not last year.
   No, not really.
2. About half, around £750.
   No, I haven't.
3. About £1,500.
4. From your bank? No, but I've had a loan from Bartley's.
5. A van for our band.
   Because all the cars were too small.
6. For two years.
   Last month? Around £400.

b Answer the following questions:

1. Who is the man sitting at the desk?
2. What does the young man want?
3. What is the name of the bank which paid for the ad?
4. Which bank does the man sitting at the desk work for?
5. Which bank has the young man had a loan from before?
6. What does the MINI BANK want the readers to believe about their bank?

198 one hundred and ninety-eight

UNIT 14 C

c What questions did the manager ask?
  ▶ Have you ever tried to get a loan from our bank before?
    First the manager asked whether the young man had ever tried to get a loan from their bank before.
  ▶ How much money did they lend you?
    After that he wanted to know how much money they had lent him.
    Go on.

d Here are some of the young man's answers in full sentences.
Report what he said.
  ▶ I haven't had a loan from your bank, but I have had a loan from Bartley's.
    The young man said that he had not had a loan from their bank, but that he had had a loan from Bartley's.
  ▶ They lent me about £1,500.
    He added that they had lent him about £1,500.
  ▶ I didn't save any money.
    He also said that he had not saved any money.

  1 I've paid back about half so far, around £750.
  2 I haven't borrowed any money from any other bank.
  3 I've decided to get a van for our band.
  4 I didn't think about getting a car because all the cars were too small.
  5 I've had my present job for 2 years.
  6 My pay last month was around £400.
  7 I didn't really expect to get a loan from you.
  8 I also went to other banks.

2 Here are some reactions to the advertisement.
They were recorded four months after the advertising campaign.

a Listen to the cassette.
Who is the first/second/third speaker:
a father, a motor-bike dealer, a son, a computer engineer, a bank manager, a mother?

b Listen to the cassette again.
Who spoke about what?
  1 the number of customers
  2 a computer
  3 the price of a motor bike
  4 the positive side of the advertisement
  5 the negative side of the advertisement
  6 a motor bike shop

c True or false? Listen to the cassette again.
  1 The number of loans has gone up from 4,591 to 5,122 at one MINI BANK branch.
  2 MINI BANK is not doing a better trade now than before.
  3 The young man hasn't paid back a loan which he had got from his mother.
  4 MINI BANK gave the young man the full loan for his moto-cross bike.
  5 The young man thinks that MINI BANK loans are a good idea.
  6 MINI BANK makes people spend their money before they have earned it, according to the young man's father.
  7 The young man's father thinks that his son's life is easier with the loan.

d Now report what the bank manager, the young man and the young man's father said.
  ▶ last March/borrow £500/from my mother.
    The young man said that last March he had borrowed £500 from his mother.

  1 our son/borrow money/for a computer
  2 the moto-cross bike/cost/£2,000
  3 the number of the bank's customers/rise/by about 10%
  4 Mum and Dad/not lend/any money
  5 loans for young people/go up/by 21%
  6 on Wednesday/my son/buy/moto-cross bike

one hundred and ninety-nine 199

UNIT 14

1 Advertising – facts and opinions

Advertising is very expensive. A sixty-second TV commercial can cost £50,000 and a direct-mail campaign to 100,000 households costs £30,000 just for postage. All advertisements try to influence people. Commercial ads, for example, want the public to buy certain products.

To be successful, advertisers have to choose the correct medium and the correct time. In winter, for example, there are a lot of ads telling us to buy medicine against colds. Products designed for mass consumption are advertised on TV or in newspapers. But how can you sell something like pop records or peanut butter? In this case a teenage magazine or junk mail would probably be a better answer.

Advertisers hope to create a positive image for their product. Just think of a young man on a beach, surrounded by beautiful women and holding up a soft drink. This soft drink can be linked to an active and successful social life.

You shouldn't believe everything you see in ads, however. The "young attractive girl" showing her super fingernails in a TV ad could be three women. The face belongs to one woman, the fingernails to another, and the soft voice you hear to a third.

So we see, advertising uses tricks. Is that bad? Andrew Horn, 28, manager at IAC (International Advertising Company) looks at it like this: "We give useful information about products and give the public the chance to compare prices and quality. Of course, we persuade people to buy products and as a result mass production has become necessary. So, in the end, we help to provide work for a lot of people. But ads do not only influence people to buy something, they also try to protect them. For example, in the past, we spent quite a bit of time on writing texts for anti-ads. Our company designed the advertising campaigns against smoking and drink-driving ..."

a Which of the following opinions can you find in the text?

1. Advertising can cost a lot.
2. Famous sportsmen advertise for certain products.
3. Successful ads depend on the right time.
4. All ads want people to buy something.
5. Advertising informs about products, too.
6. Products designed for mass consumption are usually advertised by junk mail.
7. A lot of ads are linked with positive images.
8. Anti-ads do not try to influence people.

b Can you do these tasks?

1. What are the costs of advertising on TV and through direct mail in your money?
2. What products are mainly advertised on TV and in newspapers?
3. Through which medium would an advertising agency try to sell pop records? Say why.
4. Give an example of a positive image in advertising.
5. Give an example of the use of tricks in advertising.
6. What did Andrew Horn say about anti-ads in his company?
7. Explain the difference between a commercial ad and an anti-ad.
8. Make a list of the positive and the negative sides of advertising, as they are mentioned in the text.

UNIT 14

c Find words which have the same meaning as the following expressions from the text:
1 TV commercial
2 products
3 correct
4 beautiful
5 chance
6 company

d Find the opposites of the following expressions from the text:
1 expensive
2 buy
3 against
4 better
5 answer
6 positive
7 soft
8 active
9 useful
10 in the past

e Report what Andrew Horn said about advertising.
▶ He said/explained/added ...

f Make one sentence out of two.
1 The public should buy a lot of products.
That is what the advertisers want.
The advertisers want ...

2 You should buy ALASKA skis.
That is what Jean Kelly advises on TV.
Jean Kelly advises ...

3 People should stop smoking.
Perhaps anti-ads can help them.
Perhaps anti-ads can help ...

g Now translate the text on advertising into German.

2 What else do you know about advertising?

a Can you do these tasks?
1 Give more examples of advertising which depend on the seasons of the year.
2 Do you think that advertising on TV and on the radio has anything to do with the time of day? Give reasons.
3 How would you try to sell your cassette-recorder?
4 How do you think a local shopkeeper would try to sell fashion clothes?
5 Think of some products which are linked with positive images. Give examples.
6 Have you ever bought anything simply because you had read or heard about it through advertising?
7 Give more examples of anti-ads.

b An average household receives about half a kilo of ads (direct mail, junk mail etc) per week. Therefore people have started to put NO ADS stickers on their letter boxes. Would you do the same? Why? Why not?

3 Radio advertising

a Listen to the cassette and answer the following questions:
1 What are the names of the products in the ads?
2 What kind of products are they?
3 What are the slogans?

b Listen to the cassette again.
1 How often can you hear each name in each of the ads?
2 What groups of people are the ads addressing?
3 What arguments are given to persuade people to buy these products?
4 What else do the advertisers use to influence people?

c What do you think about these ads?

S1 UNIT 14

Waste disposal: a consumer problem?

In the course of a year the average British family throws away six trees worth of paper, 55 kilos of metal and 45 kilos of plastics. For the country as a whole that is 20 million tons. Most of this 'rubbish' is useful. Filling holes in the ground with materials which we could use again is therefore not very sensible. Landfill sites produce dangerous gases and are also a threat to water supplies.

Recycling makes sense because it
- regenerates the environment
- conserves our resources
- reduces pollution and litter
- cuts energy costs
- generates jobs
- creates profitable industry

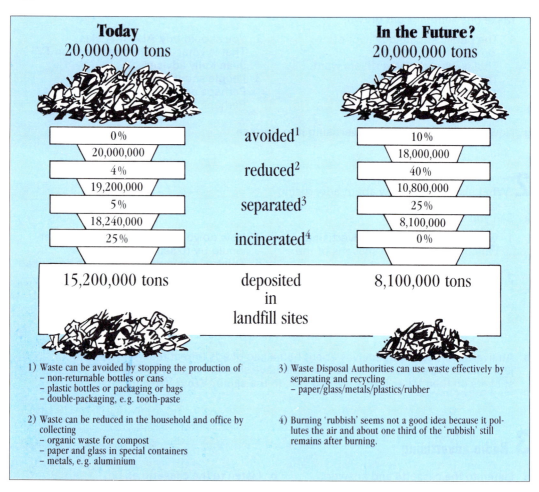

Today 20,000,000 tons

	avoided[1]	
0% / 20,000,000		10% / 18,000,000
4% / 19,200,000	reduced[2]	40% / 10,800,000
5% / 18,240,000	separated[3]	25% / 8,100,000
25%	incinerated[4]	0%

15,200,000 tons — deposited in landfill sites — 8,100,000 tons

In the Future? 20,000,000 tons

1) Waste can be avoided by stopping the production of
   - non-returnable bottles or cans
   - plastic bottles or packaging or bags
   - double-packaging, e.g. tooth-paste

2) Waste can be reduced in the household and office by collecting
   - organic waste for compost
   - paper and glass in special containers
   - metals, e.g. aluminium

3) Waste Disposal Authorities can use waste effectively by separating and recycling
   - paper/glass/metals/plastics/rubber

4) Burning 'rubbish' seems not a good idea because it pollutes the air and about one third of the 'rubbish' still remains after burning.

a Define the following nouns:
1 landfill site
2 waste
3 compost
4 container

b Make sentences with the following verbs:
1 regenerate
2 conserve
3 recycle
4 deposit

c You want to replace your old fridge but you don't want to simply throw it away. Think of the different parts. What material can be recycled?

d What can you do to avoid/reduce waste?

Eggs and Salmonella – the Facts.

Today eggs are a valuable part of a balanced diet. But a lot of people are worried because they have heard or read about people who have fallen ill after eating eggs. What are the facts?

The number of cases of food poisoning from salmonella in eggs is very small compared to the number of eggs eaten in Britain every day – about 30 million on average. So far there have been only 49 cases of salmonella resulting from the consumption of eggs. The Government and industry are fighting the problem and have made new rules for egg producers.

But, of course, people want to know – is it safe to eat eggs? The Government has therefore asked its Chief Medical Officer to advise the public about the use of eggs. Here is his advice:

1. For healthy people there is very little risk from eggs which have been cooked – whether you like them boiled, fried, scrambled or poached.

2. For certain groups of people – that is, the elderly, the sick, babies and pregnant women – eggs should be completely cooked until the white and the yolk are solid.

3. But nobody should eat raw eggs or uncooked food made from them – for example, home-made mayonnaise or home-made ice-cream.

The Chief Medical Officer adds:

> Meals with eggs in them should be eaten as soon as possible after cooking. If the meal is not eaten immediately, it should be kept in the fridge.

Please follow this advice.

H. M. GOVERNMENT

---

a True or false?

1. Many people think it may be dangerous to eat eggs.
2. These days eggs are not so important for a healthy diet.
3. Salmonella can cause food poisoning.
4. The number of cases of food poisoning is relatively big.
5. The Government has told doctors what to do about salmonella.
6. If you want to make a meal with eggs which you want to eat the next day, you should keep it cool.
7. Nobody should worry about eating raw eggs.

b Find the words or expressions in the text which have the same meaning.

1. illness resulting from eating something bad
2. good mixture of healthy foods
3. expecting a baby
4. some tips
5. older people
6. a kitchen appliance which keeps your food cold
7. people who are ill
8. animal products which have not been cooked
9. the Government's top doctor
10. the yellow part of an egg

c Answer the following questions:

1. Why have some people become ill after eating eggs?
2. There are about 60 million people living in Britain. How many eggs does each person eat on average per week?
3. What has the Government done about the problem of salmonella?
4. Is it dangerous for healthy people to eat eggs?
5. Why do you think old and young people, the sick and the pregnant should be careful about eating eggs?

UNIT 14

A year of success?

ANDERSON is a big multinational group. Its headquarters are in London. Because of its world-wide activities it has branches in nearly every country.

The ANDERSON Group has never been in better shape

Our shareholders can look back on a year of success

Reports on our activities in 1988 from our divisions:

MINING
Main locations: Zimbabwe and Zambia.
Result: We improved our profits.

AGRICULTURE
Main locations: Malawi, Kenya, Zambia, Mozambique, California and Texas.
Result: Our activities, which include cattle ranches, tea plantations and large-scale vegetable production, showed good results.

MOTOR VEHICLE DISTRIBUTION
Main locations: England, Kenya, Zambia.
Result: Our distributors representing the world's biggest manufacturers sold more cars and trucks than in 1987.

1988 AT A GLANCE

	1988	1987
Turnover	£4,516m	£3,216m
Profit before tax	£220m	£200m
Total dividends	£123m	£102m
Face value of one share	25p	25p
Market value of one share as per 31-12-88	£3,30	

TRADE
Location: West Germany.
Result: Because of the weak dollar, buying and selling on an international level was extremely difficult. But DUISBURG, STEEL, now known as ANDERSON DUISBURG, had an extremely good year. Their steel sales went up and their import and export business increased considerably.

HOTELS
Main locations: England, Kenya, California.
Result: Our Duchess Group proved very successful.

PRINTING AND PUBLISHING
Main locations: England, Scotland.
Result: The money invested in a new printing plant for our British papers was well spent.
Our printing business on the whole should show some growth in 1989.

FREIGHT
Location: Switzerland.
Result: HÜGLI & SÖHNE, owned partly by us, did much better than in the year before.

OIL AND GAS
Location: California.
Result: Profits did not quite reach those achieved in 1987.

---

a Which ANDERSON divisions could deal with the following?

b Which ANDERSON division do you think was the most successful/the least successful in 1988? Give reasons.

c Match the following definitions with the words at the top of the ANDERSON ad.

- an amount of money which you gain when you are paid more for something than it costs you to make it
- the amount of money which something is worth
- the equal parts into which a company's capital is divided
- the value of the goods and services which a company has sold during a special period of time
- part of a company's profits which is paid to people who have shares in the company

to-infinitive after verb and object

| Verb + Objekt + *to*-Infinitiv | Einige Verben treten oft mit Objekt und *to*-Infinitiv auf. |

June **told her friend to check** the unit price.
The shopkeeper **asked him not to touch** the apples.
Advertisers **want the consumer to buy** more products.
They **warned me to be** careful.
I **warned them not to touch** the engine.

Zu diesen Verben gehören:
advise, ask, expect, help,
persuade, want, warn, tell.
warn to = „ermahnen …"
warn not to = „davor warnen …"

Participle constructions

Relativsätze werden häufig durch kürzere Partizipialkonstruktionen ersetzt.
Es gibt zwei verschiedene Möglichkeiten:

1. mit Partizip Präsens (*ing*-Form)

The body copy is a longer text **giving** more details about the product.

The body copy is a longer text which gives more details about the product.

Diese Konstruktion entspricht einem aktiven Relativsatz.

2. mit Partizip Perfekt (3. Form)

Information **given** to the consumer should be correct.

Information which is given to the consumer should be correct.

Diese Konstruktion entspricht einem passiven Relativsatz.

Reported speech (III) – Einleitendes Verb im Past Tense

Steht das einleitende Verb (z. B. *say, think/ask, want to know*) im *Past Tense,* erfolgt beim Verb in der indirekten Rede eine Rückverschiebung.

Statement		Reported statement	
Bank manager:	We **gave** the young man a loan.	The bank manager **said** that they **had given** the young man a loan.	*Past Tense*-Formen werden zu *Past Perfect*-Formen.
Brian:	I **haven't borrowed** any money from the bank.	Brian **said** he **hadn't borrowed** any money from the bank.	*Present Perfect*-Formen werden zu *Past Perfect*-Formen.

Question		Reported question	
Bank manager:	**Have** you **borrowed** money from another bank?	The manager **wanted to know if** Brian **had borrowed** money from another bank.	Indirekte Entscheidungsfragen werden mit *if* oder *whether* eingeleitet.
Bank manager:	**Did** you **save** any money?	The manager **asked whether** Brian **had saved** any money.	Die Umschreibung mit *did* wird in der indirekten Frage durch die *Past Perfect*-Form ersetzt.
Brian:	**Why did** you **ring** my employer?	Brian **asked why** the manager **had rung** his employer.	

UNIT 15

English as an international language

I have to interview people from all over the world.

I work on energy projects in East Africa. All the technical details are in English.

Jenny from America

Kurt from Germany

I'm often in Europe on business. We generally hold our meetings in English.

I talk to the nurses in English.

Makoto from Japan   Asha from India

My students come from many different countries to learn English here.

I always talk to the tower in English.

Penny from Britain

Kimran from the Philippines

Which places are shown in the pictures?
Which person goes with which place?
What do you think the people's jobs are?
Why do you think many people have to use English in their jobs?

UNIT 15 A

1 At a language school

Many people have to learn English for many different reasons. Melanie Schmidt from Frankfurt is a trainee office worker, and in her job she often has to use English. Her English is not that good so she has decided to go on a language course in Britain in her summer holidays. She also wants to stay with a family.

Here are parts of two language school brochures she has received.

Bristol School of English

Our school was founded in 1981. Since then we have offered full-time summer courses (2, 4, 6 weeks) to students from all over the world.
Our school has places for up to 80 people who want to study English seriously.
If you decide to come to our school, we will first test your English and then you will be put into the RIGHT class for YOU (beginners, intermediate or advanced). There are never more than 10 students in one class.
The course fees include almost everything – even the books (they are given out on loan if you don't want to buy them).
At the weekends you will be able to go on excursions, which are free of charge.
Accommodation is arranged with local families.

The basic timetable is:
09.30 – 11.00: Grammar practice and vocabulary development
11.30 – 13.00: Reading and writing practice
14.15 – 15.45: either Conversation or Special English

Our special courses, which we introduced 5 years ago, are at all levels.
They include Business English, Technical English, Medical English, Hotel and Restaurant English and English for Journalists.

LONDON INTERNATIONAL SCHOOL

Founded in 1979
One of London's largest language schools with over 500 students

Length of part-time summer courses:
2, 4, 6 and 8 weeks

Classes:
max. class size 15

Teaching:
4 hours daily (mornings)

Course fees include:
tests, certificates,
registration, welfare
services (books not included)

Activities:
trips and visits in the afternoons
(small extra charge)

Accommodation:
either in guest houses
or in hotels

Special courses (advanced level only):
Business English
English for Doctors
English for Engineers
English for University Students
English for Teachers
(NEW COURSE)

a Answer the following questions on the Bristol School:
1. When did the school start to offer English courses?
2. How many students can attend the school?
3. If you went to this school, what would the teachers do first?
4. What do the course fees include?
5. Where do the students live when they attend this school?
6. What will the students do in the afternoon?
7. Do you have to be very good at English to attend this school?
8. What did the school introduce 5 years ago?

b Rewrite the London School brochure in full sentences.

c Which school do you think Melanie chooses? Give reasons.

A UNIT 15

2 On the first day at the language school in Bristol, the teacher is asking the students some general questions in order to find out which courses are best for them.

Teacher: Melanie, I see you're training to be an office worker in Frankfurt, aren't you?
Melanie: Yes, I am.
Teacher: Björn, you've trained to be a male nurse, haven't you?
Björn: Yes, I have.
Teacher: You'll only be here for two weeks to learn general English, won't you, Suburo?
Suburo: Yes, I will. I must be back in Tokyo in two weeks.
Teacher: Gabriela, you want to write for a newspaper in Rio, don't you?
Gabriela: Yes, I do.
Teacher: Kahraman, I see you trained to be a car mechanic in Istanbul. You didn't have English then, did you?
Kahraman: No, I didn't.

a True or false?
1 Melanie is training to be an office worker, isn't she?
2 Björn has already studied medicine, hasn't he?
3 Suburo won't be at the school in a month, will he?
4 Gabriela wants to study engineering, doesn't she?
5 Kahraman learnt some technical English at school, didn't he?

b Find the missing question tags. Then answer the questions.
Gabriela comes from South America, ①?
Björn hasn't worked in a hospital yet, ②?
Melanie isn't French, ③?
Kahraman learnt English at work, ④?
Suburo won't be in Europe in two weeks, ⑤?
The students have come from all over the world, ⑥?
Gabriela, you aren't training to be a film star, ⑦?
Melanie, you have already learnt some English in Germany, ⑧?

c Which special courses do you think the students are taking at the school?

3

REGISTRATION FORM

Family name Mr/Mrs/**Ms** _Schmidt_
First name(s) _Melanie_
Nationality _German_
Course dates From _1st Aug_ to _14th Aug_
Address in Britain _39 Denny Road, Bristol_
Tel. no. _79008_
Profession _trainee office worker_
How long have you studied English? _6 years_
Have you taken the Cambridge English exam?   YES ☐   NO ☑
Have you been to Britain before?   YES ☐   NO ☑
Where will you need English in future? _in the office_
Will you buy your own books for the course?   YES ☐   NO ☑
How will you pay for the course?   by cheque ☐   by credit card ☐   in cash ☑

UNIT 15 A

The teacher is talking to Melanie. He is checking her English so that he can put her in a suitable course.

Teacher: You're Melanie Schmidt from Germany, aren't you?
Melanie: Yes, I am.
Teacher: You're training to be an office worker, aren't you?
Melanie: Yes, that's right.
Teacher: And you've studied English for 6 years, haven't you?
Melanie: Yes, I have.
Teacher: You'll need English in your future job, won't you?
Melanie: Yes. That's why I want to do this course.

a Now you are the teacher. Ask Melanie some more questions. The registration form on page 64 will help you.

b Here is some information from the registration forms of two students.

Ms Michiko Tanaka
Japan
1st August to 30th August
29 Clifton Road
trainee nurse
9 years
no Cambridge exam
never
in the hospital
own books
by credit card

Mr John Mgabi
Nigeria
1st August to 21st August
15 Bath Street
trainee computer operator
12 years
Cambridge exam
three times
in his job
own books
by cheque

Ask these two people similar questions.

4 Some interesting facts about the English language

a Listen to the cassette and find out the correct information.

1 Over 25/250 million people use English as their mother tongue in the world today.
2 People speak about 4,000/14,000 words an hour in normal conversations.
3 A person can read 14,000/40,000 words an hour at normal speed.
4 The word 'kiosk' comes from Swedish/Turkish.
5 The word 'sherry' came from a wrong pronunciation of the Danish/Spanish word 'Jerez'.
6 The Normans introduced a lot of Spanish/French words into the English language.
7 William Shakespeare, the famous English poet, used more than 1,500/15,000 different words in his dramas.
8 British people use about 1,000/10,000 different words in normal everyday conversations.

b Now work with your partner and discuss the facts.

▶ Over 250 million people use English as their mother tongue in the world today, don't they? That's right./No, ...

B UNIT 15

1 While Melanie is at the language school, she is staying with a West Indian family. Mr Marley left his home in Jamaica in the 1950s in order to work in Britain. Melanie is talking to him about his experiences in Britain.

Melanie: You know, I can understand the language here much better now than when I first arrived. We learn English at school but here in England it sounds quite different.

Mr Marley: Yes, we had the same problem when we first came here. Of course, we spoke English in Jamaica – if we hadn't spoken English, it would have been even harder for us here in the beginning. But our dialect was quite different to the one they speak here in Bristol.

Melanie: Why do people speak English in Jamaica?

Mr Marley: Well, you see the British took people from Africa to work in the West Indies as slaves. If they hadn't done that, these people would never have spoken English. Gradually, the West Indian slaves lost their African culture and became influenced by the British culture. They also developed their own dialects of English.

Melanie: But at least you could speak English when you came to Britain.

Mr Marley: Of course, but even then, it wasn't easy for our new neighbours. They couldn't understand us at all at first. But they were very patient. If they hadn't been so patient, we would have felt very isolated. We were lucky. However, some British people don't like the way we immigrants speak. They think that Black English isn't as good as standard English.

Melanie: Do you miss Jamaica?

Mr Marley: Of course, the sun especially. But if we had stayed there, we wouldn't have had the same opportunities. I probably wouldn't have got such a good job if we hadn't moved here. And we West Indians try to keep some of our own traditions even in Britain, like the Carnival every year in Notting Hill in London.

Melanie: I'm glad I'm staying with you. If the school had sent me to another family, I wouldn't have learnt as much. I expect I would still think that the British all drink tea at four and speak with an Oxford accent.

a Something is wrong with these sentences. Can you correct them?

1. Melanie still finds it difficult to understand the way the British speak English.
2. The Jamaican dialect and the Bristol dialect are almost the same.
3. As a child Mr Marley did not speak English.
4. The British took African slaves to the West Indies in order to teach them English.
5. The Marleys did not get to know their British neighbours because they did not understand them.
6. All British people are as friendly as the Marleys' neighbours.
7. The Marleys like Britain because it is so sunny.
8. There are better opportunities to get a good job in Jamaica.
9. Melanie would have liked to stay with another family.
10. Melanie believes that all the British drink tea at four.

UNIT 15 B

b Find the correct pairs.

1 If the Marleys hadn't spoken a dialect, 2 If Mr Marley hadn't wanted a good job, 3 If Mr Marley had stayed in Jamaica, 4 If there hadn't been a slave trade, 5 If the Marleys had had unfriendly neighbours, 6 If Melanie had stayed in a hotel,	he wouldn't have left Jamaica. it would have been harder for them to live in Britain. people in the West Indies wouldn't have begun to speak English. she wouldn't have learnt so much about immigrant dialects. it would have been easier for them when they arrived. he would have enjoyed better weather.

c Make sentences with 'if'.

▶ Melanie wanted to learn more English and so she went to a language school.
If she hadn't wanted to learn more English, she wouldn't have gone to a language school.

▶ Melanie's English wasn't good enough for her office job, that's why she needed a course in Business English.
If her English had been good enough for her office job, she wouldn't have needed a course in Business English.

1 She went to a language school in Bristol, that's how she met the Marleys.
2 She didn't learn all her English vocabulary and so she didn't get a good mark in the first test.
3 She talked to Mr Marley, that's how she learnt about West Indian history.
4 She missed the bus on Monday and so she didn't get to school on time.
5 She didn't want to go back home after the end of the course, that's why she stayed another week.
6 She talked to people from Bristol as often as possible and so she improved her English quickly.

2 Here is an example of an immigrant dialect. It is a West Indian dialect, which is well known from reggae music.

Inglan is a bitch
by Linton Kwesi Johnson

w'en mi jus' come to Landan toun
mi use to work pan di andahgroun
but workin' pan di andahgroun
y'u don't get fi know your way aroun'

Inglan is a bitch
dere's no escapin' it
Inglan is a bitch
dere's no runnin' whey fram it

well mi dhu day wok an' mi dhu nite wok
mi dhu clean wok an' mi dhu dutty wok
dem sey dat black man is very lazy
but if y'u si how mi wok y'u woulda sey mi crazy

In standard English, this is what the first verse says:

When I had just come to London town
I used to work on the underground
but working on the underground
you don't get to know your way around.

a Can you translate the rest of the poem into standard English? You can use the words in the box.

I	escaping	away	England	do
there	running	work	they	
	dirty	night	would	
say	from	you	that	see

b Now answer the following questions:

1 What was Linton Kwesi Johnson's first job?
2 Does he like Britain?
3 How does he describe the different kinds of work?
4 How do some British people describe Black people?
5 Does Linton Kwesi Johnson agree with this view of Black people?

UNIT 15

1 American English

When you visit America for the first time, you may get confused by some American words even if your English is quite good.

a Do you know what these signs mean?

b Here are some more American words you may come across in the States. Do you know what they mean? Ask your partner. If you can't decide, you can use the definitions in the box.

1 avgas   4 fish story
2 busboy   5 night letter
3 dirt farmer 6 rock pig

> a story which is hard to believe
> a fan of rock music, especially of heavy metal
> aviation gasoline (petrol for aeroplanes)
> a farmer who works his own land
> a waiter's assistant in a restaurant, who clears tables, brings water etc
> a telegram which is sent at night for delivery the next day at a cheaper rate than a regular telegram

2 Traveling in the States

Melanie Schmidt from Frankfurt is visiting the United States for the first time. Melanie's American friend Cathy has just welcomed her:

Melanie: How great to be in New York at last!
Cathy: Yeah, New York is really fantastic.
Melanie: Where do we go first, Cathy? I've got all this luggage with me.
Cathy: With all that baggage we'd better drive downtown first and find a hotel for the night.
Melanie: OK, Cathy.
Cathy: But before we get onto the freeway, we'll have to get some gas.

Melanie: Let me try my English on the receptionist.
Cathy: Right. You talk to the front clerk. I'll go to the restroom in the meantime.
Melanie: OK, if you're tired. See you later ... Have you got two rooms with a bath, if possible, on the first floor?
Receptionist: I'm sorry. Our restaurant is on the first floor. I can only offer you rooms with a bath on the second floor. But we have an elevator.
Melanie: But the restaurant is over there!
Receptionist: I'm sorry, it seems a little complicated, miss. What we call the first floor is called ground floor in British English, I think.
Melanie: I see. So we have to take the lift.
Receptionist: Right. – What's your last name, miss?
Melanie: My surname's Schmidt.

Cathy: What would you like to have?
Melanie: I'm not very hungry, I'll just have some chips.
Cathy: French fries for my friend and a hamburger for me, please. – Anything to drink?
Melanie: A coke, please.
Cathy: A can of coke and a tomato juice. – What are you going to do in your vacation here, Melanie?
Melanie: Well, when I'm on holiday, I really like to relax for a while.
Cathy: I've gotten us two tickets for the movie theater tonight. They're showing the brand-new Dustin Hoffman movie, you know.
Melanie: A film would be all right. No more sightseeing for today, please.
Cathy: OK. I'm going to get us some candy before we go there.

UNIT 15 C

a Answer these questions:
1 Where do the three dialogues take place?
2 Why is it sometimes difficult for Melanie to understand Americans?

b Can you find the American expressions for these words?
1 luggage
2 receptionist
3 ground floor
4 first floor
5 lift
6 surname
7 chips
8 holidays
9 film

c Can you find the British expressions for these words?
1 downtown
2 freeway
3 gas
4 restroom
5 I've gotten
6 movie theater
7 candy

d What is the American spelling of these British words?
1 theatre
2 centre
3 labour
4 neighbour
5 colour
6 travelling

e Listen to the cassette again. How do Americans pronounce these words?
1 New York
2 bath
3 floor
4 last
5 tomato
6 better
7 clerk
8 complicated
9 going to

3 After two weeks Melanie has learnt a lot of American English. So she writes a letter to her old English teacher in Frankfurt, and she uses all the new American expressions.

Rewrite this letter in British English.
Replace the underlined expressions.
Then translate the letter into German.

6/20/90

Dear Mr Rosenkranz

Greetings from America! I must say I've really enjoyed my <u>vacation</u> here in the US. I've seen many places and I've tried so many things here: the <u>railroads</u>, the <u>subways</u> and the <u>freeways</u>. I even rented <u>an automobile</u> for some days in order to see the Grand Canyon. I stayed at a motel for one night and then I took a flight along the Colorado River early in the morning. The <u>colors</u> of the canyon are spectacular! But of course, the trip was quite expensive so I was glad I had my <u>traveler's checks</u> with me. Soon my stay here will be over. Yesterday I went <u>downtown</u> L.A., where I bought some souvenirs at the local <u>stores</u>. You'd be surprised to see what I've <u>gotten</u> for you. Tuesday night I'm <u>gonna</u> check in at the airport. I hope I'll manage to take all the <u>baggage</u> with me.

Yours,
Melanie Schmidt

4 Here are some American advertisements. Explain what they mean.

The Old General Store
Gateway Candies
All your favorites to choose

Houses 4 sale
U come by
Downtown L.A.
5 Park Lane

● **Tonite!** ●
Burger &
French Fries
only 99c
at Linda's Place

Free Movie with this ad!
Mon thru Fri
until Aug. 5
VIDEO CENTER

UNIT 15

1

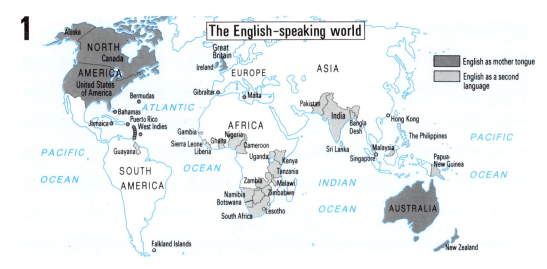

1 In which countries is English spoken as a first language?
2 On which continents is English spoken as a first or second language?
3 In some African countries and in some Asian countries (e.g. India), there are many groups of people who speak different languages. Why do they speak English as a second (or official) language?
4 About 500 million people can also speak English as a foreign language. Why do you think they have learnt it?

2 English all over the world

Nowadays, more and more people are travelling to other countries, either for business or pleasure. A lot of these people agree that English is very useful in their travels. As Jasper Bürli from Switzerland, who is employed as an engineer, points out, "some people don't like the idea, but the fact is that English has become the world language, hasn't it? I've travelled all over the world – in the African bush and in the Malaysian jungle, but English has always been very helpful. I need it for my work and to talk to the locals. In my opinion, that's the main argument for learning it."

Or, as Nadine Dufrais, a French girl who has started her own business, making and importing jewellery, puts it, "I was hopeless at English at school, but if I hadn't learnt it, I would never have been able to start this business. You can't learn every foreign language, can you? But in a lot of places you can get by with English."

Gabi Müller from West Germany agrees with her. Gabi, a waitress in a hotel in the Philippines, was unemployed after she had finished school, so she decided to go abroad to find employment. "Lots of languages borrow words from English", she says. "In Malaysia, when I saw the sign 'teksi', I knew straight away what it was. Or in Thailand, when I needed toothpaste, I asked for colgate – that's what they call all makes of toothpaste. Here in the Philippines, it's even more interesting. They completely mix up two languages, their own and English."

Gabi is quite right. In the Philippines it is not unusual to hear everybody, not only businessmen or engineers, talk in English. They do this because there are over 80 dialects of their own language. So people from different parts of the country often cannot understand one another. English, which was introduced to them after the Second World War by the Americans, was a good way of solving this problem. Sometimes you may hear one person say something in Tagalog, the main Philippine dialect, and another person answer in English. Or parts of a sentence are in English and parts are in Tagalog. They call this mixture 'Taglish' and they are proud of it. Some Filipinos even say that theirs is the third-largest English-speaking country in the world, after the US and the UK.

UNIT 15 T

a Answer these questions:

1. Who works as an engineer?
2. Who has been to Malaysia and Thailand?
3. Where did Nadine learn English?
4. Where do they speak 'Taglish'?
5. What kind of language is 'Taglish'?
6. What are the two largest English-speaking countries?
7. Why do most people in the Philippines talk in English?
8. Why did Gabi leave Germany?

b Complete these sentences:

1. If Jasper had not been able to speak English, ...
2. If Nadine had learnt another foreign language instead of English, ...
3. If Gabi had stayed in West Germany, ...
4. If someone had spoken to Gabi in Tagalog, ...
5. If Gabi had not been unemployed, ...
6. If the Americans had not introduced English to the Philippines, ...
7. If there had only been one dialect in the Philippines, ...

c Make as many nouns as possible from the words in the list. You can use the endings in the box.

1. engine
2. wait
3. argue
4. employ
5. busy
6. please
7. mix

-ure
-ness
-ress
-er
-ture
-ment

d Now make as many adjectives as possible from the words in this list. You can use the endings in the box.

1. hope
2. fun
3. use
4. value
5. employ
6. help
7. interest

-y
-ed
-ing
-ful
-less
-able

e Here are some advertisements. Can you find the correct endings for the words in brackets?

1. Experienced (engine) wanted for work on building project in Nigeria.

2. Secretary wanted for top international firm in Manila. Knowledge of word processing (help).

3. Out of work? We can offer (employ) in the computer industry.

4. Tonight at 8.00 p.m. (Interest) adventure film!

5. (Hope) at languages? Our new teaching method guarantees success.

6. (Wait) needed. Four afternoons a week.

3 English on the job

You will find the names of three people in the list below.
You will hear these people talk about their jobs.

Name	Age	Country	Company	Job	Where did they learn English?	What do they need English for?
Nilima Tagore						
Tanizaki Hayato						
Britta Lagerkvist						

a Make a list like this in your exercise book, listen to the cassette and complete the list.

How old are the three people?
Where are they from?
What's their job?

b Listen to the cassette again and complete the rest of your list.

Where did the three people learn English?
What exactly do they need it for?

UNIT 15

Civil engineering

1 What is a civil engineer?

We can see the work of civil engineers everywhere – roads, bridges, tunnels, dams and all kinds of buildings. What must they be able to do? First they have to survey a site. Then they prepare the technical drawings and estimate the total costs of the building or structure. And finally they have to supervise the work. So we can say they must be 'all-rounders'. They must know about mechanical, electrical and chemical engineering. During their training they learn all these things, both in a drawing office and on a building site.

Look at the pictures.
What is the civil engineer doing here?

2 This advertisement appeared in a German newspaper last week.

TECHNICIAN needed
to assist Civil Engineer for West African Project

Requirements: applicants should
- be aged 20–30
- have passed exams at College of Further Education
- have some experience in civil engineering
- have a good knowledge of German and English

We offer:
- 2-year contract (renewable)
- competitive salary
- fringe benefits (flight paid etc.)
- excellent working conditions

Those interested should enclose full personal and career details in English.

Write to   **Mr Clark (Personnel Manager)
Billstone Ltd.
P.O. Box 698, Birmingham, England**

Two Germans want to apply for the job.
Here are some of their details:

```
Jörg Schulte
21
college of F.E.exams
3 years experience in a building firm
good English
single
hobbies:  reading
```

```
Karsten Nölle
29
college exams
5 years experience in an electronic firm
reasonable English
married, 2 children
hobbies:  sports
```

Which one would you choose? Give reasons.

3 Jörg is interested in the technician's job.
Can you write a letter of application for him?

Start your letter like this:	Dear Sir, I would like to apply for the job of technician …
Write your curriculum vitae including:	date and place of birth/status/education/ qualifications/job training and experience/ interests and hobbies/plans for the future
End your letter like this:	Looking forward to hearing from you, Yours faithfully,

UNIT 15 S2

You want to help?

1 This is an advertisement from VSO (Voluntary Service Overseas).

Answer these questions:
1 Who is this VSO advertisement addressed to?
2 How does VSO want to help the Third World?
3 Why do you think the Third World needs this kind of help?

You can give the Third World a lot more than money.

Business and Social
Business Administrators ☐
Small Business Advisers ☐
Architects ☐
Town Planners ☐
Community Workers ☐
Banking Trainers ☐

Health
Doctors ☐
Midwives ☐
Nurses ☐
Nutritionists ☐

Many people want to help the Third World. But not many have the kind of skills and professions which are most needed.
If you want to help and you have the training and experience to work in one of the jobs listed here, please complete and return this form to
Enquiries Unit, VSO, 317 Putney Bridge Road, London SW15 2PN. Tel. 01-780 1331.

VSO
Helping the Third World help itself.

Technical
Builders ☐
Engineers ☐
Mechanics ☐
Technical teachers ☐
Electricians ☐

Education
English teachers ☐
Science teachers ☐
Maths teachers ☐
Teacher trainers ☐

---

2 Nursing in Sri Lanka

Mary O'Brien from Ireland replied to the VSO advertisement. She is now working as a nurse in Sri Lanka.

Mary well remembers the day she set off for Sri Lanka. "Of course I was a bit nervous, I didn't know how it would be to work in a strange country. But I was also excited and happy. You see, it's what I've always wanted to do. Even when I was little, I played nurse to my dolls when they were ill. I bandaged their legs, and I put sticking plaster on their hands.

I had finished my training as a nurse, so I was qualified to do the job and I really wanted the chance to go out and help people. Being a nurse out here is a great challenge because the conditions are tougher than in Ireland. But you get a lot of satisfaction when you know you've really made someone feel better. Of course, the day to day life on the wards is similar. You take the patients' temperature and pulse rates. You give them their medicine or take them for treatment – some have to be X-rayed or have injections. Sometimes on the surgical wards, you have to get a patient ready for an operation. When the doctor or consultant comes, I go round the ward with him or her and make notes of any changes in the treatment.

I enjoy the work here. I have more time to get involved with the patients, and I also train new nurses. So in lots of ways I feel that I am really helping people."

a Look at the text and make a list of the jobs a nurse does.

b Complete these sentences.

   1 After Mary had answered the VSO advertisement, she ...
   2 Mary felt nervous before she left because ...
   3 Although Mary felt nervous, she ...
   4 If Mary hadn't done her training as a nurse in Ireland first, she ...
   5 Mary finds satisfaction in her job because ...
   6 While Mary goes round the wards with the doctor, she ...
   7 Mary not only looks after patients, she ...

c Write a letter of application for one of the jobs listed in the VSO advertisement. For details of how to write your letter, look at page 72.

UNIT 15

Women in Business

THE WOMAN'S INTERNATIONAL MONTHLY MAGAZINE

Go into Europe with a B.A.P.

**Are you a secretary?
Are you an office worker?
Do you want to reach
a better position
in business?**

If your answer is "yes", then you could be a candidate for our "High Flyer Competition Of The Year".

The prize is a place on the 10-month Business Administration Programme (B.A.P.) at LeClerk Business School in Paris, France. A B.A.P. can be the key to a better business position.

There is a lot of competition for places on its courses, and the degree is even more important today in the single European market. Companies will need an international outlook more than ever before.

We want to help more women reach better business posts and realize what they are really able to do. That is why we will pay the winner's full course fees, plus living expenses during the course – a package worth £18,000.

The course is intensive and there will be plenty of hard work. It is highly practical: You will learn to address customers from abroad, to plan and organize meetings, to establish international business connections and to set up business contracts. Students come from all over the world and work groups have to learn the special difficulties (and advantages) of working together with different nationalities and cultures.

But it is not all work, there is plenty of fun, too, with an active social life and the Eiffel Tower only half an hour away.

English is the main language used on the programme and you will need a good knowledge of it. You must also have done professional training, and you should have three to five years' work experience.

For these reasons, and as we want to promote young women, applicants must be aged between 23 and 35.

---

a Answer the following questions:

1. Why are they looking for women in this article?
2. What qualifications must the applicants have?
3. What is the prize?
4. What can people learn at the business school?
5. Why is English important at the school?
6. Why do you think English is important in the European market?

b Jessica Schilling is interested in the B.A.P. competition.
Write a letter of application for her.
For details of how to write your letter, look at page 72.
Use the following prompts:

Address:	Lange Str. 55, 5000 Köln
Age:	25
Qualifications:	3 years' trainee office worker in an industrial firm
	3 years' experience in the sales department
Languages:	good knowledge of German and English, a little French
Hobbies:	reading, tennis
Future plans:	work abroad
	get to know other people and countries

UNIT 15 G

Question tags

Frageanhängsel sind kurze Fragen, die an das Ende eines Aussagesatzes angehängt werden.
Sie werden im Deutschen zum Beispiel mit „nicht?", „oder?", „nicht wahr?" wiedergegeben.

You're training to be an office worker, **aren't you**? Michaela **can** speak English, **can't she**? Björn **has** already studied medicine, **hasn't he**?	Im Frageanhängsel wird das Hilfsverb des Aussagesatzes wieder aufgenommen. Im bejahten Aussagesatz wird das Frageanhängsel verneint.
Gabi, you **want** to write for a newspaper, **don't you**? Suburo **trained** to be a mechanic, **didn't he**?	Enthält der Aussagesatz kein Hilfsverb, wird mit einer Form von *do* umschrieben.
You **won't** forget your school report, **will you**? The school **isn't** far from Oxford Street, **is it**? The school **doesn't** offer Medical English, **does it**?	Im verneinten Aussagesatz wird das Frageanhängsel bejaht.

Conditional sentences (III)

if-Sätze drücken Bedingungen aus.

if-Teil	Hauptsatz
If Mr Marley **had stayed** in Jamaica, If Melanie **hadn't gone** to Britain,	he **would have enjoyed** better weather. she **wouldn't have met** Mr Marley.
Past Perfect	*would have* + Partizip Perfekt

Für den Sprecher ist das Gesagte nicht mehr erfüllbar, da es sich auf die abgeschlossene Vergangenheit bezieht. Er betont, daß es sich um rein theoretische Überlegungen handelt.

American and British English

Unterschiedliche Schreibung/Formbildung:

American English	British English
trave**l**ing cent**er**, theat**er** col**o**r, lab**o**r, neighb**o**r dial**og** progra**m**	trave**ll**ing cent**re**, theat**re** col**ou**r, lab**ou**r, neighb**ou**r dial**ogue** progra**mme**
(to) get, got, **gotten**	(to) get, got, **got**

Welche Schreibung in der internationalen Geschäftssprache angewandt wird, hängt häufig von wirtschaftlichen, politischen und kulturellen Bindungen einzelner Länder zu den USA oder Großbritannien ab.
In der Computerfachsprache hat sich z.B. die amerikanische Schreibung von *program* weltweit – auch im britischen Englisch – durchgesetzt.

Unterschiedlicher Wortschatzgebrauch:

American English	British English
apartment	flat
check	bill
fall	autumn
smart	clever
store	shop
subway	underground

REVISION 3
Unit 11

61 Put the following sentences into the passive.

The customs officer talks about these problems:

1. Every day people break the rules.
2. They do not declare the goods properly.
3. They bring in plants.
4. They even smuggle in dogs.
5. They import too much alcohol.

But the officers are well trained:

6. They do not accept wrong information.
7. They make spot checks.*
8. They open handbags.
9. They unpack a lot of parcels.
10. They check most of the luggage.
11. They arrest people with explosives.

*spot checks = Stichproben

62 Here are some things which happened at the port of Lagos yesterday. Write complete passive sentences.

1. Coffee/load/onto a German ship.
2. Electronic equipment/take/through customs.
3. A blue container/drop/into the sea.
4. Diplomats from Britain/not check/ at the customs.
5. Fresh fish/sell/on the docks/in the morning.
6. One warehouse/not lock/in the evening.
7. Crates/put/onto lorries.
8. A British ship with chemical waste/not unload.
9. Containers from Switzerland/take/to a special area.
10. Lorries which were too heavy/not stop.
11. A drunken tanker captain/arrest.

63 Look at some of the things which are normally done in an office. Can they be done by the cleaners or should they be done by the secretaries?

1. collect waste paper
2. read the telexes
3. check the automatic answering machine
4. clean the carpets
5. switch on the computers

Which of the following things can be done by the repairmen and which have to be done by the office staff?

6. fix broken windows
7. order goods
8. set the correct heating temperature
9. arrange meetings with foreign visitors
10. fit new light switches
11. check import papers from other firms

Now say what shouldn't be done by the cleaners and the repairmen because it's not their job.

64 During a talk on cotton production and the manufacturing of textiles, a shopkeeper was asked a lot of questions. Here are the answers. What were the questions? Ask for the words in **bold type**. Use the interrogative pronouns in the box.

where	what
when	how
where	why

1. **40 years ago** cotton was picked by hand.
2. Today it is picked **by machines**.
3. **Clothes** cannot be imported duty-free into Britain.
4. A lot of clothes are made **in Asia**.
5. Our textile industry should be protected **because of unemployment**.
6. Most clothes are designed **in Britain**.

65 Gordon Walker, the managing director of Canned Food Ltd, is worried about his firm.

1. "We work day and night, but our profits are going down all the time."
2. "I'm in my office 24 hours a day, but I don't get the results I want."
3. "How can I change our situation?"
4. "I must get the answers to a few questions and then everything will be OK."
5. "Why can our competitors sell their fruit more cheaply?"
6. "Where did they buy their fruit?"
7. "Why didn't they transport it to Britain by plane?"
8. "Should Canned Food Ltd reduce its prices to sell more?"
9. "Have other firms had the same problems as we are having at present?"
10. "I'm sure we'll be in a better position when we have found the answers."

Report what Gordon Walker says about himself and his firm and what he wants to know.

Unit 12

REVISION 3

66 CANDY Ltd, a chocolate factory, wants to introduce robots.
The workers at CANDY's are worried. Here is one of them:

1 "I work at CANDY's."
2 "I'm married and I have two children."
3 "If they introduce these new robots, I'll probably lose my job."
4 "As my wife doesn't go out to work, we'll have no money at all."
5 "But the managers can't be very clever."
6 "Somebody tells them they'll make more profits and so they want to buy robots."
7 "Of course, robots aren't men so they won't go on strike, but they are made by men and so they'll break down."

Report what the worker said about himself and CANDY Ltd.

67 Tina Lesmy, a shop-steward at CANDY's, asked the managers some questions in a letter to them.

1 "How many workers does one robot replace?"
2 "How many workers will become redundant?"
3 "Are there any plans for the people who will become redundant?"
4 "What is your experience with robots?"
5 "Do you have contacts with firms which have robots?"
6 "When can we have a general meeting with you?"
7 "Will production increase after the installation of robots?"
8 "Why don't you show any interest in your workers' future?"
9 "Will work be easier with robots?"

Report what Tina wanted to know.

68 Linda, new in town, asked Joe a few questions at a local disco.

1 "Are there any good pubs here?"
2 "Is there a leisure centre here?"
3 "Have you got a car?"
4 "Will you come here again tomorrow?"
5 "Can you pick me up for work?"
6 "Where do you buy your clothes?"
7 "Do you like working at CANDY's?"
8 "Do you go to local football matches?"

In his answers Joe said that
– he went every Saturday.
– he could.
– he had.
– there were.
– he bought them at LEWIS's.
– he wouldn't.
– there wasn't.
– he did.

Can you match Linda's questions with Joe's answers?

69 Put in the correct relative pronouns.

Brenda and Hilda want to open a CD shop. Brenda, ① is older than Hilda, is very optimistic. Hilda, ② parents are completely against the idea, wants to start as soon as possible. They would like to rent the small shop on Drake Street, ③ owner has just retired. The price of £400 a month, ④ he is asking, is very high and his wife, ⑤ only interest seems to be money, wants even more. The girls, ⑥ dream could come true if they had the shop, have decided to fight for it. They really want to get into the CD market, ⑦ promises to be interesting.

70 Scunthorpe, a town in the north of England, is heading for a good future after years of problems.
Join the following sentences with relative pronouns:

1 Scunthorpe is getting back on its feet. Its population is about 62,000.
2 In the late 70s and early 80s, about 13,000 people lost their jobs. They had worked in the steelworks.
3 In the late 80s, new high-tech firms came to Scunthorpe. Its offer of cheap building sites was very attractive.
4 Then the job situation got better. It had been one of the worst in England.
5 The unemployment rate fell by half. It had been 18% in 1983.
6 The new economic development has had a lot of positive effects. They can be seen everywhere.

REVISION 3

Unit 13

71 A lot of things went wrong at the Cleveland Youth Club last year.

1. They didn't provide snacks in the evening.
2. They closed the club at 6 o'clock in the evening.
3. They didn't hold general meetings.
4. They didn't elect a chairman.
5. They didn't invite pop groups.
6. They didn't organize dances.
7. They let adults in.
8. They sold alcoholic drinks.
9. They didn't charge membership fees.

But next year everything will be changed.
▶ In the evening snacks ...

72 Mickey Gladowsky and his wife Jane have just moved into an old house. A lot of things haven't been done for a long time. Mickey and Jane are discussing what to do first.

We should
– cut the grass in the garden because it ① for ages.
– water the plants in front of the house because they ② since Friday.
– renew the roof insulation because ③ since 1972.
– paint the ceilings because ④ for years.
– insulate the pipes because ⑤ since 1920.
– clean the stove because ⑥ for a long time.
– paper the walls because ⑦ since George Washington's times.

Complete the sentences and fill in the correct form of the verb (Present Perfect passive).

73 Here are parts of a conversation.
Rewrite the sentences and express the same meaning.
Join the sentences with 'although', 'in order to', 'so that', 'because' and leave out the words in **bold type**.

1. "You'll have to wash your shoes with water. **Then** they'll look clean again."
2. "We'll have to do sports **if we want** to lose weight."
3. "He had an accident. **The reason**? He had drunk too much."
4. "Turn round. **Then** I can see your face."
5. "They couldn't start their car. **But think**: they had worked all day on it."
6. "You must come earlier **if you want** to get something to eat."

74 How does the speaker go on?
Complete the sentences with 'it' or 'they' and fill in the correct form of the verb.

Look at	her hair. her trousers.	① ②	(be) too long.
Listen to	this information. these statements. his advice. the news.	③ ④ ⑤ ⑥	(be) interesting.
Let's buy	some fruit. some vegetables. some food.	⑦ ⑧ ⑨	(look) nice.
Don't stare at	my jeans. my clothes. my skirt.	⑩ ⑪ ⑫	(be) clean.

222 two hundred and twenty-two

Unit 14

REVISION 3

75 Mike Rollerson from Illinois, employed by ANCHORAGE OIL,
planned to rent an old house in Anchorage.
But before he decided to move into the house, he wanted to talk
to the owners and to the oil company about some problems.
These were his ideas:

1 The oil company should pay part of the rent. (expect)
2 The owners should fill the gaps around the doors and windows. (want)
3 The owners should put in a modern heating system. (advise)
4 The owners should improve the insulation of the walls. (persuade)
5 The owners should lag the pipes. (want)
6 His employers should take over all future repairs. (expect)

Write about Mike's ideas.
Use the verbs in brackets.

▶ The oil company should help me. (expect)
He expected the oil company ...

76 Work on the oilfields in Alaska is very dangerous.
Mike Curruthers, assistant manager at ANCHORAGE OIL,
has written down some rules to tell workers what to do or not to do.

1 Anybody who works outside must wear gloves and cover his face.
2 Gloves which are worn on the sites should be padded*.
3 Leaks which are discovered on the pipelines must be reported as soon as possible.
4 Emergency crews who go out to deal with leaks should be in radio contact with the management.
5 Controllers who monitor the pipelines should check their equipment regularly.
6 Crews who are called out on an emergency must inform the stand-by crews.

Use participle constructions to shorten the sentences.

* padded = gepolstert

77 Later at night Curruthers is watching the local news on TV.
Here are the headlines:

1 Workers selling alcohol to Eskimos will be sent home.
2 Eskimos don't show interest in jobs offered by oil company.
3 Helicopters transporting emergency crews will work day and night.
4 ANCHORAGE OIL spokesman announces cheaper rates for oil transported by ship.
5 "Language spoken by Eskimos will disappear", says Dr. David B. Turner of New York University.
6 Sheriff warns of fish caught near Anchorage.

Rewrite the headlines. Use relative clauses.

78 In a TV interview Michael Henderson asked Fiona Watnik,
project manager at ALTERNATIVE ENERGIES INC., about her work.

M.: **I've heard about your new tidal energy project** in the Bay of Fundy. Have you already started?
F.: Started to build? No. But **we've finished our preparations**.
M.: What preparations?
F.: Well, **we've worked out the exact costs** and – very important – **we've managed to get the support of a lot of people in Canada** and near the Bay of Fundy.
M.: Really? **Weren't most people against it?**
F.: **At first it appeared so, but in May they had a discussion on TV. There the Energy Minister and the Mayor of Truro supported the project.**
M.: Hm, **that's new. What reasons did they give for their support**?
F.: Well, **the Minister didn't see any other way to produce alternative energy and the Mayor was happy about the new jobs which we promised**.
M.: **Was anybody against the project?**
F.: Yeah, a local resident, a certain Mr James. But listen, **didn't you watch the discussion**?
M.: **No, I didn't. I was in Europe in May.** So, **what arguments did he use**?
F.: **He spoke about the negative effects of the project on the wildlife** ...

Report the conversation.
Use only the sentences in **bold type**.

REVISION 3

Unit 15

79 Match the question tags in the box with the sentences.

You don't like a watch squeaking at you, ①?
They've got a Harakiri jeep, ②?
I'm not interested in advertising, ③?
We saw the commercials on TV, ④?
You won't forget our meeting, ⑤?
A slogan should be short and catchy, ⑥?
Headlines can be shortened, ⑦?
The artist will bring the illustrations tomorrow, ⑧?
Ms Walker wasn't at the product presentation, ⑨?
Princess Di has got a nice pair of jeans, ⑩?
Allen doesn't work at the advertising agency any more, ⑪?
You always have an egg for breakfast, ⑫?

```
            can't they
am I                    do you
            don't you
            didn't we
does he                 was she
            hasn't she
            haven't they
will you                won't she
            shouldn't it
```

80 Mrs Wagner from MRS WAGNER'S PIES is not happy about the advertisement which an advertising agency has produced for her firm. She is complaining to the manager. What would have happened if ...? Put in the correct form of the verbs in brackets.

1 If you had produced a better ad, we (sell) more pies.
2 If you (use) our logo, the readers would have recognized the product easily.
3 The readers (remember) our product if you had found a better slogan.
4 More people would have read the body copy if the headline (be) shorter.
5 If the body copy (give) more details about the product, it (be) more informative.
6 If you (use) a more interesting visual, more readers (look) at the ad.
7 If you (use) a photo, the ad (not be) so boring.
8 You (not make) so many mistakes if you (listen) to me.

The manager replies:
9 If you (pay) us in dollars instead of pies, we (produce) a better ad.

81

> **Advice to consumers**
> 1 If you compare prices, you will find the cheapest product.
> 2 You will save a lot of money if you go to the sales.
> 3 If you work out the unit price, you won't pay too much.
> 4 You will see a lot of bargains if you look in discount shops.
> 5 You won't make a mistake if you get information about different products.
> 6 If you read WHICH, you won't buy bad products.

Mr Bloomer didn't know about this WHICH brochure so he got everything wrong. If he had read it, he would have got everything right.

▶ If he had compared prices, he ...

Ms Craft had the brochure so she got everything right. If she hadn't read the brochure, she wouldn't have got everything right.

▶ If she hadn't compared prices, she ...

82 Put in the correct form of the verbs in brackets.

Every day people (buy) lots of things they (not need). Who really (need) an electric toothbrush, for example? It is the job of advertising agencies to make us believe that we (want) certain products.
That is why at this very moment they (try) to "create" new markets. At the same time, they (make up) ads and commercials for new products.
People (sell) things for a long, long time and they (advertise) for almost as long. Thousands of years ago, people (begin) to make more things than they (need) for themselves. They also (see) that it (be) more effective for one person to do the farming and another to make the bread and so on. And of course they (want) to sell their products. So what (do) they then? Well, after the baker (make) the bread, he (put) a sign outside the door to show he had bread for sale. And so advertising (be born).
Today a lot of people (be) against advertising. But advertising (have) its good points. Take our towns, for example. They would look very boring if we (not have) colourful advertising. And we (not have) any information about different products if there (be) no ads. As a well-known slogan goes: "If they don't know it, they (not buy) it."

224 two hundred and twenty-four

Units 11–15

REVISION 3   R

83 Students at the Bristol School of English are talking to each other.
Fill in the correct form of the verbs.

– Giorgio, are you going to stay with an English family?
– Yes, I am. If (1 not stay) with an English family, I won't learn as much.

– Peter, do you always do your homework?
– No, not really. I wouldn't have any time to go out if I (2 do).

– Nadine, did you register for the Business English class?
– Yes, I did. If I hadn't taken Business English, my firm (3 not offer) to pay for the course.

– Does Nicole want to take the test?
– Yes, she does. If she doesn't take the test, she (4 not be able to) get a certificate.

– Did Olaf pass his exams?
– No, I don't think he did. He's still at the school. If he (5 pass) his exams, he (6 go home) yesterday.

– Did Jean-Pierre really stay up until three o'clock this morning?
– I don't know. But I think he did. He (7 be on time) for the course this morning if he (8 not get home) so late.

84 Pierre, a student at the Bristol School of English, has prepared a talk on the English language. Here are the most important sentences from his notes:

Some historical facts about Britain and the English language:
1 In the 6th and 7th centuries, the Angles* and the Saxons** brought Germanic dialects to Britain.
2 The Normans introduced French as an official language in the 11th century.
3 In the 13th century English dialects replaced French again.

English today:
4 Most former English colonies use English as an official language.
5 All over the world, schools teach English as the first foreign language.
6 You can hear English all over the world.

Where I can see dangers:
7 People will not speak native languages any more.
8 The English language will also influence the way of life of many nations.

Reactions by other nations or ethnic groups:
9 In some French dictionaries they don't list English expressions.
10 According to Hispanics in the US, states with many Hispanics should introduce Spanish as a second official language.

Put the sentences into the passive.

*Angles = Angeln
**Saxons = Sachsen

85 During his language course at the Bristol school of English, Peter from Hamburg stayed with a local family. Here is part of a conversation he had with Mrs Fletcher, his British host.

1 Mrs Fletcher: "Peter, have you ever been to America?"
2 Peter: "Yes, I have. I was there three years ago and I liked it very much."
3 Mrs Fletcher: "Didn't you have any difficulties with their language?"
4 Peter: "I didn't have too much trouble. I was in Boston and there the grammar and the pronunciation don't seem to be much different from the British English I learnt at school."
5 Mrs Fletcher: "But aren't some of the words different?"
6 Peter: "Sure they are. I once had a funny problem with one word. I only had it though because my native language is German."
7 Mrs Fletcher: "Tell me about it, please."
8 Peter: "OK. I wanted to put my case away. My American host told me to put it in the closet in the bedroom. It took me hours before I realized that he didn't mean the toilet but the built-in wardrobe. But can I put one question to you in American English? Maybe you'll find the right answer."
9 Mrs Fletcher: "Go ahead."
10 Peter: "Where can I wash my hands, please?"
11 Mrs Fletcher: "Oh, I see what you mean. You want the toilet."
12 Peter: "That's right. In Boston people always asked this question when they wanted to go to the toilet."

Now report their conversation.

two hundred and twenty five   225

VOCABULARY

Basic vocabulary · Grundwortschatz

A

a, an	ein(e)
able	fähig
about	herum; hinsichtlich
above	oberhalb
accident	Unfall
across	(quer) über
(to) act	handeln
address	Adresse
aeroplane	Flugzeug
afraid	ängstlich
(to) be afraid	Angst haben, sich fürchten
after	nach
afternoon	Nachmittag
again	wieder
against	gegen
age	Alter
ago	vor
(to) agree	übereinstimmen
air	Luft
airport	Flughafen
all	alle(s); ganz
almost	fast, beinahe
alone	allein
along	entlang
already	schon
also	auch
although	obwohl
always	immer
among	zwischen, unter
and	und
angry	wütend
animal	Tier
another	noch ein(e); ein(e) andere(r, s)
answer	Antwort
(to) answer	(be)antworten
any	irgendeine(r, s)
anybody	irgend jemand
anyone	irgend jemand
anything	irgend etwas
(to) appear	(er)scheinen
apple	Apfel
arm	Arm
around	herum; um; ungefähr
(to) arrive	ankommen
as	wie; da; als
(to) ask	fragen
at	an; auf; bei; in; zu
attention	Aufmerksamkeit
aunt	Tante
autumn	Herbst
away	weg
awful	furchtbar

B

baby	Baby, Kleinkind
back	Rücken; zurück
bad	schlecht; schlimm
bag	Tüte; Tasche
(to) bake	backen
baker	Bäcker(in)
ball	Ball
bank	Bank (Geldinstitut)
bath	Bad
bathroom	Badezimmer
(to) be	sein
beautiful	schön
because	weil
(to) become	werden
bed	Bett
bedroom	Schlafzimmer
before	bevor, ehe
(to) begin	beginnen
behind	hinter
(to) believe	glauben
(to) belong	gehören
between	zwischen
bicycle	Fahrrad
big	groß
bike	Fahrrad
bill	Rechnung
bird	Vogel
birthday	Geburtstag
bit	Stückchen
black	schwarz
blackboard	(Wand)tafel
blood	Blut
blue	blau
board	Brett
boat	Boot
body	Körper
(to) boil	kochen
book	Buch
(to) book	buchen
born	geboren
boss	Chef
both	beide
bottle	Flasche
bottom	Boden
box	Schachtel, Karton; Kiste, Kasten
boy	Junge
bread	Brot
break	Pause
(to) break	(zer)brechen
breakfast	Frühstück
bridge	Brücke
(to) bring	(her-, mit)bringen
broad	breit
brother	Bruder
brown	braun
brush	Bürste, Pinsel
(to) brush	bürsten
(to) build	bauen
building	Gebäude
(to) burn	brennen
bus	Omnibus
business	Geschäft
but	aber
butcher	Fleischer(in), Metzger(in)
butter	Butter
(to) buy	kaufen
by	durch, mit Hilfe von; bei, neben; bis

VOCABULARY

C

café	Café
cake	Kuchen
call	(An)ruf; Telefongespräch
(to) call	(an)rufen; nennen
camera	Kamera
camp	Lager
(to) camp	zelten, lagern
can	Büchse, Dose
can	können
capital	Großbuchstabe; Hauptstadt
car	Wagen
card	Karte
care	Sorge
(to) care	sorgen
careful	sorgfältig
(to) carry	tragen
cat	Katze
(to) catch	fangen
cause	Ursache
(to) cause	verursachen
centre	Zentrum, Mittelpunkt
certain	sicher
certainly	sicherlich
chair	Stuhl
chalk	Kreide
change	Wechsel(geld); (Ver)änderung
(to) change	wechseln; (sich) (ver)ändern
cheap	billig
cheese	Käse
child	Kind
chocolate	Schokolade
(to) choose	(aus)wählen
Christmas	Weihnachten
church	Kirche
cigarette	Zigarette
cinema	Kino
city	(Innen)stadt
class	Klasse; Unterricht(sstunde)
classroom	Klassenzimmer
clean	sauber
(to) clean	reinigen, säubern
clear	klar
(to) clear	säubern
clever	klug
clock	Uhr
(to) close	schließen
clothes	Kleider
cloud	Wolke
club	Verein, Club
coat	Mantel
coffee	Kaffee
coin	Münze
cold	Erkältung; kalt
colour	Farbton, Farbe
comb	Kamm
(to) comb	kämmen
(to) come	kommen
cook	Koch, Köchin
(to) cook	kochen
copy	Kopie
(to) copy	abschreiben; kopieren
corner	Ecke
correct	richtig
(to) correct	richtigstellen; korrigieren
cost	Kosten
(to) cost	kosten
(to) count	zählen; ins Gewicht fallen
counter	Ladentisch
country	Land
cow	Kuh
cross	Kreuz
(to) cross	überqueren
crossing	Kreuzung
crowd	Menschenmenge
crowded	dichtgedrängt, voll
cry	Schrei
(to) cry	schreien; weinen
cup	Tasse
cut	Schnitt
(to) cut	schneiden

D

dance	Tanz
(to) dance	tanzen
danger	Gefahr
dangerous	gefährlich
dark	dunkel
darkness	Dunkelheit
date	Datum; Zeitpunkt
daughter	Tochter
day	Tag
dead	tot
dear	lieb
death	Tod
deep	tief
desk	Schreibtisch
(to) dictate	diktieren
dictation	Diktat
dictionary	Wörterbuch
(to) die	sterben
different	verschieden
difficult	schwierig
dining-room	Eßzimmer
dinner	(Mittag-, Abend)essen
dirty	schmutzig
(to) discuss	diskutieren
discussion	Diskussion
(to) dislike	nicht mögen
distance	Entfernung
(to) do	tun, machen
doctor	Arzt, Ärztin
dog	Hund
door	Tür
down	hinunter; unten
(to) draw	ziehen; zeichnen
dream	Traum
(to) dream	träumen
dress	Kleid(ung)
(to) dress	anziehen
drink	Getränk, etw. zum Trinken
(to) drink	trinken
(to) drive	fahren
driver	Fahrer(in)
dry	trocken
(to) dry	trocknen
during	während

VOCABULARY

E

each	jede(r, s)
each other	einander, sich
ear	Ohr
early	früh
easy	leicht
(to) eat	essen
egg	Ei
either . . . or	entweder . . . oder
empty	leer
end	Ende
(to) end	(be)enden
(to) enjoy	genießen, sich freuen an
enough	genug
(to) enter	eintreten
evening	Abend
ever	jemals
every	jede(r, s)
everybody	jeder(mann), alle
everyone	jeder(mann), alle
everything	alles
exact	genau
exam	Prüfung
examination	Prüfung
example	Beispiel
excuse	Entschuldigung
(to) excuse	(sich) entschuldigen
exercise	Übung
expensive	teuer
(to) explain	erklären
extra	besonders
eye	Auge

F

face	Gesicht
fact	Tatsache
fair	gerecht; angemessen
fall	Fall
(to) fall	fallen
false	falsch
family	Familie
far	weit
farm	Bauernhof
farmer	Landwirt(in)
fast	schnell
fat	dick
father	Vater
(to) feel	(sich) fühlen
few	wenige
field	Feld
(to) fill	füllen
film	Film
(to) film	filmen
(to) find	finden
fine	schön; gut
finger	Finger
(to) finish	beenden
fire	Feuer
first	zuerst, zunächst
fish	Fisch
(to) fish	fischen, angeln
flat	Wohnung; flach
floor	Fußboden; Stockwerk
flower	Blume
fly	Fliege
(to) fly	fliegen
(to) follow	folgen
food	Nahrung, Essen
foot	Fuß
for	für
(to) forget	vergessen
fork	Gabel
form	Form; Klasse
(to) form	formen, bilden
free	frei
friend	Freund(in)
from	von
front	Vorderseite
in front of	vor
fruit	Obst
full	voll
fun	Spaß

G

game	Spiel
garage	Garage; Autowerkstatt
garden	Garten
gate	Tor
gentleman	Herr
(to) get	bekommen, erhalten; besorgen
girl	Mädchen
(to) give	geben
glad	froh
glass	Glas
glasses	Brille
(to) go	gehen, fahren
good	gut
goodbye	Auf Wiedersehen!
government	Regierung
grandfather	Großvater
grandmother	Großmutter
great	großartig
green	grün
grey	grau
grocer	Lebensmittelhändler
ground	Boden
(to) grow	wachsen
grown-up	erwachsen; Erwachsene(r)
guest	Gast

H

hair	Haar
hairdresser	Friseur, Friseuse
half	Hälfte; halb
ham	Schinken
hand	Hand
(to) hand	reichen
handbag	Handtasche
handkerchief	Taschentuch
(to) happen	geschehen
happy	glücklich
hard	hart; schwierig, anstrengend
hat	Hut
(to) have	haben
he	er
head	Kopf
headache	Kopfweh
(to) hear	hören
heart	Herz
heavy	schwer
hello	hallo
help	Hilfe
(to) help	helfen

VOCABULARY

her	ihr(e), sie	kind	Art; freundlich
here	hier	king	König
herself	sie selbst	kiss	Kuß
high	hoch	(to) kiss	küssen
him	ihm, ihn	kitchen	Küche
himself	er selbst	knee	Knie
his	sein(e)	knife	Messer
(to) hold	halten	knock	Schlag
hole	Loch	(to) knock	klopfen
holiday	Ferien	(to) know	wissen, kennen
home	Wohnung; Heimat; nach Hause		
homework	Hausaufgaben	**L**	
hope	Hoffnung	lady	Dame
(to) hope	hoffen	lamp	Lampe
horse	Pferd	land	Land
hot	heiß	(to) land	landen
hotel	Hotel	language	Sprache
hour	Stunde	large	groß
house	Haus	last	letzte(r, s)
housewife	Hausfrau	late	spät
how	wie	laugh	Lachen
hungry	hungrig	(to) laugh	lachen
hurry	Eile	lazy	faul
(to) hurry	sich beeilen	(to) learn	lernen
(to) hurt	(sich) verletzen; schmerzen	(to) leave	(ver)lassen, weggehen
husband	(Ehe)mann	left	links
		leg	Bein
I		lemon	Zitrone
I	ich	lesson	Unterrichtsstunde
ice-cream	Eis	(to) let	lassen, zulassen
idea	Gedanke, Vorstellung, Idee	letter	Brief; Buchstabe
		lie	Lüge
if	wenn, falls	(to) lie	lügen; liegen
ill	krank	life	Leben
important	wichtig	light	Licht, Lampe; hell; leicht
in	in		
indeed	tatsächlich	(to) light	anzünden; beleuchten
(to) inform	benachrichtigen	(to) like	mögen
information	Information, Auskunft	like	wie
		line	Linie; Zeile
inside	innen	lip	Lippe
instead	anstatt	list	Liste
interest	Interesse; Zins(en)	(to) list	auflisten
interesting	interessant	(to) listen	zuhören
into	in, hinein	little	klein; wenig
(to) introduce	vorstellen	a little	ein bißchen
invitation	Einladung	(to) live	leben, wohnen
(to) invite	einladen	living-room	Wohnzimmer
island	Insel	long	lange
it	es	look	Blick
its	sein(e), ihr(e)	(to) look	schauen; aussehen
		lord	Herr
J		(to) lose	verlieren
jacket	Jacke	lot	Menge
jam	Marmelade	loud	laut
job	Arbeit	love	Liebe
(to) join	sich anschließen, beitreten	(to) love	lieben
		lovely	hübsch
journey	Reise	low	niedrig
juice	Saft	luck	Glück
jump	Sprung	lucky	glücklich
(to) jump	hüpfen, springen	lunch	Mittagessen
just	genau; soeben; nur		
		M	
K		machine	Maschine
(to) keep	(be)halten	madam	Gnädige Frau
key	Schlüssel	magazine	Zeitschrift
		(to) make	machen

VOCABULARY

man	Mann; Mensch, Menschheit
many	viele
map	Landkarte
marmalade	Orangenmarmelade
(to) marry	heiraten
match	Streichholz; Wettkampf/-spiel
(to) match	zusammenbringen, verbinden
may	dürfen
maybe	vielleicht
me	mich, mir
meal	Mahlzeit
(to) mean	bedeuten, meinen
meaning	Bedeutung
meat	Fleisch
(to) meet	(sich) treffen; kennenlernen
meeting	Treffen
middle	Mitte
milk	Milch
minute	Minute
(to) miss	vermissen; verfehlen, verpassen
Miss	Fräulein
Mr	Herr
Mrs	Frau
Ms	Frau
mistake	Fehler
money	Geld
month	Monat
moon	Mond
morning	Morgen
mother	Mutter
mouth	Mund
(to) move	bewegen
movement	Bewegung
much	viel
music	Musik
must	müssen
my	mein(e)
myself	ich selbst

N

name	Name
(to) name	benennen
near	nahe
necessary	notwendig
neck	Hals
need	Bedürfnis; Not(lage)
(to) need	benötigen; brauchen
neither . . . nor . . .	weder . . . noch . . .
never	nie
new	neu
news	Nachrichten, Neuigkeit
newspaper	Zeitung
next	nächste(r, s)
nice	nett
night	Nacht, Abend
no	kein; nein
noise	Lärm
noisy	geräuschvoll
nose	Nase
not	nicht
nothing	nichts
now	jetzt
number	Zahl

O

o'clock	Uhr *(Zeitangabe)*
of	von
off	von . . . weg
often	oft
old	alt
on	auf
once	einmal; früher
only	nur; einzige(r, s)
open	offen
(to) open	öffnen
or	oder
order	Befehl; Bestellung
(to) order	befehlen; bestellen
other	andere(r, s)
our	unser
ourselves	wir selbst
out	aus
over	vorüber; über; mehr als
own	eigen
(to) own	besitzen
owner	Besitzer(in)

P

page	Seite
pair	Paar
paper	Papier; Zeitung
parents	Eltern
park	Park
(to) park	parken
part	Teil
party	Party
pass	Paß
(to) pass	vorbeigehen
passenger	Fahrgast
passport	Paß
pay	Lohn
(to) pay	(be)zahlen
pen	Füllhalter
pencil	Bleistift
penny	Penny
people	Leute; Volk
perhaps	vielleicht
petrol	Benzin
phone	Telefon
(to) phone	telefonieren
picture	Bild
piece	Stück
pipe	Pfeife; Röhre
place	Platz; Ort
plan	Plan
(to) plan	planen
plane	Flugzeug
plate	Teller
platform	Bahnsteig
play	(Schau)spiel
(to) play	spielen
player	Spieler(in)
please	bitte
plum	Pflaume
pocket	(Hosen)tasche
point	Punkt
(to) point	zeigen
police	Polizei
policeman	Polizist
poor	arm
possible	möglich
postcard	Postkarte

230 two hundred and thirty

VOCABULARY V

postman	Briefträger	round	Runde; rund; herum
post office	Postamt	rubber	Gummi
pot	Topf	(to) run	laufen
potato	Kartoffel		
pound	Pfund	**S**	
power	Kraft	sad	traurig
(to) practise	üben	safe	sicher
present	Geschenk; anwesend, gegenwärtig	safety	Sicherheit
		salt	Salz
press	Presse	same	gleiche(r, s); der-, die-, dasselbe
(to) press	pressen, drücken	sand	Sand
pretty	hübsch	(to) say	sagen
price	Preis	school	Schule
(to) pronounce	aussprechen	sea	Meer
pronunciation	Aussprache	seat	Sitz
(to) pull	ziehen	second	Sekunde
pupil	Schüler	(to) see	sehen
(to) push	schieben	(to) seem	scheinen
(to) put	setzen, stellen, legen	self	selbst
		(to) sell	verkaufen
Q		(to) send	schicken, senden
quarter	Viertel	sentence	Satz
queen	Königin	(to) serve	bedienen
question	Frage	(to) set	stellen, setzen
quick	schnell	several	mehrere
quiet	ruhig	shall	sollen
quite	ganz; ziemlich	she	sie
		sheet	(Papier)blatt, Bogen
R		(to) shine	scheinen, leuchten
radio	Radio	ship	Schiff
railway	Eisenbahn	shirt	(Herren)hemd
rain	Regen	shoe	Schuh
(to) rain	regnen	shop	Geschäft
rainy	regnerisch	(to) shop	einkaufen
rather	ziemlich	short	kurz
(to) reach	erreichen	shoulder	Schulter
(to) read	lesen	shout	Schrei
ready	fertig	(to) shout	rufen, brüllen
real	wirklich	show	Show, Vorstellung
really	tatsächlich	(to) show	zeigen
reality	Wirklichkeit	(to) shut	schließen
reason	Grund	sick	krank
record	Rekord; Schallplatte	side	Seite
red	rot	since	seit
(to) remain	bleiben	(to) sing	singen
(to) remember	sich erinnern an	sir	Herr
repair	Reparatur	sister	Schwester
(to) repair	reparieren	(to) sit	sitzen
(to) repeat	wiederholen	skirt	Rock
report	Bericht	sky	Himmel
(to) report	berichten	sleep	Schlaf
rest	Rest	(to) sleep	schlafen
restaurant	Restaurant	slow	langsam
result	Ergebnis	small	klein
return	Wiederkehr	smell	Geruch
rich	reich	(to) smell	riechen
ride	Ritt; Fahrt	smile	Lächeln
(to) ride	reiten; fahren	(to) smile	lächeln
right	Recht; rechts; richtig; unmittelbar, direkt	smoke	Rauch
		(to) smoke	rauchen
		snow	Schnee
ring	Ring; Anruf	(to) snow	schneien
(to) ring	klingeln; anrufen	so	deshalb, also, folglich; so
(to) rise	aufstehen		
river	Fluß	soap	Seife
road	Landstraße	sock	Socke
roof	Dach	soft	weich
room	Zimmer	some	einige

VOCABULARY

somebody	jemand
someone	jemand
something	etwas
sometimes	manchmal
son	Sohn
song	Lied
soon	bald
sorry	betrübt; tut mir leid, Entschuldigung!
(to) speak	sprechen
(to) spell	buchstabieren
(to) spend	ausgeben; verbringen
spoon	Löffel
sport	Sport
spring	Frühling
stamp	Briefmarke
(to) stand	stehen
star	Stern
start	Anfang
(to) start	anfangen
state	Staat; Zustand
station	Bahnhof
stay	Aufenthalt
(to) stay	bleiben; sich aufhalten; wohnen
still	(den)noch
stone	Stein
stop	Halt, Haltestelle
(to) stop	anhalten
story	Geschichte
street	Straße
strike	Streik
(to) strike	schlagen
strong	stark
study	Studium
(to) study	studieren
subject	Fach
such	solche(r, s)
suddenly	plötzlich
sugar	Zucker
suit	Anzug
(to) suit	passen
summer	Sommer
sun	Sonne
supper	Abendessen
sure	sicher, natürlich
sweet	süß
(to) swim	schwimmen
switch	Schalter
(to) switch	schalten

T

table	Tisch
(to) take	nehmen
talk	Gespräch
(to) talk	reden
tall	hoch(gewachsen), groß; hohe(r, s)
taxi	Taxi
tea	Tee
(to) teach	lehren
teacher	Lehrer(in)
team	Mannschaft
telephone	Telefon
television	Fernseher, Fernsehen
(to) tell	erzählen
terrible	schrecklich
than	als
thank	Dank
(to) thank	danken
thanks	danke
that	daß; jene(r, s), welche(r, s)
the	der, die, das
their	ihr(e)
themselves	sie selbst
then	dann; damals
there	dort
therefore	deshalb
these	diese
they	sie
thick	dick
thin	dünn
thing	Ding
(to) think	denken, meinen, glauben
thirsty	durstig
this	diese(r, s)
those	jene
though	obwohl, aber, jedoch
through	durch
(to) throw	werfen
thus	so
ticket	(Fahr)karte
till	bis
time	Zeit
times	Mal(e)
tired	müde
to	zu, bis
tobacco	Tabak
today	heute
together	zusammen
toilet	WC
tomato	Tomate
tomorrow	morgen
tongue	Zunge
tonight	heute nacht/abend
too	zu sehr; auch
tooth	Zahn
top	Spitze
toward(s)	in Richtung
tower	Turm
town	Stadt
traffic	Verkehr
traffic light(s)	Ampel
train	Zug
(to) translate	übersetzen
translation	Übersetzung
travel	Reise
(to) travel	reisen, fahren
tree	Baum
trip	Kurzreise
trouble	Schwierigkeit(en)
trousers	Hose
true	wahr, richtig
(to) try	versuchen
turn	Drehung
(to) turn	drehen

U

umbrella	Regenschirm
uncle	Onkel
under	unter
(to) understand	verstehen
until	bis

232 two hundred and thirty-two

VOCABULARY V

up	hinauf	white	weiß
upon	auf	who	wer
us	uns	whole	ganz
use	Gebrauch	whom	wem, wen
(to) use	gebrauchen	whose	wessen
		why	warum
V		wife	(Ehe)frau
very	sehr	will	werden
village	Dorf	(to) win	gewinnen
visit	Besuch	wind	Wind
(to) visit	besuchen	(to) wind	aufziehen
voice	Stimme	window	Fenster
		wish	Wunsch
W		(to) wish	wünschen
(to) wait	warten	with	mit
waiter	Kellner	within	innerhalb
waitress	Kellnerin	without	ohne
(to) wake up	aufwachen; wecken	woman	Frau
		wonderful	wunderbar
walk	Spaziergang	wood	Holz, Wald
(to) walk	gehen	word	Wort
wall	Wand, Mauer	work	Arbeit
(to) want	wollen	(to) work	arbeiten
warm	warm	worker	Arbeiter(in)
(to) wash	waschen	world	Welt
watch	Armbanduhr	(to) write	schreiben
(to) watch	beobachten, sehen	wrong	falsch
water	Wasser		
way	Weg	**Y**	
we	wir	year	Jahr
(to) wear	tragen *(Kleidung)*	yellow	gelb
weather	Wetter	yes	ja
week	Woche	yesterday	gestern
well	gut	yet	jedoch; schon
what	was	you	du, Sie; dir, dich; ihr, euch; Ihnen, Sie
when	wann; als		
where	wo(hin)	young	jung
whether	ob	your	dein(e, r)
which	welche(r, s)	yourself	du/Sie selbst
while	während	yourselves	ihr/Sie selbst

Phonetic alphabet · Lautschrift

[ː] bedeutet, daß der vorangehende Laut lang ist

[ˈ] bedeutet, daß die folgende Silbe eine Hauptbetonung erhält

[ˌ] bedeutet, daß die folgende Silbe eine Nebenbetonung erhält

[iː]	meet [miːt]	[ʊ]	good [gʊd]	[b]	by [baɪ]	[s]	son [sʌn]
[ɑː]	father [ˈfɑːðə]	[ə]	father [ˈfɑːðə]	[t]	teacher [ˈtiːtʃə]	[z]	his [hɪz]
[ɔː]	daughter [ˈdɔːtə]	[eɪ]	name [neɪm]	[d]	daughter [ˈdɔːtə]	[ʃ]	she [ʃiː]
[uː]	school [skuːl]	[aɪ]	my [maɪ]	[k]	clock [klɒk]	[ʒ]	television [ˈtelɪˌvɪʒn]
[ɜː]	firm [fɜːm]	[ɔɪ]	toilet [ˈtɔɪlɪt]	[g]	good [gʊd]	[h]	he [hiː]
[ɔ̃ː]	restaurant [ˈrestɔ̃ːŋ]	[əʊ]	show [ʃəʊ]	[tʃ]	teacher [ˈtiːtʃə]	[m]	my [maɪ]
		[aʊ]	now [naʊ]	[dʒ]	job [dʒɒb]	[n]	now [naʊ]
[ɪ]	in [ɪn]	[ɪə]	here [hɪə]	[f]	firm [fɜːm]	[ŋ]	evening [ˈiːvnɪŋ]
[e]	yes [jes]	[eə]	where [weə]	[v]	evening [ˈiːvnɪŋ]	[l]	like [laɪk]
[æ]	thanks [θæŋks]	[ʊə]	tourist [ˈtʊərɪst]	[θ]	thanks [θæŋks]	[r]	room [ruːm]
[ʌ]	son [sʌn]	[p]	pub [pʌb]	[ð]	this [ðɪs]	[w]	where [weə]
[ɒ]	job [dʒɒb]					[j]	yes [jes]

V VOCABULARY

Unit 1

Contextual vocabulary · Unitbegleitendes Wörterverzeichnis

Alle **halbfett** hervorgehobenen englischen Wörter gehören zum verbindlichen Lernwortschatz. Sie müssen aktiv beherrscht werden, denn sie werden in späteren Units als bekannt vorausgesetzt.
Normal gedruckte englische Wörter sind entweder nur für das Textverständnis in der jeweiligen Unit aufgeführt und werden deshalb in späteren Units nicht als bekannt vorausgesetzt, oder sie stellen Internationalismen (wie z.B. *container, film star, pop music*) und *cognates* (wie z.B. *mouse, shoemaker, windmill*) dar. Solche Wörter bedeuten keine besondere Lernbelastung. Sie werden deshalb nur einmal aufgeführt, auch wenn sie in späteren Units wieder gebraucht werden.

UNIT 1

St

(to) be from ['bɪ frəm]	sein/kommen aus
Britain ['brɪtn]	Großbritannien
United Kingdom [juːˈnaɪtɪd ˈkɪŋdəm]	Vereinigtes Königreich
England ['ɪŋɡlənd]	England
Scotland ['skɒtlənd]	Schottland
Northern Ireland [ˈnɔːðən ˈaɪələnd]	Nordirland
Wales [weɪlz]	Wales

A1

student ['stjuːdnt]	Student(in); *hier:* Schüler(in)
college ['kɒlɪdʒ]	höh. Lehranstalt, Internat; *hier:* Berufsfachschule
first [fɜːst]	erste(r, s)
secretary ['sekrətrɪ]	Sekretär(in)
(to) sit down ['sɪt ˈdaʊn]	sich setzen
Well then – let's see. ['wel ðen lets 'siː]	Nun – dann wollen wir mal sehen.
of course [əv ˈkɔːs]	selbstverständlich
first name ['fɜːst ˌneɪm]	Vorname
High Street ['haɪ ˌstriːt]	Hauptstraße
registration card [ˌredʒɪˈstreɪʃn ˌkaːd]	(An)meldekarte; *hier:* Schülerkarteikarte
there is/are [ðər ˈɪz] [ðər ˈaː]	es gibt, es ist/sind vorhanden, da ist/sind

A2

How are things? [haʊ ə ˈθɪŋz]	Wie stehts?
all right [ˌɔːlˈraɪt]	in Ordnung
at the moment [ət ðə ˈməʊmənt]	im Augenblick
on holiday [ɒn ˈhɒlədɪ]	im Urlaub
at home [ət ˈhəʊm]	zu Hause, daheim
at work [ət ˈwɜːk]	bei der Arbeit
How are you? [haʊ ˈɑː juː]	Wie geht es Dir/Ihnen?
Yours [jɔːz]	Dein(e), Euer (Eure), Ihr(e)

A4

on the phone [ɒn ðə ˈfəʊn]	am Apparat, am Telefon
part of ['paːt_əv]	ein Teil von
whose [huːz]	wessen
Is that you? [ɪz ðæt ˈjuː]	Bist du das?

B1

girlfriend [ˈɡɜːlfrend]	(feste) Freundin
photo [ˈfəʊtəʊ]	Foto(grafie), Aufnahme
originally [əˈrɪdʒənəlɪ]	ursprünglich
cousin [ˈkʌzn]	Cousin(e)
mechanic [mɪˈkænɪk]	Mechaniker(in)
them [ðəm]	sie, ihnen
out of work [ˌaʊt_əv ˈwɜːk]	arbeitslos
nurse [nɜːs]	Krankenschwester
hospital [ˈhɒspɪtl]	Krankenhaus

B2

tourist [ˈtʊərɪst]	Tourist(in), Urlauber(in)
tourist information centre [ˈtʊərɪst ˌɪnfəˈmeɪʃn ˌsentə]	Fremdenverkehrsbüro
(to) ask about sth [ˈaːsk əˈbaʊt]	sich nach etw erkundigen
(to) be lost [bɪ ˈlɒst]	sich nicht zurechtfinden
lots of [ˈlɒts_əv]	eine Menge, viel(e)
things you can do [ˈθɪŋz juː kən ˈduː]	Dinge, die man machen/unternehmen kann
for example [fər_ɪɡˈzaːmpl]	zum Beispiel
leisure centre [ˈleʒəˌsentə]	Freizeitzentrum
squash [skwɒʃ]	Squash
table tennis [ˈteɪbl ˌtenɪs]	Tischtennis
swimming-pool [ˈswɪmɪŋpuːl]	Schwimmbad/-becken
disco [ˈdɪskəʊ]	Disko
place [pleɪs]	Platz, Ort; *hier:* Lokal
copy [ˈkɒpɪ]	Kopie, Exemplar; *hier:* Ausgabe
really [ˈrɪəlɪ]	tatsächlich, wirklich; *hier:* eigentlich
ice-skating [ˈaɪsˌskeɪtɪŋ]	Schlittschuhlauf(en)
fan [fæn]	Anhänger, Fan
ice-skating rink [ˈaɪsˌskeɪtɪŋ ˌrɪŋk]	Schlittschuhbahn, Eislaufstadion
one [wʌn]	eine(r, s)
this evening [ðɪs ˈiːvnɪŋ]	heute abend
fantastic [fænˈtæstɪk]	fantastisch, großartig
What time …? [wɒt ˈtaɪm]	Um wieviel Uhr? Wann?
evening newspaper [ˈiːvnɪŋ ˈnjuːsˌpeɪpə]	Abendzeitung
university [ˌjuːnɪˈvɜːsətɪ]	Universität

Unit 2

VOCABULARY

B 3

where to go, what to see ['weə tə 'gəʊ, 'wɒt tə 'siː]	etwa: wo man hingehen … was man sich anschauen kann; hier: Sehenswürdigkeiten	in the same way [ɪn ðə 'seɪm 'weɪ]	auf die gleiche Weise

T 1

Australia [ɒ'streɪljə] — Australien
capital ['kæpɪtl] — Hauptstadt
sightseeing trip ['saɪt‿siːɪŋ trɪp] — Besichtigungsreise; hier: Stadtrundfahrt
tour [tʊə] — Reise, Tour, Fahrt
palace ['pælɪs] — Palast
(to) go shopping ['gəʊ 'ʃɒpɪŋ] — einkaufen gehen
in front of [ɪn 'frʌnt‿əv] — vor
history ['hɪstrɪ] — Geschichte, Geschichts-
kilogram ['kɪləgræm] — Kilogramm
pigeon ['pɪdʒɪn] — Taube
Italian [ɪ'tæljən] — italienisch; Italiener(in); Italienisch
busy ['bɪzɪ] — geschäftig
main [meɪn] — Haupt-
shopping ['ʃɒpɪŋ] — Einkauf(en), Einkaufs-

parking area ['pɑːkɪŋ ‿eərɪə] — Parkplätze
post office ['pəʊst‿ɒfɪs] — Postamt
theatre ['θɪətə] — Theater
football ['fʊtbɔːl] — Fußball
football ground ['fʊtbɔːl‿graʊnd] — Fußballplatz
symbol ['sɪmbl] — Symbol, Zeichen
central Manchester ['sentrəl 'mæntʃɪstə] — Innenstadt von Manchester

C 1

travelling ['trævlɪŋ] — Reisen
British ['brɪtɪʃ] — britisch; (die) Briten
youth hostel ['juːθ‿hɒstl] — Jugendherberge
boyfriend ['bɔɪfrend] — (fester) Freund
English ['ɪŋglɪʃ] — englisch; Engländer(in); Englisch
Irish ['aɪərɪʃ] — irisch; Ire, Irin; Irisch/Gälisch
Swedish ['swiːdɪʃ] — schwedisch; Schwede, Schwedin, Schwedisch
German ['dʒɜːmən] — deutsch; Deutsche(r); Deutsch
America [ə'merɪkə] — Amerika
France [frɑːns] — Frankreich
Italy ['ɪtəlɪ] — Italien
Norway ['nɔːweɪ] — Norwegen
Sweden ['swiːdn] — Schweden

T 2

note [nəʊt] — Notiz, Aufschrieb, Anmerkung, Vermerk
mountain ['maʊntɪn] — Berg
factory ['fæktrɪ] — Fabrik
farming ['fɑːmɪŋ] — Landwirtschaft; Ackerbau und Viehzucht
fishing ['fɪʃɪŋ] — Fischfang
lake [leɪk] — See
oil [ɔɪl] — Öl
whisky ['wɪskɪ] — Whisky
tweed [twiːd] — Wollstoff
monster ['mɒnstə] — Ungeheuer, Monster
golf course ['gɒlf‿kɔːs] — Golfplatz
sheep [ʃiːp] — Schaf(e)
cattle ['kætl] — Rinder, Vieh
coal [kəʊl] — Kohle
wool [wʊl] — Wolle
mining ['maɪnɪŋ] — Bergbau; Arbeit im Bergwerk
industry ['ɪndəstrɪ] — Industrie

C 2

in the evening [ɪn ðɪ 'iːvnɪŋ] — am Abend
(to) lay the table ['leɪ ðə 'teɪbl] — den Tisch decken
jug [dʒʌg] — Krug, Kanne
not … yet [nɒt 'jet] — noch nicht

UNIT 2

St

computer [kəm'pjuːtə] — Computer, Rechner
computer programmer [kəm'pjuːtə 'prəʊgræmə] — Programmierer(in)
hairstylist ['heə‿staɪlɪst] — Damenfriseur/-friseuse
joiner ['dʒɔɪnə] — Schreiner(in), Tischler(in)
painter ['peɪntə] — Maler(in)
shop-assistant ['ʃɒpə‿sɪstənt] — Verkäufer(in)
typist ['taɪpɪst] — Stenotypist(in)
airline ['eəlaɪn] — Luftverkehrsgesellschaft
airline stewardess ['eəlaɪn stjʊə‿des] — Stewardeß
electrician [ˌɪlek'trɪʃn] — Elektriker(in)
office worker ['ɒfɪs‿wɜːkə] — Büroangestellte(r)

C 3

sight [saɪt] — Sehenswürdigkeit
nearby [ˌnɪə'baɪ] — in der Nähe, nahe gelegen
closed [kləʊzd] — geschlossen, zu
on Sundays [ɒn 'sʌndɪz] — sonntags
beach [biːtʃ] — Strand
ferry ['ferɪ] — Fähre
cathedral [kə'θiːdrəl] — Kathedrale, Dom, Münster
(to) be famous for [bɪ 'feɪməs fə] — berühmt sein für/wegen
bell [bel] — Glocke
metre ['miːtə] — Meter
north [nɔːθ] — nördlich; Nord(en)
castle ['kɑːsl] — Schloß, Burg
west [west] — westlich; West(en)
south [saʊθ] — südlich; Süd(en)
east [iːst] — östlich; Ost(en)
classmate ['klɑːsmeɪt] — Klassenkamerad(in)

two hundred and thirty-five 235

VOCABULARY

Unit 2

A1

electric cooker [ɪˈlektrɪk ˈkʊkə] — Elektroherd
(to) type [taɪp] — Schreibmaschine schreiben, tippen
(to) program [ˈprəʊgræm] — programmieren
tool [tuːl] — Werkzeug
(to) plant [plɑːnt] — (ein)pflanzen
vegetables [ˈvedʒtəblz] — Gemüse
(to) calculate [ˈkælkjʊleɪt] — aus-/berechnen
course [kɔːs] — Kurs, Lehrgang
French [frentʃ] — französisch; Französisch

metalwork [ˈmetlwɜːk] — Metallbearbeitung
business studies [ˈbɪznɪs ˌstʌdɪz] — Volks- und Betriebswirtschaftslehre
home economics [ˈhəʊm ˌiːkəˈnɒmɪks] — Hauswirtschaftslehre
woodwork [ˈwʊdwɜːk] — Holzbearbeitung
secretarial studies [ˌsekrəˈteərɪəl ˌstʌdɪz] — Sekretärinnenausbildung; Sekretariatspraxis

electronics [ˌɪlekˈtrɒnɪks] — Elektronik
computer studies [kəmˈpjuːtə ˌstʌdɪz] — Datenverarbeitung, EDV

A2

(to) want him to go [ˈwɒnt hɪm tə ˈgəʊ] — wollen, daß er geht
(to) be like [bɪ ˈlaɪk] — sein wie
I see [aɪ ˈsiː] — hier: ich verstehe
(to) train to be [ˈtreɪn tə ˈbiː] — ausgebildet werden zu, eine Lehre machen

A3

busy [ˈbɪzi] — arbeitsreich, geschäftig
timetable [ˈtaɪmˌteɪbl] — Stundenplan
in the morning [ɪn ðə ˈmɔːnɪŋ] — morgens, am Morgen
past [pɑːst] — nach
mathematics, maths [ˌmæθəˈmætɪks, mæθs] — Mathematik, Mathe
typing [ˈtaɪpɪŋ] — Schreibmaschineschreiben
football training [ˈfʊtbɔːl ˌtreɪnɪŋ] — Fußballtraining

A4

coffee bar [ˈkɒfiˌbɑː] — Cafeteria
Why's that? [ˈwaɪz ˈðæt] — Warum das denn?
What's it like? [ˈwɒtsˌɪt ˈlaɪk] — Wie ist das so?
(to) learn how to do sth [ˈlɜːn haʊ tə ˈduː] — lernen etw zu tun
Long time no see. [ˈlɒŋ taɪm nəʊ ˈsiː] — Lange nicht gesehen!
these days [ˈðiːz ˈdeɪz] — heutzutage; hier: zur Zeit
money [ˈmʌni] — Geld; hier: Bezahlung
better than [ˈbetə ðən] — besser als
(to) go out with sb [ˈgəʊ ˈaʊt wɪð] — hier: mit jdm gehen/befreundet sein
in fact [ɪn ˈfækt] — tatsächlich, in der Tat
on holiday [ɒn ˈhɒlədɪ] — im Urlaub

nowadays [ˈnaʊədeɪz] — heutzutage
(to) imagine [ɪˈmædʒɪn] — sich vorstellen
well paid [ˈwelˈpeɪd] — gut bezahlt

B1

(to) talk about sth/sb [ˈtɔːk əˈbaʊt] — sich über jdn/etw unterhalten
diary [ˈdaɪərɪ] — Tagebuch, Kalender
trainee [treɪˈniː] — Auszubildende(r); Praktikant(in)
concert [ˈkɒnsət] — Konzert
tennis [ˈtenɪs] — Tennis
class [klɑːs] — hier: Unterrichtsstunde

B2

(to) talk to sb [ˈtɔːk tə] — mit jdm reden/sprechen
exactly [ɪgˈzæktlɪ] — genau
(to) pick sb up [ˈpɪk ˈsʌmbədɪ ˈʌp] — jdn abholen/mitnehmen
on the way [ɒn ðə ˈweɪ] — auf dem Weg, unterwegs
Come on! [ˈkʌmˈɒn] — Mach schon!
by the way [baɪ ðə ˈweɪ] — übrigens
(to) get sth for sb [get] — etw für jdn besorgen
(to) bring sb/sth with you [brɪŋ] — jdn/etw mitbringen
not be friends with sb [ˈnɒt bɪ ˈfrendz wɪð] — nicht gut zu sprechen sein auf jdn
mad [mæd] — verrückt, wütend
See you. [ˈsiː juː] — Tschüs!
See you tomorrow. [ˈsiː juː təˈmɒrəʊ] — Bis morgen!
(to) go by bus [ˈgəʊ baɪ ˈbʌs] — mit dem Bus fahren
the next day [ðə ˈneks ˈdeɪ] — am nächsten Tag
What can I get you? [ˈwɒt kənˌaɪ ˈget juː] — Was darf ich dir besorgen/mitbringen?
Here you are. [ˈhɪə juː ˈɑː] — Hier bitte!
another thing [əˈnʌðə ˈθɪŋ] — noch etwas
Friday night [ˈfraɪdɪ ˈnaɪt] — Freitagabend
(to) look after sb/sth [ˈlʊkˈɑːftə] — sich um jdn/etw kümmern

B3

kick off [ˈkɪkɒf] — Anstoß
judo [ˈdʒuːdəʊ] — Judo
match [mætʃ] — Spiel, Wettkampf
weekend [ˌwiːˈkend] — Wochenende
programme [ˈprəʊgræm] — Programm

C1

(to) milk [mɪlk] — melken

C2

farming course [ˈfɑːmɪŋˌkɔːs] — Kurs in Landwirtschaftslehre
equipment [ɪˈkwɪpmənt] — Ausrüstung, Gerät(e)
screwdriver [ˈskruːˌdraɪvə] — Schraubenzieher
spanner [ˈspænə] — Schraubenschlüssel
typewriter [ˈtaɪpˌraɪtə] — Schreibmaschine
(to) lend sth to sb [lend] — jmd etw leihen

Unit 3

VOCABULARY

spade [speɪd]	Spaten	
cookbook ['kʊkbʊk]	Kochbuch	
pocket calculator ['pɒkɪt 'kælkjʊleɪtə]	Taschenrechner	

C 3

problem ['prɒbləm]	Problem
term [tɜːm]	Zeitraum; *hier:* Schulhalbjahr
section ['sekʃn]	Abteilung
sports [spɔːts]	Sport, Sport-
Spanish ['spænɪʃ]	Spanisch
Russian ['rʌʃn]	Russisch
history ['hɪstrɪ]	Geschichte
geography [dʒɪ'ɒgrəfɪ]	Geographie
civic studies ['sɪvɪk ˌstʌdɪz]	Gemeinschaftskunde
drama ['drɑːmə]	Schauspiel
physics ['fɪzɪks]	Physik
chemistry ['kemɪstrɪ]	Chemie
biology [baɪ'ɒlədʒɪ]	Biologie
hairstyling ['heəˌstaɪlɪŋ]	Friseurhandwerk
Get it? [get_ɪt]	Kapiert?
(to) hate [heɪt]	hassen
needn't ['niːdnt]	nicht brauchen/müssen
foreign ['fɒrən]	fremd, ausländisch
(to) be good at sth [bɪ 'gʊd_ət]	gut sein in etw
sign [saɪn]	Zeichen, Schild
(to) photocopy ['fəʊtəˌkɒpɪ]	photokopieren
mustn't ['mʌsnt]	nicht dürfen
(to) drop [drɒp]	wegwerfen, fallenlassen
litter ['lɪtə]	Abfall, Abfälle

C 4

principal ['prɪnsəpl]	Schulleiter(in)
rule [ruːl]	Vorschrift, Regel
(to) speak up ['spiːk_ˈʌp]	lauter sprechen
tidy ['taɪdɪ]	aufgeräumt, sauber
cleaner ['kliːnə]	Gebäudereiniger(in)
basket ['bɑːskɪt]	Korb; *hier:* Abfallbehälter
pub [pʌb]	Kneipe, Wirtschaft
cafeteria [ˌkæfɪ'tɪərɪə]	Cafeteria
lunch ticket ['lʌnʃ ˌtɪkɪt]	Essensbon/-marke
snack [snæk]	Imbiß, kleine Mahlzeit
tie [taɪ]	Krawatte, Schlips
overalls ['əʊvərɔːlz]	Arbeitsanzug, Overall
free period [ˌfriː 'pɪərɪəd]	Freistunde
study room ['stʌdɪˌruːm]	Studier-/Arbeitszimmer
outside [ˌaʊt'saɪd]	außerhalb, draußen
beginning [bɪ'gɪnɪŋ]	Beginn, Anfang
smoking ['sməʊkɪŋ]	Rauchen
by [baɪ]	*hier:* nicht später als

T

YTS (Youth Training Scheme) ['waɪ ˌtiː ˈes]	staatliches Programm zur Berufsausbildung Jugendlicher
school-leaver [skuːlˈliːvə]	Schulabgänger(in)
skill [skɪl]	Fertigkeit; *hier:* Berufsausbildung, Qualifikation
(to) earn [ɜːn]	(Geld) verdienen
at the same time [ət ðə ˌseɪm ˈtaɪm]	gleichzeitig, zur gleichen Zeit
Watch out! [wɒtʃ_ˈaʊt]	Aufgepaßt! Achtung!
Japan [dʒə'pæn]	Japan
competitor [kəm'petɪtə]	Konkurrent(in)
Europe ['jʊərəp]	Europa
(to) train [treɪn]	eine Ausbildung machen, ausbilden; üben
(to) take sth away ['teɪk_ə'weɪ]	etw wegnehmen
trade [treɪd]	Handel, Gewerbe, Handwerk; *hier:* Geschäft
not much longer ['nɒt ˌmʌtʃ 'lɒŋgə]	nicht mehr lange
typical ['tɪpɪkl]	typisch
a sixteen-year-old [ə ˌsɪkstiːn jɪər_ˈəʊld]	ein(e) Sechzehnjährige(r)
in this way [ɪn 'ðɪs ˌweɪ]	so, auf diese Art und Weise
chance [tʃɑːns]	Chance
firm [fɜːm]	Firma
(to) take part in sth [teɪk 'pɑːt_ɪn]	teilnehmen an etw
(to) look for sb/sth ['lʊk fə]	nach jdm/etw suchen
(to) be worth it/sth [bɪ 'wɜːθ_ɪt]	sich lohnen, etw wert sein
(to) get sth back [get ˌsʌmθɪŋ 'bæk]	etwas zurückholen/-bekommen
abroad [ə'brɔːd]	im/ins Ausland
(to) be over [bɪ 'əʊvə]	vorüber/vorbei sein
(to) work with sb/sth ['wɜːk wɪð]	(zusammen)arbeiten mit jdm; arbeiten mit etw
this summer ['ðɪs ˌsʌmə]	in diesem Sommer
at first [ət 'fɜːst]	zuerst
at present [ət 'preznt]	zur Zeit, im Augenblick
Be careful! [bɪ 'keəfʊl]	Vorsicht! Achtung!
a good point [ə ˌgʊd 'pɔɪnt]	ein überzeugender Punkt

F 1

commercial college [kə'mɜːʃl ˌkɒlɪdʒ]	Wirtschafts(ober)schule, (höhere) Handelsschule
(to) organize ['ɔːgənaɪz]	organisieren; *hier:* erstellen
economics [ˌiːkə'nɒmɪks]	Wirtschaftslehre
politics ['pɒlɪtɪks]	Gemeinschaftskunde
religious instruction [rɪˌlɪdʒəs_ɪn'strʌkʃn]	Religion
ethics ['eθɪks]	Ethik
(to) take place ['teɪk ˌpleɪs]	stattfinden

UNIT 3

St

and all that [ənd_ˌɔːl 'ðæt]	und alles, was dazugehört
gymnastics [dʒɪm'næstɪks]	Turnen, Gymnastik
rugby ['rʌgbɪ]	Rugby
wrestling ['reslɪŋ]	Ringen
basketball ['bɑːskɪtbɔːl]	Basketball
volleyball ['vɒlɪbɔːl]	Volleyball
swimming ['swɪmɪŋ]	Schwimmen

two hundred and thirty-seven 237

VOCABULARY

Unit 3

high jump ['haɪdʒʌmp] — Hochsprung
weight-lifting ['weɪt,lɪftɪŋ] — Gewichtheben
long jump ['lɒŋdʒʌmp] — Weitsprung
water polo ['wɔːtə,pəʊləʊ] — Wasserball
ice-hockey ['aɪs,hɒkɪ] — Eishockey
riding ['raɪdɪŋ] — Reiten

A 1

local hero ['ləʊkl 'hɪərəʊ] — Lokalmatador
local ['ləʊkl] — hiesig, einheimisch
interviewer ['ɪntəvjuːə] — Interviewer(in)
studio ['stjuːdɪəʊ] — Studio, Atelier, Senderaum
freestyle ['friːstaɪl] — Freistil
champion ['tʃæmpjən] — Sieger(in), Meister(in)
Congratulations. [kən,grætjʊ'leɪʃnz] — Herzlichen Glückwunsch!
Thank you very much. ['θæŋk jʊ 'verɪ 'mʌtʃ] — Vielen Dank.
exactly [ɪg'zæktlɪ] — genau
(to) come from ['kʌm frɒm] — kommen aus/von
pool [puːl] — Schwimmbecken
normally ['nɔːməlɪ] — normalerweise
five days a week ['faɪv 'deɪz ə 'wiːk] — fünf Tage in der Woche
(to) tell sb about sth [tel] — jdm von/über etw erzählen/berichten
fitness ['fɪtnɪs] — (gute) Form, (körperliche) Kondition
length [leŋθ] — Bahn, Länge
mile [maɪl] — Meile
start [stɑːt] — Start
long-distance [,lɒŋ'dɪstəns] — Langstrecke
sprint [sprɪnt] — Kurzstrecke, Sprint
What about...? ['wɒt ə'baʊt] — Wie steht's mit...?
competition [,kɒmpə'tɪʃn] — Wettkampf; Konkurrenz
usually ['juːʒʊəlɪ] — gewöhnlich, normalerweise
spare time ['speə 'taɪm] — Freizeit
hobby ['hɒbɪ] — Steckenpferd, Hobby
(to) go riding ['gəʊ 'raɪdɪŋ] — reiten
(to) have to do sth ['hæv tə 'duː] — etw machen müssen
interview ['ɪntəvjuː] — Unterredung, Interview
so far [səʊ 'fɑː] — bisher, bis jetzt; *hier:* einstweilen
(to) get up [get 'ʌp] — aufstehen
(to) contrast with [kən'trɑːst wɪð] — gegenüberstellen, vergleichen mit

A 3

puck [pʌk] — Puck, Scheibe
stick [stɪk] — Stock
soccer ['sɒkə] — Fußball(spiel)
oval ['əʊvl] — oval
windsurfer ['wɪnd,sɜːfə] — Windsurfer(in)
jogger ['dʒɒgə] — Jogger(in)
skate [skeɪt] — Schlittschuh
skier ['skiːə] — Skifahrer(in)
hockey ['hɒkɪ] — Hockey

racket ['rækɪt] — Tennisschläger
skater ['skeɪtə] — Schlittschuhläufer(in)
running shoe ['rʌnɪŋ ,ʃuː] — Laufschuh

A 4

cycling ['saɪklɪŋ] — Radfahren
athletics [æθ'letɪks] — Leichtathletik
body building ['bɒdɪ,bɪldɪŋ] — Bodybuilding
dancing ['dɑːnsɪŋ] — Tanzen
skiing ['skiːɪŋ] — Skifahren
windsurfing ['wɪnd,sɜːfɪŋ] — Windsurfen
jogging ['dʒɒgɪŋ] — Joggen

B 1

(to) keep fit ['kiːp 'fɪt] — sich in Form halten
(to) skate [skeɪt] — Schlittschuh laufen
once a week ['wʌns ə 'wiːk] — einmal in der Woche
times [taɪmz] — -mal, Mal(e)
(to) relax [rɪ'læks] — sich entspannen
twice [twaɪs] — zweimal
every other day ['evrɪ ˌʌðə 'deɪ] — jeden zweiten Tag

B 2

(to) describe sb/sth [dɪ'skraɪb] — jdn/etw beschreiben
bench [bentʃ] — Bank
on the spot [ɒn ðə 'spɒt] — auf der Stelle
(to) bend down ['bend 'daʊn] — (sich) beugen
(to) watch TV ['wɒtʃ tiː'viː] — fernsehen
circuit programme ['sɜːkɪt ,prəʊgræm] — Zirkeltrainingsprogramm

B 3

slim [slɪm] — schlank
(to) watch one's weight ['wɒtʃ wʌnz 'weɪt] — auf sein Gewicht achten
alcohol ['ælkəhɒl] — Alkohol
chocolates ['tʃɒklɪts] — Pralinen, Konfekt
some kind of ['sʌm 'kaɪnd əv] — irgendein(e, r)
on the move [ɒn ðə 'muːv] — in Bewegung
shopping bag ['ʃɒpɪŋ,bæg] — Einkaufstüte/-tasche
(to) be overweight [bɪ ,əʊvə'weɪt] — Übergewicht haben
spaghetti [spə'getɪ] — Spaghetti
cream-cake [,kriːm'keɪk] — Sahnetorte
nearly ['nɪəlɪ] — beinahe
all day ['ɔːl 'deɪ] — den ganzen Tag
from time to time [from 'taɪm tə 'taɪm] — von Zeit zu Zeit
packet ['pækɪt] — Packung
orange ['ɒrɪndʒ] — Orange
banana [bə'nɑːnə] — Banane
carrot ['kærət] — Möhre, Karotte
wine [waɪn] — Wein
beer [bɪə] — Bier

Unit 3

VOCABULARY

C1

Highland Games ['haɪlənd 'geɪmz]	schottische Hochlandwettkämpfe
(to) take part in sth [teɪk 'pɑːt_ɪn]	teilnehmen an etw
dancing competition ['dɑːnsɪŋ ˌkɒmpɪˌtɪʃn]	Tanzmeisterschaften
piping competition ['paɪpɪŋ ˌkɒmpɪˌtɪʃn]	Dudelsackpreisblasen
event [ɪ'vent]	Ereignis, Veranstaltung; *hier:* Disziplin
tossing the caber ['tɒsɪŋ ðə 'keɪbə]	(Baum)stammwerfen
caber ['keɪbə]	(Baum)stamm
feet [fiːt]	Füße; *hier:* Fuß *(Maßeinheit)*
(to) weigh [weɪ]	wiegen
pound [paʊnd]	Pfund
kilo ['kiːləʊ]	Kilo
athlete ['æθliːt]	(Leicht)athlet(in)
(to) have to [hæv tə]	müssen
as far as [əz 'fɑːr_əz]	so weit wie
(to) turn in a circle ['tɜːn ɪn ə 'sɜːkl]	sich im Kreis drehen
(to) hit [hɪt]	schlagen; *hier:* treffen
(to) be made of [bɪ 'meɪd_əv]	bestehen aus, gemacht sein aus

C2

sportsman ['spɔːtsmən]	Sportler
height [haɪt]	Größe
weight [weɪt]	Gewicht
statement ['steɪtmənt]	Aussage

C3

(to) draw [drɔː]	zeichnen
beard [bɪəd]	Bart
cap [kæp]	Mütze
kilt [kɪlt]	Schottenrock
scarf [skɑːf]	Schal
(to) have sth on ['hæv 'sʌmθɪŋ 'ɒn]	etw anhaben
wide [waɪd]	breit, weit, ausgedehnt

C4

tip [tɪp]	Rat(schlag), Tip
at once [ət 'wʌns]	sofort; *hier:* auf einmal
(to) check with sb ['tʃek wɪð]	sich be-/absprechen mit jdm
(to) get sth up to ['get_ʌp tuː]	*hier:* steigern/hochtreiben auf
pulse [pʌls]	Puls
fresh [freʃ]	frisch
(to) get out ['get_'aʊt]	hinauskommen, herauskommen
afterwards ['ɑːftəwədz]	danach
leaflet ['liːflɪt]	Faltblatt, Broschüre, Prospekt

C5

bathing-cap ['beɪðɪŋˌkæp]	Bademütze

T

fort [fɔːt]	Fort
flea [fliː]	Floh
American [ə'merɪkən]	amerikanisch; Amerikaner(in); Amerikanisch
bear [beə]	Bär
European [ˌjʊərə'piːən]	europäisch; Europäer(in)
(to) pick up sth [pɪk_'ʌp]	etw aufheben/-sammeln
footballer ['fʊtbɔːlə]	Fußballspieler
helmet ['helmɪt]	Helm
padding ['pædɪŋ]	Polsterung
ft (foot) [fʊt]	Fuß *(Maßeinheit)*
in (inch) [ɪntʃ]	Inch, Zoll *(Maßeinheit)*
at the age of [ət ði 'eɪdʒ_əv]	im Alter von
attraction [ə'trækʃn]	Anziehungskraft; *hier:* Attraktion
a cool million [ə 'kuːl 'mɪljən]	eine satte Million
dollar ['dɒlə]	Dollar
thousands [θaʊzndz]	Tausende
favourite ['feɪvrɪt]	Lieblings-
hamburger ['hæmbɜːgə]	Hamburger, Frikadelle
up to ['ʌp tə]	bis zu
jumbo ['dʒʌmbəʊ]	Riesen-
ambition [æm'bɪʃn]	Wunsch, Ehrgeiz
championship ['tʃæmpjənʃɪp]	Meisterschaft
in a way [ɪn_ə 'weɪ]	in gewisser Hinsicht
rough [rʌf]	grob; *hier:* rücksichtslos
as well [əz 'wel]	auch; *hier:* ebenso
nickname ['nɪkneɪm]	Spitzname
all over the place [ɔːl_'əʊvə ðə 'pleɪs]	überall
officially [ə'fɪʃəli]	offiziell, förmlich
amateur ['æmətə]	Amateur(in)
motoring ['məʊtərɪŋ]	Autofahren
steak [steɪk]	Steak
earnings ['ɜːnɪŋz]	Einkommen
(to) compare [kəm'peə]	vergleichen
star [stɑː]	Stern; *hier:* Star
everywhere ['evrɪweə]	überall
reporter [rɪ'pɔːtə]	Reporter(in)
article ['ɑːtɪkl]	Artikel
manager ['mænɪdʒə]	Manager(in), Geschäftsführer(in)
(to) introduce sb to sth/sb [ˌɪntrə'djuːs]	jdm etw/jdn vorstellen

F

motor racing ['məʊtəˌreɪsɪŋ]	Autorennen
finish ['fɪnɪʃ]	Schluß, Ende; *hier:* Ziel
tyre ['taɪə]	Reifen
square [skweə]	Quadrat; *hier:* Feld
(to) miss [mɪs]	verfehlen, verpassen; *hier:* aussetzen
one turn ['wʌn 'tɜːn]	eine Runde
(to) overtake [ˌəʊvə'teɪk]	überholen
engine ['endʒɪn]	Maschine, Motor
the engine stalls [ði 'endʒɪn 'stɔːlz]	der Motor stottert/stirbt

VOCABULARY

Unit 4

pit [pɪt] — Graben, Grube; *hier:* Box
spectator [spek'teɪtə] — Zuschauer(in)
Whose turn is it? ['huːz 'tɜːn ɪz_ɪt] — Wer ist an der Reihe?
It's my turn. [ɪts 'maɪ 'tɜːn] — Ich bin dran.

UNIT 4

St

media ['miːdjə] — Medien
daily ['deɪlɪ] — täglich
daily newspaper ['deɪlɪ 'njuːsˌpeɪpə] — Tageszeitung
business ['bɪznɪs] — Geschäft; *hier:* Wirtschaft(steil)
home news ['həʊmˌnjuːz] — Inlandsnachrichten
cookery ['kʊkərɪ] — Kochen, Kochkunst
crossword ['krɒswɜːd] — Kreuzworträtsel
entertainment [ˌentə'teɪnmənt] — Unterhaltung
foreign news ['fɒrɪnˌnjuːz] — Auslandsnachrichten
gardening ['gɑːdnɪŋ] — Gartenarbeit; Gartenbau

A1

print-out ['prɪntaʊt] — (Computer)ausdruck
survey ['sɜːveɪ] — Untersuchung, Umfrage
now and then ['naʊ_ən 'ðen] — hin und wieder, ab und zu
television [telɪ'vɪʒn] — Fernseher, Fernsehen
video ['vɪdɪəʊ] — Video

A2

grandad ['grændæd] — Opa
grandma ['grænmɑː] — Oma
comic ['kɒmɪk] — Comicheft
pop music ['pɒpˌmjuːzɪk] — Popmusik, Schlagermusik
western ['westən] — Western, Wildwestfilm
thriller ['θrɪlə] — Thriller, Krimi
classical ['klæsɪkl] — klassisch
(to) report about sb/sth [rɪ'pɔːt_əˌbaʊt] — über jdn/etw berichten

A3

disc jockey ['dɪskˌdʒɒkɪ] — Diskjockey
cleaner ['kliːnə] — Gebäudereiniger(in)
editor ['edɪtə] — Redakteur(in)
telex ['teleks] — Fernschreiben/-schreiber, Telex
technical ['teknɪkl] — technisch
technical engineer ['teknɪklˌendʒɪ'nɪə] — Techniker(in)
(to) service ['sɜːvɪs] — bedienen; *hier:* warten
teenage magazine ['tiːneɪdʒˌmægəˌziːn] — Jugendmagazin; *hier:* Programm/Sendung für Jugendliche
listener ['lɪsnə] — Zuhörer(in)
power cut ['paʊəˌkʌt] — Stromausfall

A4

latest ['leɪtɪst] — späteste(r, s), neueste(r, s), letzte(r, s)

case [keɪs] — Fall
(to) give sb trouble/a hard time ['gɪv 'trʌbl/ ə 'hɑːd 'taɪm] — jdm Schwierigkeiten machen
(to) come round ['kʌm 'raʊnd] — vorbeikommen/-schauen
regularly ['regjʊləlɪ] — regelmäßig
right now ['raɪt 'naʊ] — im Augenblick, zur Zeit
(to) stay with sb ['steɪ wɪð] — sich aufhalten/wohnen/übernachten bei jdm
caravan ['kærəvæn] — Wohnwagen
drug [drʌg] — Droge
good points ['gʊd 'pɔɪnts] — *hier:* gute Seiten
unpaid [ˌʌn'peɪd] — unbezahlt
Yours sincerely ['jɔːz sɪn'sɪəlɪ] — mit freundlichen Grüßen (Briefschluß)

A5

personal ['pɜːsnl] — persönlich
(to) go on the air ['gəʊ ɒn ðɪ 'eə] — auf Sendung gehen
(to) take over sb's role ['teɪk 'əʊvə 'sʌmbədɪz 'rəʊl] — jds Rolle übernehmen
(to) present sth [prɪ'zent] — etw darbieten, übergeben, schenken, präsentieren
sheepdog ['ʃiːpdɒg] — Schäferhund
(to) run after ['rʌn_'ɑːftə] — hinterherrennen
kitten ['kɪtn] — Kätzchen
winner ['wɪnə] — Sieger(in)
the whole of this week [ðə 'həʊl_əv 'ðɪs 'wiːk] — die ganze Woche lang
(to) offer ['ɒfə] — anbieten
fireman ['faɪəmən] — Feuerwehrmann
(to) risk [rɪsk] — aufs Spiel setzen, riskieren
(to) serve sb sth [sɜːv] — jdm etw servieren
all the year round ['ɔːl ðə 'jɪə 'raʊnd] — das ganze Jahr über

A6

(to) milk [mɪlk] — melken
(to) feed [fiːd] — füttern
cowshed ['kaʊʃed] — Kuhstall
customer ['kʌstəmə] — Kunde, Kundin

B1

sort [sɔːt] — Sorte, Marke
(to) be on [bɪ 'ɒn] — *hier:* gesendet werden, auf dem Programm stehen
channel ['tʃænl] — Kanal; *hier:* Programm
comedy ['kɒmɪdɪ] — Komödie
religious [rɪ'lɪdʒəs] — religiös
quiz game ['kwɪzˌgeɪm] — Quiz
documentary [ˌdɒkjʊ'mentrɪ] — Tatsachenbericht/-film
educational programme [ˌedjuː'keɪʃənl 'prəʊgræm] — *etwa:* Erziehungs- und Bildungsprogramm
song of praise ['sɒŋ_əv 'preɪz] — Lobgesang
cathedral [kə'θiːdrəl] — Kathedrale, Dom
mastermind ['mɑːstəmaɪnd] — *etwa:* (geistige) Kapazität

VOCABULARY

Unit 4

(to) have a good laugh ['hæv_ə 'gʊd 'lɑːf] — (herzlich) lachen
international [ˌɪntəˈnæʃənl] — international
at war [ət 'wɔː] — im Krieg(szustand)
swimmer ['swɪmə] — Schwimmer(in)

B 2

(to) think about sth/sb ['θɪŋk_ə'baʊt] — halten von jdm/etw, denken über jdn/etw
TV (television) [ˌtiːˈviː] — Fernsehen
viewer ['vjuːə] — Zuschauer
popular ['pɒpjʊlə] — populär; *hier:* beliebt
entertaining [ˌentəˈteɪnɪŋ] — unterhaltsam, unterhaltend
informative [ɪnˈfɔːmətɪv] — lehrreich, informativ, aufschlußreich
play [pleɪ] — Schauspiel, Theater-/Bühnenstück
chart [tʃɑːt] — Tabelle
less [les] — weniger
least [liːst] — am wenigsten

B 3

(to) advertise ['ædvətaɪz] — werben für
viewing figure ['vjuːɪŋ ˌfɪgə] — Einschaltquote
better ['betə] — besser
best [best] — beste(r,s)
company ['kʌmpənɪ] — Gesellschaft, Firma
product ['prɒdʌkt] — Erzeugnis, Produkt
worse [wɜːs] — schlechter, schlimmer
worst [wɜːst] — am schlechtesten, schlimmste(r,s)
even ['iːvn] — sogar, selbst
midnight ['mɪdnaɪt] — Mitternacht
advertising ['ædvətaɪzɪŋ] — Werbung, Reklame

B 4

(to) have a close look at sth/sb ['hæv_əˈkləʊs 'lʊk_ət] — jdn/etw genau anschauen
welcome ['welkəm] — willkommen
(to) share [ʃeə] — teilen
housework ['haʊswɜːk] — Hausarbeit
Cornish Pasties ['kɔːnɪʃ 'pæstɪz] — kornische Pasteten *(Gebäck aus Blätterteig und Füllung)*
first of all ['fɜːst_əv_ˈɔːl] — zuallererst
ingredients [ɪnˈgriːdjənts] — Zutaten
quantity ['kwɒntətɪ] — Menge
recipe ['resɪpɪ] — (Koch)rezept
pastry ['peɪstrɪ] — Teig
flour ['flaʊə] — Mehl
margarine [ˌmɑːdʒəˈriːn] — Margarine
filling ['fɪlɪŋ] — Füllung
beef [biːf] — Rindfleisch
onion ['ʌnjən] — Zwiebel
pepper ['pepə] — Pfeffer

C 1

announcement [əˈnaʊnsmənt] — Ansage, Durchsage
store [stɔː] — *AE:* Geschäft, Laden
salon ['sælɒn] — Salon

fur [fɜː] — Pelz
weekly ['wiːklɪ] — wöchentlich
(to) give away sth ['gɪv_əˈweɪ] — etw verschenken/ kostenlos abgeben
beauty treatment ['bjuːtɪ ˌtriːtmənt] — Schönheitsbehandlung

C 2

famous ['feɪməs] — berühmt, sehr bekannt
place [pleɪs] — Ort; *hier:* Sehenswürdigkeit
on the corner of [ɒn ðə ˈkɔːnər_əv] — an der Ecke von
(to) tell sb the way ['tel ˌsʌmbədɪ ðə ˈweɪ] — jdm den Weg zeigen
straight [streɪt] — gerade, geradewegs, geradeaus
(to) turn left/right ['tɜːn 'left/'raɪt] — nach links/rechts abbiegen
on your left/right [ɒn jɔː 'left/'raɪt] — auf Ihrer linken/ rechten Seite
position [pəˈzɪʃn] — Stellung; *hier:* Lage

T 1

papers ['peɪpəz] — Zeitungen
dailies ['deɪlɪz] — Tageszeitungen
probably ['prɒbəblɪ] — wahrscheinlich
event [ɪˈvent] — Ereignis
by [baɪ] — *hier:* mit Hilfe von; über
(news) agency ['njuːz_ˌeɪdʒənsɪ] — (Nachrichten)agentur
such as ['sʌtʃ_əz] — wie zum Beispiel
(to) take a look at sb/sth ['teɪk_əˈlʊk_ət] — einen Blick werfen auf jdn/etw
production [prəˈdʌkʃn] — Herstellung, Fertigung, Produktion
(to) collect [kəˈlekt] — sammeln
on the telex ['ɒn ðə 'teleks] — über Fernschreiber
assistant editor [əˈsɪstənt ˈedɪtə] — Redaktionsassistent(in)
article ['ɑːtɪkl] — Artikel
layout man ['leɪaʊtˌmæn] — Layouter, Entwurfgrafiker
size [saɪz] — Größe
proof-reader ['pruːfˌriːdə] — Korrektor(in)
printer ['prɪntə] — Drucker(in)
(to) operate ['ɒpəreɪt] — in Betrieb/Gang sein, funktionieren; *hier:* Druckpresse bedienen

(printing-)press ['prɪntɪŋˌpres] — Druckpresse/-maschine
edition [ɪˈdɪʃn] — Ausgabe, Auflage
van [væn] — Lieferwagen
(to) deliver [dɪˈlɪvə] — (aus)liefern
newspaper shop ['njuːzpeɪpəˌʃɒp] — Kiosk, Zeitungshändler
(to) go on [ˈgəʊ 'ɒn] — vor sich gehen, passieren; weitermachen

well-known [ˌwelˈnəʊn] — bekannt
well-liked [ˌwelˈlaɪkt] — beliebt
(to) work [wɜːk] — *hier:* bedienen

VOCABULARY

Unit 5

T 2

upset [ʌpˈset]	fassungslos, aufgeregt
number-plate [ˈnʌmbəˌpleɪt]	Nummernschild
pretty [ˈprɪtɪ]	schön, hübsch; *hier:* ziemlich
like this [laɪk ˈðɪs]	so, auf diese Art und Weise
still [stɪl]	*hier:* immer noch
a bit of [ə ˈbɪt əv]	ein bißchen
darling [ˈdɑːlɪŋ]	Liebling
pleasure [ˈpleʒə]	Freude, Vergnügen
number-plate centre [ˈnʌmbəˌpleɪt ˌsentə]	*etwa:* Zulassungsstelle
rule [ruːl]	Vorschrift
motor-bike [ˈməʊtəˌbaɪk]	Motorrad
scooter [ˈskuːtə]	Motorroller
on the road [ɒn ðə ˈrəʊd]	unterwegs

F

left-hand/right-hand side [ˈlefthænd/ ˈraɪthænd ˈsaɪd]	links/rechts, linke/rechte Seite
in the centre [ɪn ðə ˈsentə]	in der Mitte, im Mittelpunkt, im Zentrum
background [ˈbækɡraʊnd]	Hintergrund
foreground [ˈfɔːɡraʊnd]	Vordergrund
(to) guess [ɡes]	(er)raten, vermuten

UNIT 5

A1

(to) spend [spend]	verbringen
grandad [ˈɡrændæd]	Opa
inhabitant [ɪnˈhæbɪtənt]	Einwohner(in)
old-fashioned [ˌəʊldˈfæʃnd]	altmodisch
in those days [ɪn ˈðəʊz ˈdeɪz]	damals
cart [kɑːt]	(Pferde)wagen, Karre(n)
lorry [ˈlɒrɪ]	Lastwagen
central heating [ˌsentrəl ˈhiːtɪŋ]	Zentralheizung
nothing like that [ˈnʌθɪŋ laɪk ˈðæt]	nichts Derartiges
nothing at all [ˈnʌθɪŋ ət ˈɔːl]	überhaupt nichts
unhappy [ʌnˈhæpɪ]	unglücklich
(to) be interested in sb/sth [bɪ ˈɪntrɪstɪd ɪn]	sich für jdn/etw interessieren
hunting [ˈhʌntɪŋ]	Jagen; Jagd
grandma [ˈɡrænmɑː]	Oma

A3

curious [ˈkjʊərɪəs]	neugierig
fisherman [ˈfɪʃəmən]	Fischer
out at sea [ˈaʊt ət ˈsiː]	draußen auf dem Meer, auf hoher See
trawler [ˈtrɔːlə]	Fischdampfer
what else [ˈwɒt ˈels]	was sonst (noch)

A 4

comfortable [ˈkʌmftəbl]	bequem
from all over the world [frəm ˈɔːl ˈəʊvə ðə ˈwɜːld]	aus der ganzen Welt
pollution [pəˈluːʃn]	Umweltverschmutzung

A 5

supermarket [ˈsuːpəˌmɑːkɪt]	Supermarkt

A 6

neighbour [ˈneɪbə]	Nachbar(in)
(to) move into/in [ˈmuːv ˌɪntə]	einziehen
not long ago [ˈnɒt ˈlɒŋ əˈɡəʊ]	vor kurzem, unlängst
shock [ʃɒk]	Schreck, Schock
normal [ˈnɔːməl]	normal, gewöhnlich
funny-looking [ˈfʌnɪˌlʊkɪŋ]	komisch (aussehend)
bean [biːn]	Bohne
windmill [ˈwɪndmɪl]	Windmühle
smell [smel]	Geruch; *hier:* Gestank
polluted [pəˈluːtɪd]	verschmutzt, umweltbelastet
crowded [ˈkraʊdɪd]	überfüllt *(mit Menschen)*
(to) decide [dɪˈsaɪd]	sich entscheiden, beschließen
way of life [ˈweɪ əv ˈlaɪf]	Lebensweise, Lebensstil, Lebensart
(to) move to the country [ˈmuːv tə ðə ˈkʌntrɪ]	aufs Land ziehen
wholefood [ˈhəʊlfuːd]	Vollwertkost/-nahrung
above all [əˈbʌv ˈɔːl]	vor allem
alternative [ɔːlˈtɜːnətɪv]	alternativ; Alternative
electricity [ˌɪlekˈtrɪsətɪ]	Strom, Elektrizität

B 1

bed and breakfast place [ˈbed ən ˈbrekfəst ˌpleɪs]	Frühstückspension
seaside resort [ˈsiːsaɪd rɪˈzɔːt]	Seebad, Badeort
landlady [ˈlænˌleɪdɪ]	(Haus-, Gast-, Pensions-)wirtin
oil tanker [ˈɔɪl ˌtæŋkə]	Öltanker
(to) get onto [ˈɡet ˌɒntə]	gelangen auf
storm [stɔːm]	Sturm
(to) do some shopping [ˈduː səm ˈʃɒpɪŋ]	Einkäufe machen
(to) sink [sɪŋk]	sinken, untergehen
last night [ˌlɑːst ˈnaɪt]	gestern abend, letzte Nacht
rock [rɒk]	Fels
signal [ˈsɪɡnl]	Signal, Zeichen
helicopter [ˈhelɪkɒptə]	Hubschrauber
government [ˈɡʌvəmənt]	Regierung
(to) call in [ˈkɔːl ˌɪn]	herbeiholen
army [ˈɑːmɪ]	Armee, Heer
(to) blame sb for sth [bleɪm]	jdm Vorwürfe machen
could you? [ˈkʊd juː]	oder?
that year [ˈðæt ˈjɪə]	in dem/jenem Jahr

Unit 5

VOCABULARY

B 2

somewhere else [ˈsʌmweərˌels] — anderswo(hin)

environment [ɪnˈvaɪərənmənt] — Umgebung, Umwelt
(to) put sth up [pʊt] — aufstellen, errichten
sign [saɪn] — Zeichen, Schild
(to) remind sb to do sth [rɪˈmaɪnd] — jdn daran erinnern, etw zu tun
tidy [ˈtaɪdi] — ordentlich, sauber, gepflegt
rubbish [ˈrʌbɪʃ] — Müll, Abfall, Abfälle
rubbish bin [ˈrʌbɪʃˌbɪn] — Mülleimer
control [kənˈtrəʊl] — Kontrolle
central [ˈsentrəl] — in der Mitte gelegen, zentral, Haupt-
(to) have a swim [ˈhævˌə ˈswɪm] — schwimmen gehen
museum [mjuːˈzɪəm] — Museum
fish and chips [ˈfɪʃˌən ˈtʃɪps] — gebackener Fisch und Pommes frites

B 3

plastic [ˈplæstɪk] — Kunststoff, Plastik
bottle bank [ˈbɒtlˌbæŋk] — Glascontainer, Behälter für Glasabfall
special [ˈspeʃl] — besondere(r,s), gesondert
container [kənˈteɪnə] — Behälter
total points [ˈtəʊtl ˈpɔɪnts] — Gesamtpunktzahl
(to) keep up [ˈkiːpˌˈʌp] — beibehalten, weitermachen
active [ˈæktɪv] — hier: tätig, lebendig, aktiv
carefully [ˈkeəfʊli] — sorgfältig, aufmerksam

C 1

earth [ɜːθ] — Erde
group [gruːp] — Gruppe
(to) protect sb/sth from [prəˈtekt] — jdn/etw schützen vor
acid rain [ˈæsɪd ˈreɪn] — saurer Regen
healthy [ˈhelθi] — gesund
waste [weɪst] — Abfall
transport [ˈtrænspɔːt] — Transport, Verkehr
energy [ˈenədʒi] — Energie
nuclear energy [ˈnjuːklɪərˌˈenədʒi] — Atomenergie
action [ˈækʃn] — Maßnahme, Handlung, Tat, Aktion
(to) save [seɪv] — retten; hier: sparen
(to) protest about sb/sth [prəˈtest] — gegen etw/jdn protestieren
(to) fight [faɪt] — kämpfen
form [fɔːm] — Form, Gestalt, Figur
project [ˈprɒdʒekt] — Projekt, Vorhaben
power station [ˈpaʊəˌsteɪʃn] — Kraftwerk
chemical [ˈkemɪkl] — Chemikalie
motorway [ˈməʊtəweɪ] — Autobahn
past [pɑːst] — Vergangenheit
in a lot of ways [ɪnˌə ˈlɒtˌəv ˈweɪz] — auf vielfältige Art und Weise

C 2

should [ʃʊd] — sollte
battery [ˈbætəri] — Batterie
(to) ride [raɪd] — reiten; hier: fahren
(to) accept [əkˈsept] — annehmen, akzeptieren
recycled [ˌriːˈsaɪkld] — wiederverwertet
recycled paper [ˈriːsaɪkld ˈpeɪpə] — Umweltschutzpapier
writing paper [ˈraɪtɪŋ ˈpeɪpə] — Brief-/Schreibpapier
toilet roll [ˈtɔɪlɪtˌrəʊl] — Toilettenpapierrolle, Klopapier
spray [spreɪ] — Sprühdose/-mittel, Spray
Good luck! [ˈgʊd ˈlʌk] — Viel Erfolg! Viel Glück!
detail [ˈdiːteɪl] — Einzelheit, Detail

C 3

some more [səm ˈmɔː] — weitere
envelope [ˈenvələʊp] — Briefumschlag
pink [pɪŋk] — rosa
orange [ˈɒrɪndʒ] — orange(farben); Orange
sticker [ˈstɪkə] — Aufkleber
order [ˈɔːdə] — Ordnung, Reihenfolge; hier: Auftrag, Bestellung
article [ˈɑːtɪkl] — Artikel, Gegenstand
total [ˈtəʊtl] — Gesamtsumme
(to) write down [ˈraɪt ˈdaʊn] — aufschreiben

T

(to) surprise [səˈpraɪz] — überraschen
member [ˈmembə] — Mitglied
coal-fired power station [ˈkəʊlfaɪəd ˈpaʊəˌsteɪʃn] — Kohlekraftwerk
protester [prəˈtestə] — Demonstrant(in)
main gate [ˈmeɪn ˈgeɪt] — Haupttor
(to) block [blɒk] — blockieren
railway line [ˈreɪlweɪˌlaɪn] — Eisenbahnlinie/-gleis
(to) take ten minutes [ˈteɪk ˈten ˈmɪnɪts] — zehn Minuten brauchen
demonstrator [ˈdemɒnstreɪtə] — Demonstrant(in)
(to) climb up [ˈklaɪmˌʌp] — hinaufklettern
(to) hang [hæŋ] — hängen
banner [ˈbænə] — Fahne, Transparent
in the field of [ɪn ðə ˈfiːldˌəv] — auf dem Gebiet von
health [helθ] — Gesundheit
(to) go on [ˈgəʊ ˈɒn] — weitergehen; andauern
(to) promise [ˈprɒmɪs] — versprechen
a discussion on [ə dɪsˈkʌʃnˌɒn] — eine Diskussion über
summary [ˈsʌməri] — Zusammenfassung, Inhaltsangabe
(to) reply [rɪˈplaɪ] — erwidern, entgegnen
headline [ˈhedlaɪn] — Schlagzeile
woodland [ˈwʊdlənd] — Wald(gebiet)
smog [smɒg] — Dunstglocke, Smog
radioactive waste [ˌreɪdɪəʊˈæktɪv ˈweɪst] — Atommüll
(to) damage [ˈdæmɪdʒ] — beschädigen, schaden
in my opinion [ɪn ˈmaɪ əˈpɪnjən] — meines Erachtens, meiner Meinung nach

V VOCABULARY

Unit 6

UNIT 6

St

nation ['neɪʃn]	Nation, Volk, Staat
(to) spot [spɒt]	entdecken, erblicken
Brit [brɪt]	Engländer(in), Brite, Britin
Australian [ɒˈstreɪljən]	australisch; Australier(in)
Polish [ˈpəʊlɪʃ]	polnisch; Pole, Polin; Polnisch
Pakistani [ˌpɑːkɪˈstɑːnɪ]	pakistanisch; Pakistani, Pakistaner(in)
Chinese [ˌtʃaɪˈniːz]	chinesisch; Chinese, Chinesin; Chinesisch
South African [ˌsaʊθˈæfrɪkən]	südafrikanisch; Südafrikaner(in)

A1

(to) pass by [ˈpɑːs baɪ]	vorüber-/vorbeigehen an
Indian [ˈɪndjən]	indisch; Inder(in)
(to) move in(to) [ˈmuːv ˈɪntə]	einziehen
next door [ˌneks ˈdɔː]	nebenan
Come on! [ˈkʌm ˈɒn]	Na, na!; Geh mir doch weg!
foreigner [ˈfɒrənə]	Ausländer(in)
Wait a minute! [ˈweɪt ə ˈmɪnɪt]	Augenblick mal!
(to) let sth go to the dogs [ˈlet ˈsʌmθɪŋ ˈgəʊ tə ðə ˈdɒgz]	etw herunterkommen lassen
(to) renovate [ˈrenəveɪt]	renovieren
(to) notice [ˈnəʊtɪs]	bemerken, wahrnehmen
(to) paint [peɪnt]	(an)streichen
(to) do sth to sth [duː]	etw an etw machen
round the corner [ˈraʊnd ðə ˈkɔːnə]	um die Ecke
(to) fix sth [fɪks]	etw reparieren/in Ordnung bringen
curtain [ˈkɜːtn]	Vorhang
I think so [aɪ ˈθɪŋk səʊ]	Ich glaube/denke schon
(to) mend [mend]	reparieren, ausbessern
back door [ˌbækˈdɔː]	Hintertür
dustbin [ˈdʌstbɪn]	Mülleimer
(to) make sth look nice [ˈmeɪk ˈsʌmθɪŋ lʊk ˈnaɪs]	etw hübsch aussehen lassen
a few times [ə ˈfjuː ˈtaɪmz]	ein paarmal
chance [tʃɑːns]	Gelegenheit, Chance
(to) paper [ˈpeɪpə]	tapezieren
pipe [paɪp]	Wasserleitung
ceiling [ˈsiːlɪŋ]	(Zimmer)decke

A2

good afternoon [ˈgʊd ˌɑːftəˈnuːn]	guten Tag
how do you do [ˈhaʊ də ˌjuː ˈduː]	guten Tag (bei Vorstellung)
unemployed [ˌʌnɪmˈplɔɪd]	arbeitslos
I'm sorry [aɪm ˈsɒrɪ]	es tut mir leid
job centre [ˈdʒɒbˌsentə]	Arbeitsvermittlungsstelle
(to) come back from [ˈkʌm ˈbæk frəm]	zurückkommen von
(to) close down [ˈkləʊz ˈdaʊn]	stillegen, schließen
unfortunate [ʌnˈfɔːtʃnət]	bedauerlich
(to) apply for [əˈplaɪ fə]	sich bewerben um
at least [ət ˈliːst]	wenigstens, mindestens
oh dear [ˈəʊ ˈdɪə]	O je! Meine Güte!
savings [ˈseɪvɪŋz]	Ersparnisse
for now [fə ˈnaʊ]	für heute; im Moment
bank manager [ˈbæŋkˌmænɪdʒə]	Bankdirektor(in)
saucer [ˈsɔːsə]	Untertasse
table-cloth [ˈteɪblˌklɒθ]	Tischtuch/-decke

A3

perfect [ˈpɜːfɪkt]	vollkommen, perfekt
next door neighbour [ˈneksdɔːˈneɪbə]	Nachbar(in) von nebenan
marvellous [ˈmɑːvləs]	wunderbar, großartig
(to) run out [ˈrʌn ˈaʊt]	*hier:* ablaufen
job situation [ˈdʒɒb sɪtjʊˌeɪʃn]	Lage auf dem Arbeitsmarkt

A4

(to) do some repairs [ˈduː səm rɪˈpeəz]	einige Reparaturarbeiten machen
material [məˈtɪərɪəl]	Baustoff, Material
budget [ˈbʌdʒɪt]	Etat, Budget
per [pə]	pro

B1

advice [ədˈvaɪs]	Beratung, Rat
CAB [ˌsiːˌeɪˈbiː] [kæb]	öffentliche Beratungsstelle
throughout [θruːˈaʊt]	überall in
adviser [ədˈvaɪzə]	Berater(in)
(to) deal with sth [diːl wɪð]	sich mit etw befassen
immigrant [ˈɪmɪgrənt]	Einwanderer(in)
(to) take a seat [ˈteɪk ə ˈsiːt]	sich setzen, Platz nehmen
What can I do for you? [ˈwɒt kən aɪ ˈduː fɔː ˌjuː]	Was kann ich für Sie tun?
next to [ˈnekstə]	(direkt) neben
arrival [əˈraɪvl]	Ankunft
relative [ˈrelətɪv]	Verwandte(r)
What's your problem? [ˈwɒts jɔː ˈprɒbləm]	Wo fehlt es Ihnen?
interview [ˈɪntəvjuː]	Interview, Befragung
employment [ɪmˈplɔɪmənt]	Beschäftigung
let me see [ˈlet mɪ ˈsiː]	wir wollen mal sehen, laß mich mal sehen

B2

town hall [ˈtaʊnˈhɔːl]	Rathaus
dragon [ˈdrægən]	Drache

B5

for ages [fərˈeɪdʒɪz]	eine Ewigkeit, seit Ewigkeiten
cartoon [kɑːˈtuːn]	Karikatur
(to) shave [ʃeɪv]	(sich) rasieren
Easter [ˈiːstə]	Ostern

VOCABULARY

Unit 6

C1

(to) stand as (a candidate) ['stænd əz ə 'kændɪdət]	kandidieren	
independent [ˌɪndɪ'pendənt]	(politisch) Unabhängige(r)	
election [ɪ'lekʃn]	Wahl	
local election ['ləʊkl ɪ'lekʃn]	Kommunalwahl	
home town ['həʊm 'taʊn]	Heimatstadt	
speech [spiːtʃ]	Rede	
(to) have a good look round/at sth ['hæv ə 'gʊd 'lʊk raʊnd/ət]	sich gründlich um-/ansehen	
the unemployed [ðɪ ˌʌnɪm'plɔɪd]	die Arbeitslosen	
not any of us ['nɒt 'enɪ əv ʌs]	keiner von uns	
modern ['mɒdn]	modern	
congress centre ['kɒŋgres ˌsentə]	Kongreßzentrum	
council ['kaʊnsl]	Stadtrat, Rat(sversammlung)	
(to) provide sth for sb [prə'vaɪd]	jdm etw zur Verfügung stellen	
playground ['pleɪgraʊnd]	Spielplatz	
tennis court ['tenɪskɔːt]	Tennisplatz	
furniture ['fɜːnɪtʃə]	Möbel	
youth centre ['juːθ ˌsentə]	Jugendhaus/-zentrum	
nursery school ['nɜːsrɪ ˌskuːl]	Kindergarten	
wider ['waɪdə]	breiter, weiter	
(to) contrast [kən'trɑːst]	gegenüberstellen	

C3

(to) be happy about sth ['hæpɪ ə'baʊt]	über etw glücklich sein
situation [ˌsɪtjʊ'eɪʃn]	Lage
(to) do a survey of sth ['duː ə 'sɜːveɪ əv]	einen Bericht/eine Untersuchung von/über etw machen
(to) multiply by ['mʌltɪplaɪ baɪ]	malnehmen/multiplizieren mit

T1

(to) elect [ɪ'lekt]	wählen
Member of Parliament ['membər əv 'pɑːləmənt]	Abgeordnete(r) des Unterhauses
political [pə'lɪtɪkl]	politisch
party ['pɑːtɪ]	Partei
the Conservatives [kən'sɜːvətɪvz]	die Konservative Partei
the Labour Party ['leɪbə ˌpɑːtɪ]	die Labour Party
vote [vəʊt]	(Wahl)stimme
candidate ['kændɪdət]	Kandidat
(to) run [rʌn]	hier: regieren
unemployment [ˌʌnɪm'plɔɪmənt]	Arbeitslosigkeit
far too high ['fɑː tuː 'haɪ]	viel zu hoch
(to) go down ['gəʊ 'daʊn]	sinken
(to) go up ['gəʊ 'ʌp]	steigen
per cent [pə'sent]	Prozent
number of police ['nʌmbər əv pə'liːs]	hier: Polizeistärke
(to) increase [ɪn'kriːs]	zunehmen, ansteigen
(to) reduce [rɪ'djuːs]	vermindern, reduzieren
crime [kraɪm]	Verbrechen
(to) mean it ['miːn ɪt]	dahinterstehen, es ernst meinen
future ['fjuːtʃə]	Zukunft
Youth Training Scheme [ˌjuːθ 'treɪnɪŋ ˌskiːm]	staatliches Programm zur Berufsausbildung Jugendlicher
education [ˌedjuː'keɪʃn]	Bildung, Ausbildung
(to) decrease [dɪ'kriːs]	abnehmen, weniger/geringer werden
(to) accept [ək'sept]	aufnehmen, akzeptieren
Asia ['eɪʃə]	Asien
(to) be fair to sb [bɪ 'feə tə]	gerecht/fair gegenüber jdm sein
(to) slow down ['sləʊ 'daʊn]	verlangsamen
immigration [ˌɪmɪ'greɪʃn]	Einwanderung
pension ['penʃn]	Rente, Pension
(to) vote [vəʊt]	wählen
law and order ['lɔː ən 'ɔːdə]	Recht und Ordnung

T2

Asian ['eɪʃn]	asiatisch; Asiat(in)
African ['æfrɪkən]	afrikanisch; Afrikaner(in)
(to) immigrate ['ɪmɪgreɪt]	einwandern
(to) solve [sɒlv]	lösen
coloured person ['kʌləd ˌpɜːsn]	Farbige(r)
(to) exist [ɪg'zɪst]	vorhanden sein, existieren
Germany ['dʒɜːmənɪ]	Deutschland

T3

figure ['fɪgə]	Zahl, Ziffer
past [pɑːst]	vergangene(r, s), letzte(r, s)
(to) come down to ['kʌm 'daʊn]	sinken auf
second lowest ['sekənd 'ləʊɪst]	zweitniedrigste(r,s)
rate [reɪt]	Rate
(to) turn away ['tɜːn ə'weɪ]	wegschicken, abweisen
tens of thousands ['tenz əv 'θaʊzndz]	Zehntausende

S1

do it yourself ['duː ɪt jɔː'self]	Heimwerken
homeowner ['həʊmˌəʊnə]	Hausbesitzer(in)
(to) recommend [ˌrekə'mend]	empfehlen
basic ['beɪsɪk]	grundlegend, Grund-
tool-kit ['tuːlkɪt]	Werkzeugsatz/-kasten
screwdriver ['skruːˌdraɪvə]	Schraubenzieher
spanner ['spænə]	Schraubenschlüssel
angle-grinder ['æŋglˌgraɪndə]	Winkelschleifer

VOCABULARY

Unit 7

jigsaw ['dʒɪgsɔː]	Stich-/Laubsäge	(to) take off [teɪk 'ɒf]	abziehen
power drill ['paʊədrɪl]	elektrische Bohrmaschine	ideal [aɪ'dɪəl]	Ideal; ideal
test lamp ['testlæmp]	Prüflampe	private ['praɪvɪt]	privat
pipe wrench ['paɪprentʃ]	Rohrzange	(to) turn on ['tɜːn 'ɒn]	ein-/anschalten
jump lead ['dʒʌmpliːd]	Starthilfekabel	button ['bʌtn]	Knopf
hammer ['hæmə]	Hammer	beginner [bɪ'gɪnə]	Anfänger(in)
pliers ['plaɪəz]	Draht-/Kneifzange	all-round [ˌɔːl'raʊnd]	all-/vielseitig
crossword puzzle ['krɒswɜːd ˌpʌzl]	Kreuzworträtsel	model ['mɒdl]	Modell
frame [freɪm]	Rahmen	washing powder ['wɒʃɪŋ ˌpaʊdə]	Waschmittel/-pulver
nut [nʌt]	(Schrauben)mutter	video recorder ['vɪdɪəʊrɪ ˌkɔːdə]	Videorecorder
practical ['præktɪkl]	praktisch	T-shirt ['tiːʃɜːt]	T-Shirt
disc [dɪsk]	(Schleif)scheibe		
metal ['metl]	Metall		
battery ['bætərɪ]	Batterie		
(to) drill [drɪl]	bohren		
nail [neɪl]	Nagel		
(to) bend [bend]	biegen, krümmen		
wire ['waɪə]	Draht, Leitung		
(to) check [tʃek]	überprüfen		
electric [ɪ'lektrɪk]	elektrisch		
(to) tighten ['taɪtn]	anziehen, festziehen		
(to) loosen ['luːsn]	lösen, losdrehen		
screw [skruː]	Schraube		

UNIT 7

St

history ['hɪstrɪ]	Geschichte
now and then ['naʊ ən 'ðen]	heute und damals

A1

all the best ['ɔːl ðə 'best]	zum Wohl!
Cheers! [tʃɪəz]	Prost!
bar [bɑː]	Bar
strange [streɪndʒ]	fremd; *hier:* komisch, merkwürdig
opening hours ['əʊpnɪŋ ˌaʊəz]	Öffnungszeiten
traditional [trə'dɪʃənl]	traditionell; *hier:* traditionsbewußt
school uniform ['skuːl 'juːnɪfɔːm]	Schulkleidung/-uniform
that sort of thing ['ðæt sɔːt əv 'θɪŋ]	dergleichen
tradition [trə'dɪʃn]	Überlieferung, Tradition
(to) sound a good idea [ˌsaʊnd ə 'gʊd aɪ'dɪə]	nicht schlecht klingen
Englishman ['ɪŋglɪʃmən]	Engländer
Highland Games ['haɪlənd 'geɪmz]	schottische Hochlandwettkämpfe

A2

shoemaker ['ʃuːˌmeɪkə]	Schuhmacher(in)
and so on [ən 'səʊ ɒn]	und so weiter, usw
local history ['ləʊkl 'hɪstrɪ]	Lokal-/Ortsgeschichte
sign [saɪn]	Schild
dragon ['drægən]	Drache
(to) kill [kɪl]	töten
century ['sentʃʊrɪ]	Jahrhundert
tea shop ['tiːʃɒp]	Teeladen/-stube
(to) bring down ['brɪŋ 'daʊn]	senken
Bobby ['bɒbɪ]	Polizist
(to) start [stɑːt]	*hier:* gründen
short form ['ʃɔːt fɔːm]	Kurzform
horse rider ['hɔːsˌraɪdə]	Reiter(in)
sword [sɔːd]	Schwert
description [dɪ'skrɪpʃn]	Beschreibung
in the same way [ɪn ðə 'seɪm 'weɪ]	auf die gleiche Art und Weise

S 2

British Empire ['brɪtɪʃ 'empaɪə]	Britisches Weltreich
from all over the world [frəm 'ɔːl ˌəʊvə ðə 'wɜːld]	aus aller Welt
especially [ɪs'peʃlɪ]	besonders
amongst [ə'mʌŋst]	unter, zwischen
(to) get married ['get 'mærɪd]	heiraten
(to) cater for ['keɪtə fə]	mit Speisen und Getränken versorgen
lunchtime ['lʌnʃtaɪm]	Essenszeit, Mittagszeit
take away ['teɪk ə'weɪ]	zum Mitnehmen
cash [kæʃ]	Bargeld
plastic money ['plæstɪk ˌmʌnɪ]	Plastikgeld
credit card ['kredɪt ˌkɑːd]	Kreditkarte
fully licensed ['fʊlɪ 'laɪsənst]	mit Schankerlaubnis für alkoholische Getränke

S 3

consumer [kən'sjuːmə]	Verbraucher, Konsument
household ['haʊshəʊld]	Haushalt
speciality [ˌspeʃɪ'ælɪtɪ]	Spezialität
automatic [ˌɔːtə'mætɪk]	automatisch
(dish)washer ['dɪʃˌwɒʃə]	Spülmaschine
down payment ['daʊn 'peɪmənt]	Anzahlung
special offer ['speʃl 'ɒfə]	Sonderangebot
summer sale ['sʌmə 'seɪl]	Sommerschlußverkauf
cash [kæʃ]	Bargeld
drill [drɪl]	Bohrer, Bohrmaschine
instalment [ɪn'stɔːlmənt]	Rate
discount ['dɪskaʊnt]	Preisnachlaß, Rabatt
advertisement [əd'vɜːtɪsmənt]	Anzeige, Reklame
payment ['peɪmənt]	Zahlung
goods [gʊdz]	Waren
banknote ['bæŋknəʊt]	Geldschein, Banknote

VOCABULARY

Unit 7

A 3
the day before yesterday [ðə ˈdeɪ bɪˌfɔː ˈjestədɪ] — vorgestern
flea market [ˈfliːˌmɑːkɪt] — Flohmarkt
lunchtime [ˈlʌnʃtaɪm] — Mittagszeit, Mittagspause

A 4
real [rɪəl] — wirklich, echt
sandwich [ˈsænwɪdʒ] — belegtes Brot
accent [ˈæksənt] — Aussprache, Akzent
best wishes [ˌbest ˈwɪʃɪz] — alles Gute

B 1
talk show [ˈtɔːkʃəʊ] — Gesprächsrunde, Talk-Show
interviewer [ˈɪntəvjuːə] — Gesprächsleiter(in)
rock singer [ˈrɒkˌsɪŋə] — Rocksänger(in)
charity promoter [ˈtʃærətɪprəˌməʊtə] — Wohltätigkeitsveranstalter
up till now [ˌʌp tɪl ˈnaʊ] — bis jetzt
sixties [ˈsɪkstɪz] — Sechziger(jahre)
journalist [ˈdʒɜːnəlɪst] — Journalist(in)
pop star [ˈpɒpstɑː] — Popstar
hit record [ˈhɪtˌrekɔːd] — Hitplatte
(to) organize [ˈɔːgənaɪz] — organisieren
in this way [ɪn ˈðɪs ˈweɪ] — so, auf diese Art und Weise
Third World [ˌθɜːd ˈwɜːld] — Dritte Welt
(to) make sb Sir [ˌmeɪk ˈsʌmbədɪ ˈsɜː] — jdn zum Ritter schlagen
on TV [ˌɒn ˌtiːˈviː] — im Fernsehen
a couple of [ə ˈkʌpl_əv] — mehrere, ein paar
sailor [ˈseɪlə] — Matrose, Seefahrer(in)
writer [ˈraɪtə] — Schriftsteller(in)
(to) sail across [ˌseɪl əˈkrɒs] — mit dem Schiff überqueren
on sb's own [ɒn ˈsʌmbədɪz ˈəʊn] — alleine, auf sich gestellt
woman sailor [ˌwʊmən ˈseɪlə] — weiblicher Matrose, Seefahrerin
(to) take up sth [ˌteɪk ˈʌp] — etw anfangen/in Angriff nehmen
sailing [ˈseɪlɪŋ] — Segeln
(to) give up sth [ˌgɪv ˈʌp] — etw aufgeben
on the radio [ˌɒn ðə ˈreɪdɪəʊ] — im Radio
main occupation [ˌmeɪn ˌɒkjʊˈpeɪʃn] — Hauptbeschäftigung
at sea [ət ˈsiː] — auf See
title [ˈtaɪtl] — (Adels)titel
for quite a while [fə ˌkwaɪt ə ˈwaɪl] — ziemlich lange
astronaut [ˈæstrənɔːt] — Astronaut(in), Raumfahrer(in)
introduction [ˌɪntrəˈdʌkʃn] — Einführung; hier: Vorstellung
USA (United States of America) [ˌjuːesˈeɪ] — Vereinigte Staaten (von Amerika)
test pilot [ˈtestˌpaɪlət] — Testpilot(in)
professor [prəˈfesə] — Professor(in)
engineering [ˌendʒɪˈnɪərɪŋ] — Maschinenbau
chairman [ˈtʃeəmən] — Vorsitzender, Präsident
company [ˈkʌmpənɪ] — Gesellschaft, Firma
on business [ɒn ˈbɪznɪs] — geschäftlich

B 2
career [kəˈrɪə] — Laufbahn, Karriere
racing driver [ˈreɪsɪŋˌdraɪvə] — Rennfahrer(in)
experience [ɪksˈpɪərɪəns] — Erfahrung

B 3
film star [ˈfɪlmstɑː] — Filmstar, berühmte(r) Filmschauspieler(in)
candidate [ˈkændɪdət] — Kandidat, Bewerber
biography [baɪˈɒgrəfɪ] — Lebenslauf, Biographie
California [ˌkælɪˈfɔːnjə] — Kalifornien
(to) get married [ˌget ˈmærɪd] — (sich) (ver)heiraten
politics [ˈpɒlɪtɪks] — Politik
(to) protest against sth [prəˈtest əˈgenst] — gegen etw protestieren
Vietnam [ˌvjetˈnæm] — Vietnam
war [wɔː] — Krieg
atomic bomb [əˈtɒmɪk ˈbɒm] — Atombombe
(to) guess [ges] — vermuten, raten
date of birth [ˌdeɪt əv ˈbɜːθ] — Geburtsdatum
birthplace [ˈbɜːθpleɪs] — Geburtsort

C 1
right now [ˌraɪt ˈnaʊ] — jetzt (gerade)
old-fashioned [ˌəʊldˈfæʃnd] — altmodisch
market [ˈmɑːkɪt] — Markt
hall [hɔːl] — Halle
over there [ˌəʊvə ˈðeə] — dort drüben
area [ˈeərɪə] — Gebiet
all fields [ˌɔːl ˈfiːldz] — lauter Felder
monk [mʌŋk] — Mönch
(to) grow [grəʊ] — hier: anbauen
the one [ðə ˈwʌn] — der-/die-/dasjenige
anyway [ˈenɪweɪ] — jedenfalls, wie dem auch sei
(to) throw sb out [θrəʊ] — jdn hinauswerfen, vertreiben
simply [ˈsɪmplɪ] — einfach
trade [treɪd] — Handel
in a way [ɪn ə ˈweɪ] — in gewissem Sinn
feeling [ˈfiːlɪŋ] — hier: Atmosphäre
street entertainer [ˈstriːtentəˌteɪnə] — Straßenkünstler(in)
stall [stɔːl] — (Verkaufs)stand
all sorts of things [ˌɔːl sɔːts əv ˈθɪŋz] — alle möglichen Dinge
later on [ˌleɪtər ˈɒn] — später
since then [sɪns ˈðen] — seither
no longer [ˌnəʊ ˈlɒŋgə] — nicht mehr

C 2
dancer [ˈdɑːnsə] — Tänzer(in)
guitar [gɪˈtɑː] — Gitarre
guitar-player [gɪˈtɑːˌpleɪə] — Gitarrenspieler(in)
(to) be a quiet talker [bɪ ə ˈkwaɪət ˈtɔːkə] — leise sprechen
smoker [ˈsməʊkə] — Raucher(in)
(to) be a fast talker [bɪ ə ˈfɑːst ˈtɔːkə] — schnell sprechen

VOCABULARY

Unit 7

wrong note ['rɒŋ 'nəʊt]	falscher Ton	exhaust [ɪg'zɔ:st]	Auspuff
piano [pɪ'ænəʊ]	Klavier, Piano	bumper ['bʌmpə]	Stoßstange
(to) put one's fingers in one's ears ['pʊt wʌnz 'fɪŋɡəz_ɪn wʌnz_ɪəz]	sich die Ohren zuhalten	number-plate ['nʌmbə‚pleɪt]	Nummernschild
		workshop ['wɜ:kʃɒp]	Werkstatt
tasty ['teɪstɪ]	lecker, schmackhaft	service ['sɜ:vɪs]	Inspektion
(to) step on sth ['step_ɒn]	auf etw treten	service check ['sɜ:vɪs‚tʃek]	Wartung
toe [təʊ]	Zeh(e)	pressure ['preʃə]	Druck
all kinds of ['ɔ:l 'kaɪndz_əv]	alle möglichen	tread [tred]	Profil
		(to) remove [rɪ'mu:v]	abmontieren
glove [ɡlʌv]	Handschuh	rear [rɪə]	Hinter-; hinten
toy [tɔɪ]	Spielzeug	(to) balance ['bæləns]	auswuchten
Scotsman ['skɒtsmən]	Schotte	(to) fill up [‚fɪl_'ʌp]	auffüllen
bagpipe ['bæɡpaɪp]	Dudelsack	(to) get out [‚ɡet_'aʊt]	herausbekommen
		spare wheel ['speə 'wi:l]	Reserverad
T1		flat [flæt]	platt
motor museum ['məʊtəmju:‚zɪəm]	Automobilmuseum	(to) work [wɜ:k]	*hier:* funktionieren
vehicle ['vi:ɪkl]	Fahrzeug	**S2**	
(to) play an important part ['pleɪ ən_ɪm'pɔ:tənt 'pɑ:t]	eine wichtige Rolle spielen	home help ['həʊm 'help]	Haushaltshilfe
		motor transport ['məʊtə 'trænspɔ:t]	Beförderung mit dem Auto
hundreds ['hʌndrədz]	Hunderte	independent [‚ɪndɪ'pendənt]	unabhängig
stage coach ['steɪdʒkəʊtʃ]	Postkutsche	social services ['səʊʃl 'sɜ:vɪsɪz]	staatliche Fürsorge
steam [sti:m]	Dampf	voluntary ['vɒləntrɪ]	freiwillig
steam-engine ['sti:m‚endʒɪn]	Dampfmaschine	organization [‚ɔ:ɡənaɪ'zeɪʃn]	Organisation
steam coach ['sti:mkəʊtʃ]	Dampfkutsche	Meals on Wheels ['mi:lz_ɒn 'wi:lz]	Essen auf Rädern
(to) travel ['trævl]	*hier:* zurücklegen	(to) hoover ['hu:və]	staubsaugen
(to) have to ['hæv tə]	müssen	carpet ['kɑ:pɪt]	Teppich
(to) invent [ɪn'vent]	erfinden	ironing ['aɪənɪŋ]	Bügeln
wheel [wi:l]	Rad	(to) polish ['pɒlɪʃ]	polieren
not even [‚nɒt 'i:vn]	nicht einmal	(to) tidy up [‚taɪdɪ_'ʌp]	aufräumen
at that time [ət 'ðæt 'taɪm]	damals, zu der Zeit	(to) wash [wɒʃ]	*hier:* wischen
heating ['hi:tɪŋ]	Heizung	washing up [‚wɒʃɪŋ_'ʌp]	Geschirrspülen, Abwasch
mass production [‚mæsprə'dʌkʃn]	Massenproduktion	**S3**	
(to) be able to [bɪ 'eɪbl tə]	können, fähig/in der Lage sein	(to) rent [rent]	mieten
beetle ['bi:tl]	Käfer	daily ['deɪlɪ]	täglich
compact car ['kɒmpækt 'kɑ:]	Kompaktwagen	weekly ['wi:klɪ]	wöchentlich
		(to) include [ɪn'klu:d]	einschließen
(to) consume [kən'su:m]	verbrauchen	full insurance ['fʊl_ɪn'ʃʊərəns]	Vollkaskoversicherung
as a result [əz_ə rɪ'zʌlt]	mit dem Ergebnis, daß	VAT (value added tax) [‚vi:eɪ'ti:]	Mehrwertsteuer
(to) work badly ['wɜ:k 'bædlɪ]	schlecht funktionieren	hirer ['haɪərə]	Mieter(in)
T2		car rental ['kɑ:‚rentl]	Autovermietung
racing ['reɪsɪŋ]	Rennfahren	desk [desk]	Schalter
race [reɪs]	Rennen	clerk [klɑ:k]	Angestellte(r)
at the beginning [ət ðə bɪ'ɡɪnɪŋ]	anfangs, am Anfang	kind [kaɪnd]	Art, Sorte, Typ
engineer [‚endʒɪ'nɪə]	Ingenieur(in)	Would you like to ...? ['wʊd jʊ 'laɪk tə]	Würden Sie gerne ...?
racing car ['reɪsɪŋ‚kɑ:]	Rennwagen	(to) hire out ['haɪər_'aʊt]	vermieten
car racing ['kɑ:‚reɪsɪŋ]	Autorennen	(credit) card ['kredɪt‚kɑ:d]	Kreditkarte
S1		cheque book ['tʃek‚bʊk]	Scheckheft
bonnet ['bɒnɪt]	Motorhaube	(to) pay cash [‚peɪ 'kæʃ]	bar bezahlen
headlight ['hedlaɪt]	Scheinwerfer	mileage ['maɪlɪdʒ]	gefahrene Meilen, zurückgelegte Strecke
mirror ['mɪrə]	(Rück)spiegel		
boot [bu:t]	Kofferraum		
windscreen-wiper ['wɪnskri:n‚waɪpə]	Scheibenwischer	mileage chart ['maɪlɪdʒ‚tʃɑ:t]	Entfernungstabelle

Unit 8

VOCABULARY

(to) make out ['meɪk_'aʊt]	ausstellen
final amount ['faɪnl_ə'maʊnt]	Endsumme, Endbetrag

UNIT 8

St

service ['sɜːvɪs]	Dienstleistung, Kundendienst
advertisement [əd'vɜːtɪsmənt]	Anzeige, Reklame
cab [kæb]	Taxi
estate agent [ɪs'teɪt͵eɪdʒənt]	Grundstücks-/Immobilienmakler(in)
recovery service [rɪ'kʌvərɪ͵sɜːvɪs]	Abschlepp-/Bergungsdienst
24 hour ['twentɪfɔːr͵aʊə]	rund um die Uhr
emergency [ɪ'mɜːdʒənsɪ]	Notfall/-lage
emergency service [ɪ'mɜːdʒənsɪ͵sɜːvɪs]	Not-/Hilfsdienst
coach hire ['kəʊtʃ͵heɪə]	Reisebusvermietung
paint [peɪnt]	Farbe, Anstrich
wallpaper ['wɔːl͵peɪpə]	Tapete
in the middle of [ɪn ðə 'mɪdl_əv]	inmitten, mittendrin
(to) break down ['breɪk_'daʊn]	kaputtgehen, eine Panne haben
(to) finish with sb ['fɪnɪʃ wɪð]	mit jdm Schluß machen
(to) baby-sit ['beɪbɪsɪt]	Kinder hüten
(to) go red ['gəʊ 'red]	rot werden, rot anlaufen
(to) swallow ['swɒləʊ]	schlucken

A 1

receptionist [rɪ'sepʃənɪst]	Empfangsdame, Portier
(to) let [let]	hier: vermieten
balcony ['bælkənɪ]	Balkon
football ground ['fʊtbɔːl͵graʊnd]	Fußballplatz
rent [rent]	Miete
landlord (landlady) ['lænlɔːd/'lænleɪdɪ]	Hausbesitzer(in), Vermieter(in)
jeans [dʒiːnz]	Jeans
(to) replace sb/sth [rɪ'pleɪs]	jdn/etw ersetzen

A 2

couple ['kʌpl]	(Ehe)paar
advantage [əd'vɑːntɪdʒ]	Vorteil
disadvantage [͵dɪsəd'vɑːntɪdʒ]	Nachteil
ideal [aɪ'dɪəl]	ideal

A 4

(to) make it ['meɪk_ɪt]	es schaffen
at last [ət 'lɑːst]	endlich, schließlich
cooker ['kʊkə]	Herd
fridge [frɪdʒ]	Kühlschrank
washing-machine ['wɒʃɪŋmə͵ʃiːn]	Waschmaschine
downstairs [daʊn'steəz]	die Treppe herunter; hier: ein Stockwerk tiefer
second-hand [͵sekənd'hænd]	gebraucht
Love [lʌv]	hier: liebe Grüße

A 5

(to) record sth [rɪ'kɔːd]	aufzeichnen, aufnehmen
(to) control sb/sth [kən'trəʊl]	regeln, kontrollieren
(to) take up ['teɪk_'ʌp]	hochbringen/-befördern

B 1

daytime ['deɪtaɪm]	Tages-; tagsüber
complaint [kəm'pleɪnt]	Beschwerde, Klage

B 2

(to) lock in ['lɒk_ɪn]	einschließen

B 3

daily routine ['deɪlɪ ruː'tiːn]	normaler Tagesablauf
(to) greet sb [griːt]	jdn (be)grüßen
reception [rɪ'sepʃn]	Empfang, Rezeption

B 4

brochure ['brəʊʃə]	Broschüre, Faltblatt
British Tourist Authority ['brɪtɪʃ 'tʊərɪst ɔː'θɒrɪtɪ]	Britisches Fremdenverkehrsamt
Roman ['rəʊmən]	Römer(in); römisch
(to) put up ['pʊt_'ʌp]	errichten
cathedral [kə'θiːdrəl]	Kathedrale, Dom, Münster
Norman ['nɔːmən]	Normanne, Normannin; normannisch
(to) be worth sth [bɪ 'wɜːθ]	etw wert sein
moreover [mɔː'rəʊvə]	darüber hinaus, außerdem
(to) stay at ['steɪ ət]	bleiben; hier: absteigen, unterkommen
attractive [ə'træktɪv]	hübsch, attraktiv
excellent ['eksələnt]	ausgezeichnet, hervorragend
staff [stɑːf]	Personal, Mitarbeiter
stay [steɪ]	Aufenthalt
enjoyable [ɪn'dʒɔɪəbl]	angenehm
(to) contact sb ['kɒntækt]	sich mit jdm in Verbindung setzen
anytime ['enɪtaɪm]	jederzeit

B 5

(to) prefer sb/sth to sb/sth [prɪ'fɜː]	jdn/etw jdm/einer Sache vorziehen
camping ['kæmpɪŋ]	Camping, Zelten
caravan ['kærəvæn]	Wohnwagen
caravan park ['kærəvæn͵pɑːk]	etwa: Campingplatz für Wohnwagen
coast [kəʊst]	Küste
especially [ɪ'speʃlɪ]	speziell, besonders
close to ['kləʊs tə]	in der Nähe von, nahe bei
harbour ['hɑːbə]	Hafen

two hundred and forty-nine 249

VOCABULARY

Unit 8

C1

double decker ['dʌbl'dekə]	Doppeldecker(bus)
mini bus ['mɪnɪˌbʌs]	Kleinbus
fare [feə]	Fahrgeld/-preis
(to) enjoy doing sth [ɪn'dʒɔɪ 'duːɪŋ]	etw gerne tun
visitor ['vɪzɪtə]	Besucher(in)
hooligan ['huːlɪɡən]	Rowdy
worried ['wʌrɪd]	besorgt; beunruhigt
(to) get on/off ['ɡet ɒn/ɒf]	ein-/aussteigen
two-way radio ['tuːweɪ 'reɪdɪəʊ]	Sprechfunkanlage
old age pensioner ['əʊldeɪdʒ 'penʃənə]	Pensionär(in), Rentner(in)
(to) suppose [sə'pəʊz]	annehmen, vermuten
just like ['dʒʌst laɪk]	genauso wie
all in all ['ɔːl ɪn 'ɔːl]	alles in allem
(to) prefer doing sth [prɪ'fɜː]	etw lieber machen; es vorziehen, etw zu tun
(to) be gone [bɪ 'ɡɒn]	hier: vorüber/vorbei sein

C2

(to) run out ['rʌn 'aʊt]	hinaus-/herauslaufen
(to) brake [breɪk]	bremsen
in time [ɪn 'taɪm]	rechtzeitig
(to) fall down ['fɔːl 'daʊn]	hinfallen
(to) interview sb ['ɪntəvjuː]	jdn befragen
witness ['wɪtnɪs]	Zeuge, Zeugin
police officer [pə'liːsˌɒfɪsə]	Polizeibeamter/-beamtin
reg. (registered) ['redʒɪstəd]	amtlich zugelassen
(to) continue [kən'tɪnjuː]	fortfahren/-setzen
finally ['faɪnəlɪ]	schließlich, endlich

C3

fire bell ['faɪəˌbel]	Feuerglocke, Feueralarm

C4

coach [kəʊtʃ]	(Reise)bus
luggage ['lʌɡɪdʒ]	Gepäck
(to) be confused [bɪ kən'fjuːzd]	verwirrt/irritiert sein
case [keɪs]	Koffer
label ['leɪbl]	Aufkleber, Anhänger
(to) say [seɪ]	hier: besagen, geschrieben stehen
surfboard ['sɜːfbɔːd]	Surfbrett
racket ['rækɪt]	Schläger

T1

ambulance ['æmbjʊləns]	Rettungs-/Krankenwagen
organization [ˌɔːɡənaɪ'zeɪʃn]	Organisation, Unternehmen
(to) dial ['daɪəl]	wählen (Telefon)
fire-brigade ['faɪəbrɪˌɡeɪd]	Feuerwehr
rescue ['reskjuː]	Rettung
lifeboat ['laɪfbəʊt]	Rettungsboot
coastguard ['kəʊsɡɑːd]	Küstenwache
(to) want [wɒnt]	hier: brauchen, benötigen
operator ['ɒpəreɪtə]	Telefonist(in)
(to) keep calm ['kiːp 'kɑːm]	Ruhe bewahren, ruhig bleiben
(to) lift [lɪft]	heben, anheben
handset ['hændset]	(Telefon)hörer
(to) connect sb to sb [kə'nekt]	jdn mit jdm verbinden
(to) replace [rɪ'pleɪs]	hier: auflegen
false [fɔːls]	hier: mißbräuchlich
law [lɔː]	Gesetz
(to) risk [rɪsk]	riskieren, aufs Spiel setzen
(to) test [test]	prüfen
(to) include [ɪn'kluːd]	einschließen
(to) pull up sb ['pʊl 'ʌp]	jdn herauf-/hochziehen
boot [buːt]	Stiefel
rubber ['rʌbə]	Gummi
fire-engine ['faɪər'endʒɪn]	Feuerwehrauto
ladder ['lædə]	Leiter
ambulanceman ['æmbjʊlənsˌmæn]	Sanitäter

T2

past [pɑːst]	vorüber/vorbei an
jewellery ['dʒuːəlrɪ]	Juwelen, Schmuck
(to) wonder ['wʌndə]	sich fragen
stocking ['stɒkɪŋ]	Strumpf
experience [ɪk'spɪərɪəns]	Erlebnis, Erfahrung
(to) ask for ['ɑːsk fə]	bitten um, fragen nach
(to) retell [ˌriː'tel]	noch einmal erzählen, nacherzählen

S1

(to) turn on ['tɜːn 'ɒn]	an-/einschalten
cable ['keɪbl]	Kabel, Leitung
main cable ['meɪn 'keɪbl]	Hauptleitung/-kabel
underground ['ʌndəɡraʊnd]	unterirdisch
district ['dɪstrɪkt]	Bezirk, Gebiet
above ground [ə'bʌv 'ɡraʊnd]	oberirdisch
pylon ['paɪlən]	Hochspannungsmast
meter ['miːtə]	Zähler
(to) measure ['meʒə]	messen
master switch ['mɑːstəˌswɪtʃ]	Hauptschalter
(to) cut off ['kʌt 'ɒf]	abschalten
fuse [fjuːz]	Sicherung
fuse box ['fjuːzˌbɒks]	Sicherungskasten
(to) break [breɪk]	unterbrechen
circuit ['sɜːkɪt]	Stromnetz, Stromkreis
fault [fɔːlt]	Fehler
wiring circuit ['waɪərɪŋˌsɜːkɪt]	Leitungsnetz
function ['fʌŋkʃn]	Funktion, Aufgabe
voltage ['vəʊltɪdʒ]	Spannung
volt [vəʊlt]	Volt
(to) shrink [ʃrɪŋk]	schrumpfen, schwinden
(to) flicker ['flɪkə]	flackern
appliance [ə'plaɪəns]	Vorrichtung, (elektrisches) Gerät
watt [wɒt]	Watt
current ['kʌrənt]	elektrischer Strom
(to) flow [fləʊ]	fließen
amp [æmp]	Ampere

VOCABULARY

Unit 9

physics ['fɪzɪks]	Physik
properly ['prɒpəlɪ]	richtig, ordentlich, angemessen
electricity bill [ɪlek'trɪsətɪ ˌbɪl]	Stromrechnung
unit ['juːnɪt]	Einheit
light bulb [ˌlaɪt ˌbʌlb]	Glühbirne
oven ['ʌvn]	Herd
figure ['fɪgə]	Zahl(enangabe), Ziffer
(to) be on [bɪ 'ɒn]	eingeschaltet sein

S 2

food for thought ['fuːd fə 'θɔːt]	etwa: Stoff zum Nachdenken
(to) check [tʃek]	überprüfen, kontrollieren
(to) see [siː]	zusehen, dafür sorgen
on time [ɒn 'taɪm]	pünktlich
(to) expect [ɪk'spekt]	erwarten
well-prepared [ˌwelprɪ'peəd]	gut zubereitet
well-balanced [ˌwel'bælənst]	gut ausgewogen
(to) make sure [meɪk 'ʃʊə]	sicherstellen, gewährleisten
balance ['bæləns]	Gleichgewicht
protein ['prəʊtiːn]	Protein, Eiweiß(stoffe)
carbohydrate [ˌkɑːbəʊ'haɪdreɪt]	Kohlehydrat
fat [fæt]	Fett
mineral ['mɪnərəl]	Mineral(stoff)
vitamin ['vɪtəmɪn]	Vitamin
source [sɔːs]	Quelle
cereal ['sɪərɪəl]	Getreide
(to) supply with [sə'plaɪ wɪð]	versorgen mit
dairy ['deərɪ]	Molkerei
foods [fuːdz]	Nahrungsmittel
(to) contain [kən'teɪn]	enthalten
pea [piː]	Erbse
lamb [læm]	Lammfleisch
nut [nʌt]	Nuß
beef [biːf]	Rindfleisch
rice [raɪs]	Reis
lettuce ['letɪs]	(Kopf)salat
noodle ['nuːdl]	Nudel
sausage ['sɒsɪdʒ]	Wurst
cream [kriːm]	Sahne, Rahm
pork [pɔːk]	Schweinefleisch
onion ['ʌnjən]	Zwiebel
liver ['lɪvə]	Leber
lentil ['lentɪl]	Linse
cabbage ['kæbɪdʒ]	Kohl
carrot ['kærət]	Karotte, Mohrrübe
bean [biːn]	Bohne

S 3

Girobank ['dʒaɪrəʊˌbæŋk]	Girokasse der Post in GB
(to) be open long hours [bɪ ˌəʊpən 'lɒŋ ˌaʊəz]	lange Öffnungszeiten haben
current account ['kʌrənt əˌkaʊnt]	Girokonto
cheque-book ['tʃek ˌbʊk]	Scheckheft
(to) draw [drɔː]	abheben
choice [tʃɔɪs]	Wahl, Auswahl
every other business day ['evrɪ ˌʌðə 'bɪznɪs ˌdeɪ]	jeden zweiten Werktag
cheque card ['tʃek ˌkɑːd]	Scheckkarte
a time [ə 'taɪm]	auf einmal
cash machine ['kæʃməˌʃiːn]	Bankomat
credit ['kredɪt]	Kredit
buying power ['baɪɪŋ ˌpaʊə]	Kaufkraft
worldwide [ˌwəːld'waɪd]	weltweit
travel agency ['trævlˌeɪdʒənsɪ]	Reisebüro
plastic money ['plæstɪkˌmʌnɪ]	Plastikgeld
savings account ['seɪvɪŋzəˌkaʊnt]	Sparkonto

UNIT 9

St

technology [tek'nɒlədʒɪ]	Technik
critical ['krɪtɪkl]	kritisch
vacancy ['veɪkənsɪ]	freie/offene/unbesetzte Stelle
robot ['rəʊbɒt]	Roboter

A 1

prediction [prɪ'dɪkʃn]	Vorhersage
gas(oline) ['gæsəliːn]	AE: Benzin
space [speɪs]	(Welt)raum
not … any more [nɒt … enɪ 'mɔː]	keine … mehr, nicht … mehr
illness ['ɪlnɪs]	Krankheit
airliner ['eəlaɪnə]	Verkehrsflugzeug
sound [saʊnd]	Klang; hier: Schall
cash [kæʃ]	Bargeld
credit ['kredɪt]	Kredit
credit card ['kredɪt ˌkɑːd]	Kreditkarte
transport ['trænspɔːt]	Verkehr(swesen)
medicine ['medsɪn]	Medizin, Arznei
(to) come true ['kʌm 'truː]	wahr werden, eintreffen

A 2

ad [æd]	(Werbe)anzeige
PC ['piː 'siː]	Personalcomputer
fantastic [fæn'tæstɪk]	fantastisch, großartig
specifications [ˌspesɪfɪ'keɪʃnz]	technische Daten
memory ['memərɪ]	Gedächtnis; hier: Speicher
hard disk [ˌhɑːd 'dɪsk]	Festplatte
disk drive ['dɪsk ˌdraɪv]	Laufwerk
printer ['prɪntə]	Drucker
(to) turn on/off ['tɜːn ˌɒn/ɒf]	ein-/ausschalten
floppy disk [ˌflɒpɪ 'dɪsk]	Diskette, Floppy
monitor ['mɒnɪtə]	Bildschirmgerät, Monitor
mouse [maʊs]	Maus
screen [skriːn]	Bildschirm
cursor ['kɜːsə]	Schreibmarke, Laufzeiger
keyboard ['kiːbɔːd]	Tastatur
pocket money ['pɒkɪtˌmʌnɪ]	Taschengeld

VOCABULARY

Unit 9

vocabulary [vəˈkæbjʊləri] — Wortschatz
(to) check [tʃek] — überprüfen, kontrollieren
spelling [ˈspelɪŋ] — Rechtschreibung
(to) improve [ɪmˈpruːv] — verbessern
chess [tʃes] — Schach
algebra [ˈældʒəbrə] — Algebra
Spanish [ˈspænɪʃ] — Spanisch
(to) go on [gəʊ ˈɒn] — fortfahren, weitermachen

A 3

suburb [ˈsʌbɜːb] — Vorstadt/-ort
Come on! [ˈkʌm ˈɒn] — *hier:* Sei doch nicht so!
(to) mean [miːn] — dahinterstehen, es so meinen
quite a bit [ˈkwaɪt ə ˈbɪt] — ganz schön viel
(to) sound [saʊnd] — klingen, sich anhören
reasonable [ˈriːznəbl] — vernünftig
(to) give some money towards [gɪv səm ˈmʌni təˈwɔːdz] — Geld beisteuern zu
Mom [mɒm] — *AE:* Mama

A 4

flow chart [ˈfləʊ tʃɑːt] — Fluß-/Ablaufdiagramm
dead end [ˈded ˈend] — Sackgasse
well done [ˈwel ˈdʌn] — Gut gemacht!
statement [ˈsteɪtmənt] — Aussage, Behauptung

B 1

multi-media [ˌmʌltɪˈmiːdjə] — Medienverbund, Multimedia
(to) bite [baɪt] — (durch)beißen
cable [ˈkeɪbl] — (Strom)kabel
electric shock [ɪˈlektrɪk ˈʃɒk] — elektrischer Schlag
(to) put sth on [pʊt] — etw anziehen/aufsetzen
earphone [ˈɪəfəʊn] — Kopfhörer
(to) damage [ˈdæmɪdʒ] — beschädigen
video recorder [ˈvɪdɪəʊrɪˌkɔːdə] — Videorecorder
video camera [ˈvɪdɪəʊˌkæmrə] — Videokamera
(to) fall off [ˈfɔːl ˈɒf] — herunterfallen
shelf [ʃelf] — Regal
salesman [ˈseɪlzmən] — Verkäufer

B 2

recording [rɪˈkɔːdɪŋ] — (Ton)aufnahme
digital [ˈdɪdʒɪtl] — digital
(cassette) recorder [kæˈsetrɪˌkɔːdə] — (Kassetten)recorder
(to) work [wɜːk] — arbeiten; *hier:* funktionieren, laufen
(cassette) deck [kæˈsetˌdek] — (Kassetten)deck
(to) connect [kəˈnekt] — verbinden, anschließen
microphone [ˈmaɪkrəfəʊn] — Mikrophon
(to) plug in [ˈplʌg ˈɪn] — einstecken, anschließen
(to) release [rɪˈliːs] — loslassen, lösen
pause [pɔːz] — Pause
key [kiː] — *hier:* Taste
play [pleɪ] — *hier:* Wiedergabe

(to) turn up [ˈtɜːn ˈʌp] — aufdrehen
volume level [ˈvɒljuːm ˌlevl] — Lautstärke
record [ˈrekɔːd] — *hier:* Aufnahme

B 3

rhythm [ˈrɪðm] — Rhythmus
print-out [ˈprɪntaʊt] — (Computer)ausdruck
biorhythm chart [ˈbaɪəʊˌrɪðmˌtʃɑːt] — Biorhythmusdiagramm
(to) work sth out [wɜːk] — etw ausarbeiten/ herstellen
fit [fɪt] — in Form
weak [wiːk] — schwach
physical [ˈfɪzɪkl] — körperlich
high [haɪ] — Höhe, Höhepunkt
low [ləʊ] — Tiefe, Tiefpunkt
emotional [ɪˈməʊʃənl] — seelisch, gefühlsmäßig
mind [maɪnd] — Geist, Verstand, Gedächtnis
mental [ˈmentl] — geistig
curve [kɜːv] — Kurve
analysis [əˈnæləsɪs] — Analyse
practical [ˈpræktɪkl] — praktisch
(to) have got sth on [həv ˈgɒt ˈsʌmθɪŋ ˈɒn] — etw vorhaben
(to) pick [pɪk] — heraussuchen, auswählen
(to) take [teɪk] — *hier:* brauchen, dauern
stupid [ˈstjuːpɪd] — dumm
according to [əˈkɔːdɪŋ tə] — laut, gemäß, nach
(to) go climbing [gəʊ ˈklaɪmɪŋ] — Bergsteigen gehen
serious [ˈsɪərɪəs] — ernst
mainly [ˈmeɪnlɪ] — hauptsächlich
dinner-dance [ˈdɪnəˌdɑːns] — Abendgesellschaft mit Tanz
driving lesson [ˈdraɪvɪŋˌlesn] — Fahrstunde
test [test] — Prüfung, Klassenarbeit
(to) take part in [teɪk ˈpɑːt ˌɪn] — teilnehmen an
fun-run [ˈfʌnrʌn] — Volkslauf
Dad [dæd] — Papa
rose bush [ˈrəʊz ˌbʊʃ] — Rosenstrauch/-stock

B 4

warning [ˈwɔːnɪŋ] — Warnung, (Er)mahnung
fragile [ˈfrædʒaɪl] — zerbrechlich
Beware of the dog! [bɪˈweər əv ðə ˈdɒg] — Vorsicht, bissiger Hund!
slippery [ˈslɪpəri] — rutschig, glatt
inflammable [ɪnˈflæməbl] — *hier:* leicht entzündbar

C 1

microwave (oven) [ˈmaɪkrəʊweɪvˌʌvn] — Mikrowellenherd
(to) joke [dʒəʊk] — scherzen, einen Witz machen
dear [dɪə] — mein Lieber, meine Liebe *(Anrede)*
(to) be tired of sth [bɪ ˈtaɪəd ˌəv] — etw satt haben, etw leid sein
sir [sɜː] — mein Herr *(höfliche Anrede)*

Unit 9 — VOCABULARY

not ... either ['nɒt ... 'aɪðə] — auch nicht
(to) waste [weɪst] — verschwenden, vergeuden
direction [dɪ'rekʃn] — Richtung
photo ['fəʊtəʊ] — Foto(grafie)

C 2

(to) mind sth [maɪnd] — etw dagegen haben

C 3

waste [weɪst] — Verschwendung

T

satellite ['sætəlaɪt] — Satellit
communication [kə,mju:nɪ'keɪʃn] — Nachrichtenübermittlung
(to) take a picture ['teɪk_ə_'pɪktʃə] — eine Aufnahme machen
in many ways [ɪn 'meni 'weɪz] — in vielerlei Hinsicht
(to) predict sth [prɪ'dɪkt] — etw voraussagen
(to) communicate [kə'mju:nɪkeɪt] — in Verbindung treten, sich verbinden lassen
(to) transmit [trænz'mɪt] — senden, übermitteln
conversation [,kɒnvə'seɪʃn] — Gespräch, Unterhaltung
drawing ['drɔ:ɪŋ] — Zeichnung
mirror [mɪrə] — Spiegel
aerial ['eərɪəl] — Antenne
station ['steɪʃn] — hier: Sender, Sendestation
(to) reflect [rɪ'flekt] — reflektieren, zurücksenden
(to) carry ['kærɪ] — hier: übermitteln
at one time [ət 'wʌn 'taɪm] — gleichzeitig
(to) increase [ɪn'kri:s] — vermehren, steigern
solar cell [,səʊlə 'sel] — Sonnenzelle
(to) cover sb/sth ['kʌvə] — jdn/etw bedecken
(to) produce [prə'dju:s] — erzeugen, produzieren
(to) go off course ['gəʊ ɒf 'kɔ:s] — vom Kurs abweichen
motor ['məʊtə] — Motor
(to) succeed [sək'si:d] — Erfolg haben
at the top [ət ðə 'tɒp] — oben
importance [ɪm'pɔ:tns] — Bedeutung, Wichtigkeit
opposite ['ɒpəzɪt] — Gegenteil, entgegengesetzter Begriff
(to) decrease [dɪ'kri:s] — verringern
flying saucer [,flaɪɪŋ 'sɔ:sə] — Fliegende Untertasse
video tape ['vɪdɪəʊ,teɪp] — Videoband
Pa [pɑ:] — Papa
Got it. ['gɒt_ɪt] — Kapiert.
guess [ges] — hier: etwa, na ja
vacation [və'keɪʃn] — AE: Ferien, Urlaub
sun-bathing ['sʌnbeɪðɪŋ] — Sonnenbaden, sich sonnen
savings ['seɪvɪŋz] — Ersparnisse
(to) imagine [ɪ'mædʒɪn] — sich vorstellen

S 1

CAD (computer aided design) [,sɪ: eɪ 'di:] — computerunterstützte(r) Gestaltung/Entwurf
draftsman ['drɑ:ftsmən] — technischer Zeichner
drawing-board ['drɔ:ɪŋbɔ:d] — Zeichenbrett
shape [ʃeɪp] — Form, Umriß
object ['ɒbdʒekt] — Gegenstand
two-dimensional [,tu:dɪ'menʃnl] — zweidimensional
figure ['fɪgə] — Abbildung
circle ['sɜ:kl] — Kreis
area ['eərɪə] — Fläche
square [skweə] — Quadrat-
(to) select [sɪ'lekt] — (aus)wählen
command [kə'mɑ:nd] — Befehl
(to) enlarge [ɪn'lɑ:dʒ] — vergrößern
(to) reduce [rɪ'dju:s] — verkleinern
circle area ['sɜ:kl ,eərɪə] — Kreisfläche
circular ['sɜ:kjʊlə] — kreisförmig
rectangular [rek'tæŋgjʊlə] — rechteckig
dimension [dɪ'menʃn] — Dimension
(to) create [krɪ'eɪt] — hervorrufen
effect [ɪ'fekt] — Ergebnis; Eindruck
depth [depθ] — Tiefe
screen [skri:n] — Bildschirm
rectangle ['rektæŋgl] — Rechteck
measurement ['meʒəmənt] — Maß
height [haɪt] — Höhe
width [wɪdθ] — Breite
length [leŋθ] — Länge
(to) hold [həʊld] — enthalten, fassen
straight [streɪt] — gerade

S 2

appliance [ə'plaɪəns] — Vorrichtung, (elektrisches) Gerät
dishwasher ['dɪʃwɒʃə] — Geschirrspülmaschine
fridge-freezer [,frɪdʒ'fri:zə] — Kühl-/Gefrierkombination
fan cooker ['fæn,kʊkə] — Umluftherd
ceramic hob [sə'ræmɪk 'hɒb] — Keramikplatte
cooker hood ['kʊkə,hʊd] — Dunstabzugshaube
sink [sɪŋk] — Ausguß, Spülbecken
sink and draining-board unit ['sɪŋk_ən 'dreɪnɪŋbɔ:d ,ju:nɪt] — Spüle mit Abtropfvorrichtung
cupboard ['kʌbəd] — Schrank
function ['fʌŋkʃn] — Funktion, Aufgabe
(to) remove [rɪ'mu:v] — entfernen
(to) heat up ['hi:t_ʌp] — erhitzen
(to) store [stɔ:] — lagern, aufbewahren
utensil [ju:'tensl] — Gerät, Werkzeug
dishes ['dɪʃɪz] — Geschirr
cutlery ['kʌtlərɪ] — Besteck
(to) provide [prə'vaɪd] — zur Verfügung stellen
work area ['wɜ:k,eərɪə] — Arbeitsfeld/-bereich
pan [pæn] — Pfanne
stool [stu:l] — Hocker
freezer ['fri:zə] — Gefrierschrank
bottom cupboard ['bɒtəm ,kʌbəd] — Unterschrank
top cupboard ['tɒp ,kʌbəd] — Oberschrank
(to) design [dɪ'zaɪn] — entwerfen

VOCABULARY

Unit 10

S 3

document	['dɒkjʊmənt]	Dokument, Papier
overseas	[ˌəʊvə'siːz]	nach Übersee
TELEFAX	['telɪfæks]	telefonischer Fernkopierer
employee	[ˌemplɔɪ'iː]	Angestellte(r), Arbeitnehmer(in)
TELETEX	['telɪteks]	elektronische Schrift- und Bildübermittlung
memo	['meməʊ]	Notiz, Aufzeichnung
receiver	[rɪ'siːvə]	Empfänger
mail box	['meɪl ˌbɒks]	elektronischer Briefkasten
space	[speɪs]	Platz
(to) store	[stɔː]	ablegen, lagern
amount	[ə'maʊnt]	Menge
short code dialling	['ʃɔːtkəʊd ˌdaɪəlɪŋ]	Kurzwahlsystem
memory	['meməri]	Speicher
Corp (Corporation)	['kɔːpəreɪʃn]	AE: GmbH
Ltd (Limited)	['lɪmɪtɪd]	BE: GmbH
ring-when-free-system	['rɪŋwen'friː ˌsɪstəm]	telefonische Rückrufautomatik
person	['pɜːsn]	Person
(to) put down	['pʊt 'daʊn]	auflegen
receiver	[rɪ'siːvə]	(Telefon)hörer
(to) pick up	[pɪk_'ʌp]	abnehmen
note	[nəʊt]	Notiz
partner	['pɑːtnə]	Geschäftspartner(in)
round-table discussion	[ˌraʊnd'teɪbl dɪsˌkʌʃn]	Gespräch am runden Tisch, Gesprächsrunde
supplier	[sə'plaɪə]	Lieferant(in)
(to) phone back	['fəʊn 'bæk]	zurückrufen

UNIT 10

St

goods	[gʊdz]	Waren, Güter

A1

by ship	[baɪ 'ʃɪp]	mit dem Schiff
passenger dock	['pæsɪndʒəˌdɒk]	Passagieranlegestelle
customs	['kʌstəmz]	Zoll(behörde)
(to) have to	['hæv tə]	müssen
channel	['tʃænl]	Durchgang, Passage
(to) depend (on)	[dɪ'pend ˌɒn]	abhängen von; hier: darauf ankommen
(to) declare	[dɪ'kleə]	verzollen, angeben
well	[wel]	hier: nun denn
perfume	['pɜːfjuːm]	Parfüm
(to) be allowed to	[bɪ ə'laʊd tə]	dürfen
duty-free	[ˌdjuːtɪ'friː]	zollfrei
gram	[græm]	Gramm
(to) take in	['teɪk_'ɪn]	hier: mitnehmen, hereinbringen
sort	[sɔːt]	Art, Sorte, Marke
Oh dear!	['əʊ 'dɪə]	oje!
customs officer	['kʌstəmzˌɒfɪsə]	Zollbeamter/-beamtin
duty	['djuːtɪ]	Zoll(gebühr)
basket	['bɑːskɪt]	Korb
Good heavens!	['gʊd 'hevnz]	Um Himmels willen!
regulation	[ˌregjʊ'leɪʃn]	Vorschrift
strict	[strɪkt]	streng
(to) smuggle in sb/sth	['smʌglˌ'ɪn]	jdn/etw schmuggeln
over there	[ˌəʊvə 'ðeə]	dort drüben
limit	['lɪmɪt]	Grenze (des Erlaubten)
tax	[tæks]	Steuer
allowance	[ə'laʊəns]	hier: Höchstmenge, Freibetrag
alcoholic	[ˌælkə'hɒlɪk]	alkoholisch
proof	[pruːf]	Alkoholgehalt
tobacco	[tə'bækəʊ]	Tabak
cigar	[sɪ'gɑː]	Zigarre
plant	[plɑːnt]	Pflanze
gold coin	['gəʊld 'kɔɪn]	Goldmünze
explosives	[ɪk'spləʊsɪvz]	Sprengstoff

A 2

import-export firm	['ɪmpɔːt 'ekspɔːt ˌfɜːm]	Import-Export Firma
terrific	[tə'rɪfɪk]	klasse, unheimlich gut
(to) get	[get]	hier: besorgen
(to) bring in	['brɪŋ_'ɪn]	einführen
luckily	['lʌkɪlɪ]	glücklicherweise
cactus	['kæktəs]	Kaktus
(to) take sth through	['teɪk 'sʌmθɪŋ 'θruː]	hier: mitnehmen

A 3

flight	[flaɪt]	Flug
(to) check in	['tʃek_'ɪn]	einchecken, sich bei der Flugabfertigung melden
(to) unpack	[ˌʌn'pæk]	auspacken
seat-belt	['siːtbelt]	Sicherheitsgurt
washroom	['wɒʃruːm]	Waschraum, Toilette
emergency landing	[ɪ'mɜːgənsɪ 'lændɪŋ]	Notlandung
(to) get into	['get_'ɪntʊ]	einsteigen, betreten
(to) get out of	['get_'aʊt_əv]	aussteigen, verlassen
engine trouble	['endʒɪn ˌtrʌbl]	Maschinenschaden
instruction	[ɪn'strʌkʃn]	Anweisung

B1

(to) carry	['kærɪ]	hier: transportieren, befördern
cargo	['kɑːgəʊ]	Ladung, Fracht
dock worker	['dɒkˌwɜːkə]	Dock-/Hafenarbeiter
(to) load/unload	[ləʊd/ˌʌn'ləʊd]	be-/entladen
port	[pɔːt]	Hafen
warehouse	['weəhaʊs]	Lager(haus)
(to) store	[stɔː]	lagern
(to) deliver	[dɪ'lɪvə]	ausliefern
cocoa	['kəʊkəʊ]	Kakao
Nigeria	[naɪ'dʒɪərɪə]	Nigeria
onto	['ɒntʊ]	auf
MS	['em'es]	Motorschiff
after	['ɑːftə]	nachdem

Unit 10

VOCABULARY

B 2

system	[ˈsɪstəm]	System, Methode
type	[taɪp]	Art, Sorte, Typ
packing	[ˈpækɪŋ]	Verpackung
crate	[kreɪt]	Kiste, Kasten, Korb
(to) pack	[pæk]	(ver)packen
no. (number)	[ˈnʌmbə]	Zahl, Anzahl
tonne	[tʌn]	metrische Tonne
amount	[əˈmaʊnt]	Summe, Betrag, Anzahl
(to) pass through	[ˈpɑːs ˈθruː]	passieren
Commonwealth	[ˈkɒmənwelθ]	das Britische Commonwealth
EC (European Community)	[ˌiːˈsiː]	EG, Europäische Gemeinschaft
(to) import	[ɪmˈpɔːt]	einführen, importieren
(to) export	[eksˈpɔːt]	ausführen, exportieren
used to	[ˈjuːst tə]	pflegte(n), (ein)mal

B 3

docklands	[ˈdɒklændz]	Hafenviertel
introduction	[ˌɪntrəˈdʌkʃn]	Einführung
square mile	[ˌskweə ˈmaɪl]	Quadratmeile
(to) turn into sth	[ˈtɜːn_ˈɪntʊ]	sich verwandeln in etw
slum	[slʌm]	Elendsviertel/-quartier
area	[ˈeərɪə]	Fläche, Gebiet
(to) invest	[ɪnˈvest]	(Geld) anlegen, investieren
(to) modernize	[ˈmɒdənaɪz]	modernisieren
block of flats	[ˈblɒk_əv ˈflæts]	Wohnhaus/-block
however	[haʊˈevə]	jedoch
hi tech	[ˌhaɪˈtek]	Hochtechnologie
(to) clear	[klɪə]	hier: abreißen, beseitigen
jet	[dʒet]	Düsenflugzeug
(to) move away	[muːvˌəˈweɪ]	wegziehen
(to) knock down	[ˈnɒk ˈdaʊn]	hier: abreißen

C 1

Californian	[ˌkælɪˈfɔːnjən]	kalifornisch; Kalifornier(in)
managing director	[ˈmænɪdʒɪŋ dɪˈrektə]	Generaldirektor(in)
head of department	[ˈhed_əv dɪˈpɑːtmənt]	Abteilungsleiter(in)
profit	[ˈprɒfɪt]	Gewinn
cotton	[ˈkɒtn]	Baumwoll-; Baumwolle
sale	[seɪl]	Verkauf
private	[ˈpraɪvɪt]	privat; Privat-
beef	[biːf]	Rindfleisch
(to) install	[ɪnˈstɔːl]	einrichten, aufstellen, installieren
video typewriter	[ˌvɪdɪəʊ ˈtaɪpraɪtə]	Bildschirmschreibmaschine
wine	[waɪn]	Wein
general administration	[ˈdʒenrəl ədˌmɪnɪˈstreɪʃn]	Hauptverwaltung
like this	[laɪk ˈðɪs]	folgendermaßen

non-food design	[ˌnɒnˈfuːd dɪˈzaɪn]	Non-food-Gestaltung, Formgebung
quality	[ˈkwɒlətɪ]	Qualität
(to) be compared	[bɪ kəmˈpeəd]	etwa: zum Vergleich
origin	[ˈɒrɪdʒɪn]	Herkunft
per unit	[pə ˈjuːnɪt]	pro Einheit
Argentina	[ˌɑːdʒənˈtiːnə]	Argentinien
Austria	[ˈɒstrɪə]	Österreich
China	[ˈtʃaɪnə]	China
GDR	[ˌdʒiː diː ˈɑː]	DDR
India	[ˈɪndjə]	Indien
Portugal	[ˈpɔːtʃʊgl]	Portugal
South Korea	[ˌsaʊθkəˈrɪə]	Südkorea
Spain	[speɪn]	Spanien
Sri Lanka	[ˌsriːˈlæŋkə]	Sri Lanka
Taiwan	[ˈtaɪˈwɑːn]	Taiwan

C 2

(to) dictate sth	[dɪkˈteɪt]	etw diktieren
Hong Kong	[ˌhɒŋˈkɒŋ]	Hongkong
delivery	[dɪˈlɪvərɪ]	Belieferung, Auslieferung, Lieferung
(to) receive	[rɪˈsiːv]	empfangen, erhalten
(to) expect	[ɪkˈspekt]	erwarten
(to) try hard	[ˈtraɪ ˈhɑːd]	sich bemühen, anstrengen
on time	[ɒn ˈtaɪm]	termingemäß, rechtzeitig
grateful	[ˈgreɪtfʊl]	dankbar
(to) cooperate	[kəʊˈɒpəreɪt]	mitwirken, zusammenarbeiten
cooperation	[kəʊˌɒpəˈreɪʃn]	Zusammenarbeit

T 1

Soviet Union	[ˈsəʊɪətˈjuːnjən]	Sowjetunion
(to) pick	[pɪk]	hier: pflücken
by hand	[baɪ ˈhænd]	von Hand
(to) press	[pres]	pressen
bale	[beɪl]	Ballen
clothing	[ˈkləʊðɪŋ]	(Be)kleidung
that is why	[ˈðæts ˈwaɪ]	deshalb
exclusive	[ɪkˈskluːsɪv]	vornehm, elegant, exklusiv
(to) spin	[spɪn]	spinnen
raw	[rɔː]	roh, unbearbeitet
acrylic	[əˈkrɪlɪk]	Akrylfaser
(to) weave	[wiːv]	weben
cloth	[klɒθ]	Tuch
(to) cut out	[ˈkʌt_ˈaʊt]	ausschneiden
T-shirt	[ˈtiːʃɜːt]	T-Shirt
(to) sew	[səʊ]	nähen
automatic	[ˌɔːtəˈmætɪk]	automatisch
agency	[ˈeɪdʒənsɪ]	Geschäftsstelle, Vertretung, Agentur
all over the world	[ˈɔːl_əʊvə ðə ˈwɜːld]	auf der ganzen Welt
by plane	[baɪ ˈpleɪn]	mit dem Flugzeug
directly	[dɪˈrektlɪ]	unmittelbar, direkt
department store	[dɪˈpɑːtmənt stɔː]	Kaufhaus
textile factory	[ˈtekstaɪlˌfæktrɪ]	Textilfabrik

VOCABULARY

Unit 11

T 2
connection	[kə'nekʃn]	Verbindung, Beziehung

T 4
interest	['ɪntrɪst]	*hier:* Zinsen

S 1
trade	[treɪd]	Gewerbe
detached	[dɪ'tætʃt]	freistehend; Einzel-
semi-detached (house)	[,semɪdɪ'tætʃt 'haʊs]	Doppelhaus(hälfte)
terraced (house)	['terəst ,haʊs]	Reihenhaus
row	[rəʊ]	Reihe
apartment	[ə'pɑ:tmənt]	Appartement
joined to	['dʒɔɪnd tə]	verbunden mit
building site	['bɪldɪŋ ,saɪt]	Baustelle
carpenter	['kɑ:pəntə]	Bauschreiner(in), Zimmermann
bricklayer	['brɪkleɪə]	Maurer(in)
plumber	['plʌmə]	Klempner(in), Flaschner(in)
roofer	['ru:fə]	Dachdecker(in)
decorator	['dekəreɪtə]	Dekorationsmaler(in)
(to) put in	['pʊt _ɪn]	verlegen
wiring	['waɪərɪŋ]	elektrische Leitungen
wooden	['wʊdn]	hölzern; Holz-
tile	[taɪl]	Ziegel
material	[mə'tɪərɪəl]	Baustoff

S 2
fashion	['fæʃn]	Mode
(to) design	[dɪ'zaɪn]	entwerfen, gestalten
style	[staɪl]	Stil
successful	[sək'sesfʊl]	erfolgreich
flowery	['flaʊərɪ]	geblümt
sleeve	[sli:v]	Ärmel
tight	[taɪt]	eng (anliegend)
waist	[weɪst]	Taille
full	[fʊl]	weit
countryside	['kʌntrɪsaɪd]	Landschaft
country-look	['kʌntrɪlʊk]	*etwa:* ländlicher/ rustikaler Stil
interior furnishing	[ɪn'tɪərɪə 'fɜ:nɪʃɪŋ]	Innenarchitektur, Raumausstattung
decoration	[,dekə'reɪʃn]	Dekorierung, Dekoration
loose-fitting	[,lu:s'fɪtɪŋ]	weit geschnitten
thread	[θred]	Faden, Garn
underneath	[,ʌndə'ni:θ]	darunter
blouse	[blaʊz]	Bluse
shorts	[ʃɔ:ts]	Shorts, kurze Hose
(to) label	['leɪbl]	bezeichnen
feature	['fi:tʃə]	Merkmal, Charakteristikum

S 3
trading nation	['treɪdɪŋ ,neɪʃn]	Handelsnation
(to) increase	[ɪn'kri:s]	zunehmen, ansteigen
network	['netwɜ:k]	Netz
motorway	['məʊtəweɪ]	Autobahn
door-to-door	[,dɔ:tə'dɔ:]	von Haus zu Haus
ton	[tʌn]	Tonne
economical	[,i:kə'nɒmɪkl]	wirtschaftlich
machinery	[mə'ʃi:nərɪ]	Maschinen(teile)
ferry	['ferɪ]	Fähre
(to) play a part in	['pleɪ ə 'pɑ:t_ɪn]	eine Rolle spielen bei
the Continent	[ðə 'kɒntɪnənt]	das europäische Festland
air freight	['eə,freɪt]	Luftfracht
shipment	['ʃɪpmənt]	(Schiff)transport, Verschiffung
by sea	[baɪ 'si:]	auf dem Seeweg
means of transport	['mi:nz_əv 'trænspɔ:t]	Transportmittel
(to) mention	['menʃn]	erwähnen
main	[meɪn]	Haupt-

UNIT 11

A 1
(to) arrange	[ə'reɪndʒ]	arrangieren; *hier:* verabreden
wide range	['waɪd 'reɪndʒ]	große Auswahl, umfangreiches Angebot
household	['haʊshəʊld]	Haushalt
(to) welcome	['welkəm]	begrüßen, willkommen heißen
stores	[stɔ:z]	Lager
steel	[sti:l]	Stahl
casing	['keɪsɪŋ]	Gehäuse, Verkleidung
sheet	[ʃi:t]	*hier:* Blech
(to) transport	[træn'spɔ:t]	transportieren, befördern
shop-floor	[,ʃɒp'flɔ:]	Fabrik-/Werkshalle
metal	['metl]	Metall-
fork-lift truck	['fɔ:klɪft ,trʌk]	Gabelstapler
production line	[prə'dʌkʃn,laɪn]	Fertigungsstraße, Fließband
(to) put sth together	['pʊt sʌmθɪŋ tə'geðə]	etw zusammensetzen/ montieren
(to) spray	[spreɪ]	ver-, besprühen; spritzlackieren
paint	[peɪnt]	(Anstrich)farbe, Lack
oven	['ʌvn]	Ofen
motor	['məʊtə]	(Elektro)motor
(to) pack	[pæk]	(ver)packen
dealer	['di:lə]	Händler
Australia	[ɒ'streɪljə]	Australien

A 2
North Pole	[,nɔ:θ 'pəʊl]	Nordpol
toilet paper	['tɔɪlət,peɪpə]	Toilettenpapier
hair-drier	['heə,draɪə]	Haartrockner, Fön

A 3
office	['ɒfɪs]	Büro, Dienststelle, Amt
income	['ɪŋkəm]	Einkommen
wage	[weɪdʒ]	Lohn
last but not least	['lɑ:st bət 'nɒt 'li:st]	nicht zuletzt; nicht zu vergessen
purpose	['pɜ:pəs]	Zweck, Ziel; Absicht, Vorhaben
(to) employ	[ɪm'plɔɪ]	beschäftigen
(to) provide	[prə'vaɪd]	beschaffen, liefern; zur Verfügung stellen
old people's home	[,əʊld 'pi:plz ,həʊm]	Altersheim

Unit 11 VOCABULARY

(to) develop [dɪˈveləp] — entwickeln, ausarbeiten, ausbauen
youth club [ˈjuːθˌklʌb] — Jugendklub/-haus
kindergarten [ˈkɪndəˌgɑːtn] — Kindergarten
(to) increase [ɪnˈkriːs] — vermehren; *hier:* erhöhen
pension [ˈpenʃn] — Pension, Rente
facility [fəˈsɪlətɪ] — Gelegenheit, Möglichkeit, Einrichtung
else [els] — sonst, weiter, außerdem

A 4
device [dɪˈvaɪs] — Vorrichtung, Gerät
food-mixer [ˈfuːdˌmɪksə] — Mixer, Rührgerät
drier [ˈdraɪə] — Trockenapparat, (Wäsche)trockner
photo-copier [ˈfəʊtəʊˌkɒpɪə] — Fotokopierer
pan [pæn] — Pfanne
dishwasher [ˈdɪʃˌwɒʃə] — Geschirrspülmaschine

B 1
machine operator [məˈʃiːnˌɒpəreɪtə] — Maschinenarbeiter(in)
test [test] — Test, Prüfung
personnel manager [ˌpɜːsəˈnelˌmænədʒə] — Personalchef(in)
registration card [ˌredʒɪsˈtreɪʃnˌkɑːd] — Anmeldeschein/-karte; Personalkarte
training centre [ˈtreɪnɪŋˌsentə] — Schulungs-/Ausbildungszentrum
(to) call in [ˈkɔːlˌɪn] — hereinrufen/-bitten
general knowledge [ˈdʒenrəlˈnɒlɪdʒ] — Allgemeinbildung
(to) discover [dɪsˈkʌvə] — entdecken
steam-engine [ˈstiːmˌendʒɪn] — Dampfmaschine
president [ˈprezɪdənt] — Präsident(in)
(to) print [prɪnt] — drucken

B 2
(to) recognize [ˈrekəgnaɪz] — (wieder)erkennen
(to) suggest [səˈdʒest] — vorschlagen, anregen, empfehlen
(to) design [dɪˈzaɪn] — konstruieren, entwerfen
architect [ˈɑːkɪtekt] — Architekt(in)
work area [ˈwɜːkˌeərɪə] — Arbeitsfläche/-bereich
word processor [ˈwɜːdˌprəʊsesə] — Textverarbeitungsanlage; Speicherschreibmaschine
(to) reduce [rɪˈdjuːs] — vermindern, verringern, reduzieren
routine [ruːˈtiːn] — Routine-; gewohnheitsmäßig
telefax [ˈtelɪfæks] — Telefax
(to) install [ɪnˈstɔːl] — installieren, einrichten, aufstellen
up-to-date [ˈʌptəˈdeɪt] — modern, neuzeitlich, auf dem neuesten Stand
relaxation area [ˌriːlækˈseɪʃnˌeərɪə] — Erholungs-/Pausenbereich

restroom [ˈrestruːm] — Aufenthalts-/Pausenraum
(to) redecorate [riːˈdekəreɪt] — neu streichen/tapezieren
canteen [kænˈtiːn] — Kantine
wholefood [ˈhəʊlfuːd] — Vollwertkost/-nahrung
menu [ˈmenjuː] — Speisekarte, Speisenfolge
tea-lady [ˈtiːˌleɪdɪ] — Frau, die in Betrieben und Büros Tee macht
(to) supply [səˈplaɪ] — versorgen, beliefern
carpet [ˈkɑːpɪt] — Teppich(boden)

C 1
(to) face [feɪs] — sich gegenübersehen, gegenüberstehen
financial [faɪˈnænʃl] — finanziell
difficulty [ˈdɪfɪkəltɪ] — Schwierigkeit
management [ˈmænɪdʒmənt] — Betriebs-/Geschäftsleitung
automation [ˌɔːtəˈmeɪʃn] — Automation, Automatisierung
employee [ˌemplɔɪˈiː] — Arbeitnehmer(in), Arbeiter(in), Angestellte(r)
redundant [rɪˈdʌndənt] — überflüssig, arbeitslos
union [ˈjuːnjən] — Gewerkschaft
(to) support [səˈpɔːt] — unterstützen
robot [ˈrəʊbɒt] — Roboter, Automat
work-force [ˈwɜːkfɔːs] — Belegschaft(sstärke)
leader [ˈliːdə] — (An)führer, Vorsitzende(r)
(to) be of the opinion [ˈbiː əv ðɪ əˈpɪnjən] — der Meinung/Ansicht sein

C 2
reaction [rɪˈækʃn] — Reaktion, Entgegnung, Erwiderung
(to) fight for sth [ˈfaɪt fə] — um/für etw kämpfen
working conditions [ˈwɜːkɪŋ kənˌdɪʃnz] — Arbeitsbedingungen
shop-steward [ˌʃɒpˈstjʊəd] — gewerkschaftliche(r) Vertrauensmann/-frau
(to) represent [ˌreprɪˈzent] — vertreten
(to) rent [rent] — mieten
part-time [ˌpɑːtˈtaɪm] — Teilzeit
(to) take over [ˈteɪkˌəʊvə] — übernehmen

C 3
(to) be prepared to [bɪ prɪˈpeəd tə] — vorbereitet/bereit sein
a number of [ə ˈnʌmbər əv] — eine Anzahl/Reihe von

T 1
crisis [ˈkraɪsɪs] — Krise
steelworks [ˈstiːlwɜːks] — Stahlwerk(e)
publicity [pʌˈblɪsətɪ] — Öffentlichkeits(arbeit); Werbe-
(to) interest [ˈɪntrəst] — interessieren, gewinnen (für)
spot [spɒt] — Fleck(en), Stelle, Ort
motorway [ˈməʊtəweɪ] — Autobahn

VOCABULARY

Unit 12

recently [ˈriːsəntlɪ]	vor kurzem, neulich	CAM (computer-aided manufacturing) [ˌsiː eɪ ˈem]	computerunterstützte Fertigung
catastrophe [kəˈtæstrəfɪ]	Unglück, Katastrophe		
immediately [ɪˈmiːdjətlɪ]	sogleich, unverzüglich	computer-controlled [kəmˈpjuːtə kənˈtrəʊld]	computergesteuert
non-steel [ˌnɒnˈstiːl]	nicht stahlverarbeitend; metallfrei, nicht-metallisch	finished product [ˈfɪnɪʃt ˈprɒdʌkt]	Endprodukt
industrial estate [ɪnˈdʌstrɪəl ɪˈsteɪt]	Industriegebiet	(to) monitor [ˈmɒnɪtə]	überwachen
cosmetics [kɒzˈmetɪks]	Schönheitspflegemittel	(to) respond [rɪˈspɒnd]	antworten; reagieren
potato crisps [pəˈteɪtəʊ ˈkrɪsps]	Kartoffelchips	feedback [ˈfiːdbæk]	Rückkoppelung, Rück-meldung, Bestätigung

S 2

(to) wonder [ˈwʌndə]	sich fragen, gern wissen mögen
success [səkˈses]	Erfolg
scheme [skiːm]	Plan, Projekt, Programm
(to) complete [kəmˈpliːt]	vervollständigen, vollenden, fertigstellen
(to) pull sth down [ˈpʊl sʌmθɪŋ ˈdaʊn]	abreißen/-brechen
(to) decrease [dɪˈkriːs]	abnehmen, weniger/geringer werden
completion [kəmˈpliːʃn]	Ergänzung, Vollendung, Fertigstellung

(to) function [ˈfʌŋkʃn]	funktionieren, arbeiten
check-out till [ˈtʃekaʊt tɪl]	(Laden)kasse
bar code [ˈbɑːkəʊd]	Balken-/Strichkode
laser scanner [ˈleɪzəˌskænə]	Laser-Lesegerät
display screen [dɪˈspleɪˌskriːn]	*hier:* Bildschirm, der den Betrag anzeigt
receipt [rɪˈsiːt]	Kassenbon, Quittung
tin [tɪn]	Büchse
baked beans [ˈbeɪkt ˈbiːnz]	gebackene Bohnen
memory [ˈmemərɪ]	Speicher
stripe [straɪp]	Streifen
assistant [əˈsɪstənt]	Verkäufer(in)
cornflakes [ˈkɔːnfleɪks]	Corn-flakes
(to) melt [melt]	schmelzen

T 2

below [bɪˈləʊ]	unter(halb)
person [ˈpɜːsn]	Person
all my life [ˈɔːl maɪ ˈlaɪf]	mein ganzes Leben lang, in meinem ganzen Leben
(to) fry [fraɪ]	braten
(to) go out on a date [ˈgəʊ ˈaʊt ˌɒn ə ˈdeɪt]	zu einer Verabredung/ einem Treffen gehen
boring [ˈbɔːrɪŋ]	langweilig
except [ɪkˈsept]	außer, ausgenommen
(to) be one's scene [bɪ wʌnz ˈsiːn]	jds Fall sein
steady girlfriend [ˈstedɪ ˈgɜːlfrend]	feste Freundin
lipstick [ˈlɪpstɪk]	Lippenstift
electrical [ɪˈlektrɪkl]	elektrisch
back home [ˈbæk ˈhəʊm]	daheim, zu Hause
patient [ˈpeɪʃnt]	geduldig

S 3

economy [ɪˈkɒnəmɪ]	Wirtschaft
population [ˌpɒpjʊˈleɪʃn]	Bevölkerung
per head [pəˈhed]	pro Kopf
inflation [ɪnˈfleɪʃn]	Inflation
agriculture [ˈægrɪkʌltʃə]	Landwirtschaft
rate [reɪt]	Rate, Quote
standard of living [ˈstændəd əv ˈlɪvɪŋ]	Lebensstandard
because of [bɪˈkɒz əv]	wegen

UNIT 12

St

United States [juːˈnaɪtɪd ˈsteɪts]	Vereinigte Staaten
square [skweə]	Quadrat(-)
kilometer [ˈkɪləʊˌmiːtə]	*AE:* Kilometer
source [sɔːs]	Quelle, Herkunft
immigration [ˌɪmɪˈgreɪʃn]	Einwanderung(s-)
Hispanic [hɪˈspænɪk]	spanisch(en Ursprungs); Spanisch sprechend
Indian [ˈɪndjən]	indianisch; Indianer(in)
Poland [ˈpəʊlənd]	Polen
Mexico [ˈmeksɪkəʊ]	Mexiko
Cuba [ˈkjuːbə]	Kuba
Venezuela [ˌveneˈzweɪlə]	Venezuela
graph [græf]	Graphik, Diagramm
population [ˌpɒpjʊˈleɪʃn]	Bevölkerung(szahl)
state [steɪt]	Staat

S 1

(to) manufacture [ˌmænjʊˈfæktʃə]	produzieren, herstellen
process [ˈprəʊses]	Prozeß, Vorgang, Ablauf
mechanical [məˈkænɪkl]	mechanisch
(to) weld [weld]	schweißen
biscuit [ˈbɪskət]	Keks
flexible [ˈfleksəbl]	flexibel, anpassungsfähig
(to) equip [ɪˈkwɪp]	ausstatten, ausrüsten, versehen mit
audio [ˈɔːdɪəʊ]	Hör-, Gehör-
visual [ˈvɪzjʊəl]	visuell; Seh-, Sicht-
touch [tʌtʃ]	Berührung(s-)
sensor [ˈsensə]	Sensor, (Meß)fühler
complex [ˈkɒmpleks]	komplex, kompliziert; verwickelt, schwierig
complicated [ˈkɒmplɪkeɪtɪd]	kompliziert, schwierig

A 1

director [dɪˈrektə]	Leiter(in), Direktor(in)
impression [ɪmˈpreʃn]	Eindruck, Impression

Unit 12 VOCABULARY

comment	[kɒment]	Kommentar, Stellungnahme
opinion	[əˈpɪnjən]	Meinung, Ansicht
murder	[ˈmɜːdə]	Mord
robbery	[ˈrɒbəri]	Raub(überfall)
gun	[gʌn]	Gewehr, Schußwaffe
(to) protest against sth	[prəˈtest əgenst]	gegen etw protestieren
free sale	[friː ˈseɪl]	freier/ungehinderter Verkauf
anti-gun movement	[ˈæntɪˌgʌn ˌmuːvmənt]	US-amerikanische Bewegung gegen privaten Schußwaffenbesitz
friendly	[ˈfrendli]	freundlich, hilfsbereit
helpful	[ˈhelpfʊl]	gefällig, hilfsbereit; hilfreich, nützlich
kindness	[ˈkaɪndnəs]	Freundlichkeit, Gefälligkeit
voluntary	[ˈvɒləntri]	freiwillig
charity	[ˈtʃærəti]	(Nächsten)liebe; Wohltätigkeit(sverein); gutes Werk
positive	[ˈpɒzətɪv]	positiv, wohlwollend
(to) afford	[əˈfɔːd]	sich leisten
all over	[ˈɔːl ˌəʊvə]	überall in
(to) search through sth	[ˈsɜːtʃ θruː]	etw (gründlich) durchsuchen
garbage can	[ˈgɑːbɪdʒ ˌkæn]	AE: Müll-/Abfalleimer
social security	[ˌsəʊʃl sɪˈkjʊərəti]	Sozialversicherung
health insurance	[ˈhelθ ɪnˌʃʊərəns]	Krankenversicherung
(to) think up sth	[ˌθɪŋk ˈʌp]	sich etw einfallen lassen, etw erfinden
such as	[ˈsʌtʃ əz]	wie zum Beispiel, wie beispielsweise
speed limit	[ˈspiːd ˌlɪmɪt]	Geschwindigkeitsbegrenzung; hier: Höchstgeschwindigkeit
negative	[ˈnegətɪv]	negativ, ablehnend
crime rate	[ˈkraɪm ˌreɪt]	Verbrechensrate
friendliness	[ˈfrendlinəs]	Freundlichkeit, Entgegenkommen, Hilfsbereitschaft
fantastic	[fænˈtæstɪk]	fantastisch
(to) worry	[ˈwʌri]	(sich) Sorgen machen, (sich) beunruhigen

A 2

newsletter	[ˈnjuːzˌletə]	Rundschreiben, Mitteilungsblatt
party	[ˈpɑːti]	hier: Gruppe
(to) welcome	[ˈwelkəm]	begrüßen, willkommen heißen
speaker	[ˈspiːkə]	Sprecher(in)
(to) add	[æd]	addieren, hinzufügen

A 3

pleasant	[pleznt]	angenehm
statistics	[stəˈtɪstɪks]	Statistik(en)
floor space	[ˈflɔːˌspeɪs]	Grund-/Nutzfläche
square feet	[ˈskweəˈfiːt]	Quadratfuß
aerobics	[eəˈrəʊbɪks]	Aerobic
parade	[pəˈreɪd]	Parade, Festumzug
fee	[fiː]	Gebühr, Beitrag
adult	[ˈædʌlt]	Erwachsene(r)
senior	[ˈsiːnɪə]	Senior(in)
available	[əˈveɪləbl]	vorhanden, erreichbar, vorrätig
pre-school	[ˈpriːskuːl]	Vorschul-
program	[ˈprəʊgræm]	AE: Veranstaltung, Programm
series	[ˈsɪəriːz]	Serie, Reihe
squash	[skwɒʃ]	Squash(sport)
kid	[kɪd]	Kind, Jugendliche(r) (umgangssprachlich)

B 1

poverty	[ˈpɒvəti]	Armut
poverty level	[ˈpɒvətiˌlevl]	Armutsgrenze, Existenzminimum

B 2

unemployment benefits	[ˌʌnɪmˈplɔɪmənt ˌbenɪfɪts]	Arbeitslosengeld/-unterstützung
(to) depend on	[dɪˈpend ɒn]	abhängen von, abhängig sein von
(to) pay into sth	[ˈpeɪ ˌɪntə]	in etw einzahlen
pension scheme	[ˈpenʃnˌskiːm]	(Alters)versorgungsplan; Rentenversicherung
handicapped	[ˈhændɪkæpt]	behindert
welfare benefits	[ˈwelfeə ˌbenɪfɪts]	Sozialleistung/-hilfe/-unterstützung
food stamp	[ˈfuːdˌstæmp]	Lebensmittelmarke/-gutschein
labour market	[ˈleɪbəˌmɑːkɪt]	Arbeitsmarkt
color	[ˈkʌlə]	AE: (Haut)farbe
retirement	[rɪˈtaɪəmənt]	Ruhestand, Verrentung
regular	[ˈregjʊlə]	regulär, regelmäßig
sum	[sʌm]	Summe, Betrag
at all	[ətˈɔːl]	überhaupt
Mexican	[ˈmeksɪkən]	mexikanisch; Mexikaner(in)
illegally	[ɪˈliːgəli]	illegal
nobody	[ˈnəʊbədi]	niemand

B 3

social worker	[ˈsəʊʃl ˌwɜːkə]	Sozialarbeiter(in)
helper	[ˈhelpə]	Helfer(in)
(to) be brief	[bɪ ˈbriːf]	sich kurz fassen
line	[laɪn]	hier: (Menschen)schlange
(to) hand out sth	[ˈhændˌaʊt]	etw austeilen
soup	[suːp]	Suppe
ladleful	[ˈleɪdlfʊl]	Schöpflöffel voll
just a second	[ˈdʒʌst ə ˈsekənd]	einen Augenblick
bowl	[bəʊl]	Schüssel, Schale
hamburger	[ˈhæmbɜːgə]	Hamburger, Frikadelle
section	[ˈsekʃn]	Abteilung, Unterteilung, Abschnitt
(to) pass	[pɑːs]	reichen
spoonful	[ˈspuːnfʊl]	Eßlöffel voll
French fries	[ˌfrentʃˈfraɪz]	AE: Pommes frites
pea	[piː]	Erbse

VOCABULARY

Unit 12

(to) guess [ges] — raten, glauben, vermuten
gravy ['greɪvɪ] — (Braten)soße
(to) pour [pɔː] — (aus)schütten, (aus)gießen, einschenken

general rule ['genrəl 'ruːl] — allgemeine (Verhaltens)regel, Richtlinie, Grundsatz
dishes ['dɪʃɪz] — Geschirr
for a while [fər_ə 'waɪl] — ein Weilchen, eine Zeitlang
guy [gaɪ] — Typ(e), Kerl
(to) breathe [briːð] — (durch)atmen; *hier:* sich erholen

C1

(to) look upon sb/sth ['lʊk_ə'pɒn] — jdn/etw betrachten als, halten für
surprise [sə'praɪz] — Überraschung
successful [sək'sesfʊl] — erfolgreich
semester [sə'mestə] — Semester
cleaner ['kliːnə] — Raumpfleger(in)
assistant [ə'sɪstənt] — Assistent(in); Verkäufer(in)
medical school ['medɪkl ˌskuːl] — medizinische Fakultät/Hochschule
technician [tek'nɪʃn] — Techniker, Facharbeiter
secret ['siːkrət] — Geheimnis
bright idea ['braɪt_aɪ'dɪə] — glänzender Einfall
promotion [prə'məʊʃn] — *etwa:* (Werbe)aktion, (Sonder)angebot
expectant mother [ɪk'spektənt 'mʌðə] — werdende Mutter
(to) stand for sth ['stænd fə] — an Stelle von/für etw stehen; *hier:* heißen, bedeuten
degree [dɪ'griː] — Grad
in addition [ɪn_ə'dɪʃn] — außerdem, darüber hinaus
completely [kəm'pliːtlɪ] — vollkommen, vollständig, völlig
foundation [faʊn'deɪʃn] — Stiftung
earnings ['ɜːnɪŋz] — Einkünfte; Gewinn, Ertrag
aim [eɪm] — Ziel
millionaire [ˌmɪljə'neə] — Millionär
support [sə'pɔːt] — Unterstützung
famous ['feɪməs] — berühmt
fight [faɪt] — Kampf, Auseinandersetzung
illiteracy [ɪ'lɪtərəsɪ] — Analphabetentum
rate [reɪt] — Rate, Quote
teenager ['tiːnˌeɪdʒə] — Jugendliche(r)
Labor Department ['leɪbədɪˌpɑːtmənt] — *AE:* Arbeitsamt
press conference ['presˌkɒnfərəns] — Pressekonferenz
(to) be willing [ˌbɪ 'wɪlɪŋ] — willens/bereit sein

C2

(to) manufacture [ˌmænjʊ'fæktʃə] — herstellen, erzeugen
showroom ['ʃəʊruːm] — Vorführ-/Ausstellungsraum
software ['sɒftweə] — Software, (Computer)programme

T1

impossible [ɪm'pɒsəbl] — unmöglich, nicht möglich
productivity [ˌprɒdʌk'tɪvətɪ] — Produktivität, Leistung(svermögen)
Department of Health and Human Services [dɪ'pɑːtmənt_əv 'helθ_ənd 'hjuːmən 'sɜːvɪsɪz] — (US-amerikanisches) Gesundheits- und Sozialministerium
(to) publish ['pʌblɪʃ] — veröffentlichen
(to) present [prɪ'zent] — präsentieren, vorstellen
myth [mɪθ] — Mythos, Märchen; *hier:* Vorurteil
contribution [ˌkɒntrɪ'bjuːʃn] — Beitrag
(to) enable [ɪ'neɪbl] — befähigen, ermöglichen, in die Lage versetzen
productive [prə'dʌktɪv] — produktiv, leistungsfähig
data ['deɪtə] — Daten, Angaben, Werte
opposite ['ɒpəzɪt] — Gegenteil
(to) make up ['meɪk_ʌp] — bilden, darstellen, stellen
statement ['steɪtmənt] — Aussage, Behauptung
(to) think sth over ['θɪŋk sʌmθɪŋ_'əʊvə] — sich etw überlegen, nachdenken über etw
(to) retire [rɪ'taɪə] — in Pension/Rente gehen
truth [truːθ] — Wahrheit
(to) base sth on sth ['beɪs sʌmθɪŋ_ɒn] — etw auf etw stützen/gründen

T2

(to) make way for ['meɪk 'weɪ fə] — Platz machen für
(to) refuse [rɪ'fjuːz] — sich weigern
(to) fire sb ['faɪə] — jdn entlassen
(to) take sb to court ['teɪk ˌsʌmbədɪ tə 'kɔːt] — jdn verklagen, gegen jdn prozessieren
court case ['kɔːtˌkeɪs] — Gerichtsverfahren
ex-employer ['eksˌem'plɔɪə] — früherer Arbeitgeber
judge [dʒʌdʒ] — Richter(in)
court [kɔːt] — Gericht(shof)
(to) limit ['lɪmɪt] — begrenzen, ein-/beschränken
(to) take sth easy ['teɪk sʌmθɪŋ 'iːzɪ] — *hier:* etw ruhig angehen lassen
life-time ['laɪftaɪm] — Lebenszeit, Lebensdauer; *hier:* Leben
(to) deserve [dɪ'zɜːv] — verdienen
(to) speak up ['spiːk_ʌp] — lauter sprechen/reden
(to) carry on ['kærɪ_ɒn] — weitermachen, fortfahren
politician [ˌpɒlɪ'tɪʃn] — Politiker

S1

(to) assemble [ə'sembl] — montieren, zusammenbauen
(to) launch [lɔːntʃ] — abschießen/-feuern, starten
space shuttle ['speɪsˌʃʌtl] — Raumfähre
fuel tank ['fjʊəlˌtæŋk] — Brennstofftank
booster rocket ['buːstəˌrɒkɪt] — Startrakete
adventure [əd'ventʃə] — Abenteuer
rocket ['rɒkɪt] — Rakete

VOCABULARY

Unit 13

spectacular [spek'tækjʊlə] — spektakulär, sensationell
flight deck ['flaɪtˌdek] — Cockpit, Besatzungsraum
liftoff ['lɪftɒf] — Abheben, Start
heat tile ['hiːtˌtaɪl] — Hitzekachel
external [ek'stɜːnl] — äußerlich; Außen(bord)-fest; Feststoff-
solid ['sɒlɪd]
crew [kruː] — Mannschaft, Besatzung
compartment [kəm'pɑːtmənt] — Abteilung, Abteil, Raum
commander [kə'mɑːndə] — Kommandant, Flugkapitän
flight controls ['flaɪtkənˌtrəʊlz] — Bord-/Fluginstrumente
authentic [ɔː'θentɪk] — authentisch; Original-
various ['veərɪəs] — verschieden(artig)
wing [wɪŋ] — Flügel, Tragfläche
red-hot [ˌred'hɒt] — rotglühend; glühend heiß
cool [kuːl] — kühl, kalt
shield [ʃiːld] — Schild

S 2

campaign [kæm'peɪn] — Kampagne, Feldzug, Aktion
(to) draw attention to sth ['drɔː_ə'tenʃn tə] — die Aufmerksamkeit auf etw ziehen/lenken
lack [læk] — Mangel
(to) lead to ['liːd tə] — führen zu
(to) result in [rɪ'zʌlt_ɪn] — resultieren, zur Folge haben
illiteracy [ɪ'lɪtərəsɪ] — Analphabetentum
(to) hang about ['hæŋ_ə'baʊt] — herumhängen/-lungern
prospect ['prɒspekt] — Chance, Aussicht
(to) confront [kən'frʌnt] — konfrontieren, gegenüberstellen
(to) take a look at sth ['teɪk_ə_'lʊk_ət] — einen Blick auf etw werfen
elementary school [ˌelɪ'mentərɪ ˌskuːl] — Grundschule
inner-city [ˌɪnə'sɪtɪ] — innerstädtisch; Innenstadt-
single-parent ['sɪŋgl'peərnt] — alleinerziehend; Alleinerziehende(r)
average ['ævrɪdʒ] — Durchschnitt(s)-
prize [praɪz] — Preis *(Gewinn)*
volunteer [ˌvɒlən'tɪə] — Freiwillige(r)
fairy tale ['feərɪteɪl] — Märchen
role-model ['rəʊlˌmɒdl] — Rollenvorbild
after-school ['ɑːftə'skuːl] — nach Unterrichtsschluß; außerschulisch
heroin ['herəʊɪn] — Heroin

S 3

development [dɪ'veləpmənt] — Entwicklung
namely ['neɪmlɪ] — nämlich
increase ['ɪnkriːs] — Zunahme, Zuwachs
(to) predict [prɪ'dɪkt] — voraus-/vorhersagen
(to) decrease [dɪ'kriːs] — abnehmen
bar graph ['bɑːˌgræf] — Stab-/Balkendiagramm
line graph ['laɪnˌgræf] — Kurvendiagramm
solution [sə'luːʃn] — Lösung
ups and downs ['ʌps_ən'daʊnz] — Auf- und Abbewegungen
(to) stand for ['stænd fə] — stehen für; darstellen
blue collar ['bluːˌkɒlə] — Arbeiter-
white collar ['waɪtˌkɒlə] — Angestellten-

UNIT 13

St

input ['ɪnpʊt] — Input
public service ['pʌblɪk 'sɜːvɪs] — öffentliche Dienstleistung
luxury goods ['lʌkʃərɪˌgʊdz] — Luxuswaren/-artikel
source [sɔːs] — Quelle
lighting ['laɪtɪŋ] — Beleuchtung

A 1

Alaska [ə'læskə] — Alaska
Russia ['rʌʃə] — Rußland
because of [bɪ'kɒz_əv] — wegen
climate ['klaɪmət] — Klima
relatively ['relətɪvlɪ] — verhältnismäßig
unproductive [ˌʌnprə'dʌktɪv] — unergiebig, unproduktiv
lumbering ['lʌmbərɪŋ] — Holzfällen, Holzfällerei
discovery [dɪs'kʌvərɪ] — Entdeckung
economic [ˌiːkə'nɒmɪk] — ökonomisch, wirtschaftlich; Wirtschafts-
(to) transform [træns'fɔːm] — um-/verwandeln, verändern
reserve [rɪ'zɜːv] — Reserve, Vorkommen
Trans Alaska Pipeline ['trænz_ə'læskə 'paɪplaɪn] — Transalaska-Rohrleitung/-Pipeline
oilfield ['ɔɪlfiːld] — Ölfeld/-vorkommen
technologically [ˌteknə'lɒdʒɪkəlɪ] — *hier:* in technischer Hinsicht, technisch gesehen
moon landing ['muːnˌlændɪŋ] — Mondlandung
newcomer ['njuːˌkʌmə] — Neuankömmling
(to) attract [ə'trækt] — anziehen, anlocken, reizen
(to) create [kriː'eɪt] — (er)schaffen

A 2

Arctic Circle ['ɑːktɪk 'sɜːkl] — nördlicher Polarkreis
extreme [ɪk'striːm] — außergewöhnlich; Extrem, Gegensatz
temperature ['temprətʃə] — Temperatur
condition [kən'dɪʃn] — Bedingung; Lage
line [laɪn] — (Schreib)zeile
(to) let sb know ['let sʌmbədɪ 'nəʊ] — jdm Bescheid geben
stand-by ['stændbaɪ] — Bereitschaft(sdienst)
crew [kruː] — Mannschaft, Besatzung
(to) call out ['kɔːl_aʊt] — herbeirufen, alarmieren
leak [liːk] — Leck
damage ['dæmɪdʒ] — Schaden, Beschädigung
(to) take sth off ['teɪk sʌmθɪŋ_ɒf] — ausziehen, ablegen
ice-cold ['aɪs'kəʊld] — eiskalt

VOCABULARY

Unit 13

(to) get better [get 'betə] — sich erholen, gesund werden
accomodation [ə,kɒmə'deɪʃn] — Unterkunft
a bit [ə bɪt] — ein bißchen, ein wenig
controller [kən'trəʊlə] — Kontrolleur
operations control center [,ɒpə'reɪʃnz kən'trəʊl ,sentə] — etwa: Steuerzentrale
(to) monitor ['mɒnɪtə] — überwachen
(to) get to work ['get tə 'wɜːk] — sich an die Arbeit machen
site [saɪt] — Stelle, Stätte, Ort
(to) touch [tʌtʃ] — berühren, anfassen
frost bite ['frɒstbaɪt] — Erfrierung(en)
pay [peɪ] — Bezahlung, Verdienst

A3

Eskimo ['eskɪməʊ] — Eskimo-
boom [buːm] — Boom, wirtschaftlicher Aufschwung
Alaskan [ə'læskən] — Alaska-
proud [praʊd] — stolz
main [meɪn] — hauptsächlich; Haupt-
activity [æk'tɪvəti] — Tätigkeit, Beschäftigung
wooden hut ['wʊdn 'hʌt] — Holzhütte
igloo ['ɪgluː] — Iglu, Schneehütte
fur [fɜː] — Pelz
parka ['pɑːkə] — Parka
anorak ['ænəræk] — Anorak, Windjacke
(to) hunt [hʌnt] — jagen
completely [kəm'pliːtli] — vollkommen, völlig
self-sufficient [,selfsə'fɪʃnt] — unabhängig, autark
outsider [,aʊt'saɪdə] — Außenseiter
culture ['kʌltʃə] — Kultur
(to) destroy [dɪ'strɔɪ] — zerstören
development [dɪ'veləpmənt] — Entwicklung
apartment house [ə'pɑːtmənt,haʊs] — Wohn-, Mietshaus
fast food ['fɑːstfuːd] — Fastfood, Schnellimbiß
bar [bɑː] — Bar
native language ['neɪtɪv 'læŋgwɪdʒ] — Muttersprache
stranger ['streɪndʒə] — Fremde(r)
kind of ['kaɪnd əv] — Art, Sorte
prediction [prɪ'dɪkʃn] — Voraus-/Vorhersage
foreign-made ['fɒrɪn,meɪd] — im Ausland hergestellt
promise ['prɒmɪs] — Versprechen
(to) raise [reɪz] — anheben
TV station [,tiː'viː,steɪʃn] — Fernsehsender
living conditions ['lɪvɪŋkən,dɪʃnz] — Lebensbedingungen, -umstände
standard of living ['stændəd əv 'lɪvɪŋ] — Lebensstandard

B1

Canadian [kə'neɪdjən] — kanadisch
channel ['tʃænl] — Kanal; hier: Programm
tide [taɪd] — Ebbe und Flut; Gezeiten
Canada ['kænədə] — Kanada
tidal energy ['taɪdl ,enədʒi] — Gezeitenenergie
turbine ['tɜːbaɪn] — Turbine
dam [dæm] — Damm
(to) come in ['kʌm 'ɪn] — hereinkommen; hier: steigen
(to) go out ['gəʊ 'aʊt] — (hin)ausgehen; hier: zurückgehen
in order to [ɪn 'ɔːdə] — um zu
(to) generate ['dʒenəreɪt] — erzeugen
(to) function ['fʌŋkʃn] — funktionieren, arbeiten
bay [beɪ] — Bucht
billion ['bɪljən] — AE: Milliarde; BE: Billion
coastline ['kəʊstlaɪn] — Küste(nlinie)

B2

various ['veərɪəs] — verschiedene
mayor [meə] — Bürgermeister
resident ['rezɪdənt] — Ein-/Bewohner
minister ['mɪnɪstə] — Minister
resource [rɪ'sɔːs] — Ressource, Vorrat, Vorkommen
meter ['miːtə] — Meter
tidal range ['taɪdl 'reɪndʒ] — Gezeitenunterschied; (Tiden)hub
(to) make the most of sth ['meɪk ðə 'məʊst əv] — das Beste aus etw machen
on the other hand [ɒn ðɪ 'ʌðə ,hænd] — and(e)rerseits
effect [ɪ'fekt] — Auswirkung, Effekt
wildlife ['waɪldlaɪf] — natürliche Tier- und Pflanzenwelt
permanently ['pɜːmənəntli] — dauernd, ständig
(to) flood [flʌd] — (über)fluten
feeding ground ['fiːdɪŋ,graʊnd] — Futterplatz
bird lover ['bɜːd,lʌvə] — Vogelschützer/-liebhaber
point of view [,pɔɪnt əv 'vjuː] — Stand-/Gesichtspunkt
(to) protect sb/sth [prə'tekt] — jdn/etw (be)schützen
difference ['dɪfrəns] — Unterschied
(to) suffer ['sʌfə] — leiden, in Mitleidenschaft gezogen werden
manageress [,mænɪdʒə'res] — Geschäftsführerin
ugly ['ʌgli] — häßlich
builder ['bɪldə] — Bauunternehmer(in)

C1

coupon ['kuːpɒn] — Kupon, Abschnitt
(to) heat [hiːt] — heizen
massive ['mæsɪv] — massiv, groß, gewaltig
waste [weɪst] — Verschwendung
solution [sə'luːʃn] — Lösung
Energy Council ['enədʒi,kaʊnsl] — etwa: Energieberatungsstelle
(to) call on sb ['kɔːl ɒn] — jdn besuchen
chimney ['tʃɪmni] — Schornstein
draft [drɑːft] — Zug(luft)
(to) ask sb about sth ['ɑːsk sʌmbədi ə,baʊt] — jdn über etw befragen
insulation [,ɪnsjʊ'leɪʃn] — Isolierung, Dämmung

Unit 13 VOCABULARY

(to) use up [juːz ˈʌp]	verbrauchen
(to) put sth in [ˈpʊt sʌmθɪŋ ˌɪn]	einbauen
central heating [ˈsentrəl ˈhiːtɪŋ]	Zentralheizung
step [step]	Schritt, Stufe
Freefone [ˈfriːfəʊn]	gebührenfreier Anruf
energy doctor [ˈenədʒɪˌdɒktə]	etwa: Energieberater(in)
(to) send sth in [ˈsend sʌmθɪŋ ˌɪn]	etw einschicken
double glazing [ˈdʌbl ˈɡleɪzɪŋ]	Isolierglas/-verglasung
gap [ɡæp]	Lücke, Spalt
(to) lag [læɡ]	isolieren, abdichten
(to) insulate [ˈɪnsjʊleɪt]	isolieren, dämmen
gas [ɡæs]	Gas
worthwhile [ˌwɜːθˈwaɪl]	lohnend, der Mühe wert
(to) cool off [ˈkuːl ˈɒf]	abkühlen

C 2

Department of Energy [dɪˈpɑːtmənt ɒv ˈenədʒɪ]	Energieministerium
fuel [fjʊəl]	Brennstoff, Heizmaterial
(to) waste [weɪst]	verschwenden
air conditioning [ˈeəkənˌdɪʃənɪŋ]	Klimatisierung, Klimaanlage
blind [blaɪnd]	Rolladen, Rollo
(to) pull sth down [ˈpʊl sʌmθɪŋ ˈdaʊn]	etw herunterziehen/-lassen
gadget [ˈɡædʒɪt]	Apparat, Vorrichtung, Gerät
whenever [wenˈevə]	jedesmal/immer wenn
even though [ˈiːvn ˈðəʊ]	obwohl, obgleich
out of action [ˈaʊt əv ˈækʃn]	außer Betrieb
naturally [ˈnætʃrəli]	natürlich, auf natürliche Art und Weise
sense [sens]	Sinn; Bewußtsein
common sense [ˈkɒmən ˈsens]	gesunder Menschenverstand; Vernunft
wet [wet]	naß

T 1

risk [rɪsk]	Risiko, Gefahr
warning [ˈwɔːnɪŋ]	Warnung; Warn-
geyser [ˈɡiːzə]	Geysir
hot spring [ˈhɒt ˈsprɪŋ]	heiße Quelle, Thermalquelle
volcano [vɒlˈkeɪnəʊ]	Vulkan
right below [ˈraɪt bɪˈləʊ]	genau/direkt unter(halb)
geothermal [ˌdʒiːəʊˈθɜːml]	Erdwärme-
steam [stiːm]	Dampf
nature [ˈneɪtʃə]	Natur
(to) harm [hɑːm]	(be)schädigen, schaden; verletzen
absolutely [ˈæbsəluːtli]	absolut, vollkommen, völlig
down under [ˈdaʊn ˈʌndə]	(in) Australien/Neuseeland
solar collector [ˈsəʊlə kəˌlektə]	Sonnenkollektor
sunlight [ˈsʌnlaɪt]	Sonnenlicht
(to) convert [kənˈvɜːt]	umwandeln
efficiently [ɪˈfɪʃəntli]	wirksam, rationell, wirtschaftlich
sunshine [ˈsʌnʃaɪn]	Sonnenschein
New Zealand [ˌnjuːˈziːlənd]	Neuseeland
countryside [ˈkʌntrɪsaɪd]	Land(schaft)
according to [əˈkɔːdɪŋ]	gemäß, nach, laut
Denmark [ˈdenmɑːk]	Dänemark
Brazil [brəˈzɪl]	Brasilien
region [ˈriːdʒən]	Region, Gebiet, Gegend
(to) pollute [pəˈluːt]	verschmutzen

T 2

(to) mention [ˈmenʃn]	erwähnen
cowshed [ˈkaʊʃed]	Kuhstall
windy [ˈwɪndi]	windig
diesel [ˈdiːzl]	Diesel
(to) demonstrate [ˈdemənstreɪt]	demonstrieren
(to) dismiss [dɪsˈmɪs]	entlassen
miner [ˈmaɪnə]	Bergmann
mine [maɪn]	Bergwerk, Grube

T 3

(to) lead to [liːd]	führen zu

S 1

light heating oil [ˈlaɪt ˈhiːtɪŋ ˌɔɪl]	leichtes Heizöl
kW-hr (kilowatt per hour) [ˈkɪləʊwɒt per ˈaʊə]	Kilowattstunde
investment costs [ɪnˈvestmənt ˌkɒsts]	Investitionskosten
bio-mass [ˈbaɪəʊˌmæs]	Biomasse
dung [dʌŋ]	Dung
available [əˈveɪləbl]	vorhanden, verfügbar
heat exchanger [ˈhiːt ɪksˌtʃeɪndʒə]	Wärmetauscher, Wärmeumwälzpumpe
(to) cool [kuːl]	kühlen
solid fuel [ˈsɒlɪd ˈfjʊəl]	Festbrennstoff
straw [strɔː]	Stroh

S 2

energy giver [ˈenədʒɪˌɡɪvə]	Energiespender
spinach [ˈspɪnɪdʒ]	Spinat
salad [ˈsæləd]	Salat
joule [dʒuːl]	Joule
baked potato [ˈbeɪkt pəˈteɪtəʊ]	gebackene Kartoffel
organ [ˈɔːɡən]	(Körper)organ
(to) measure [ˈmeʒə]	messen
(to) contain [kənˈteɪn]	enthalten
expert [ˈekspɜːt]	Experte, Fachmann
average [ˈævrɪdʒ]	Durchschnitt(s-)
output [ˈaʊtpʊt]	Ausstoß; Verbrauch
(to) pump [pʌmp]	pumpen

S 3

home improvement [ˈhəʊm ɪmˈpruːvmənt]	Wohnungsrenovierung
loan [ləʊn]	Darlehen
repayment [rɪˈpeɪmənt]	Rückzahlung

V VOCABULARY

Unit 14

life insurance ['laɪf_ɪnʃʊərəns]	Lebensversicherung
term [tɜːm]	Ausdruck, Begriff
(to) lend [lend]	(ver)leihen
straight away ['streɪt_əˌweɪ]	direkt, unmittelbar
security [sɪ'kjʊərətɪ]	Sicherheit, Bürgschaft
period ['pɪərɪəd]	Periode, Zeitraum
(to) take out ['teɪk_'aʊt]	herausnehmen; in Anspruch nehmen
(to) insure [ɪn'ʃʊə]	versichern
(to) have a word with sb ['hæv_ə 'wɜːd wɪð]	ein Gespräch mit jdm führen
branch manager ['brɑːntʃˌmænɪdʒə]	Zweigstellenleiter
agent ['eɪdʒənt]	Agent, Vertreter
clerk [klɑːk]	Angestellter
suitable [suːtəbl]	geeignet, passend
(to) sound [saʊnd]	tönen, klingen; sich anhören
personal loan [ˌpɜːsnl 'ləʊn]	persönliches Darlehen
(to) borrow ['bɒrəʊ]	sich (aus)leihen
application form [ˌæplɪ'keɪʃnˌfɔːm]	Antragsformular
in what way [ɪn wɒt 'weɪ]	wie, auf welche Weise
on top of [ɒn 'tɒp_əv]	zusätzlich, zuzüglich
(to) manage ['mænɪdʒ]	leiten
interest rate ['ɪntrəstˌreɪt]	Zinssatz/-rate
(to) repay [rɪ'peɪ]	zurückzahlen

UNIT 14

St

solid ['sɒlɪd]	fest; massiv, gediegen
(to) tick [tɪk]	ticken
method ['meθəd]	Methode, Vorgehen
(to) appeal to [ə'piːl]	an jdn/etw appellieren, jdn/etw ansprechen
(to) think of ['θɪŋk_əv]	denken an; einfallen

A1

consumer [kən'sjuːmə]	Verbraucher(in)
shopper [ʃɒpə]	Käufer(in)
tip [tɪp]	Tip, Hinweis, Ratschlag
trap [træp]	Falle
impulsive [ɪm'pʌlsɪv]	impulsiv, unüberlegt
shape [ʃeɪp]	Form, Gestalt
bright [braɪt]	hell, leuchtend
(to) persuade [pə'sweɪd]	überreden, bewegen, überzeugen
(to) advise [əd'vaɪz]	(be)raten
stomach ['stʌmək]	Magen
discount ['dɪskaʊnt]	Preisnachlaß, Rabatt
reduction [rɪ'dʌkʃn]	Verringerung; Ermäßigung, (Preis)nachlaß
at one time [ət 'wʌn 'taɪm]	auf einmal
(to) enable [ɪ'neɪbl]	ermöglichen, befähigen, in die Lage versetzen
item ['aɪtəm]	Artikel
shopkeeper [ʃɒpˌkiːpə]	Ladeninhaber(in)
bargain ['bɑːgɪn]	vorteilhaftes Geschäft, günstiger Kauf
collection [kə'lekʃn]	Kollektion
original [ə'rɪdʒənl]	Original-; ursprünglich
tag [tæg]	(Preis)schild
especially [ɪ'speʃəlɪ]	speziell, besonders
unit ['juːnɪt]	Grund-/Maßeinheit
laboratory [lə'bɒrətrɪ]	Labor(atorium)
advertiser ['ædvətaɪzə]	Inserent(in); Werbefachmann/-frau
Consumer Advice Council [kən'sjuːmər_əd'vaɪsˌkaʊnsl]	Verbraucherberatung(sstelle)

A2

special offer ['speʃl_'ɒfə]	Sonderangebot
cream [kriːm]	*hier:* (Gesichts)creme
(to) warn [wɔːn]	ermahnen; warnen

A3

p (penny/pence) [piː]	britische Währungseinheit
yoghurt ['jɒgət]	Joghurt
chicken ['tʃɪkɪn]	Küken, Hähnchen; Hühnerfleisch
pie [paɪ]	Pastete, Torte
value ['væljuː]	(Gegen)wert
washing-powder ['wɒʃɪŋˌpaʊdə]	Waschpulver
alarm clock [ə'lɑːmˌklɒk]	Wecker
p & p (postage and packing) ['pəʊstɪdʒ_ən 'pækɪŋ]	Porto und Verpackung
v (volt) [vəʊlt]	Volt
superb [suː'pɜːb]	hervorragend, ausgezeichnet
live [laɪv]	lebendig; direkt, live
pp (per person) [pə 'pɜːsn]	pro Person
incl (including) [ɪn'kluːdɪŋ]	einschließlich
VAT (Value Added Tax) [ˌviːeɪ'tiː]	Mehrwertsteuer
d.b.b. (dinner, bed and breakfast) ['dɪnə 'bed_ən 'brekfəst]	Halbpension
min (minimum) ['mɪnɪməm]	Mindest-
solarium [səʊ'leərɪəm]	Solarium
sauna ['sɔːnə]	Sauna
(to) measure ['meʒə]	messen
additional [ə'dɪʃənl]	zusätzlich; Extra-

B1

winner ['wɪnə]	Sieger, Gewinner
(to) squeak [skwiːk]	quiek(s)en, piep(s)en
(to) bleep [bliːp]	piep(s)en
(to) flash [flæʃ]	blitzen
(to) manufacture [ˌmænjʊ'fæktʃə]	herstellen
craftsman ['krɑːftsmən]	Handwerker; Könner
extract ['ekstrækt]	Auszug
body copy ['bɒdɪˌkɒpɪ]	Hauptteil/-text
function ['fʌŋkʃn]	Funktion, Aufgabe
reader ['riːdə]	Leser(in)
(to) contain [kən'teɪn]	enthalten
basic ['beɪsɪk]	grundlegend; Grund-

Unit 14

message ['mesɪdʒ] — Botschaft, Mitteilung, Nachricht
logo ['ləʊgəʊ] — Firmenemblem/-zeichen
brand name ['brænd͵neɪm] — Markenname
slogan ['sləʊgən] — Slogan, Werbespruch
catchy ['kætʃɪ] — eingängig
phrase [freɪz] — Redewendung, Redensart
visual ['vɪʒʊəl] — visuell; Bildelement
illustration [͵ɪləˈstreɪʃn] — Illustration, Bebilderung

B 3

(to) ban [bæn] — verbieten
commercial [kəˈmɜːʃl] — Werbespot/-sendung
prize [praɪz] — Preis *(Gewinn)*
agency ['eɪdʒənsɪ] — Agentur, Büro
flexible ['fleksəbl] — flexibel, beweglich, anpassungsfähig

B 4

trade mark [treɪdmɑːk] — Markenname
simple ['sɪmpl] — einfach
funny ['fʌnɪ] — lustig, komisch

B 5

jeep [dʒiːp] — Geländewagen
reliable [rɪˈlaɪəbl] — zuverlässig
actually ['æktʃʊəlɪ] — wirklich, tatsächlich

C 1

loan [ləʊn] — Darlehen
(to) pay back ['peɪ 'bæk] — zurückzahlen
(to) borrow ['bɒrəʊ] — sich (aus)leihen
(to) manage ['mænɪdʒ] — fertig-/zuwege bringen, schaffen
band [bænd] — Kapelle, Band

C 2

campaign [kæmˈpeɪn] — (Werbe)aktion/-kampagne
motor-bike ['məʊtəbaɪk] — Motorrad
dealer ['diːlə] — Händler
moto-cross ['məʊtəʊkrɒs] — Moto-Cross; Gelände-
(to) pay off ['peɪ 'ɒf] — abzahlen
according to [əˈkɔːdɪŋ] — nach, laut, gemäß

T 1

direct mail ['dɪrektˌmeɪl] — *etwa:* Brief-/Wurfsendung
postage ['pəʊstɪdʒ] — Porto, Versand(kosten)
public ['pʌblɪk] — öffentlich; Öffentlichkeit
medium ['miːdɪəm] — Medium, Mittel; (Werbe)träger
mass consumption [͵mæskənˈsʌmpʃn] — Massenverbrauch
(to) advertise ['ædvətaɪz] — werben; Werbung machen
peanut butter ['piːnʌt ͵bʌtə] — Erdnußbutter/-creme
junk mail ['dʒʌŋk͵meɪl] — Postwurfsendung

image ['ɪmɪdʒ] — Image, Bild, Vorstellung
(to) surround [səˈraʊnd] — umgeben
(to) hold sth up ['həʊld ˈsʌmθɪŋ ˈʌp] — in die Höhe halten, hochhalten
soft drink ['sɒftˌdrɪŋk] — alkoholfreies Getränk
(to) link [lɪŋk] — verbinden, verknüpfen
fingernail ['fɪŋgəneɪl] — Fingernagel
trick [trɪk] — Trick
useful ['juːsfʊl] — nützlich
in the end [ɪn ðɪ 'end] — schließlich, endlich
(to) influence ['ɪnflʊəns] — beeinflussen
anti-ad ['æntɪˌæd] — Werbung gegen etwas
drink-driving ['drɪŋk͵draɪvɪŋ] — *etwa:* Fahren unter Alkoholeinfluß
ski [skiː] — Ski

T 2

season ['siːzn] — Jahreszeit, Saison
fashion ['fæʃn] — Mode
average ['ævərɪdʒ] — durchschnittlich; Durchschnitts-
sticker ['stɪkə] — Aufkleber

T 3

(to) pull on ['pʊl ˈɒn] — anziehen
spot [spɒt] — *hier:* Pickel, Flecken
forehead ['fɒrɪd] — Stirn
Big Dipper ['bɪg 'dɪpə] — Großer Bär *(Gestirn)*
chin [tʃɪn] — Kinn
acne ['æknɪ] — Akne
(to) light up [laɪt ˈʌp] — (auf)leuchten
strength [streŋθ] — Stärke, Kraft
horrible ['hɒrəbl] — schrecklich
stop-watch ['stɒpwɒtʃ] — Stoppuhr
waterproof ['wɔːtəpruːf] — wasserdicht
(to) address [əˈdres] — sich wenden an, ansprechen

S 1

waste disposal ['weɪstdɪ͵spəʊzl] — Abfall-/Müllbeseitigung
in the course of [ɪn ðə ˈkɔːs əv] — im Lauf(e) von
(to) throw away ['θrəʊ əˈweɪ] — wegwerfen
plastic ['plæstɪk] — Kunststoff, Plastik
as a whole [əz ə 'həʊl] — im ganzen, insgesamt
sensible ['sensəbl] — vernünftig
landfill site ['lændfɪl͵saɪt] — Müllhalde, Deponie
threat [θret] — Bedrohung, Gefahr
supply [səˈplaɪ] — Vorrat, Vorkommen
recycling [͵riːˈsaɪklɪŋ] — Wiederverwertung/-aufbereitung
(to) make sense ['meɪk 'sens] — vernünftig/sinnvoll sein
(to) regenerate [rɪˈdʒenəreɪt] — regenerieren, erneuern
(to) conserve [kənˈsɜːv] — konservieren, bewahren
resources [rɪˈsɔːsɪz] — natürliche Vorkommen, Bodenschätze, Ressourcen
litter ['lɪtə] — Abfall, Müll
profitable ['prɒfɪtəbl] — einträglich, gewinnbringend/-trächtig
(to) avoid [əˈvɔɪd] — vermeiden

VOCABULARY

Unit 15

(to) separate ['sepəreɪt]	trennen
(to) incinerate [ɪn'sɪnəreɪt]	verbrennen
(to) deposit [dɪ'pɒzɪt]	(ab)lagern, deponieren
non-returnable [ˌnɒnrɪ'tɜːnəbl]	Einweg-
can [kæn]	*AE:* Büchse, Dose
packaging ['pækɪdʒɪŋ]	Verpackung
double-packaging ['dʌbl 'pækɪdʒɪŋ]	doppelte Verpackung
organic [ɔː'gænɪk]	organisch
compost ['kɒmpɒst]	Kompost
aluminium [ˌæljʊ'mɪnjəm]	Aluminium
Waste Disposal Authority ['weɪst dɪs'pəʊzl_ɔː,θɒrətɪ]	Abfallbeseitigungsbehörde
effectively [ɪ'fektɪvlɪ]	wirksam
(to) recycle [ˌriː'saɪkl]	wiederverwerten/-aufbereiten

S 2

salmonella [ˌsælmə'nelə]	Salmonellen
valuable ['væljʊəbl]	wertvoll
diet ['daɪət]	Diät; Ernährung
(to) fall ill ['fɔːl_ɪl]	krank werden
food poisoning ['fuːd,pɔɪzənɪŋ]	Lebensmittelvergiftung
consumption [kən'sʌmpʃn]	Verbrauch; Genuß, Verzehr
(to) fight [faɪt]	(be)kämpfen
Chief Medical Officer ['tʃiːf 'medɪkl_'ɒfɪsə]	*etwa:* oberster Amtsarzt
fried (egg) ['fraɪd_eg]	Spiegel-(Ei)
scrambled (egg) ['skræmbld]	Rühr-(Ei)
poached (egg) [pəʊtʃt]	pochiertes/verlorenes (Ei)
the elderly [ðɪ 'eldəlɪ]	ältere Menschen
pregnant ['pregnənt]	schwanger
white [waɪt]	*hier:* Eiweiß
yolk [jəʊk]	Eigelb, Dotter
uncooked [ˌʌn'kʊkt]	ungekocht, roh
home-made ['həʊmmeɪd]	hausgemacht
mayonnaise [ˌmeɪə'neɪz]	Mayonnaise
(to) cause [kɔːz]	verursachen
cool [kuːl]	kühl, kalt; gekühlt
(to) result [rɪ'zʌlt]	resultieren, zur Folge haben
mixture ['mɪkstʃə]	Mischung

S 3

multinational [ˌmʌltɪ'næʃənəl]	multinational
headquarters ['hed,kwɔːtəz]	Hauptquartier, Zentrale
world-wide ['wɜːldwaɪd]	weltweit
shareholder ['ʃeə,həʊldə]	Aktionär
(to) look back on ['lʊk 'bæk_ɒn]	zurückschauen/-blicken auf
at a glance [ət_ə 'glɑːns]	auf einen Blick
turnover ['tɜːn,əʊvə]	Umsatz
profit before tax ['prɒfɪt bɪfɔː 'tæks]	Gewinn vor Steuer
dividend ['dɪvɪdend]	Dividende
face value ['feɪs,væljuː]	Nenn-/Nominalwert
share [ʃeə]	Aktie; Anteil
market value ['mɑːkɪt,væljuː]	Markt-/Kurs-/Verkehrswert
division [dɪ'vɪʒn]	*hier:* Geschäftsbereich
location [ləʊ'keɪʃn]	Stelle, Standort
cattle ranch ['kætl,rɑːntʃ]	Rinderzuchtfarm
plantation [plæn'teɪʃn]	Plantage, Pflanzung
large-scale ['lɑːdʒ'skeɪl]	groß(angelegt), umfangreich, großflächig
motor vehicle ['məʊtə'viːɪkl]	Motorfahrzeug
distribution [ˌdɪstrɪ'bjuːʃn]	Verteilung
distributor [dɪ'strɪbjʊtə]	Verteiler
manufacturer [ˌmænjʊ'fæktʃərə]	Hersteller
truck [trʌk]	Lastwagen
level ['levl]	Ebene, Niveau
considerably [kən'sɪdərəblɪ]	beträchtlich
(to) prove [pruːv]	beweisen
publishing ['pʌblɪʃɪŋ]	Verlagswesen; Verlags-, Druckerei
printing plant ['prɪntɪŋ,plɑːnt]	
on the whole [ɒn ðə 'həʊl]	im großen (und) ganzen
growth [grəʊθ]	Wachstum
freight [freɪt]	Fracht
partly ['pɑːtlɪ]	teilweise, zum Teil
(to) achieve [ə'tʃiːv]	erreichen
(to) deal with ['diːl wɪð]	sich befassen mit
(to) gain [geɪn]	gewinnen
(to) be worth [bɪ 'wɜːθ]	wert sein
equal ['iːkwəl]	gleich
(to) divide [dɪ'vaɪd]	(auf)teilen

UNIT 15

St

generally ['dʒenərəlɪ]	im allgemeinen
East Africa ['iːst_'æfrɪkə]	Ostafrika

A1

trainee [treɪ'niː]	Auszubildende(r); Praktikant(in)
(to) found [faʊnd]	gründen
full-time [ˌfʊl'taɪm]	ganztägig; Ganztags-
beginner [bɪ'gɪnə]	Anfänger(in)
intermediate [ˌɪntə'miːdjət]	Mittelstufe(n-)
advanced [əd'vɑːnst]	fortgeschritten
on loan [ɒn 'ləʊn]	leihweise
excursion [ɪk'skɜːʃn]	Exkursion, Ausflug
free of charge ['friː_əv 'tʃɑːdʒ]	kostenlos
timetable ['taɪm,teɪbl]	Stundenplan
grammar ['græmə]	Grammatik
practice ['præktɪs]	Übung(en)
conversation [ˌkɒnvə'seɪʃn]	Konversation, Unterhaltung
level ['levl]	Niveau, Stufe
daily ['deɪlɪ]	täglich
certificate [sə'tɪfɪkət]	Zertifikat, Abschlußzeugnis
welfare service ['welfeə,sɜːvɪs]	*etwa:* soziale Leistungen
guest house ['gesthaʊs]	Gästehaus, Pension
(to) attend [ə'tend]	besuchen, teilnehmen

VOCABULARY

Unit 15

A 2

general	[ˈdʒenərəl]	allgemein
(to) find out	[ˌfaɪndˈaʊt]	herausfinden, feststellen
male nurse	[ˌmeɪl ˈnɜːs]	Krankenpfleger

A 3

nationality	[ˌnæʃəˈnælətɪ]	Nationalität
profession	[prəˈfeʃn]	Beruf
Cambridge English exam	[ˈkeɪmbrɪdʒ ˈɪŋlɪʃ ɪgˌzæm]	Englischprüfungsmodell aus Cambridge
cheque	[tʃek]	Scheck
suitable	[ˈsuːtəbl]	passend, geeignet

A 4

mother tongue	[ˈmʌðəˌtʌŋ]	Muttersprache
speed	[spiːd]	Geschwindigkeit, Tempo
kiosk	[ˈkiːɒsk]	Kiosk
Turkish	[ˈtɜːkɪʃ]	türkisch; Türkisch
Danish	[ˈdeɪnɪʃ]	dänisch; Dänisch
sherry	[ˈʃerɪ]	Sherry
pronunciation	[prəˌnʌnsɪˈeɪʃn]	Aussprache
Norman	[ˈnɔːmən]	Normanne
poet	[ˈpəʊɪt]	Dichter
everyday	[ˈevrɪdeɪ]	alltäglich, üblich

B 1

West Indian	[ˌwestˈɪndjən]	westindisch
Jamaica	[dʒəˈmeɪkə]	Jamaika
experience	[ɪkˈspɪərɪəns]	Erfahrung; Erlebnis
(to) sound	[saʊnd]	klingen
dialect	[ˈdaɪəlekt]	Dialekt, Mundart
Africa	[ˈæfrɪkə]	Afrika
West Indies	[ˌwestˈɪndɪz]	Westindien
gradually	[ˈgrædʒʊəlɪ]	allmählich, Schritt für Schritt
patient	[ˈpeɪʃnt]	geduldig
isolated	[ˈaɪsəleɪtɪd]	isoliert, auf sich allein gestellt
standard English	[ˈstændəd ˌɪŋlɪʃ]	hochsprachliches Englisch
opportunity	[ˌɒpəˈtjuːnɪtɪ]	Möglichkeit, (günstige) Gelegenheit
carnival	[ˈkɑːnɪvl]	Karneval
Jamaican	[dʒəˈmeɪkən]	jamaikisch, jamaikanisch
(to) get to know	[ˌget tə ˈnəʊ]	kennenlernen
sunny	[ˈsʌnɪ]	sonnig
slave trade	[ˈsleɪvˌtreɪd]	Sklavenhandel
unfriendly	[ˌʌnˈfrendlɪ]	unfreundlich
mark	[mɑːk]	(Zeugnis)note

B 2

reggae	[ˈregeɪ]	Reggae
verse	[vɜːs]	Strophe, Vers
underground	[ˈʌndəgraʊnd]	U-Bahn
(to) escape	[ɪˈskeɪp]	entkommen/-fliehen
view	[vjuː]	(Aus)sicht; Ansicht, Meinung, Auffassung

C 1

(to) confuse	[kənˈfjuːz]	verwirren
restroom	[ˈrestruːm]	AE: Toilette
gas station	[ˈgæsˌsteɪʃn]	AE: Tankstelle
the States	[steɪts]	die (Vereinigten) Staaten
(to) come across	[ˈkʌm əˌkrɒs]	begegnen, über den Weg laufen
avgas	[ˈavgæs]	AE: Flugbenzin
busboy	[ˈbʌsbɔɪ]	AE: Hilfskellner
dirt farmer	[ˈdɜːtˌfɑːmə]	AE: Farmer, der sein Land selbst bestellt
fish story	[ˈfɪʃˌstɔːrɪ]	AE: Angler-/Jägerlatein
night letter	[ˈnaɪtˌletə]	AE: (verbilligtes) Nachttelegramm
rock pig	[ˈrɒkˌpɪg]	AE: Rock-Fan/-Anhänger
(to) work	[wɜːk]	(be)arbeiten
(to) clear	[klɪə]	(ab)räumen
telegram	[ˈtelɪgræm]	Telegramm

C 2

baggage	[ˈbægɪdʒ]	AE: Gepäck
downtown	[ˌdaʊnˈtaʊn]	AE: in der/die Stadtmitte
freeway	[ˈfriːweɪ]	AE: (gebührenfreie) Schnellstraße; Autobahn
front clerk	[ˈfrʌntˌklɑːk]	AE: Empfangschef/-dame
in the meantime	[ɪn ðə ˈmiːntaɪm]	in der Zwischenzeit
first floor	[ˌfɜːst ˈflɔː]	AE: Erdgeschoß
second floor	[ˌsekənd ˈflɔː]	AE: erster Stock, erste Etage
elevator	[ˈelɪveɪtə]	AE: Aufzug
complicated	[ˈkɒmplɪkeɪtɪd]	schwierig, kompliziert
ground floor	[ˌgraʊnd ˈflɔː]	Erdgeschoß
lift	[lɪft]	Aufzug
last name	[ˈlɑːstˌneɪm]	AE: Zu-/Nach-/Familienname
surname	[ˈsɜːneɪm]	Zu-/Nach-/Familienname
French fries	[ˌfrentʃ ˈfraɪz]	AE: Pommes frites
coke	[kəʊk]	Cola
movie theater	[ˈmuːvɪˌθɪətə]	AE: Kino
sightseeing	[ˈsaɪtˌsiːɪŋ]	Besichtigung von Sehenswürdigkeiten
candy	[ˈkændɪ]	AE: Süßigkeiten
labour	[ˈleɪbə]	Arbeit

C 3

railroad	[ˈreɪlrəʊd]	AE: Eisenbahn
subway	[ˈsʌbweɪ]	AE: U-Bahn
automobile	[ˈɔːtəməʊbiːl]	AE: Auto, Wagen
motel	[məʊˈtel]	Motel
color	[ˈkʌlə]	AE: Farbe
spectacular	[spekˈtækjʊlə]	aufsehenerregend, imposant
traveler's check	[ˈtrævələzˌtʃek]	AE: Reisescheck
souvenir	[ˌsuːvəˈnɪə]	Souvenir, Andenken

VOCABULARY

C 4

general store ['dʒenərəl 'stɔː]	AE: Gemischtwarenladen
favorite ['feɪvərɪt]	Lieblings-
(to) come by [ˌkʌm 'baɪ]	vorbeikommen
thru [θruː]	AE: durch; bis

T 1

continent ['kɒntɪnənt]	Kontinent, Festland
official [ə'fɪʃl]	offiziell; Amts-
foreign language ['fɒrən ˌlæŋgwɪdʒ]	Fremdsprache

T 2

Switzerland ['swɪtsələnd]	die Schweiz
(to) point out ['pɔɪnt ˌaʊt]	betonen; hinweisen auf
bush [bʊʃ]	Busch, Dickicht
Malaysian [məˈleɪziən]	malaysisch; Malaysier(in)
jungle ['dʒʌŋgl]	Dschungel
argument ['ɑːgjumənt]	Argument
jewellery ['dʒuːəlrɪ]	Schmuck
hopeless ['həʊpləs]	hoffnungslos
(to) get by [ˌget 'baɪ]	zurecht-/durch-/auskommen
the Philippines [ðə 'fɪlɪpiːnz]	die Philippinen
Malaysia [məˈleɪziə]	Malaysia
straight away [ˌstreɪtə'weɪ]	sogleich, unmittelbar, unverzüglich
Thailand ['taɪlænd]	Thailand
make [meɪk]	Fabrikat, Marke
(to) mix up ['mɪks ˌʌp]	(ver)mischen
unusual [ʌn'juːʒʊəl]	ungewöhnlich
Second World War ['sekənd ˌwɜːld 'wɔː]	Zweiter Weltkrieg
mixture ['mɪkstʃə]	Mischung
Filipino [ˌfɪlɪ'piːnəʊ]	Bewohner(in) der Philippinen
experienced [ɪk'spɪərɪənst]	erfahren
knowledge ['nɒlɪdʒ]	Kenntnis, Wissen
word processing ['wɜːdˌprəʊsesɪŋ]	Textverarbeitung
adventure [əd'ventʃə]	Abenteuer-
(to) guarantee [ˌgærən'tiː]	garantieren, bürgen

T 3

Japanese [ˌdʒæpə'niːz]	japanisch; Japanisch; Japaner(in)
data processing ['deɪtə ˌprəʊsesɪŋ]	Datenverarbeitung(s-)
hectic ['hektɪk]	hektisch, aufgeregt

S 1

civil engineer ['sɪvl ˌendʒɪnɪə]	Bauingenieur
tunnel ['tʌnl]	Tunnel
(to) survey [sə'veɪ]	vermessen
(to) prepare [prɪ'peə]	vorbereiten, herrichten
technical drawing ['teknɪkl 'drɔːɪŋ]	technische Zeichnung; Bau-/Konstruktionszeichnung
(to) estimate ['estɪmeɪt]	schätzen, berechnen
structure ['strʌktʃə]	Konstruktion; Bauwerk
(to) supervise ['suːpəvaɪz]	beaufsichtigen, überwachen
all-rounder [ɔːl'raʊndə]	Alleskönner
mechanical engineering [məˈkænɪkl ˌendʒɪ'nɪərɪŋ]	Maschinenbau
electrical engineering [ɪ'lektrɪkl ˌendʒɪ'nɪərɪŋ]	Elektrotechnik
chemical engineering ['kemɪkl ˌendʒɪ'nɪərɪŋ]	Chemotechnik; Industriechemie
drawing office ['drɔːɪŋ ˌɒfɪs]	Zeichenbüro
building site ['bɪldɪŋ ˌsaɪt]	Baustelle
(to) assist [ə'sɪst]	helfen, unterstützen
requirement [rɪ'kwaɪəmənt]	Erfordernis; Anforderung
applicant ['æplɪkənt]	Bewerber(in)
aged [eɪdʒd]	alt
college of further education ['kɒlɪdʒ əv 'fɜːðə ˌedjuː'keɪʃn]	etwa: Fachhochschule
contract ['kɒntrækt]	Vertrag
renewable [rɪ'njuːəbl]	verlängerbar
competitive [kəm'petətɪv]	wettbewerbsbetont
salary ['sælərɪ]	Gehalt (Verdienst)
fringe benefits ['frɪndʒ ˌbenɪfɪts]	außertarifliche/ zusätzliche Leistungen
interested ['ɪntrəstɪd]	interessiert
(to) enclose [ɪn'kləʊz]	beifügen, beilegen
single ['sɪŋgl]	ledig, unverheiratet
letter of application [ˌletər əv ˌæplɪ'keɪʃn]	Bewerbungsschreiben
curriculum vitae [kə'rɪkjʊləm 'viːtaɪ]	Lebenslauf
status ['steɪtəs]	Familienstand
qualification [ˌkwɒlɪfɪ'keɪʃn]	Qualifikation
Yours faithfully ['jɔːz 'feɪθfʊlɪ]	Mit freundlichen Grüßen (Briefende)

S 2

VSO (Voluntary Service Overseas) [ˌviː es 'əʊ]	Name einer britischen Hilfsorganisation
(to) address to [ə'dres]	sich wenden an
Third World [ˌθɜːd 'wɜːld]	Dritte Welt
nursing ['nɜːsɪŋ]	Krankenpflege
Sri Lanka [ˌsriː 'læŋkə]	Sri Lanka
(to) set off ['set ˌɒf]	sich aufmachen
nervous ['nɜːvəs]	nervös, aufgeregt
(to) excite [ɪk'saɪt]	aufregen, erregen
doll [dɒl]	Puppe
(to) bandage ['bændɪdʒ]	verbinden, einen Verband anlegen
sticking plaster ['stɪkɪŋ ˌplɑːstə]	Heftpflaster
(to) qualify ['kwɒlɪfaɪ]	sich qualifizieren, sich als geeignet erweisen
challenge ['tʃælɪndʒ]	Herausforderung
tough [tʌf]	schwierig, hart
satisfaction [ˌsætɪs'fækʃn]	Befriedigung
day to day [ˌdeɪ tə 'deɪ]	alltäglich, üblich
ward [wɔːd]	(Kranken)station
(to) take sb's temperature ['teɪk sʌmbədɪz 'temprətʃə]	jds Temperatur/ Fieber messen

VOCABULARY V

pulse rate ['pʌls,reɪt]	Pulsfrequenz	(to) realize ['rɪəlaɪz]	verwirklichen; feststellen
(to) X-ray ['eksreɪ]	röntgen	plus [plʌs]	plus; zuzüglich
treatment ['tri:tmənt]	Behandlung	living expenses	Lebenshaltungskosten, Unterhalt
injection [ɪn'dʒekʃn]	Injektion, Spritze	['lɪvɪŋɪk,spensɪz]	
surgical ['sɜ:dʒɪkl]	chirurgisch; Chirurgie-	package ['pækɪdʒ]	Paket; Pauschale
patient ['peɪʃnt]	Patient	intensive [ɪn'tensɪv]	intensiv, gründlich
(to) get ready [get 'redɪ]	herrichten, vorbereiten	plenty ['plentɪ]	eine Menge
operation [ˌɒpə'reɪʃn]	Operation	(to) address [ə'dres]	ansprechen
consultant [kən'sʌltənt]	Berater(in); Facharzt, -ärztin	(to) establish [ɪ'stæblɪʃ]	hier: knüpfen
(to) get involved with [get_ɪn'vɒlvd wɪð]	näher/besser kennenlernen; eingehen auf	(to) set up [set_ʌp]	aufsetzen
(to) go round [gəʊ 'raʊnd]	die Runde machen	contract ['kɒntrækt]	Vertrag
(to) look after [lʊk 'ɑːftə]	sich kümmern um	social ['səʊʃl]	sozial, gesellschaftlich; gesellig
letter of application ['letər_əv,æplɪ'keɪʃn]	Bewerbungsschreiben	professional training [prə'feʃnl 'treɪnɪŋ]	Berufsausbildung
		work experience [ˈwɜːk_ɪk'spɪərɪəns]	Berufserfahrung

S 3

high flyer [ˌhaɪ'flaɪə]	Erfolgsmensch	(to) promote [prə'məʊt]	fördern, voranbringen
business administration ['bɪznɪs_əd,mɪnɪ'streɪʃn]	Betriebs-/Geschäftsverwaltung	applicant ['æplɪkənt]	Bewerber(in)
		(to) be aged [bɪ 'eɪdʒd]	alt sein
degree [dɪ'griː]	(Abschluß)diplom	qualification [ˌkwɒlɪfɪ'keɪʃn]	Qualifikation
single ['sɪŋgl]	einheitlich; Einheits-		
outlook ['aʊtlʊk]	Ausblick; Zielsetzung	letter of application ['letər_əv,æplɪ'keɪʃn]	Bewerbungsschreiben
post [pəʊst]	Posten; Stelle	sales department [ˈseɪlzdɪ,pɑːtmənt]	Verkaufsabteilung

Alphabetical word list · Alphabetisches Wortregister

Das alphabetische Wortregister enthält mit Ausnahme des Fachwortschatzes alle Wörter aus dem unitbegleitenden Wörterverzeichnis.
Die Zahlen und Buchstaben hinter den Einträgen geben die jeweilige Fundstelle an (z. B. 5, B3 = Unit 5, Schritt B3).
Bei Wörtern des verbindlichen Lernwortschatzes ist die jeweilige Fundstelle **halbfett** hervorgehoben.

A
a:
 a bit 13, **A2**
 a number of **11, C3**
above all 5, A6
abroad **2, T**
absolutely 13, T1
accent 7, A4
(to) accept *(annehmen)* **5, C2**
(to) accept *(aufnehmen)* **6, T1**
accommodation 13, A2
according to 9, B3; 13, T1; 14, C2
acid rain **5, C1**
acne 14, T3
acrylic 10, T1
action 5, C1
active 5, B3
activity 13, A3
actually 14, B5
ad **9, A2**
(to) add **12, A2**
additional 14, A3
(to) address 14, T3

adult **12, A3**
advanced 15, A1
advantage **8, A2**
adventure 15, **T2**
(to) advertise **4, B3**
advertisement **8, Starter**
advertiser 14, A1
advertising **4, B3**
advice **6, B1**
(to) advise **14, A1**
adviser 6, B1
aerial **9, T**
aerobics 12, A3
(to) afford **12, A1**
Africa 15, B1
African 6, T2
after **10, B1**
afterwards 3, **C4**
agency 10, T1; **14, B3**
aim **12, C1**
air conditioning 13, C2
airline 2, Starter
airline stewardess **2, Starter**
airliner 9, A1

alarm clock **14, A3**
Alaska 13, A1
Alaskan 13, A3
alcohol 3, B3
alcoholic 10, A1
algebra 9, A2
all:
 all day **3, B3**
 all fields 7, C1
 all in all 8, C1
 all kinds of **7, C2**
 all my life 11, T2
 all over 12, A1
 all over the place 3, T
 all over the world 10, T1
 all right 1, A2
 all sorts of things 7, C1
 all the best 7, A1
 all the year round 4, A5
allowance 10, A1
alternative **5, A6**
amateur 3, T
ambition 3, T

ambulance 8, T1
ambulanceman 8, T1
America **1, C1**
American **3, T**
amount **10, B2**
analysis 9, B3
and all that 3, Starter
and so on 7, A2
announcement **4, C1**
anorak 13, A3
another thing 2, B2
anti-ad 14, T1
anti-gun movement 12, A1
anytime **8, B4**
anyway **7, C1**
apartment house 13, A3
(to) appeal to **14, Starter**
(to) apply for **6, A2**
architect 11, B2
Arctic Circle 13, A2
area 7,C1; **10, B3**
argument 15, T2
army 5, B1

VOCABULARY

Argentina 10, C1
(to) arrange 11, **A1**
arrival 6, **B1**
article *(Artikel)*
  3, T; 4, T1
article *(Gegenstand)*
  5, **C3**
as:
  as a result 7, T1
  as far as 3, C1
  as well 3, T
Asia 6, T1
Asian 6, T2
(to) ask about sth
  1, B2; **13, C1**
(to) ask for 8, **T2**
assistant 12, **C1**
assistant editor 4, T1
astronaut 7, B1
at:
  at all 12, B2
  at first 2, **T**
  at home 1, **A2**
  at last 8, **A4**
  at least 6, **A2**
  at once 3, **C4**
  at one time
    9, T; 14, A1
  at present 2, **T**
  at sea 7, B1
  at that time 7, **T1**
  at the age of 3, **T**
  at the beginning
    7, **T2**
  at the moment 1, **A2**
  at the same time 2, T
  at the top 9, **T**
  at war 4, B1
  at work 1, **A2**
athlete 3, C1
athletics 3, A4
atomic bomb 7, B3
(to) attend 15, **A1**
(to) attract 13, **A1**
attraction 3, T
attractive 8, B4
Australia 1, T1; 11, A1
Australian 6, Starter
Austria 10, C1
automatic 10, T1
automation 11, C1
automobile 15, C3
available 12, A3
average 14, T2
avgas 15, C1

B

(to) baby-sit 8, Starter
back door 6, A1
back home 11, **T2**
background 4, Fun
baggage 15, C2
bagpipe 7, C2
balcony 8, **A1**
bale 10, T1
(to) ban 14, B3
banana 3, B3
band 14, C1
bank manager 6, A2

banner 5, T
bar 7, A1; 13, A3
bargain 14, **A1**
(to) base sth on sth
  12, T1
basic 14, B1
basket *(Abfallbehälter)*
  2, C4
basket *(Korb)* 10, **A1**
basketball 3, Starter
bathing-cap 3, C5
battery 5, C2
bay 13, **B1**
(to) be:
  (to) be a fast talker
    7, **C2**
  (to) be a quiet talker
    7, **C2**
  (to) be able to 7, **T1**
  (to) be allowed to
    10, **A1**
  (to) be brief 12, **B3**
  Be careful! 2, **T**
  (to) be compared
    10, **C1**
  (to) be confused
    8, **C4**
  (to) be fair to sb
    6, T1
  (to) be famous for
    1, **C3**
  (to) be from 1, **Starter**
  (to) be gone 8, C1
  (to) be good at sth
    2, **C3**
  (to) be happy about
    sth 6, **C3**
  (to) be interested in
    sb/sth 5, **A1**
  (to) be like 2, **A2**
  (to) be lost 1, B2
  (to) be made of 3, **C1**
  (to) be of the opinion
    11, **C1**
  (to) be on 4, B1
  (to) be one's scene
    11, **T2**
  (to) be over 2, **T**
  (to) be overweight
    3, **B3**
  (to) be prepared
    11, **C3**
  (to) be tired of sth
    9, **C1**
  (to) be willing 12, C1
  (to) be worth it/sth
    2, T1; 8, **B4**
beach 1, **C3**
bean 5, A6
bear 3, T
beard 3, **C3**
beauty treatment 4, C1
because of 13, **A1**
bed and breakfast place
  5, **B1**
beef 4, B4; 10, C1
beer 3, B3
beetle 2, C4; 7, T1
beginner 15, A1

beginning 2, **C4**
bell 1, C3
below 11, **T2**
bench 3, B2
(to) bend down 3, B2
best 4, **B3**
best wishes 7, **A4**
better 4, **B3**
better than 2, A4
Beware of the dog!
  9, B4
Big Dipper 14, T3
billion 13, B1
biography 7, B3
biology 2, C3
biorhythm chart 9, B3
bird lover 13, B2
birthplace 7, B3
(to) bite 9, **B1**
(to) blame sb for sth
  5, **B1**
(to) bleep 14, B1
blind 13, **C2**
(to) block 5, T
block of flats 10, **B3**
Bobby 7, A2
body:
  body building 3, A4
  body copy 14, B1
boom 13, A3
boot 8, **T1**
boring 11, **T2**
(to) borrow 14, **C1**
bottle bank 5, **B3**
bowl 12, **B3**
boyfriend 1, **C1**
(to) brake 8, **C2**
brand name 14, B1
Brazil 13, T1
(to) break down
  8, **Starter**
(to) breathe 12, **B3**
bright 14, **A1**
bright idea 12, C2
(to) bring:
  (to) bring down 7, A2
  (to) bring in 10, **A2**
  (to) bring sb/sth with
    2, B2
Brit 6, Starter
Britain 1, **Starter**
British 1, **C1**
British Tourist Authority
  8, B4
brochure 8, **B4**
budget 6, A4
builder 13, B2
busboy 15, C1
bush 15, T2
business 4, **Starter**
business studies 2, A1
busy 1,T1; 2, **A3**
by:
  by *(nicht später als)*
    2, **C4**
  by *(mit Hilfe von)*
    4, T1
  by hand 10, T1
  by plane 10, T1

  by ship 10, A1
  by the way 2, **B2**

C

CAB 6, B1
cab 8, Starter
caber 3, C1
cable 9, B1
cactus 10, A2
cafeteria 2, C4
(to) calculate 2, A1
California 7, B3
Californian 10, C1
(to) call:
  (to) call in
    5, B1; 11, B1
  (to) call on sb 13, **C1**
  (to) call out 13, A2
Cambridge English
  exam 15, A3
campaign 14, C2
camping 8, B5
Canada 13, B1
Canadian 13, B1
candidate 6, T1; 7, B3
canteen 11, B2
cap 3, **C3**
capital 1, **T1**
car racing 7, T2
caravan 4, A4; 8, B5
caravan park 8, B5
career 7, **B2**
carefully 5, **B3**
cargo 10, **B1**
carnival 15, B1
carpet 11, **B2**
carrot 3, B3
(to) carry:
  (to) carry *(übermitteln)*
    9, **T**
  (to) carry *(transportie-*
    ren, befördern)
    10, **B1**
  (to) carry on 12, T2
cart 5, A1
cartoon 6, B5
case *(Fall)* 4, **A4**
case *(Koffer)* 8, **C4**
cash 9, **A1**
casing 11, A1
(cassette) deck 9, B2
(cassette) recorder
  9, B2
castle 1, C3
catastrophe 11, T1
catchy 14, B1
cathedral 1, C3;
  4, B1; 8, B4
cattle 1, T2
ceiling 6, **A1**
central:
  central 5, B2
  central Manchester
    1, B3
  central heating 5, A1;
    13, C1
century 7, **A2**
certificate 15, A1
chairman 7, B1

VOCABULARY

champion 3, A1
championship 3, T
chance 2, T; 6, A1
channel *(Programm)* 4, B1; 13, B1
channel *(Durchgang, Passage)* 10, A1
charity 12, A1
charity promoter 7, B1
chart 4, **B2**
(to) check:
  (to) check 9, **A2**
  (to) check in 10, **A3**
  (to) check with sb 3, C4
cheers 7, **A1**
chemical 5, C1
chemistry 2, C3
cheque 15, A3
chess 9, A2
chicken 14, **A3**
chimney 13, C1
chin 14, T3
China 10, C1
Chinese 6, Starter
chocolates 3, B2
cigar 10, A1
circuit programme 3, B2
civic studies 2, C3
class 2, B1
classical 4, A2
classmate 1, **C3**
cleaner 2, C4; 4, A3; 12, C1
(to) clear 10, B3; 15, C1
climate 13, A1
(to) climb up 5, **T**
(to) close down 6, **A2**
close to 8, B5
closed 1, **C3**
cloth 10, **T1**
clothing 10, **T1**
coach 8, C4
coach hire 8, Starter
coal 1, **T2**
coal-fired power station 5, T
coast 8, **B5**
coastguard 8, T1
coastline 13, B1
cocoa 10, B1
coffee bar 2, A4
coke 15, C2
(to) collect 4, **T1**
collection 14, A1
college 1, **A1**
color 12, B2; 15, C3
coloured person 6, T2
(to) come:
  (to) come across 15, **C1**
  (to) come back from 6, A2
  (to) come by 15, C4
  (to) come down to 6, T3

(to) come from 3, A1
(to) come in 13, **B1**
Come on! 2, B2; 6, A1; 9, A3
(to) come round 4, **A4**
(to) come true 9, A1
comedy 4, B1
comfortable 5, **A4**
comic 4, A2
commercial:
  commercial 14, **B3**
  commercial college 2, Fun
common sense 13, **C2**
Commonwealth 10, **B2**
(to) communicate 9, **T**
communication 9, T
compact car 7, T1
company 4, B3; **7, B1**
(to) compare 3, **T**
competition 3, **A1**
competitor 2, **T**
complaint 8, B1
(to) complete 11, **T1**
completely 12, C1; 13, **A3**
completion 11, T1
complicated 15, **C2**
computer 2, **Starter**
computer programmer 2, **Starter**
computer studies 2, **A1**
concert 2, B1
condition 13, **A2**
(to) confuse 15, C1
Congratulations! 3, A1
congress centre 6, C1
(to) connect 9, **B2**
(to) connect sb to sb 8, T1
connection 10, T2
Conservatives 6, T1
(to) consume 7, T1
consumer 14, **A1**
Consumer Advice Council 14, A1
(to) contact sb 8, B4
(to) contain 14, **B1**
container 5, B3
continent 15, T1
(to) continue 8, **C2**
(to) contrast 6, C1
(to) contrast with 3, A1
contribution 12, **T1**
control 5, B2
(to) control sb/sth 8, A5
controller 13, A2
conversation 9, T; 15, A1
(to) convert 13, T1
cookbook 2, C2
cooker 8, **A4**
cookery 4, **Starter**
(to) cool off 13, C1
(to) cooperate 10, **C2**

cooperation 10, **C2**
copy 1, B2
Cornish Pasties 4, B4
cosmetics 11, T1
cotton 10, **C1**
could you? 5, B1
council 6, C1
countryside 13, T1
couple:
  couple 8, **A2**
  a couple of **7, B1**
coupon 13, C1
course 2, **A1**
court 12, **T2**
court case 12, T2
cousin 1, B1
(to) cover sb/sth 9, **T**
cowshed 4, A6; 13, T2
craftsman 14, **B1**
crate 10, B2
cream 14, A2
cream-cake 3, B3
(to) create 13, A1
credit 9, A1
credit card 9, A1
crew 13, A2
crime:
  crime 6, T1
  crime rate 12, A1
crisis 11, T1
critical 9, **Starter**
crossword 4, Starter
crowded 5, **A6**
Cuba 12, Starter
culture 13, A3
curious 5, **A3**
cursor 9, A2
curtain 6, **A1**
curve 9, B3
customer 4, **A6**
customs 10, **A1**
customs officer 10, A1
(to) cut out 10, **T1**
cycling 3, A4

D

d.b.b. 14, A3
Dad 9, B3
dailies 4, T1
daily:
  daily 4, Starter; 15, A1
  daily newspaper 4, Starter
  daily routine 8, B3
dam 13, B1
damage 13, **A2**
(to) damage 5, T; **9, B1**
dancer 7, C2
dancing 3, A4
dancing competition 3, C1
Danish 15, A4
darling 4, T2
data processing 15, T3
date of birth 7, **B3**

daytime 8, B1
dead end 9, A4
(to) deal with 6, **B1**
dealer 11, A1; 14, C2
dear 9, C1
(to) decide 5, **A6**
(to) declare 10, A1
(to) decrease 6, T1; 9, T; **11, T1**
degree 12, **C1**
(to) deliver 4, T1; 10, **B1**
delivery 10, **C2**
(to) demonstrate 13, T2
demonstrator 5, T
Denmark 13, T1
department:
  Department of Energy 13, C2
  Department of Health and Human Services 12, T1
  department store 10, **T1**
(to) depend (on) 10, A1; **12, B2**
(to) describe sb/sth 3, **B2**
description 7, A2
(to) deserve 12, **T2**
design 10, C1
(to) design 11, B2
(to) destroy 13, **A3**
detail 5, C2
(to) develop 11, **A3**
development 13, **A3**
device 11, **A4**
(to) dial 8, **T1**
dialect 15, B1
diary 2, B1
(to) dictate sth 10, C2
diesel 13, T2
difference 13, B2
difficulty 11, **C1**
digital 9, B2
dinner-dance 9, B3
direct mail 14, T1
direction 9, **C1**
directly 10, **T1**
director 12, A1
dirt farmer 15, C1
disadvantage 8, **A2**
disc jockey 4, A3
disco 1, B2
discount 14, **A1**
(to) discover 11, **B1**
discovery 13, A1
discussion 5, T
dishes 12, B3
dishwasher 11, A4
disk drive 9, A2
(to) dismiss 13, T2
(to) do:
  (to) do a survey of sth 6, C3
  (to) do some repairs 6, A4
  (to) do some shopping 5, B1

two hundred and seventy-one 271

V VOCABULARY

(to) do sth to sth 6, A1
dock worker 10, B1
docklands 10, B3
documentary 4, B1
dollar 3, T
double:
  double decker 8, C1
  double glazing 13, C1
down under 13, T1
downstairs 8, **A4**
downtown 15, C2
draft 13, C1
dragon 6, B2; 7, A2
drama 2, C3
(to) draw 2, C3
drawing 9, **T**
drier 11, A4
drink-driving 14, T1
driving lessons 9, B3
(to) drop 2, C3
drug 4, A4
dustbin 6, **A1**
duty 10, **A1**
duty-free 10, A1

E

(to) earn 2, **T**
earnings 3, T; 12, C1
earphone 9, B1
earth 5, **C1**
east 1, **C3**
East Africa 15, Starter
Easter 6, B5
EC 10, **B2**
economic 13, **A1**
economics 2, Fun
edition 4, T1
editor 4, A3
education 6, **T1**
educational programme 4, B1
effect 13, B2
efficiently 13, T1
(to) elect 6, **T1**
election 6, **C1**
electric:
  electric cooker 2, A1
  electric shock 9, B1
electrical 11, **T2**
electrician 2, **Starter**
electricity 5, **A6**
electronics 2, **A1**
elevator 15, C2
else 11, A3
emergency:
  emergency 8, **Starter**
  emergency landing 10, A3
  emergency service 8, **Starter**
emotional 9, B3
(to) employ 11, **A3**
employee 11, **C1**
employment 6, **B1**
(to) enable 12, T1; 14, **A1**
energy:
  energy 5, **C1**

Energy Council 13, C1
energy doctor 13, C1
engine 3, **Fun**
engine trouble 10, A3
engineer 7, **T2**
engineering 7, **B1**
England 1, **Starter**
English 1, **C1**
Englishman 7, **A1**
(to) enjoy doing sth 8, **C1**
enjoyable 8, **B4**
entertaining 4, B2
entertainment 4, Starter
envelope 5, **C3**
environment 5, **B2**
equipment 2, **C2**
(to) escape 15, **B2**
Eskimo 13, A3
especially 8, B5; 14, **A1**
estate agent 8, **Starter**
ethics 2, Fun
Europe 2, **T**
European 3, **T**
even:
  even 4, **B3**
  even though 13, C2
evening newspaper 1, B2
event 3, C1; 4, **T1**
every other day 3, B1
everyday 15, **A4**
everywhere 3, **T**
ex-employer 12, T2
exactly 2, B2; 3, **A1**
excellent 8, B4
except 11, **T2**
excursion 15, A1
exclusive 10, T1
(to) exist 6, **T2**
(to) expect 10, **C2**
expectant mother 12, C1
experience 7, B2; 8, T2; 15, **B1**
experienced 15, **T2**
explosives 10, A1
(to) export 10, **B2**
extract 14, B1
extreme 13, A2

F

(to) face 11, C1
facility 11, A3
factory 1, **T2**
(to) fall:
  (to) fall down 8, **C2**
  (to) fall off 9, **B1**
false 8, T1
famous 4, C2; **12, C1**
fan 1, B2
fantastic 1, B2; 9, A2; 12, A1
far:
  far too high 6, T1
fare 8, **C1**

farming 1, **T2**
farming course 2, C2
fashion 14, T2
fast food 13, A3
favorite 15, C4
favourite 3, **T**
fee 12, **A3**
(to) feed 4, **A6**
feeding ground 13, B2
feeling 7, C1
feet 3, C1
ferry 1, C3
few:
  a few times 6, A1
fight 12, C1
(to) fight:
  (to) fight 5, **C1**
  (to) fight for sth 11, **C2**
figure 6, T3
Filipino 15, **T2**
filling 4, B4
film star 7, B3
finally 8, **C2**
financial 11, C1
(to) find out 15, A2
fingernail 14, T1
finish 3, Fun
(to) finish with sb 8, **Starter**
(to) fire sb 12, T2
fire bell 8, C3
fire-brigade 8, T1
fire-engine 8, T1
fireman 4, A5
firm 2, **T**
first:
  first 1, **A1**
  first floor 15, C2
  first name 1, A1
  first of all 4, **B4**
fish:
  fish and chips 5, **B2**
  fish story 15, C1
fisherman 5, A3
fishing 1, **T2**
fit 9, B3
fitness 3, A1
five days a week 3, A1
(to) fix sth 6, **A1**
(to) flash 14, **B1**
flea 3, T
flexible 14, B3
flight 10, **A3**
(to) flood 13, B2
floor space 12, A3
floppy disk 9, A2
flour 4, B4
flow chart 9, A4
flying saucer 9, T1
food stamp 12, B2
food-mixer 11, A4
football:
  football 1, **B3**
  football ground 1, B3; 8, A1
  football training 2, A3
footballer 3, T

for:
  for ages 6, B5
  for a while 12, B3
  for example 1, **B2**
  for now 6, A2
  for quite a while 7, B1
foreground 4, Fun
forehead 14, T3
foreign:
  foreign 2, **C3**
  foreign language 15, **T1**
foreigh-made 13, A3
foreign news 4, Starter
foreigner 6, A1
fork-lift truck 11, A1
form 5, C1
fort 3, T
(to) found 15, A1
foundation 12, C1
fragile 9, B4
France 1, **C1**
free:
  free of charge 15, **A1**
  free period 2, C4
  free sale 12, A1
Freefone 13, C1
freestyle 3, A1
Freeway 15, C2
French 2, A1
French fries 12, B3; 15, C
fresh 3, **C4**
fridge 8, **A4**
friendliness 12, A1
friendly 12, **A1**
from:
  from all over the world 5, A4
  from time to time 3, B3
front clerk 15, C2
frost bite 13, A2
(to) fry 11, T2
ft (foot) 3, **T**
fuel 13, **C2**
full-time 15, **A1**
fun-run 9, B3
function 14, B1
(to) function 13, B1
funny 14, B4
funny-looking 5, A6
fur 4, C1; 13, A3
furniture 6, **C1**
future 6, **T1**

G

gadget 13, C2
gap 13, C1
garbage can 12, A1
gardening 4, **Starter**
gas 13, C1
gas(oline) 9, A1
gas station 15, C1
GDR 10, C1
general:
  general 15, **A2**
  general administration 10, C1
  general knowledge 11, B

VOCABULARY V

general rule **12, B3**
general store **15, C4**
generally **15, Starter**
(to) generate **13, B1**
geography **2, C3**
geothermal **13, T1**
German **1, C1**
Germany **6, T2**
(to) get:
  (to) get **10, A2**
  (to) get better **13, A2**
  (to) get by **15, T2**
  (to) get into **10, A3**
  Get it? **2, C3**
  (to) get married **7, B3**
  (to) get on/off **8, C1**
  (to) get onto **5, B1**
  (to) get out **3, C4**
  (to) get out of **10, A3**
  (to) get sth back **2, T**
  (to) get sth for sb **2, B2**
  (to) get to know **15, B1**
  (to) get to work **13, A2**
  (to) get up **3, A1**
  (to) get sth up to **3, C4**
geyser **13, T1**
girlfriend **1, B1**
(to) give:
  (to) give away sth **4, C1**
  (to) give sb trouble/ a hard time **4, A4**
  (to) give some money towards **9, A3**
  (to) give up sth **7, B1**
glove **7, C2**
(to) go:
  (to) go by bus **2, B2**
  (to) go climbing **9, B3**
  (to) go down **6, T1**
  (to) go off course **9, T**
  (to) go on **4, T1**; **5, T**; **9, A2**
  (to) go on the air **4, A5**
  (to) go out **13, B1**
  (to) go out on a date **11, T2**
  (to) go out with sb **2, A4**
  (to) go red **8, Starter**
  (to) go riding **3, A1**
  (to) go shopping **1, T1**
  (to) go up **6, T1**
gold coin **10, A1**
golf course **1, T2**
good:
  good afternoon **6, A2**
  a good point **2, T**
  good points **4, A4**
goods **10, Starter**
government **5, B1**
gradually **15, B1**

gram **10, A1**
grammar **15, A1**
grandad **4, A2**; **5, A1**
grandma **4, A2**; **5, A1**
graph **12, Starter**
grateful **10, C2**
gravy **12, B3**
(to) greet sb **8, B3**
ground floor **15, C2**
group **5, C1**
(to) grow **7, C1**
(to) guarantee **15, T2**
guess *(etwa, na ja)* **9, T**
(to) guess *(raten, vermuten)* **4, Fun**; **7, B3**; **12, B3**
guest house **15, A1**
guitar **7, C2**
guitar-player **7, C2**
gun **12, A1**
guy **12, B3**
gymnastics **3, Starter**

H

hair-drier **11, A2**
hairstyling **2, C3**
hairstylist **2, Starter**
hall **7, C1**
hamburger **3, T**; **12, B3**
(to) hand out sth **12, B3**
handicapped **12, B2**
handset **8, T1**
(to) hang **5, T**
harbour **8, B5**
hard disk **9, A2**
(to) harm **13, T1**
(to) hate **2, C3**
(to) have:
  (to) have a close look at sth/sb **4, B4**
  (to) have a good laugh **4, B1**
  (to) have a good look round/at sth **6, C1**
  (to) have a swim **5, B2**
  (to) have got sth on **9, B3**
  (to) have sth on **3, C3**
  (to) have to **3, C1**; **7, T1**; **10, A1**
  (to) have to do sth **3, A1**
head of department **10, C1**
headline **5, T**
health:
  health **5, T**
  health insurance **12, A1**
healthy **5, C1**
(to) heat **13, C1**
heating **7, T1**
heaven: Good heavens! **10, A1**
hectic **15, T3**
height **3, C2**
helicopter **5, B1**

helmet **3, T**
helper **12, B3**
helpful **12, A1**
Here you are. **2, B2**
hi tech **10, B3**
high:
  high **9, B3**
  high jump **3, Starter**
  High Street **1, A1**
Highland Games **3, C1**; **7, A1**
Hispanic **12, Starter**
history **1, T1**; **2, C3**; **7, Starter**
(to) hit **3, C1**
hit record **7, B1**
hobby **3, A1**
hockey **3, A3**
(to) hold sth up **14, T1**
home:
  home economics **2, A1**
  home news **4, Starter**
  home town **6, C1**
Hong Kong **10, C2**
hooligan **8, C1**
hopeless **15, T2**
horrible **14, T3**
horse rider **7, A2**
hospital **1, B1**
hot spring **13, T1**
hour:
  24 hour **8, Starter**
household **11, A1**
housework **4, B4**
how:
  How are things? **1, A2**
  How are you? **1, A2**
  how do you do **6, A2**
however **10, B3**
hundreds **7, T1**
(to) hunt **13, A3**
hunting **5, A1**

I

ice-cold **13, A2**
ice-hockey **3, Starter**
ice-skating **1, B2**
ice-skating rink **1, B2**
ideal **8, A2**
igloo **13, A3**
illegally **12, B2**
illiteracy **12, C1**
illness **9, A1**
illustration **14, B1**
image **14, T1**
(to) imagine **2, A4**; **9, T**
immediately **11, T1**
immigrant **6, B1**
(to) immigrate **6, T2**
immigration **6, T1**; **12, Starter**
(to) import **10, B2**
import-export firm **10, A2**
importance **9, T**
impossible **12, T1**
impression **12, A1**

(to) improve **9, A2**
impulsive **14, A1**
in:
  in a lot of ways **5, C1**
  in a way **3, T**; **7, C1**
  in addition **12, C1**
  in fact **2, A4**
  in many ways **9, T**
  in my opinion **5, T**
  in order to **13, B1**
  in the centre **4, Fun**
  in the end **14, T1**
  in the evening **1, C2**
  in the field of **5, T**
  in the meantime **15, C2**
  in the middle of **8, Starter**
  in the morning **2, A3**
  in the same way **1, C3**; **7, A2**
  in this way **2, T**; **7, B1**
  in those days **5, A1**
  in time **8, C2**
in (inch) **3, T**
incl **14, A3**
(to) include **8, T1**
income **11, A3**
(to) increase *(zunehmen, ansteigen)* **6, T1**
(to) increase *(vermehren, steigern)* **9, T**; **11, A3**
independent **6, C1**
India **10, C1**
Indian **6, A1**; **12, Starter**
industrial estate **11, T1**
industry **1, T2**
inflammable **9, B4**
(to) influence **14, T1**
informative **4, B2**
ingredients **4, B4**
inhabitant **5, A1**
input **13, Starter**
(to) install **10, C1**; **11, B2**
instruction **10, A3**
(to) insulate **13, C1**
insulation **13, C1**
interest **10, T4**
(to) interest **11, T1**
intermediate **15, A1**
international **4, B1**
interview **3, A1**; **6, B1**
(to) interview sb **8, C2**
interviewer **3, A1**; **7, B1**
(to) introduce sb to sth/sb **3, T**
introduction *(Vorstellung)* **7, B1**
introduction *(Einführung)* **10, B3**
(to) invent **7, T1**
(to) invest **10, B3**
Irish **1, C1**
Is that you? **1, A4**
isolated **15, B1**
Italian **1, T1**
Italy **1, C1**
item **14, A1**
It's my turn. **3, Fun**

VOCABULARY

J
Jamaica 15, B1
Jamaican 15, B1
Japan 2, T
Japanese 15, T3
jeans 8, A1
jeep 14, B5
jet 10, B3
jewellery 8, T2; 15, T2
job:
  job centre 6, A2
  job situation 6, A3
jogger 3, A3
jogging 3, A4
joiner 2, Starter
(to) joke 9, C1
journalist 7, B1
judo 2, B3
judge 12, T2
jug 1, C2
jumbo 3, T
jungle 15, T2
junk mail 14, T1
just a second 12, B3
just like 8, C1

K
(to) keep:
  (to) keep calm 8, T1
  (to) keep fit 3, B1
  (to) keep up 5, B3
key 9, B2
keyboard 9, A2
kick off 2, B3
kid 12, A3
(to) kill 7, A2
kilo 3, C1
kilogram 1, T1
kilometer 12, Starter
kilt 3, C3
kind of 13, A3
kindergarten 11, A3
kindness 12, A1
kiosk 15, A4
kitten 4, A5
(to) knock down 10, B3

L
label 8, C4
Labor Department 12, C1
laboratory 14, A1
labour:
  labour 15, C2
  labour market 12, B2
ladder 8, T1
ladleful 12, B3
(to) lag 13, C1
lake 1, T2
landlady 5, B1; 8, A1
landlord 8, A1
last:
  last but not least 11, A3
  last name 15, C2
  last night 5, B1
later on 7, C1
latest 4, A4
law 8, T1
law and order 6, T1
(to) lay the table 1, C2
layout man 4, T1
(to) lead to 13, T3
leader 11, C1
leaflet 3, C4
leak 13, A2
(to) learn how to do sth 2, A4
least 4, B2
left-hand side 4, Fun
leisure centre 1, B2
(to) lend sth to sb 2, C2
length 3, A1
less 4, B2
(to) let:
  (to) let *(vermieten)* 8, A1
  let me see 6, B1
  (to) let sb know 13, A2
  (to) let sth go to the dogs 6, A1
level 15, A1
lifeboat 8, T1
life-time 12, T2
lift 15, C2
(to) lift 8, T1
(to) light up 14, T3
lighting 13, Starter
like this *(auf diese Art und Weise)* 4, T2
like this *(folgendermaßen)* 10, C1
limit 10, A1
(to) limit 12, T2
line 12, B3; 13, A2
(to) link 14, T1
lipstick 11, T2
listener 4, A3
litter 2, C3
live 14, A3
living conditions 13, A3
(to) load/unload 10, B1
loan 14, C1
local:
  local 3, A1
  local election 6, C1
  local hero 3, A1
  local history 7, A2
(to) lock in 8, B2
logo 14, B1
long-distance 3, A1
long jump 3, Starter
(to) look:
  (to) look after sb/sth 2, B2
  (to) look for sb/sth 2, T
  (to) look upon sb/sth 12, C1
lorry 5, A1
lots of 1, B2
Love 8, A4
low 9, B3
luck:
  Good luck! 5, C2
luckily 10, A2
luggage 8, C4
lumbering 13, A1
lunch ticket 2, C4
lunchtime 7, A3
luxury goods 13, Starter

M
machine operator 11, B1
mad 2, B2
main:
  main 1, T1; 13, A3
  main gate 5, T
  main occupation 7, B1
mainly 9, B3
make 15, T2
(to) make:
  (to) make it 8, A4
  (to) make sb Sir 7, B1
  (to) make sth look nice 6, A1
  (to) make the most of sth 13, B2
  (to) make up 12, T1
  (to) make way for 12, T2
Malaysia 15, T2
Malaysian 15, T2
male nurse 15, A2
(to) manage 14, C1
management 11, C1
manager 3, T
manageress 13, B2
managing director 10, C1
(to) manufacture 12, C2; 14, B1
margarine 4, B4
mark 15, B1
market 7, C1
  flea market 7, A3
marvellous 6, A3
mass:
  mass consumption 14, T1
  mass production 7, T1
massive 13, C1
mastermind 4, B1
match 2, B3
material 6, A4
mathematics, maths 2, A3
mayor 13, B2
(to) mean it 6, T1; 9, A3
(to) measure 14, A3
mechanic 1, B1
media 4, Starter
medical school 12, C1
medicine 9, A1
medium 14, T1
member:
  member 5, T
  Member of Parliament 6, T1
memory 9, A2
(to) mend 6, A1
mental 9, B3
(to) mention 13, T2
menu 11, B2
message 14, B1
metal 11, A1
metalwork 2, A1
meter 13, B2
method 14, Starter
metre 1, C3
Mexican 12, B2
Mexico 12, Starter
microphone 9, B2
microwave (oven) 9, C1
midnight 4, B3
mile 3, A1
(to) milk 2, C1; 4, A6
million:
  a cool million 3, T
millionaire 12, C1
min 14, A3
mind 9, B3
(to) mind sth 9, C2
mine 13, T2
miner 13, T2
mini bus 8, C1
mining 1, T2
minister 13, B2
mirror 9, T
(to) miss 3, Fun
(to) mix up 15, T2
mixture 15, T2
modern 6, C1
(to) modernize 10, B3
Mom 9, A3
money 2, A4
monitor 9, A2
(to) monitor 13, A2
monk 7, C1
monster 1, T2
moon landing 13, A1
moreover 8, B4
motel 15, C3
mother tongue 15, A4
moto-cross 14, C2
motor:
  motor 9, T; 11, A1
  motor museum 7, T1
  motor racing 3, Fun
motor-bike 4, T2; 14, C2
motoring 3, T
motorway 5, C1; 11, T1
mountain 1, T2
mouse 9, A2
(to) move:
  (to) move away 10, B3
  (to) move in(to) 6, A1
  (to) move into/in 5, A6
  (to) move to the country 5, A6
movie theater 15, C2
MS 10, B1
multi-media 9, B1
(to) multiply by 6, C3
murder 12, A1
museum 5, B2
mustn't 2, C3
myth 12, T1

VOCABULARY V

N
nation 6, Starter
nationality 15, A3
native language 13, A3
naturally 13, C2
nature **13, T1**
nearby **1, C3**
nearly **3, B3**
needn't **2, C3**
negative 12, A1
neighbour **5, A6**
New Zealand 13, T1
newcomer 13, A1
(news) agency 4, T1
newsletter 12, A2
newspaper:
  evening newspaper 1, B2
  newspaper shop 4, T1
next:
  next door 6, A1
  next door neighbour 6, A3
next to **6, B1**
nickname 3, T
Nigeria 10, B1
night:
  Friday night 2, B2
  night letter 15, C1
nobody 12, B2
no longer **7, C1**
no. 10, B2
non-food 10, C1
non-steel 11, T1
normal **5, A6**
normally **3, A1**
Norman 8, B4; 15, A4
north:
  north **1, C3**
  North Pole 11, A2
Northern Ireland 1, Starter
Norway 1, C1
not:
  not . . . any more 9, A1
  not . . . either **9, C1**
  not . . . yet **1, C2**
  not any of us 6, C1
  not be friends with 2, B2
  not even **7, T1**
  not long ago 5, A6
  not much longer 2, T
note 1, T2
nothing at all 5, A1
nothing like that 5, A1
(to) notice **6, A1**
now and then *(hin und wieder, ab und zu)* 4, A1
now and then *(heute und damals)* 7, Starter
nowadays **2, A4**
nuclear energy 5, C1
number:
  number of police 6, T1
  number-plate 4, T2

number-plate centre 4, T2
nurse **1, B1**
nursery school **6, C1**

O
of course **1, A1**
(to) offer **4, A5**
office:
  office **11, A3**
  office worker **2, Starter**
official 15, T1
officially 3, T
oh dear! 6, A2
oil **1, T2**
oilfield 13, A1
oil tanker 5, B1
old:
  old age pensioner **8, C1**
  old people's home 11, A3
  old-fashioned 5, A1; 7, C1
on:
  on business **7, B1**
  on holiday 1, A2; 2, A4
  on loan 15, A1
  on sb's own **7, B1**
  on Sundays **1, C3**
  on the corner of 4, C2
  on the move 3, B3
  on the other hand 13, B2
  on the phone 1, A4
  on the radio **7, B1**
  on the road **4, T2**
  on the spot 3, B2
  on the telex **4, T1**
  on the way 7, B2
  on time **10, C2**
  on TV **7, B1**
  on your left/right **4, C2**
once a week 3, B1
one **1, B2**
one turn 3, Fun
onion 4, B4
onto **10, B1**
opening hours 7, A1
(to) operate 4, T1
operations control center 13, A2
operator 8, T1
opinion **12, A1**
opportunity **15, B1**
opposite 9, T; **12, T1**
orange 3, B3; 5, C3
order **5, C3**
organization 8, T1
(to) organize *(erstellen)* 2, Fun
(to) organize *(organisieren)* **7, B1**
origin 10, C1
original 14, A1
originally 1, B1

out:
out at sea 5, A3
out of action 13, C2
out of work **1, B1**
outside **2, C4**
outsider 13, A3
oval 3, A3
oven 11, A1
over there 7, C1; 10, A1
overalls 2, C4
(to) overtake **3, Fun**

P
p 14, A3
p & p 14, A3
Pa 9, T
(to) pack 10, B2; **11, A1**
packet 3, B3
packing 10, B2
padding 3, T
paint 8, Starter; **11, A1**
(to) paint 6, A1
painter **2, Starter**
Pakistani 6, Starter
palace 1, T1
pan **11, A4**
(to) paper 6, A1
papers 4, T1
parade 12, A3
parka 13, A3
parking area 1, B3
part of **1, A4**
part-time **11, C2**
party:
  party *(Partei)* **6, T1**
  party *(Gruppe)* 12, A2
  Labour Party 6, T1
(to) pass:
  (to) pass **12, B3**
  (to) pass by 6, A1
  (to) pass through 10, B2
passenger dock 10, A1
past:
  past *(nach)* **2, A3**
  past *(Vergangenheit)* **5, C1**
  past *(vergangene, letzte)* **6, T3**
  past *(vorüber, vorbei)* 8, T2
pastry 4, B4
patient 11, T2; **15, B1**
pause 9, B2
(to) pay:
  (to) pay back **14, C1**
  (to) pay into sth 12, B2
  (to) pay off 14, C2
PC 9, A2
pea **12, B3**
peanut butter 14, T1
pension:
  pension 6, T1; 11, A3
  pension scheme 12, B2
pepper 4, B4
per **6, A4**

per cent 6, T1
per unit 10, C1
perfect 6, A3
perfume 10, A1
permanently **13, B2**
person 11, T2
personal **4, A5**
personnel manager **11, B1**
(to) persuade **14, A1**
Philippines 15, T2
photo 1,B1; 9, C1
photo-copier 11, A4
(to) photocopy 2, C3
phrase **14, B1**
physical 9, B3
physics 2, C3
piano 7, C2
(to) pick:
  (to) pick *(heraussuchen, auswählen)* 9, B3
  (to) pick *(pflücken)* 10, T1
  (to) pick sb up 2, B2
  (to) pick up sth 3, T
pie **14, A3**
pigeon 1, T1
pink 5, C3
pipe **6, A1**
piping competition 3, C1
pit 3, Fun
place *(Lokal)* **1, B2**
place *(Sehenswürdigkeit)* 4, C2
plant **10, A1**
(to) plant **2, A1**
plastic 5, B3
play *(Schauspiel)* 4, B2
play *(Wiedergabe)* 9, B2
(to) play an important part 7, T1
playground **6, C1**
pleasant 12, A3
pleasure **4, T2**
(to) plug in 9, B2
pocket calculator **2, C2**
pocket money **9, A2**
poet 15, A4
point of view 13, B2
(to) point out **15, T2**
Poland 15, Starter
police officer 8, C2
Polish 6, Starter
political **6, T1**
politician 12, T2
politics *(Gemeinschaftskunde)* 2, Fun
politics *(Politik)* **7, B3**
(to) pollute **13, T1**
polluted 5, A6
pollution **5, A4**
pool 3, A1
pop music 4, A2
pop star 7, B1
popular **4, B2**
population **12, Starter**
port **10, B1**
Portugal 10, C1

two hundred and seventy-five **275**

VOCABULARY

position 4, C2
positive 12, A1
post office 1, B3
postage 14, T1
potato crisps 11, T1
pound 3, C1
(to) pour 12, B3
poverty:
  poverty 12, B1
  poverty level 12, B1
power cut 4, A3
power station 5, C1
pp 14, A3
practical 9, B3
practice 15, A1
pre-school 12, A3
(to) predict sth 9, T
prediction 9, A1; 13, A3
(to) prefer doing sth 8, C1
(to) prefer sb/sth to sb/sth 8, B5
(to) present sth 4, A5; 12, T1
president 11, B1
press conference 12, C1
(to) press 10, T1
pretty 4, T2
principal 2, C4
(to) print 11, B1
print-out 4, A1; 4, T1
printer 4, T1; 9, A2
printing-press 4, T1
private 10, C1
prize 14, B3
probably 4, T1
problem 2, C3
(to) produce 9, T
product 4, B3
production 4, T1
production line 11, A1
productive 12, T1
productivity 12, T1
profession 15, A3
professor 7, B1
profit 10, C1
program 12, A3
(to) program 2, A1
programme 2, B3
project 5, C1
promise 14, A3
(to) promise 5, T1
promotion 12, C1
pronunciation 15, A4
proof 10, A1
proof-reader 4, T
(to) protect sb/sth from 5, C1; 13, B2
(to) protest:
  (to) protest about sb/sth 5, C1
  (to) protest against sth 7, B3; 12, A1
protester 5, T
proud 13, A3
(to) provide 6, C1; 11, A3

pub 2, C4
public 14, T1
public service 13, Starter
publicity 11, T1
(to) publish 12, T1
puck 3, A3
(to) pull:
  (to) pull up sb 8, T1
  (to) pull on 14, T3
  (to) pull sth down 11, T1; 13, C2
pulse 3, C4
purpose 11, A3
(to) put:
  (to) put one's fingers in one's ears 7, C2
  (to) put sth in 13, C1
  (to) put sth on 9, B1
  (to) put sth together 11, A1
  (to) put sth up 5, B2
  (to) put up 8, B4

Q
quality 10, C1
quantity 4, B4
quite a bit 9, A3
quiz game 4, B1

R
race 7, T2
racing 7, T2
racing car 7, T2
racing driver 7, B2
racket 3, A3; 8 C4
radioactive waste 5, T
railroad 15, C3
railway line 5, T
(to) raise 13, A3
rate 6, T3; 12, C1
raw 10, T1
reaction 11, C2
reader 14, B1
real 7, A4
really 1, B2
reasonable 9, A3
(to) receive 10, C2
recently 11, T1
reception 8, B3
receptionist 8, A1
recipe 4, B4
(to) recognize 11, B2
record 9, B2
(to) record sth 8, A5
recording 9, B2
recovery service 8, Starter
recycled 5, C2
recycled paper 5, C2
(to) redecorate 11, B2
(to) reduce 6, T1; 11, B2
reduction 14, A1
redundant 11, C1
(to) reflect 9, T
(to) refuse 12, T2
reg. 8, C2
reggae 15, B2

region 13, T1
registration card 1, A1; 11, B1
regular 12, B2
regularly 4, A4
regulation 10, A1
relative 6, B1
relatively 13, A1
(to) relax 3, B1
relaxation area 11, B2
(to) release 9, B2
reliable 14, B5
religious 4, B1
religious instruction 2, Fun
(to) remind sb to do sth 5, B2
(to) renovate 6, A1
rent 8, A1
(to) rent 11, C2
repairs:
  (to) do some repairs 6, A4
  (to) replace *(auflegen)* 8, T1
  (to) replace sb/sth 8, A1
(to) reply 5, T
(to) report about sb/sth 4, A2
reporter 3, T
(to) represent 11, C2
rescue 8, T1
reserve 13, A1
resident 13, B2
resource 13, B2
restroom 11, B2; 15, C1
(to) retell 8, T2
(to) retire 12, T1
retirement 12, B2
rhythm 9, B3
(to) ride 5, C2
riding 3, Starter
right:
  right below 13, T1
  right-hand side 4, Fun
  right now 4, A4; 7, C1
risk 13, T1
(to) risk 4, A5; 8, T1
robbery 12, A1
robot 9, Starter; 11, C1
rock:
  rock 5, B1
  rock pig 15, C1
  rock singer 7, B1
Roman 8, B4
rose bush 9, B3
rough 3, T
round the corner 6, A1
routine 11, B2
rubber 8, T1
rubbish 5, B2
rubbish bin 5, B2
rugby 3, Starter
rule 2, C4; 4, T2

(to) run: *(regieren)* 6, T1
(to) run after 4, A5
(to) run out 6, A3; 8, C2
running shoe 3, A3
Russia 13, A1
Russian 2, C3

S
(to) sail across 7, B1
sailing 7, B1
sailor 7, B1
sale 10, C1
salesman 9, B1
salon 4, C1
sandwich 7, A4
satellite 9, T
saucer 6, A2
sauna 14, A3
(to) save 5, C1
savings 6, A2; 9, T
(to) say 8, C4
scarf 3, C3
scheme 11, T1
school-leaver 2, T
school uniform 7, A1
scooter 4, T2
Scotland 1, Starter
Scotsman 7, C2
screen 9, A2
screwdriver 2, C2
(to) search through sth 12, A1
seaside resort 5, B1
season 14, T2
seat-belt 10, A3
second:
  second floor 15, C2
  second lowest 6, T3
  Second World War 15, T2
second-hand 8, A4
secret 12, C1
secretarial studies 2, A1
secretary 1, A1
section 2, C3; 12, B3
see:
  I see 2, A2
  See you 2, B2
  See you tomorrow 2, B2
self-sufficient 13, A3
semester 12, C1
(to) send sth in 13, C1
senior 12, A3
sense 13, C2
series 12, A3
serious 9, B3
(to) serve sb sth 4, A5
service 8, Starter
(to) service 4, A3
(to) sew 10, T1
shape 14, A1
(to) share 4, B4
(to) shave 6, B5
sheep 1, T2
sheepdog 4, A5

VOCABULARY

sheet 11, A1
shelf 9, **B1**
sherry 15, A4
shock 5, A6
shoemaker 7, A2
shop-assistant **2, Starter**
shop-floor 11, A1
shop-steward 11, C2
shopkeeper **14, A1**
shopper 14, A1
shopping: **1, T1**
  (to) do some shopping 5, B1
  shopping bag 3, B3
short form 7, A2
should **5, C2**
showroom 12, C2
sight **1, C3**
sightseeing **15, C2**
sightseeing trip 1, T1
sign 2, C3; 5, B2; **7, A2**
signal 5, B1
simple 14, B4
simply **7, C1**
since then **7, C1**
(to) sink 5, B1
sir 9, C1
(to) sit down **1, A1**
site 13, A2
situation 6, C3
a sixteen-year-old 2, T
sixties 7, B1
size **4, T1**
skate 3, A3
(to) skate 3, B1
skater 3, A3
ski 14, T1
skier 3, A3
skiing 3, A4
skill **2, T**
slave trade 15, B1
slim **3, B3**
slippery 9, B4
slogan 14, B1
(to) slow down **6, T1**
slum 10, A3
smell **5, A6**
smog 5, T
smoker 7, C2
smoking 2, C4
(to) smuggle in sb/sth 10, A1
snack 2, C4
so far **3, A1**
soccer **3, A3**
social security **12, A1**
social worker **12, B3**
soft drink **14, T1**
software 12, C2
solar cell 9, T
solar collector 13, T1
solarium 14, A3
solid 14, Starter
solution **13, C1**
(to) solve **6, T2**
some kind of 3, B3
some more 5, C3

somewhere else **5, B1**
song of praise 4, B1
sorry: I'm sorry **6, A2**
sort 4, B1; 10, A1
sound **9, A1**
(to) sound 9, A3; **15, B1**
(to) sound a good idea 7, A1
soup **12, B3**
source 12, Starter; **13, Starter**
south **1, C3**
South African 6, Starter
South Korea 10, C1
souvenir 15, C3
Soviet Union **10, T1**
space **9, A1**
spade 2, C2
spaghetti 3, B3
Spain **10, C1**
Spanish 2, C3; 9, A2
spanner 2, C2
spare time **3, A1**
(to) speak up 2, C4; **12, T2**
speaker **12, A2**
special:
  special 5, B3
  special offer **14, A2**
specifications 9, A2
spectacular 15, C3
spectator 3, Fun
speech **6, C1**
speed **15, A4**
speed limit 12, A1
spelling 9, A2
(to) spend 5, A1
(to) spin 10, T1
spoonful 12, B3
sports 2, C3
sportsman 3, C2
spot *(Stelle)* **11, T1**
spot *(Pickel)* 14, T3
(to) spot 6, Starter
spray 5, C2
(to) spray 11, A1
sprint 3, A1
square 3, Fun; 12, Starter
square feet 12, A3
square mile 15, B3
squash 1, B2; 12, A3
(to) squeak 14, B1
Sri Lanka 10, C1
staff **8, B4**
stage coach 7, T1
stall 7, C1
(to) stall 3, Fun
(to) stand:
  (to) stand as a candidate 6, C1
  (to) stand for sth 12, C1
stand-by 13, A2
standard English 15, B1

standard of living 13, A3
star 3, T
start **3, A1**
(to) start **7, A2**
state 12, Starter
statement 3, C2; 9, A4; 12, T1
States 15, C1
station 9, T
statistics 12, A3
stay 8, B4
(to) stay:
  (to) stay at 8, B4
  (to) stay with sb 4, A4
steak 3, T
steady girlfriend 11, T2
steam:
  steam 7, T; **13, T1**
  steam coach 7, T1
  steam-engine 7, T1; 11, B2
steel **11, A1**
steelworks **11, T1**
step **13, C1**
(to) step on sth 7, C2
stick 3, A3
sticker 5, C3; 14, T2
still **4, T2**
stocking 8, T2
stomach **14, A1**
stop-watch 14, T3
store **4, C1**
(to) store **10, B1**
stores **11, A1**
storm **5, B1**
straight:
  straight 4, C2
  straight away **15, T2**
strange **7, A1**
stranger **13, A3**
street entertainer 7, C1
strength 14, T3
strict 10, A1
student **1, A1**
studio 3, A1
study room 2, C4
stupid 9, B3
suburb **9, A3**
subway 15, C3
(to) succeed **9, T**
success **11, T1**
successful **12, C1**
such as 4, T1; 12, A1
(to) suffer **13, B2**
(to) suggest **11, B2**
suitable 15, A3
sum 12, B2
summary 5, T
sun-bathing 9, T
sunlight 13, T1
sunny **15, B1**
sunshine 13, T1
superb 14, A3
supermarket 5, A5
(to) supply **11, B2**
support 12, C1
(to) support **11, C1**
(to) suppose **8, C1**

surfboard 8, C4
surname **15, C2**
surprise **12, C1**
(to) surprise **5, T1**
(to) surround 14, T1
survey: *(Untersuchung, Umfrage)* **4, A1**
  (to) do a survey of sth 6, C3
(to) swallow **8, Starter**
Sweden 1, C1
Swedish 1, C3
swimmer 4, B1
swimming **3, Starter**
swimming-pool 1, B2
Switzerland 15, T2
sword 7, A2
symbol 1, B3
system 10, B2

T

T-shirt 10, T1
table-cloth **6, A2**
table tennis **1, B2**
tag 14, A1
Taiwan 10, C1
(to) take: *(brauchen, dauern)* **9, B3**
  (to) take a look at sb/sth 4, T1
  (to) take a picture 9, T
  (to) take a seat 6, B1
  (to) take in 10, A1
  (to) take over 11, C2
  (to) take over sb's role 4, A5
  (to) take part in **9, B3**
  (to) take part in sth 2, T; 3, C1
  (to) take place **2, Fun**
  (to) take sb to court 12, T2
  (to) take sth away **2, T**
  (to) take sth easy 12, T2
  (to) take sth off **13, A2**
  (to) take sth through 10, A2
  (to) take ten minutes 5, T1
  (to) take up 8, A5
  (to) take up sth **7, B1**
(to) talk:
  (to) talk about sth/sb **2, B1**
  (to) talk to sb **2, B2**
talk show 7, B1
tasty **7, C2**
tax **10, A1**
tea-lady 11, B2
tea shop 7, A2
technical **4, A3**
technical engineer 4, A3
technician **12, C1**
technologically 13, A1

VOCABULARY

technology 9, **Starter**
teenage magazine 4, **A3**
teenager 12, **C1**
telefax 11, **B2**
telegram 15, **C1**
television 4, **A1**
telex 4, **A3**
(to) tell:
  (to) tell sb about sth 3, **A1**
  (to) tell sb the way 4, **C2**
temperature 13, **A2**
tennis 2, **B1**
tennis court 6, **C1**
tens of thousands 6, **T3**
term 2, **C3**
terrific 10, **A2**
test 9, **B3**; 11, **B1**
(to) test 8, **T1**
test pilot 7, **B1**
textile factory 10, **T1**
(to) thank:
  Thank you very much. 3, **A1**
that:
  that is why 10, **T1**
  that sort of thing 7, **A1**
  that year 5, **B1**
the:
  the day before yesterday 7, **A3**
  the next day 2, **B2**
  the one 7, **C1**
  the unemployed 6, **C1**
  the whole of this week 4, **A5**
theatre 1, **B3**
them 1, **B1**
there is/are 1, **A1**
these days 2, **A4**
things you can do 1, **B2**
(to) think:
  I think so 6, **A1**
  (to) think about sb/sth 4, **B2**
  (to) think of 14, **Starter**
  (to) think sth over 12, **T1**
  (to) think up sth 12, **A1**
this:
  this evening 1, **B2**
  this summer 2, **T**
thousands 3, **T**
thriller 4, **A2**
throughout 6, **B1**
(to) throw sb out 7, **C1**
thru 15, **C4**
(to) tick 14, **Starter**
tidal:
  tidal energy 13, **B1**
  tidal range 13, **B2**
tide 13, **B1**
tidy 2, **C4**; 5, **B2**
tie 2, **C4**

time:
  from time to time 3, **B3**
  long time no see 2, **A4**
  times 3, **B1**
timetable 2, **A3**; 15, **A1**
tip 3, **C4**; 14, **A1**
title 7, **B1**
tobacco 10, **A1**
toe 7, **C2**
toilet:
  toilet paper 11, **A2**
  toilet roll 5, **C2**
tonne 10, **B2**
tool 2, **A1**
tossing the caber 3, **C1**
total: *(Gesamtsumme)* 5, **C3**
  total points 5, **B3**
(to) touch 13, **A2**
tour 1, **T1**
tourist 1, **B2**
tourist information centre 1, **B2**
town hall 6, **B2**
toy 7, **C2**
trade:
  trade 2, **T**; 7, **C1**
  trade mark 14, **B4**
tradition 7, **A1**
traditional 7, **A1**
(to) train 2, **T1**
(to) train to be 2, **A2**
trainee 2, **B1**; 15, **A1**
training centre 11, **B1**
Trans Alaska Pipeline 13, **A1**
(to) transform 13, **A1**
(to) transmit 9, **T**
transport *(Transport, Verkehr)* 5, **C1**
(Verkehrswesen) 9, **A1**
(to) transport 11, **A1**
trap 14, **A1**
(to) travel 7, **T1**
traveler's check 15, **C3**
travelling 1, **C1**
trawler 5, **A3**
trick 14, **T1**
truth 7, **T1**
(to) try hard 10, **C2**
turbine 13, **B1**
Turkish 15, **A4**
turn 3, **Fun**
(to) turn:
  (to) turn away 6, **T3**
  (to) turn in a circle 3, **C1**
  (to) turn into sth 10, **B3**
  (to) turn left/right 4, **C2**
  (to) turn on/off 9, **A2**
  (to) turn up 9, **B2**
TV 4, **B2**

TV station 13, **A3**
tweed 1, **T2**
twice 3, **B1**
two-way radio 8, **C1**
type 10, **B2**
(to) type 2, **A1**
typewriter 2, **C2**
typical 2, **T**
typing 2, **A3**
typist 2, **Starter**
tyre 3, **Fun**

U
ugly 13, **B2**
underground 15, **B2**
unemployed: *(arbeitslos)* 6, **A2**
  the unemployed 6, **C1**
unemployment 6, **T1**
unemployment benefits 12, **B2**
unfortunate 6, **A2**
unfriendly 15, **B1**
unhappy 5, **A1**
union 11, **C1**
unit 14, **A1**
United Kingdom 1, **Starter**
United States 12, **Starter**
university 1, **B2**
(to) unpack 10, **A3**
unpaid 4, **A4**
unproductive 13, **A1**
unusual 15, **T2**
up:
  up till now 7, **B1**
  up to 3, **T**
up-to-date 11, **B2**
upset 4, **T2**
USA 7, **B1**
(to) use up 13, **C1**
used to 10, **B2**
useful 14, **T1**
usually 3, **A1**

V
v 14, **A3**
vacancy 9, **Starter**
vacation 9, **T**
value 14, **A3**
van 4, **T1**
various 13, **B2**
VAT 14, **A3**
vegetables 2, **A1**
vehicle 7, **T1**
Venezuela 12, **Starter**
verse 15, **B2**
video: *(Video)* 4, **A1**
  video camera 9, **B1**
  video recorder 9, **B1**
  video tape 9, **T**
  video typewriter 10, **C1**
Vietnam 7, **B3**
view 15, **B2**
viewer 4, **B2**
viewing figure 4, **B3**

visitor 8, **C1**
visual 14, **B1**
vocabulary 9, **A2**
volcano 13, **T1**
volleyball 3, **Starter**
volume level 9, **B2**
voluntary 12, **A1**
vote 6, **T1**
(to) vote 6, **T1**

W
wage 11, **A3**
(to) wait:
  wait a minute 6, **A1**
Wales 1, **Starter**
wallpaper 8, **Starter**
(to) want: *(brauchen, benötigen)* 8, **T1**
  (to) want him to go 2, **A2**
war 7, **B3**
warehouse 10, **B1**
(to) warn 14, **A2**
warning 9, **B4**; 13, **T1**
washing-machine 8, **A4**
washing-powder 14, **A3**
washroom 10, **A3**
waste *(Abfall)* 5, **C1**
waste *(Verschwendung)* 9, **C3**; 13, **C1**
(to) waste 9, **C1**; 13, **C2**
(to) watch:
  Watch out! 2, **T**
  (to) watch TV 3, **B2**
  (to) watch one's weight 3, **B3**
water polo 3, **Starter**
waterproof 14, **T3**
way of life 5, **A6**
weak 9, **B3**
(to) weave 10, **T1**
weekend 2, **B3**
weekly 4, **C1**
(to) weigh 3, **C1**
weight 3, **C2**
weight-lifting 3, **Starter**
welcome 4, **B4**
(to) welcome 11, **A1**; 12, **A2**
welfare:
  welfare benefits 12, **B2**
  welfare service 15, **A1**
well: *(nun denn)* 10, **A1**
  well done 9, **A4**
  well-known 4, **T1**
  well-liked 4, **T1**
  well paid 2, **A4**
  Well then – let's see 1, **A1**
west:
  west 1, **C3**
West Indian 15, **B1**
West Indies 15, **B1**
western 4, **A2**

VOCABULARY V

wet **13, C2**
what:
  What about? 3, A1
  What can I do for you?
    6, B1
  What can I get you?
    2, B2
  What else? **5, A3**
  What's your problem?
    6, B1
  What time? **1, B2**
  What's it like? 2, A4
wheel **7, T1**
whenever **13, C2**
where:
  where to go, what to
    see 1, B3
whisky 1, T2
wholefood 5, A6;
  11, B2
whose: *(wessen)* **1, A4**
  Whose turn is it?
  3, Fun

why:
  Why's that? 2, A4
wide:
  wide 3, C3
  wide range 11, A1
wider 6, C1
wildlife 13, B2
windsurfing 3, A4
windmill 5, A6
windsurfer 3, A3
windy 13, T2
wine 3, B3; **10, C1**
winner 4, A5; **14, B1**
witness 8, C2
woman sailor 7, B1
(to) wonder 8, T2;
  11, T1
wooden hut 13, A3
woodland 5, T
woodwork 2, A1
wool **1, T2**
word processing
  15, T2

word processor
  11, B2
work area **11, B2**
work-force **11, C1**
(to) work:
  (to) work *(bearbeiten)*
    15, C1
  (to) work *(bedienen)*
    4, T1
  (to) work *(funktionieren)*
    9, B2
  (to) work badly 7, T1
  (to) work sth out
    9, B3
  (to) work with sb/sth
    2, T
working conditions
  11, C2
world:
  from all over the world
    5, A4
  Third World 7, B1
worried 8, C1

(to) worry **12, A1**
worse **4, B3**
worst **4, B3**
worthwhile 13, C1
wrestling 3, Starter
(to) write down 5, C3
writer 7, B1
writing paper 5, C2
wrong note 7, C2

Y
yoghurt 14, A3
youth:
  youth club 11, A3
  youth hostel **1, C1**
  youth centre 6, C1
YTS/Youth Training
  Scheme 2, T; 6, T1
Yours **1, A2**
Yours sincerely **4, A4**

APPENDIX

Irregular verbs · Unregelmäßige Verben

In der folgenden Liste unregelmäßiger Verben finden sich auch solche mit „Doppelformen", das heißt Verben, die neben der unregelmäßigen auch eine regelmäßige Form besitzen.

baby-sit [ˈbeɪbɪsɪt]	baby-sat [ˈbeɪbɪsæt]	baby-sat [ˈbeɪbɪsæt]	Kinder hüten
be [biː]	was, were [wɒz, wɜː]	been [biːn]	sein
become [bɪˈkʌm]	became [bɪˈkeɪm]	become [bɪˈkʌm]	werden
begin [bɪˈgɪn]	began [bɪˈgæn]	begun [bɪˈgʌn]	beginnen
bend [bend]	bent [bent]	bent [bent]	beugen
bite [baɪt]	bit [bɪt]	bitten [ˈbɪtn]	(durch)beißen
break [breɪk]	broke [brəʊk]	broken [ˈbrəʊkən]	(zer)brechen
bring [brɪŋ]	brought [brɔːt]	brought [brɔːt]	(her-, mit)bringen
build [bɪld]	built [bɪlt]	built [bɪlt]	bauen
burn [bɜːn]	burnt (burned) [bɜːnt] [bɜːnd]	burnt (burned) [bɜːnt] [bɜːnd]	brennen
buy [baɪ]	bought [bɔːt]	bought [bɔːt]	kaufen
catch [kætʃ]	caught [kɔːt]	caught [kɔːt]	fangen
choose [tʃuːz]	chose [tʃəʊz]	chosen [ˈtʃəʊzn]	(aus)wählen
come [kʌm]	came [keɪm]	come [kʌm]	kommen
cost [kɒst]	cost [kɒst]	cost [kɒst]	kosten
cut [kʌt]	cut [kʌt]	cut [kʌt]	schneiden
deal with [ˈdiːl wɪð]	dealt [delt]	dealt [delt]	sich befassen mit
do [duː]	did [dɪd]	done [dʌn]	tun, machen
draw [drɔː]	drew [druː]	drawn [drɔːn]	ziehen; zeichnen
dream [driːm]	dreamt (dreamed) [dremt]	dreamt (dreamed) [dremt]	träumen
drink [drɪŋk]	drank [dræŋk]	drunk [drʌŋk]	trinken
drive [draɪv]	drove [drəʊv]	driven [ˈdrɪvn]	fahren
eat [iːt]	ate [et]	eaten [ˈiːtn]	essen
fall [fɔːl]	fell [fel]	fallen [ˈfɔːlən]	fallen
feed [fiːd]	fed [fed]	fed [fed]	füttern
feel [fiːl]	felt [felt]	felt [felt]	(sich) fühlen
fight [faɪt]	fought [fɔːt]	fought [fɔːt]	kämpfen
find [faɪnd]	found [faʊnd]	found [faʊnd]	finden
fly [flaɪ]	flew [fluː]	flown [fləʊn]	fliegen
forget [fəˈget]	forgot [fəˈgɒt]	forgotten [fəˈgɒtn]	vergessen
get [get]	got [gɒt]	got/(AE) gotten [gɒt] [ˈgɑːtn]	bekommen; besorgen
give [gɪv]	gave [geɪv]	given [ˈgɪvn]	geben
go [gəʊ]	went [went]	gone [gɒn]	gehen, fahren
grow [grəʊ]	grew [gruː]	grown [grəʊn]	wachsen
hang [hæŋ]	hung [hʌŋ]	hung [hʌŋ]	hängen
have [hæv]	had [hæd]	had [hæd]	haben
hear [hɪə]	heard [hɜːd]	heard [hɜːd]	hören
hit [hɪt]	hit [hɪt]	hit [hɪt]	schlagen
hold [həʊld]	held [held]	held [held]	halten
hurt [hɜːt]	hurt [hɜːt]	hurt [hɜːt]	(sich) verletzen; schmerzen
keep [kiːp]	kept [kept]	kept [kept]	(be)halten
know [nəʊ]	knew [njuː]	known [nəʊn]	wissen, kennen
lay [leɪ]	laid [leɪd]	laid [leɪd]	legen
lead [liːd]	led [led]	led [led]	führen
learn [lɜːn]	learnt (learned) [lɜːnt]	learnt (learned) [lɜːnt]	lernen
leave [liːv]	left [left]	left [left]	(ver)lassen, weggehen
lend [lend]	lent [lent]	lent [lent]	(ver)leihen
let [let]	let [let]	let [let]	(zu)lassen; vermieten

APPENDIX

lie [laɪ]	lay [leɪ]	lain [leɪn]	liegen
light [laɪt]	lit (lighted) [lɪt] [ˈlaɪtɪd]	lit (lighted) [lɪt] [ˈlaɪtɪd]	anzünden; beleuchten
lose [luːz]	lost [lɒst]	lost [lɒst]	verlieren
make [meɪk]	made [meɪd]	made [meɪd]	machen
mean [miːn]	meant [ment]	meant [ment]	bedeuten, meinen
meet [miːt]	met [met]	met [met]	(sich) treffen; kennenlernen
overtake [ˌəʊvəˈteɪk]	overtook [ˌəʊvəˈtʊk]	overtaken [ˌəʊvəˈteɪkən]	überholen
pay [peɪ]	paid [peɪd]	paid [peɪd]	(be)zahlen
put [pʊt]	put [pʊt]	put [pʊt]	setzen, stellen, legen
read [riːd]	read [red]	read [red]	lesen
ride [raɪd]	rode [rəʊd]	ridden [ˈrɪdn]	reiten; fahren
ring [rɪŋ]	rang [ræŋ]	rung [rʌŋ]	klingeln; anrufen
rise [raɪz]	rose [rəʊz]	risen [ˈrɪzn]	aufstehen
run [rʌn]	ran [ræn]	run [rʌn]	rennen
say [seɪ]	said [sed]	said [sed]	sagen
see [siː]	saw [sɔː]	seen [siːn]	sehen
sell [sel]	sold [səʊld]	sold [səʊld]	verkaufen
send [send]	sent [sent]	sent [sent]	schicken, senden
set [set]	set [set]	set [set]	setzen, stellen
sew [səʊ]	sewed [səʊd]	sewn (sewed) [səʊn] [səʊd]	nähen
shave [ʃeɪv]	shaved [ʃeɪvd]	shaved (shaven) [ʃeɪvd] [ˈʃeɪvn]	(sich) rasieren
shine [ʃaɪn]	shone [ʃɒn]	shone [ʃɒn]	scheinen, leuchten
show [ʃəʊ]	showed [ʃəʊd]	shown (showed) [ʃəʊn] [ʃəʊd]	zeigen
shrink [ʃrɪŋk]	shrank/shrunk [ʃræŋk] [ʃrʌŋk]	shrunk/shrunken [ʃrʌŋk] [ʃrʌŋkən]	schrumpfen, schwinden
shut [ʃʌt]	shut [ʃʌt]	shut [ʃʌt]	schließen
sing [sɪŋ]	sang [sæŋ]	sung [sʌŋ]	singen
sink [sɪŋk]	sank [sæŋk]	sunk [sʌŋk]	sinken, untergehen
sit [sɪt]	sat [sæt]	sat [sæt]	sitzen
sleep [sliːp]	slept [slept]	slept [slept]	schlafen
smell [smel]	smelt (smelled) [smelt]	smelt (smelled) [smelt]	riechen
speak [spiːk]	spoke [spəʊk]	spoken [ˈspəʊkən]	sprechen
spell [spel]	spelt (spelled) [spelt]	spelt (spelled) [spelt]	buchstabieren
spend [spend]	spent [spent]	spent [spent]	ausgeben; verbringen
spin [spɪn]	spun [spʌn]	spun [spʌn]	spinnen
stand [stænd]	stood [stʊd]	stood [stʊd]	stehen
strike [straɪk]	struck [strʌk]	struck [strʌk]	schlagen
swim [swɪm]	swam [swæm]	swum [swʌm]	schwimmen
take [teɪk]	took [tʊk]	taken [ˈteɪkən]	nehmen
teach [tiːtʃ]	taught [tɔːt]	taught [tɔːt]	lehren
tell [tel]	told [təʊld]	told [təʊld]	erzählen
think [θɪŋk]	thought [θɔːt]	thought [θɔːt]	denken, meinen, glauben
throw [θrəʊ]	threw [θruː]	thrown [θrəʊn]	werfen
understand [ˌʌndəˈstænd]	understood [ˌʌndəˈstʊd]	understood [ˌʌndəˈstʊd]	verstehen
wake up [ˈweɪk ˈʌp]	woke [wəʊk]	woken [ˈwəʊkən]	aufwachen; wecken
wear [weə]	wore [wɔː]	worn [wɔːn]	tragen *(Kleidung)*
weave [wiːv]	wove (weaved) [wəʊv] [wiːvd]	woven (weaved) [ˈwəʊvən] [wiːvd]	weben
win [wɪn]	won [wʌn]	won [wʌn]	gewinnen
write [raɪt]	wrote [rəʊt]	written [ˈrɪtn]	schreiben

APPENDIX

Listening comprehension texts · Hörverständnistexte

UNIT 1

Starter
- Hello, I'm Gary. I'm from Leeds. I'm sixteen years old.
- My name's Ann. I'm seventeen. I'm from Belfast.
- Hello, my name's Jill and this is my friend Al. I'm sixteen, Al's sixteen, too. We're from Edinburgh.
- I'm Derek. I'm from Cardiff. I'm fifteen years old.

A 4 a
- Manchester 799 6552.
- Leeds 413 988.
- 439 4383.
- London 749 3478.
- Manchester 639 7864.
- 875 531.
- Manchester 639 8431.
- 624 7105.
- Leeds 488 327.

C 1
- … and we're from Germany. I'm Jörg from Düsseldorf and this is Sabine, my girlfriend. Her home is in Cologne. We're here in Southampton for the first time …
- … Yes, and we're from Sweden. I'm Anna and this is my husband Sven. And you two? Where are you from?
- We're both from Paris. My name's Jeanette and this is my boyfriend, Claude. We've got English friends here in Southampton, but they're on holiday with their parents in America at the moment.
- And we're from Ireland – from Cork. This is Marie, my wife, and I'm Mick – and of course these two – our children. This is Patrick and that's Donna. The boy's three and the girl's five.

T 1 a
- So here we are. Right in front of the Houses of Parliament. That's Big Ben there.
- It's just like the picture in one of my history books. Fantastic!
- You know Big Ben is really a bell – you can hear it every hour. It's very heavy – over 13 thousand kilograms.
- Really? – Is that it now?
- Yes, that's it. Westminster Abbey is just over there – let's have a look at it – it's over 900 years old, you know.
- …
- This is Trafalgar Square and that's Nelson's Column in the middle. It's about 50 metres high.
- Are there always so many pigeons here?
- Yes, and look – lots of people have got food to give to the pigeons.
- Talking about food – I'm really hungry. Is there a good restaurant near here?
- Yes, what about an Italian restaurant? Toni's Pizza Palace is a good place.
- OK. Let's go.
- …
- This is Piccadilly Circus – a very busy place day and night. It's beautiful at night with all the lights. From here we can walk down Regent Street to Oxford Street, one of the main shopping streets in London.
- But Cathy, where's Buckingham Palace? Are we far from there?
- Yes, but there's a bus.
- …
- Well, this is it – Buckingham Palace – the home of the Queen.
- Wow, it's really big.
- Yes, it's got over 600 rooms.
- How old is it?
- It's about 300 years old.

UNIT 2

Starter *(Lösung)*
1. a hairstylist
2. a farmer
3. a joiner
4. an airline stewardess
5. a painter
6. an office worker
7. a mechanic
8. a cook

C 4
- … Now – there are some rules in our college which you must remember.
- Sorry, sir, but we can't hear you. Can you speak up a bit?
- Right. Can you understand me now?
- Yes, sir.
- Right, our lessons start at nine o'clock, so you must be in the classroom by then. After college in the afternoon, you must leave the classrooms and workshops clean and tidy. The cleaners can't do everything for you, so clean the blackboards and put the litter in the baskets.
- Where is the nearest pub, sir?
- Well, I take this as a question about food and drink. There is a cafeteria on the first floor where you can have lunch from twelve till one. You must buy your lunch tickets on Fridays. Of course, you can always buy snacks and drinks in the cafeteria during the breaks, but you mustn't take your food and drinks into the classrooms and workshops. Now, clothes: you

needn't wear a tie, of course, but in the workshops you must wear overalls and they must be clean. When you have a free period you can go to the study room on the second floor. Any questions?
– Well, sir, um sir, where can we have a smoke?
– That's a good question. You mustn't smoke inside the college building, but you can smoke outside. Another thing: the teachers are here to help you, and you can always come to us with your problems ...

UNIT 3

Starter *(Lösung)*
1 basketball
2 wrestling
3 swimming
4 gymnastics
5 weight-lifting
6 rugby
7 volleyball
8 high jump

UNIT 4

A 5
– ... and now for a really nice story. It's about a black and white sheepdog, called Deena. When she sees a cat, she runs after it. And look, what's happening today? She's looking after three little kittens. They haven't got a mother and Deena is taking over the role of a mother cat. Isn't that great?
– What a day for Janet, winner of the Chelsea Football Club Lottery. Ten years old, and for the whole of this week she's training with the Chelsea Football Team. I know she's enjoying it, and I'm sure she has got no problems because she trains with the boys in her street every day.
– "I'm selling up", says 78-year-old Mr Scott. He owns the village of Granraer on the north coast of Scotland. He's offering it for £210,000. It's got 21 empty houses and lots of land. If you're interested, phone 706 348.
– You know the men from the fire-brigade? They work long hours and they risk their lives for us. So restaurant owner Billy Jenkins is doing something for them at the moment. His staff are serving free meals and drinks to 21 firemen from Buxton. You don't believe it? Just go to the Red Lion at Nottingham Gate.
– What a Valentine's Day for Liz and Tom from Birmingham. Together they're on board the supersonic jet Concorde. They are flying to Miami. Tom, a 48-year-old architect, at the airport: "When I think how hard we work all the year round, Miami in February's not too expensive for us. We're giving these holidays as a present to each other ..."

C 1
– Good afternoon, ladies and gentlemen. This is Radio WNYK and my name is Tom Donovan. It's a beautiful afternoon here in New York City on this first day of December. I'm feeling fine and I hope you are, too. The time is 2.15 – time for our weekly look at special offers and bargains in the stores of New York City.
– Are you looking for a new TV? Well, why not try Macy's – on the corner of Broadway and 34th Street. They're selling over 200 brand-new color TVs at bargain prices from $150 to $350. That's Macy's, on the corner of Broadway and 34th. Your store for quality television equipment.
– Barron's Books on Fifth Avenue are giving away a free map of New York City if you buy a book at their store. They have over 50,000 books on sale. So why not go down to Barron's Books on Fifth Avenue at 18th Street – you're sure to find the book you're looking for.
– Are you feeling a little cold this winter? Well, you can find something to keep you warm at Frank's Fur Store on West 23rd Street. Frank's is closing and they are selling all their fur coats – yes, each and every one – at very low prices. So for a bargain-price coat, why don't you get down to Frank's Fur Store on West 23rd Street?
– A tip for dog-owners: at the Dog Beauty Salon on East 42nd Street they're offering a complete dog beauty treatment for under $30. That means cutting, shampooing and styling. Make your dog happy – take him down to the Dog Beauty Salon on East 42nd Street – he'll love you for it.
– Well, folks – that's all for now. Tune in again next week, same time, same station for the biggest and best bargains in town.

UNIT 5

A 3 b
– ... you see, Jessica, I was born in 1920.
– Where were you born?
– I was born in this house. My parents were poor and my father wasn't at home very often.
– What was your father's job?
– He was a fisherman and his work was really hard.
– How often was he out at sea?
– He was out every day, even when the weather was bad.
– What was his boat like?
– It was just a small boat. It wasn't a big trawler.
– What was your life like?
– It was a lot of fun for us children, but there was also a lot of work to do.

- What were your hobbies?
- My friends and I were good at hunting, but we weren't so good at school.
- How many children were there at your school?
- There were about 70 pupils. There were just two classes.
- What was your first job?
- At first, I was a fisherman, too. But it wasn't the right job for me. I'm a born farmer.

UNIT 8

T 2

1st boy: You know the supermarket which is at the corner of High Street and Kingston Road? Well, I was walking past there yesterday evening, when suddenly a big cloud of black smoke came out of a window ...

2nd boy: I was staying with my grandparents last summer, when I decided to visit old Mr Thomas. I knocked at the door, but there was no answer so I went round the back. When I looked through the window, I saw that he was lying on the kitchen floor ...

girl: I wanted to buy a ring for my mother last Christmas, so I went to the jewellery shop in Blackstone Street. I was looking in the window and wondering what to buy, when some men who had stockings over their heads ran out. They were carrying big black bags ...

UNIT 9

Starter *(Lösung)*
1. old telephone with a dial, new push-button telephone
2. big hand saw, chain saw
3. modern printer, manual typewriter
4. steam-engine, modern Diesel engine

A 3 b
- Hi, Carrie.
- Hi, Chuck.
- Hey Carrie, did I tell you it's my birthday next Thursday?
- Yeah, you did. About ten times. But you didn't tell me about your party. Are you going to have a party or not?
- Well, that's a bit of a problem. You see, Mom says I can either have a small present and a party or a big present and no party.
- So that means no party.
- Afraid so. Mom says they're going to give me some money as a present this year.
- That's good. What are you going to do with it?
- Well, I've got just over $400 and with the money from my parents I'm going to buy a computer. You know I've always wanted one.

B 3 b
- Hey Carrie, I think I can solve all your problems.
- How then?
- Well, I've worked out your b-i-o-rh-y-thm. You give me a list with the things you want to do and two possible days when you can do them. Come on, write your plans down, then I'll give you your print-out.
  ...
- These are your plans then, Carrie. If you go climbing on the 10th, you'll break your leg. So don't go. But if you go climbing on the 20th, you won't slip once. You see the 10th is your physical low, and the 20th is your physical high. Let's see, what about love ...

UNIT 10

T 2

Well, when I left school in Liverpool in 1980, I didn't exactly know what to do. But soon I got my first job in a big department store where I sold women's clothes. I was really enjoying the job, when they told us that 25 shop-assistants had to leave. I was one of them. Then I tried to find something else in Liverpool but there were too many young people who were looking for jobs. After I had been unemployed for half a year I moved to Birmingham because an aunt of mine lived there. She had found a job in a shop for me and so in 1982 I started at Hayman's, a very exclusive shoe shop in the city centre of Birmingham.
I didn't really enjoy it because I prefer selling things to young people. That's why I decided to go to London two years later and I started working in a boutique near Piccadilly Circus. I liked that kind of job very much – selling jeans and sweaters – That was great, you know. And I even saved some money. One day I met an old friend of mine who had gone to India soon after school. He had good business connections there so he could deliver jeans and other cheap clothes. This was why I decided to open a boutique.
After I'd talked to my bank about it, they lent me some money for a start, so I didn't have to ask my parents for help. That was back in 1986. Of course, I had to work very hard.
Today I own three boutiques here in London and I've just opened a new one in Liverpool.

APPENDIX

UNIT 11

C2 b

Linda: I've worked here for three years now. I've just rented a new flat. Of course I've bought some new furniture. If I lose my job, I'll have to sell it. That'll help me pay the rent.

Bill: I'm 51. If the company introduces robots, I'll be one of the first to go. I've just ordered a new car. I don't know how I can pay for it.

Liz and Phil: We moved into our new house last month. We have to pay 100 pounds a week for it. We don't think we'll be able to find other jobs very quickly.

Brenda: I work here part-time. The management says that all of us who work part-time here will lose our jobs. I don't know how I can pay all these bills – electricity, phone, rent …

Jack and Jill: We both work here. If the robots take over, we can pack our bags. And that holiday to Spain next year – we can forget it.

T2

Jane: My name's Jane. I've lived here in Corby all my life. It's not great but it's home. My dad worked in the steelworks but he lost his job when they closed in 1979. I was lucky. I got a job after I'd done a course at college and I like the work here in the factory. The only problem is that my clothes smell of the fat they use to fry the potatoes in. So I have to change my clothes before I go out on a date with my boyfriend. But the people here are nice and we have a lot of fun.

Eric: Hi, I'm Eric. I've only lived in Corby since 1982. My family moved here when my father opened a new business on one of the industrial estates. But I'm not very happy here. I had a lot of friends in London and there was always lots to do there. Anyway, I've got a job here now. I'm a trainee manager in my father's firm. The work's okay – it's a bit boring but the money's good. There's not much to do in Corby in the evenings except to go to the cinema or the leisure centre, and that's not really my scene.

Jimmy: Hello, my name's Jimmy and I come from Glasgow. My mother died when I was 14 so it wasn't that much fun at home. I left soon after and I've moved around quite a lot. I even lived in London for a time and worked in a bread factory. But I didn't like London, it was much too big. Corby's better, it's just the right size for me. I've got a steady girlfriend here. She thinks my job's great – I can get her cheap lipsticks and so on. The factory is a great place, too – modern and clean. The trouble is they don't pay very well.

Nancy: Hullo, I'm Nancy. I've always been interested in electrical things. I haven't got any brothers so I had to help my dad to do repairs back home in Dublin where we lived then. He's very patient my dad, he could always show me how things worked. I had a computer for my birthday when I was sixteen, but I never thought of making them until I saw an advertisement in the paper for workers here in the new computer firm. I started work a year ago and it's a really interesting job, though hard work. I'm glad we moved here because of the job, but Corby itself is too far from the coast for me. I miss the sea.

UNIT 12

B2 a

Chuck: I can't get into the labor market because I haven't got a skill. I think I'm also of the wrong color … 'cause … if there are any jobs for people without a skill, the Whites are getting them. I've never worked and so there are no unemployment benefits for me.

Brenda and Randolph: Our retirement pension is very low, because – in the past – we couldn't pay a regular sum into the pension scheme. But just imagine the people who didn't pay at all. They get no money at all.

Mickey: I had a job all right and earned good money. That's finished now, though. The local steelworks, where I used to work, closed down three years ago and I lost my job. They stopped my unemployment benefits after one year.

APPENDIX

Jaime: I came from Mexico three years ago, illegally – like most of us. I haven't even got a passport. Nobody knows that I exist. I'm not in statistics and therefore I don't even get food stamps. For me it's like this:
No work – no money – no food.

T2 a

Judge: Order, order please! Thank you ... Mr Smith, please tell the court why you're here today.

Smith: I'm here today because I want to keep my job. Everybody in this country has a right to work and I mean everybody – this is not limited to young people – I want my rights ...

Judge: Mr Hall, you are Mr Smith's ex-employer. Please give the reasons why you fired him.

Hall: Mr Smith is 66 years old. It's now time for him to take it easy. After a lifetime of work, people deserve a rest. And don't forget the young people who're looking for a job. If everybody works until they're 70 and older, there just won't be enough jobs free ...

Smith: I don't want to take away anyone's job ...
Judge: Speak up please, Mr Smith ...
Smith: I don't want to take away anyone's job. But it's my job and people are taking it away from me. Think of the top managers – they carry on working long after 65 and some politicians go on until they're eighty! Please don't take away my rights!

Judge: Well, this is a very difficult case to decide ...

UNIT 13

A2 c

Mike: I'm Mike Rollerson from Illinois. I'm a pipeline controller for an oil company in Alaska. I work at the Operations Control Center at Valdez.
The 800 mile pipeline has been monitored from here since 1978. Once a leak has been discovered, it's my job to inform our emergency crews. They get to work immediately ... The money's good here. I earn about 3,000 dollars a week. The only problem is there's not a lot to do in your spare time. And those winters ...

Ron: My name's Ron Meyer. I'm from Ohio. I've been employed here in Fairbanks for about a year now. I'm a member of an emergency crew. We repair the pipeline when there's a leak. We have to go to the site at any time – day or night. During the last 10 days we've been called out ten times. That's hard work, you know. Also we have temperatures here in winter down to –62°F. Sure we have to wear special clothing. Our gloves, for example, have to be very thick. If you touch a piece of ice-cold metal, you're in big trouble. But one of the biggest dangers is frost bite. It's so cold, you know. But the pay's good though. I earn about 2,000 dollars a week. That's why so many workers have been attracted to Alaska ...

T2

Interviewer: ... and it really works well?
Farmer: Oh, it's absolutely fantastic. It produces nearly all the electricity we need for the farmhouse and the cowsheds.
Interviewer: No problems at all?
Farmer: Well, here in Ireland, the weather is often like it is today. When it isn't windy, we start the diesel engine.

Interviewer: Why do you think you'll have to give up your job?
Fisherman: They're planning a big dam between here in South Wales and Devon. I think they want to produce electricity. I've been fishing in that area all my life. I'm 69, so I'm all right, but what'll happen to the younger ones?

Interviewer: ... and why are you demonstrating today?
Miner: They've dismissed thousands of miners in the last few years and this is still going on.
Interviewer: Why are they closing the coal mines?
Miner: They say our coal here in North-East England is too expensive.

APPENDIX

UNIT 14

C 2

Manager: Of course, we here in our local branch were very pleased with the ad. As you know, I manage the whole business here and so I know what kind of effect the ad has had on us. Well, just let me have a look at the figures again.

... here they are. Yes ... our loans for young people have gone up by 21% within the last four months. What's more, though, our overall number of customers has changed. Instead of 4,591 four months ago, it is now 5,122. So their number has risen by about 10%.

Bill: I think MINI BANK is great. I saw this fantastic moto-cross bike at Johnson's. You know, that big shop on the corner of Drake Street and Yorkshire Street. It looked just great. And only £2,000 it was. A lot of money for me, though. I really didn't have that much. So I asked my dad for some money ...
No way ... My mum didn't give me any either ... I can understand that. I borrowed £500 from her last March and haven't paid it back yet. So I went round to MINI BANK and they gave me the £1,000 I needed ...

Bill's father: A real shame this ad was. On Monday I told Bill – that's my son and he's only 19 – to be careful with his money, because he wanted a moto-cross bike and he'd already borrowed money for a computer. On Tuesday – only 24 hours later – he got himself a loan for £1,000. On Wednesday he came racing up the avenue on his brand-new bike. Since then everything he's earned has gone to pay off his loan. In my day we thought: work – save – spend. Ads like this change everything round ...

T 3

Wake in the morning
Feeling bad
Pull on your TRUE jeans
And you don't feel so sad

Pull on your TRUE jeans
You're feeling good
Pull on your TRUE jeans
And you feel like you should

TRUE the best in town! TRUE the best in town!
TRUE the best in town – TRUE TRUE TRUE!

TRUE jeans
Make yer look good – Make yer feel good
TRUE jeans – the best in town

TRUE the best in town! TRUE the best in town!
TRUE the best in town – TRUE! TRUE! TRUE!

TRUE jeans – the best in town
...

You went to bed clean
but while you slept
the spots came out like stars
you wake to find a whole constellation of spots on your face

on your forehead: the Big Dipper

on your chin: the Little Dipper

on your nose: the North Star

to win the Star Wars once and for all
get OXYTEN with benzol peroxide
the strongest acne medicine you can buy
it dries up the spots you already have
and it stops new spots from forming

it's your face

will you wake up tomorrow to find it lit up like the Milky Way
or will you get maximum strength OXYTEN
and keep the stars where they belong –
in the sky

OXYTEN stops spots
...

– What on earth's that noise?
– Oh, that's my new watch. Isn't it great?
– No, it's horrible – turn it off.
– Ah well, yes, I haven't found the right button yet. But it's a great watch – it's got a built-in stop-watch, and it's waterproof up to 250 metres and I can even play games with it.
– Does it tell the time as well?
– What?
– Does it tell the time?
– The what?
– The time, you know, one o'clock, two o'clock ...
– Ah yes, well. I haven't actually found the button for that yet ...

APPENDIX

Speaker: This watch doesn't do much – it only tells the time, but it does that superbly – better than any other watch in the world. The Winnex Solid Gold Quartz. It even ticks like watches used to do. The Winnex Solid Gold Quartz – a superb product designed and manufactured by the best British craftsmen. Especially for you.
Winnex – every one a winner.

UNIT 15

T3 a

Nilima: My name's Nilima Tagore and I'm 30. I've been working for Air India for more than 8 years now. I love my job because I like travelling very much. You see a lot of interesting places, don't you? On the plane I have to help the passengers, serve meals and drinks, give them safety instructions and so on. Of course, I must be able to speak English because most of our customers speak or at least understand English. I learnt English at school in my home town Delhi.

Tanizaki: I'm Tanizaki Hayato and I was born at the end of the Second World War. I work for a big computer company in Okinawa where I make computer programs and test them. Of course, we have to write the programs in English because we want to sell them all over the world. And not many people speak or write Japanese, do they? That's why I learnt English at college when I studied data processing.

Britta: My name's Britta Lagerkvist. I was born in 1967. You see, in Sweden all children learn English at school. I was very interested in languages so I decided to work as a secretary for an international import-export firm here in Stockholm. Of course, I had to take business and English language courses first before I could start my job. I've been working here for two years now. I must say my work's really interesting. I telephone customers in Europe and in North America, write business letters or talk to customers at the office. Sometimes work gets a bit hectic but I don't mind. It's still more fun than having a boring job, isn't it?

APPENDIX

Cardinal and ordinal numbers · Grund- und Ordnungszahlen

Cardinal numbers · Grundzahlen

0	nought, zero
1	one
2	two
3	three
4	four
5	five
6	six
7	seven
8	eight
9	nine
10	ten
11	eleven
12	twelve
13	thirteen
14	fourteen
15	fifteen
16	sixteen
17	seventeen
18	eighteen
19	nineteen
20	twenty
21	twenty-one
22	twenty-two
23	twenty-three
24	twenty-four
30	thirty
31	thirty-one
32	thirty-two
40	forty
50	fifty
60	sixty
70	seventy
80	eighty
90	ninety
100	a/one hundred
101	a/one hundred and one
182	a/one hundred and eighty-two
336	three hundred and thirty-six
1,000	a/one thousand
18,210	eighteen thousand two hundred and ten
100,000	a/one hundred thousand
1,000,000	a/one million

Ordinal numbers · Ordnungszahlen

–	
first	(1st)
second	(2nd)
third	(3rd)
fourth	(4th)
fifth	(5th)
sixth	(6th)
seventh	(7th)
eighth	(8th)
ninth	(9th)
tenth	(10th)
eleventh	(11th)
twelfth	(12th)
thirteenth	(13th)
fourteenth	(14th)
fifteenth	(15th)
sixteenth	(16th)
seventeenth	(17th)
eighteenth	(18th)
nineteenth	(19th)
twentieth	(20th)
twenty-first	(21st)
twenty-second	(22nd)
twenty-third	(23rd)
twenty-fourth	(24th)
thirtieth	(30th)
thirty-first	(31st)
thirty-second	(32nd)
fortieth	(40th)
fiftieth	(50th)
sixtieth	(60th)
seventieth	(70th)
eightieth	(80th)
ninetieth	(90th)
a/one hundredth	(100th)

APPENDIX

Instructions for the exercises · Arbeitsanweisungen

Answer the following questions (in complete/full sentences).	Beantworten Sie die folgenden Fragen (in vollständigen/ganzen Sätzen).
Ask and answer questions about ...	Stellen und beantworten Sie Fragen zu ...
Ask and answer questions like this:	Stellen und beantworten Sie Fragen nach folgendem Muster:
Ask each other the questions.	Stellen Sie sich gegenseitig die Fragen.
Ask your partner.	Fragen Sie Ihren Nachbarn/Ihre Nachbarin.
Can you answer the following questions?	Können Sie die folgenden Fragen beantworten?
Can you complete ...	Können Sie ... vervollständigen?
Can you do these tasks?	Können Sie diese Aufgaben lösen?
Can you find the missing words/the nouns/the questions?	Können Sie die fehlenden Wörter/die Nomen/die Fragen finden?
Can you take over the role?	Können Sie die Rolle übernehmen?
Can you translate ...?	Können Sie ... übersetzen?
Compare the two pictures.	Vergleichen Sie die beiden Bilder.
Complete the dialogue/the following sentences/the text.	Vervollständigen Sie den Dialog/die folgenden Sätze/den Text.
Copy ...	Schreiben Sie ... ab.
Define the words.	Geben Sie Definitionen von den Wörtern.
Do a survey.	Machen Sie eine Umfrage.
Do a short survey and report.	Machen Sie eine kurze Umfrage und berichten Sie.
Describe ...	Beschreiben Sie ...
Fill in ...	Setzen Sie ... ein.
Find out ...	Finden Sie ... heraus.
Give short answers.	Geben Sie Kurzantworten.
Go on.	Machen Sie weiter.
Go through the text again.	Gehen Sie den Text noch einmal durch.
Have a look at ...	Schauen Sie sich ... an.
Interview your partner.	Interviewen Sie Ihren Nachbarn/Ihre Nachbarin.
Join these sentences.	Verbinden Sie diese Sätze.
Listen to part of their conversation.	Hören Sie sich einen Teil ihres Gesprächs an.
Listen to the cassette (again).	Hören Sie sich die Cassette (noch einmal) an.
Look at ...	Schauen Sie sich ... an.
Make definitions ...	Bilden Sie Definitionen ...
Make a summary of the text.	Fassen Sie den Text zusammen.
Make (correct) sentences/questions/statements.	Bilden Sie (korrekte) Sätze/Fragen/Aussagen.
Make pairs ...	Bilden Sie Begriffspaare.
Match ...	Ordnen Sie ... zu.
Play the roles.	Übernehmen Sie die Rollen.
Put a short story together.	Verfassen Sie eine kurze Geschichte.
Put in ...	Setzen Sie ... ein.
Put the sentences above in the order of the text.	Bringen Sie die oben aufgeführten Sätze in die entsprechende Reihenfolge des Textes.
Put the sentences right.	Stellen Sie die Sätze richtig.
Put the text into the right order.	Bringen Sie den Text in die richtige Reihenfolge.
Replace ...	Ersetzen Sie ...
Report your answers to the class.	Berichten Sie der Klasse Ihre Antworten.
Rewrite ...	Schreiben Sie noch einmal ... auf.
Start your sentences like this:	Beginnen Sie Ihre Sätze nach folgendem Muster:
Talk about ...	Sprechen Sie über ...

APPENDIX

Tell the class about your partner.	Erzählen Sie der Klasse über Ihren Nachbarn/Ihre Nachbarin.
Tell the class/your partner ...	Erzählen Sie der Klasse; Ihrem Nachbarn/Ihrer Nachbarin ...
The opposites of ... are ...	Die gegenteiligen Begriffe von ... sind ...
Interview your partner.	Interviewen Sie Ihren Nachbarn/Ihre Nachbarin.
Translate into German.	Übersetzen Sie ins Deutsche.
True or false?	Richtig oder falsch?
Use the correct form of the words/the correct prepositions.	Benutzen Sie die korrekte Form der Wörter/die korrekten Präpositionen.
Use the expressions ...	Benutzen Sie die Ausdrücke ...
Use the following expressions in the given order:	Benutzen Sie die folgenden Ausdrücke in der vorgegebenen Reihenfolge:
Use the letters in bold type.	Benutzen Sie die hervorgehobenen Buchstaben.
Use the verbs/theses phrases.	Benutzen Sie die Verben/diese Sätze.
Which (picture) goes with which (story)?	Welches (Bild) gehört zu welcher (Geschichte)?
Which words in the text can replace the words in bold type?	Welche Wörter aus dem Text können die hervorgehobenen Wörter ersetzen?
Work with your partner.	Arbeiten Sie mit Ihrem Nachbarn/Ihrer Nachbarin.
Write down ...	Schreiben Sie ... auf.
You can use ...	Sie können ... benutzen.

APPENDIX

Grammatical terms · Grammatische Ausdrücke

Englische Begriffe	Deutsche Entsprechungen	
adjective	Adjektiv	Eigenschaftswort
adverb	Adverb	Umstandswort
adverbial clause	adverbialer Nebensatz	umstandsbeschreibender Nebensatz
article	Artikel	Geschlechtswort
auxiliary	Hilfsverb	Hilfszeitwort
cardinal number	Kardinalzahl	Grundzahl
comparison	Steigerung	–
conditional sentence	Konditionalsatz	Bedingungssatz
conjunction	Konjunktion	Bindewort
consonant	Konsonant	Mitlaut
contact clause	verkürzter Relativsatz	Kontaktsatz
definite article	bestimmter Artikel	bestimmtes Geschlechtswort
demonstrative determiner	Demonstrativbegleiter	hinweisendes Fürwort
demonstrative pronoun	Demonstrativpronomen	hinweisendes Fürwort (alleinstehend)
gerund	Gerundium	-ing-Form
if-clause	if-Satz	Bedingungssatz mit if
imperative	Imperativ	Befehlsform
indefinite article	unbestimmter Artikel	unbestimmtes Geschlechtswort
infinitive	Infinitiv	Grundform
interrogative pronoun	Interrogativpronomen	Fragewort
irregular verb	unregelmäßiges Verb	unregelmäßiges Zeitwort
main verb	Vollverb	Zeitwort
modal (auxiliary)	modales Hilfsverb	–
negation	Negation	Verneinung
noun	Nomen/Substantiv	Hauptwort
ordinal number	Ordinalzahl	Ordnungszahl
participle	Partizip	Mittelwort
participle construction	Partizipialsatz	–
passive	Passiv	Leideform
past participle	Partizip Perfekt	Mittelwort der Vergangenheit/3. Form
personal pronoun	Personalpronomen	persönliches Fürwort
plural	Plural	Mehrzahl
possessive determiner	Possessivbegleiter	besitzanzeigendes Fürwort
possessive pronoun	Possessivpronomen	besitzanzeigendes Fürwort (alleinstehend)
preposition	Präposition	Verhältniswort
pronoun	Pronomen	Fürwort
question	Interrogativsatz	Fragesatz
question tag	Frageanhängsel	–
reflexive pronoun	Reflexivpronomen	rückbezügliches Fürwort
regular verb	regelmäßiges Verb	regelmäßiges Zeitwort
relative clause	Relativsatz	–
relative pronoun	Relativpronomen	bezügliches Fürwort
reported speech	indirekte Rede	–
's-genitive	Genitiv	2. Fall
short answer	Kurzantwort	–
singular	Singular	Einzahl
statement	Aussagesatz	–
tenses	Tempora	Zeitformen

> Present Continuous
> Present Simple
> Present Perfect
> Present Perfect Continuous
>
> Past Continuous
> Past Simple
> Past Perfect
>
> *going to*-Future
> *will*-Future

verb	Verb	Zeitwort
vowel	Vokal	Selbstlaut

Quellennachweis

Fotos: AP, Frankfurt/Main: 64; Anthony Verlag, Starnberg: 88(2); Archiv für Kunst und Geschichte, Berlin: 150(1,2); Laura Ashley Manufacturing B.V., Helmond: 141; Barnaby's Picture Library, London: 8(1); 11(2,6); 15(2,3); 16(2,3); 38(1); 88(7); Bauknecht Hausgeräte GmbH, Stuttgart: 127(B,C,F,G,H); 151(1,2,3); 152(1–5); British Telecom, London: 128(2); British Tourist Authority, London: 8(7); 11(5); 16(4); Bild-Archiv des Bundesministeriums für das Post- und Fernmeldewesen, Bonn: 124(2); J. Allan Cash, London: 8(3,5,8); 9(2); 15(1); 16(5–8); 20(5); 30; 32(1,4); 36(8); 40(2); 168 *(Mickey)*; 169 *(Gretchen, Mike)*; 192(3,5,10); 206 *Makoto, Asha)*; 210(2); 218; Corby Industrial Development Centre, Corby: 158(2,4); Daimler-Benz-Archiv, Stuttgart: 96(3); Deutsches Museum, München: 96(2); dpa, Frankfurt/Main: 60; 65(2,3); 117 *(missile)*; 124(1); 150(3); 160(1); Ford-Werke AG, Köln: 96(4); fotopresent, Essen: 206 *(Kimran)*; Girobank, London: 114(1,2); Bernd Hallmann, Tübingen: Umschlagfoto (4); 36(7); 100(9,11); 102(6); 117(6); The Image Bank, München: 160(2); 168 *(Jaime, Chuck, Brenda/Randolph)*; 169 *(soup kitchen)*; 179; 181; 186(1,2); Keystone Pressedienst, Hamburg: 88(3,8); 92(2,4); 93; Jürgen Kleine, Ammerbuch: Umschlagfotos (1,2,3,5); 9(1); 11 *(Tom,* 3,4); 12; 20(3,7); 21(1–9); 22; 25; 28; 32(3,7); 36(1–4,6, 9,10); 40(1); 52(1–9); 71(1,2); 74(2–8); 83; 88(1,4–6); 90(4,5); 92(1); 94; 96(5,6); 99(3); 100(10); 102(1–5,7,8); 113; 117(1–5); 121(1–3,6); 128(1,4,5); 139(1–5); 140(3,4); 192(2,9,11); Klett Verlag für Wissen und Bildung, Stuttgart: 157(1,2, 4,5); 170; 207; Lufthansa Bildarchiv: 20(4); Uwe Neumann, Stuttgart: 53(2): Bettina Otto-Hallmann, Tübingen: 53(1); 74(1); Picturepoint, London: 20(2,6,8); 32(6,8); 38(2); 156; 157(3); 169 *(Joe, Florence)*; 172(2,5); 186(3); 192(1,6–8); 206 *(Jenny)*; 210(1); Popperfoto, London: 92(3); Presse-Foto-Baumann, Ludwigsburg: 32(2,5); Eberhard Rühle, Tübingen: 8(2,4,6); 36(5); Clive Sawyer, Crawley, Sussex: 11(1); 65(1); 82; 89; 90(1–3); 96(1); 99(1); 100(1–8); 106(1–7); 107(1–6); 108; 117(7,8); 118; 122(A–F); 132; 139(6); 140(1,2); Siemens AG, München: 127(A,D,E); Standard Elektrik Lorenz AG, Stuttgart: 128(3); Syndication International, London: 16(1); 88(9); Thomas Weccard, Kornwestheim: Umschlagfoto (4); Heiner Wessel, Frankfurt/Main: 135; Terence Wynne, Esslingen: 196; 206 *(Kurt, Penny)*; Women's Royal Voluntary Service, London: 99(2); Thomas Zörlein, Stuttgart: 20(1).

Cartoons/Zeichnungen/Piktogramme: British Telecom, London: 110/111; 124; 125; Erco Leuchten GmbH, Lüdenscheid: 17 *(fishing, wool, industry, mining, oil)*; 34(1–12); 38(1–8); Erb-Verlag, Düsseldorf: 116(3). Aus: Nikola Dischkoff, *High-Tech*; Punch Publications Ltd, London: 116(2); Rosenheimer Verlagshaus Alfred Förg GmbH & Co. KG, Rosenheim: 116(1,4). Aus: *Datenmühle; Karikaturen um den Computer*.

Realtexte/Logos: National Association of Citizens Advice Bureaux, London: 78; The Charlotte Observer, Charlotte, N.C.: 170; Corby Industrial Development Centre, Corby: 158 *(Corby Works,* 1–4,6); Crown Copyright, *reproduced with permission of the Controller of Her Majesty's Stationery Office*: 28; Fink GmbH, Herrenberg: 287; Girobank, London: 114; Jaguar Ltd, Coventry: 98 *(The Jaguar and Daimler trade marks and logos are used with the consent of Jaguar Cars Ltd, Coventry, England)*; Her Majesty's Stationery Office, Norwich: 185 *(reproduced with the permission of the Controller of Her Britannic Majesty's Stationery Office)*; 203 *(adapted by permission of the Controller of Her Britannic Majesty's Stationery Office)*; Race Today Publications, London: 211; U.S. Department of Health and Human Services, Washington, D.C.: 172; VSO, London: 217 *(VSO sends men and women to share their skills with the people of the Third World)*.

Karten: Joachim Krüger, Stuttgart: Umschlagseiten 2,3; 11; 15; 164; 179; 182; 214; London Regional Transport: 16; Peter Schimmel, München: 13.